# The Politics of International Law

Politics and law appear deeply entwined in contemporary international relations. Yet existing perspectives struggle to understand the complex interplay between these aspects of international life. In this path-breaking volume, a group of leading international relations scholars and legal theorists advance a new constructivist perspective on the politics of international law. They reconceive politics as a field of human action that stands at the intersection of issues of identity, purpose, ethics, and strategy, and define law as an historically contingent institutional expression of such politics. They explain how liberal politics has conditioned modern international law and how law 'feeds back' to constitute international relations and world politics. This new perspective on the politics of international law is illustrated through detailed case-studies of the use of force, climate change, landmines, migrant rights, the International Criminal Court, the Kosovo bombing campaign, international financial institutions, and global governance.

CHRISTIAN REUS-SMIT is Professor and Head of the Department of International Relations in the Research School of Pacific and Asian Studies at the Australian National University. He is the author of *American Power and World Order* (2004), *The Moral Purpose of the State* (1999), co-author of *Theories of International Relations* (2001), and co-editor of *Between Sovereignty and Global Governance* (1998).

CAMBRIDGE STUDIES IN INTERNATIONAL RELATIONS: 96

# The Politics of International Law

# CAMBRIDGE STUDIES IN INTERNATIONAL RELATIONS

96 *Christian Reus-Smit (ed.)*
**The politics of international law**

95 *Barry Buzan*
**From international to world society?**
English School Theory and the social structure of globalisation

94 *K. J. Holsti*
**Taming the sovereigns**
Institutional change in international politics

93 *Bruce Cronin*
**Institutions for the common good**
International protection regimes in international society

92 *Paul Keal*
**European conquest and the rights of indigenous peoples**
The moral backwardness of international society

91 *Barry Buzan and Ole Wæver*
**Regions and powers**
The structure of international security

90 *A. Claire Cutler*
**Private power and global authority**
Transnational merchant law in the global political economy

89 *Patrick M. Morgan*
**Deterrence now**

88 *Susan Sell*
**Private power, public law**
The globalization of intellectual property rights

87 *Nina Tannenwald*
**The nuclear taboo**
The United States and the non-use of nuclear weapons since 1945

86 *Linda Weiss*
**States in the global economy**
Bringing domestic institutions back in

85 *Rodney Bruce Hall and Thomas J. Biersteker (eds.)*
**The emergence of private authority in global governance**

*(List continues at the end of book)*

# The Politics of
# International Law

*Edited by*
Christian Reus-Smit
*Australian National University*

 CAMBRIDGE
UNIVERSITY PRESS

CAMBRIDGE UNIVERSITY PRESS
Cambridge, New York, Melbourne, Madrid, Cape Town, Singapore, São Paulo, Delhi

Cambridge University Press
The Edinburgh Building, Cambridge CB2 8RU, UK

Published in the United States of America by Cambridge University Press, New York

www.cambridge.org
Information on this title: www.cambridge.org/9780521546713

First published 2004
Reprinted 2005

*A catalogue record for this publication is available from the British Library*

*Library of Congress Cataloguing in Publication data*

The politics of international law / edited by Christian Reus-Smit.
    p.   cm. – (Cambridge studies in international relations: 96)
Includes bibliographical references and index.
ISBN 0 521 83766 9 – ISBN 0 521 54671 0 (pb)
1. International law – Political aspects.   2. International relations.
I. Reus-Smit, Christian, 1961–   II. Series.
KZ1250.P65   2004
341–dc22      2003065412

ISBN 978-0-521-83766-8 hardback
ISBN 978-0-521-54671-3 paperback

Transferred to digital printing 2009

# Contents

| | | |
|---|---|---|
| *List of contributors* | | ix |
| *Preface* | | xii |
| 1 | Introduction | 1 |
| | *Christian Reus-Smit* | |
| 2 | The politics of international law | 14 |
| | *Christian Reus-Smit* | |
| 3 | When states use armed force | 45 |
| | *Dino Kritsiotis* | |
| 4 | Soft law, hard politics, and the Climate Change Treaty | 80 |
| | *Robyn Eckersley* | |
| 5 | Emerging customary norms and anti-personnel landmines | 106 |
| | *Richard Price* | |
| 6 | International law, politics, and migrant rights | 131 |
| | *Amy Gurowitz* | |
| 7 | The International Criminal Court | 151 |
| | *David Wippman* | |
| 8 | The Kosovo bombing campaign | 189 |
| | *Nicholas J. Wheeler* | |
| 9 | International financial institutions | 217 |
| | *Antony Anghie* | |

*Contents*

10  Law, politics, and international governance                238
    *Wayne Sandholtz and Alec Stone Sweet*

11  Society, power, and ethics                                272
    *Christian Reus-Smit*

    *Bibliography*                                             291
    *Index*                                                    316

# List of contributors

ANTONY ANGHIE is Professor at the S. J. Quinnery School of Law at the University of Utah, where he teaches, among other subjects, international business transactions, international law and contracts. His research has focused principally on the relationship between colonialism and international law, and he has published a number of articles on this subject.

ROBYN ECKERSLEY is a Senior Lecturer in the Department of Political Science at the University of Melbourne. She is the author of *Environmentalism and Political Theory: Toward an Ecocentric Approach* (State University of New York Press, 1992); editor of *Markets, the State and the Environment: Towards Integration* (Macmillan, 1995); author of *The Green State: Rethinking Democracy and Sovereignty* (MIT Press, 2004); and co-editor with John Barry of *The State and the Global Ecological Crisis* (MIT Press, 2004).

AMY GUROWITZ is a Lecturer at the University of California at Berkeley and a postdoctoral fellow with the Travers Program in Ethics and Government Accountability. She is a recipient of an SSRC–MacArthur Fellowship in Peace and Security in a Changing World, and the author of articles in a range of journals, including *World Politics* and the *Journal of Asian Studies*.

DINO KRITSIOTIS is Reader in Public International Law at the University of Nottingham, where he has taught since October 1994. He has served as the Rapporteur of the Theory Committee of the International Law Association (British Branch) (1998–2001) and has held visiting professorships at the University of Cape Town, the Fletcher School of Law and Diplomacy at Tufts University and the University of Michigan Law School.

RICHARD PRICE is Associate Professor of Political Science at the University of British Columbia. His work has focused on the development of norms of warfare and constructivist international relations theory. He is the author of *The Chemical Weapons Taboo* (Cornell University Press, 1997), and articles in a range of journals, including *International Organization*, *Review of International Studies*, and *European Journal of International Relations*.

CHRISTIAN REUS-SMIT is Professor and Head of the Department of International Relations in the Research School of Pacific and Asian Studies at the Australian National University. He is author of *American Power and World Order* (Polity Press, 2004) and *The Moral Purpose of the State* (Princeton University Press, 1999), co-author of *Theories of International Relations* (Palgrave, 2001), and co-editor of *Between Sovereignty and Global Governance* (Macmillan, 1998). His articles have appeared in a range of journals, including *International Organization*, *Millennium*, *European Journal of International Relations*, and *Review of International Studies*. His research interests focus on international relations theory, international history, international law, international ethics, institutional theory, and the application of social theory to the study of global politics.

WAYNE SANDHOLTZ is Professor in the Department of Political Science at the University of California, Irvine, where he has been Director of the Center for Global Peace and Conflict Studies for the past two years. His chief research interest currently is the evolution of international rules, that is, how and why norms change over time. His articles have been published in a variety of leading journals, including *International Organization*, *International Studies Quarterly*, and *World Politics*.

ALEC STONE SWEET is Official Fellow, Chair of Comparative Politics, at Nuffield College, Oxford. He has published extensively on comparative law and politics, and on international law and politics. His books include *On Law, Politics, and Judicialization* (Oxford University Press, 2002) (with Martin Shapiro); *The Institutionalization of Europe* (Oxford University Press, 2001) (with Wayne Sandholtz and Neil Fligstein); *Governing with Judges: Constitutional Politics in Europe* (Oxford University Press, 2000); *European Integration and Supranational Governance* (Oxford University Press, 1998) (co-edited with Wayne Sandholtz); and *The European Court of Justice and National Courts – Doctrine and*

*Jurisprudence: Legal Change in its Social Context* (Oxford: Hart Publishing, 1998) (co-edited with Anne Marie Slaughter and Joseph Weiler).

NICHOLAS J. WHEELER is a Reader in the Department of International Politics at the University of Wales, Aberystwyth. He is co-editor of *Human Rights in World Politics* (with Tim Dunne) and author of *Saving Strangers: Humanitarian Intervention in International Society* (Oxford University Press, 2000). His research interests are theories of international society and humanitarian intervention.

DAVID WIPPMAN is Professor of Law at Cornell University, where he has been teaching public international law and human rights since 1992. In 1998–9, Wippman served as a Director in the Office of Multilateral and Humanitarian Affairs at the US National Security Council. In that capacity, he worked on war crimes issues, the International Criminal Court, economic sanctions, and UN political issues. He is the editor of *International Law and Ethnic Conflict* (Cornell University Press, 1998), and is completing a book for the American Society of International Law on humanitarian intervention.

# Preface

In late 2002 an increasingly heated debate arose within the United Nations Security Council about the merits of using force to disarm and depose Saddam Hussein's regime in Iraq. The Bush Administration gave the Council an ultimatum: uphold the rule of international law, expressed in numerous Council resolutions calling on the regime to disarm, or follow the League of Nations into the dustbin of history. If the Council would not license the use of force, the United States would lead a 'Coalition of the Willing' to defend the rule of law and protect international security. Despite the immense material resources commanded by the United States, the majority of Council members remained unpersuaded. Most did not accept that the regime posed an imminent threat to international security and favoured a strategy of deterrence combined with an invigorated system of weapons inspections. They were also suspicious of American motives. It was clear to even the most casual observer that the Bush Administration was at least as interested in regime change as it was disarmament.

The Administration's position came to be seen, therefore, not as essential to upholding the rule of international law but as a threat to that rule. When the weapons inspectors returned to Iraq their reports failed to support the Administration's claims that Iraq posed an imminent threat (thus warranting Chapter 7 action), America's not-so-veiled commitment to regime change threatened the fundamental principles of sovereignty and non-intervention, and the Administration was threatening the unilateral use of force outside of the UN framework. In the end, the United States suffered its worst diplomatic defeat in fifty years when it failed to achieve a new Council resolution licensing the use of force. Its subsequent war in Iraq successfully deposed Hussein's regime but the Bush Administration has struggled ever since to shake off an aura of illegality and illegitimacy.

This story reveals the complex interplay between politics and law in contemporary international relations. The entire process was deeply political, but law was implicated at every turn. Once the Bush Administration entered the Council process its arguments were always cast in legal terms – it was the demands of international law, so publicly flouted by the Iraqi regime, that it insisted warranted the use of force. But its interpretation of the law, and also of the regime's threat to that law, was contested by other Council members and large sectors of world society. Having lost this politico-legal debate, the Administration fell back on America's material power and acted unilaterally without the cover of international legitimacy.

This interplay between politics and law is a recurrent feature of international relations at the beginning of the twenty-first century, but our existing frameworks of understanding are poorly equipped to comprehend this phenomenon. As Chapter 1 explains, we are accustomed to thinking of politics and law as separate domains of international social life, each with their own distinctive logics. This book is an attempt to rethink the relationship between international politics and law so as to better understand the complex interconnections we see in so many issue-areas. It grew out of a long-standing conversation with my friend and colleague, Paul Keal. Both of us were deeply dissatisfied with the way in which International Relations scholars discussed politics and law, with the way in which politics was reduced to an anaemic form of strategic action and law deprived of all socially-constitutive influence. The ideas that frame this book are very much the product of our conversation, and I am deeply indebted to Paul for his friendship and insight.

The project took form around a small research workshop that Paul and I organised at the Australian National University in November 2000. With financial and administrative support from the Department of International Relations in the Research School of Pacific and Asian Studies, we brought together an extraordinary group of International Relations scholars and international lawyers. Most of our contributors participated in this event, although Wayne Sandholtz was unable to attend and Amy Gurowitz joined the project later. Richard Devetak, Hilary Charlesworth, and John Braithwaite also presented papers at the workshop, and Paul and I are immensely grateful for their invaluable contribution to the group's deliberations. The event would never have occurred had it not been for the support of John Ravenhill, then Head of the Department of International Relations. Lorraine Elliott and Greg Fry also supported the project from the outset, and played crucial roles as discussants throughout the workshop. Carolyn Bull and Malcolm Cook facilitated our discussions by providing daily rapporteurs' reports on the preceding day's deliberations, and Amy Chen was invaluable in administrative support. Most of my colleagues in the department participated in the workshop and deserve thanks for their ever-reliable support and critical interventions. Finally, I would like to express my gratitude to those who not only participated in the workshop but also provided chapters for this volume. It is ultimately their efforts that have made this project so satisfying.

Steve Smith and John Haslam have supported the project from the outset, and I am immensely grateful to both for their sage advice at critical junctures in the book's evolution. Cambridge solicited reader's reports from three leading scholars, and together these were invaluable in guiding our revisions. Mary-Louise Hickey, my department's research officer, managed the editorial process and skilfully co-edited the manuscript. Without her ever-patient assistance I would have even less hair and the book even less polish. I cannot thank her enough.

Finally, I would like to thank my partner, Heather Rae. As a member of the Department, she is thanked implicitly in preceding paragraphs. This project has been part of our life for the past three years, however, and this merits special mention. It has lurked in the corridors of our life like a mischievous gremlin, frequently inspiring conversation and debate, but also demanding far more time and energy than perhaps it merits. Just as the book bears the imprint of my conversations with Paul, so too does it bear the mark of Heather's and my ongoing discourse about the relationship between politics and norms in international relations. For this and so much more I am eternally grateful.

CHRIS REUS-SMIT
*Canberra*
*August 2003*

# 1  Introduction

*Christian Reus-Smit*

Politics and law have long been seen as separate domains of international relations, as realms of action with their own distinctive rationalities and consequences. So pervasive is this view that the disciplines of International Relations and International Law have evolved as parallel yet carefully quarantined fields of inquiry, each with its own account of distinctiveness and autonomy. Hans Morgenthau famously asserted that *the political realist 'thinks in terms of interest defined as power*, as the economist thinks in terms of interest defined as wealth; *the lawyer, of conformity of action with legal rules*; the moralist, of conformity of action with moral principles'.[1] Curiously, many scholars of international law have acquiesced in this separation. With notable exceptions, international law has been presented as a regulatory regime, external to the cut and thrust of international politics, a framework of rules and institutional practices intended to constrain and moderate political action. Legal philosophers have frequently sought to quarantine law from politics for fear that the intrusion of politics would undermine the distinctive character of law as an impartial system of rules. From both sides of the divide, therefore, international politics and law have been treated as categorically distinct, and while international law was given little space in the international relations curriculum, students of international law have learnt doctrine and process but not politics.

To many observers of contemporary international relations, this neat separation of politics and law seems increasingly anachronistic. Whether one considers the NATO intervention in Kosovo, East Timor's tortuous path to sovereign independence, the extradition proceedings

---

[1] Hans J. Morgenthau, *Politics Among Nations: The Struggle for Power and Peace*, 6th edn (New York: McGraw-Hill, 1985), p. 13 (emphasis added).

against Augusto Pinochet, the creation of the new International Criminal Court, the debate over nuclear missile defence, the conduct of the 'war against terrorism', or the standoff in the Security Council over war with Iraq, it is the complex entanglement of politics and law that stands out. In each case one struggles to locate the boundary between the political and the legal, to the point where the established concepts of politics and law no longer seem especially helpful in illuminating pressing issues, crises, events, and developments. The discourse of politics is now replete with the language of law and legitimacy as much as realpolitik, lawyers are as central to military campaigns as strategists, legal right is as much a power resource as guns and money, and juridical sovereignty, grounded in the legal norms of international society, is becoming a key determinant of state power.

It is this growing disjuncture between our established understandings of politics and law and the complexities of contemporary international relations that motivates this book. There has been much talk in recent years about the need to bridge the divide between the disciplines of International Relations and International Law.[2] Yet there has been a curious reluctance on the part of both international relations scholars and lawyers to rethink long-held assumptions about the nature of politics and law and their interrelation. There have been calls for common research agendas, for bringing together the analytical strengths of both disciplines, and for forging links between complementary theoretical paradigms, but few of these bridge-building exercises start by critically reconsidering the foundational concepts on which these bridges will be constructed. Beginning such a reconsideration is one of the primary purposes of this book. It is concerned with three interconnected questions: how should we conceptualise international politics and international law? How should we understand the relationship between the two? And, finally, how does a reconsideration of the nature of, and

---

[2] See, for example, Kenneth W. Abbott, 'Modern International Relations Theory: A Prospectus for International Lawyers', *Yale Journal of International Law* 14: 2 (1989); Robert O. Keohane, 'International Relations and International Law: Two Optics', *Harvard International Law Journal* 38: 2 (1997); Anne-Marie Slaughter Burley, 'International Law and International Relations Theory: A Dual Agenda', *American Journal of International Law* 87: 2 (1993); Anne-Marie Slaughter, Andrew S. Tulumello, and Stepan Wood, 'International Law and International Relations Theory: A New Generation of Interdisciplinary Scholarship', *American Journal of International Law* 92: 3 (1998); Robert J. Beck, 'International Law and International Relations: The Prospects for Interdisciplinary Collaboration', *Journal of International Legal Studies* 1: Summer (1995); and Anthony Clark Arend, 'Do Legal Rules Matter? International Law and International Politics', *Virginia Journal of International Law* 38: 2 (1998).

relationship between, politics and law help us to understand important issues, events, and developments in contemporary international
relations?

The answers we advance to these questions build on the insights of recent constructivist scholarship in international relations. Constructivists
argue that international politics, like all politics, is an inherently social
activity. Through politics states and other actors constitute their social
and material lives, determining not only 'who gets what when and how',
but also who will be accepted as a legitimate actor and what will pass as
rightful conduct. International politics takes place within a framework
of rules and norms, and states and other actors define and redefine these
understandings through their discursive practices. International law is
central to this framework, and like politics, constructivists see it as 'a
broad social phenomenon deeply embedded in the practices, beliefs,
and traditions of societies, and shaped by interaction among societies'.[3]
Constructivists frequently distinguish between the roles that social and
legal norms play in international life, with many suggesting that since
the latter are more codified than the former they more powerfully constitute actors' identities, interests, and actions.

To date, constructivists have devoted most of their attention to the
way in which rules and norms condition actors' self-understandings,
preferences, and behaviour, and have, as a consequence, been accused
of excessive structuralism.[4] While these criticisms are often overdrawn,
constructivists have neglected two aspects of their schema vital to this
book's project. First, their conception of politics is implied not elaborated. Alexander Wendt's *Social Theory of International Politics*[5] – which
is rightly considered a definitive constructivist work – never addresses
the question of politics directly. Nowhere do we find the equivalent of
E. H. Carr's claim that 'Political action must be based on a co-ordination
of morality and power',[6] or Morgenthau's assertion that 'International
politics, like all politics, is a struggle for power'.[7] Second, the distinction
constructivists draw between social and legal norms is inconsistent and

---

[3] Martha Finnemore and Stephen J. Toope, 'Alternatives to "Legalization": Richer Views
of Law and Politics', *International Organization* 55: 3 (2001), 743.
[4] Jeff Checkel, 'The Constructivist Turn in International Relations Theory', *World Politics*
50: 2 (1998).
[5] Alexander Wendt, *Social Theory of International Politics* (Cambridge: Cambridge University Press, 1999).
[6] E. H. Carr, *The Twenty Years' Crisis, 1919–1939: An Introduction to the Study of International
Relations*, 2nd edn (London: Macmillan, 1946), p. 97.
[7] Morgenthau, *Politics Among Nations*, p. 31.

underdeveloped. Some scholars strongly emphasise the difference,[8] others ponder whether any valid distinctions exist,[9] and still others deny categorical differences but stress the particular styles of reasoning that attend each type of norm.[10] Because of these shortcomings, constructivists have developed a substantial literature on the role of norms in international life, but have had comparatively little to say about the politics of international law.[11]

My goals in this book are thus twofold. As editor, I have sought to develop a framework for thinking about the nature of international politics, its constitutive impact on the institution of international law, and the way in which law, in turn, structures and disciplines the expression of politics. This framework is necessarily broad; it advances a set of concepts, and posits a set of relationships between aspects of international life, that help order the empirical analyses that follow, but it falls short of a 'theory'. Not only are edited volumes poorly suited to the task of theory building, I am concerned that my framework of ideas allow the empirical analyses presented by other contributors to 'breathe'. This brings us to my second goal. A relationship of fascinating complexity has evolved between international politics and law, and this relationship finds expression in diverse issue-areas. I am keen that the following chapters capture this richness. My conceptual and analytical framework is sufficiently broad to allow the other contributors to develop their own distinctive arguments about the subjects they examine. And I have included case-studies on everything from the use of force and arms control to environmental protection and migrant rights.

In developing my analytical framework, I join other international relations scholars who have sought to recover the classical conception of politics advanced by early writers in the field, such as Carr.[12] As

---

[8] Peter J. Katzenstein, *The Culture of National Security* (Ithaca: Cornell University Press, 1996).

[9] Martha Finnemore, 'Are Legal Norms Distinctive?', *New York University Journal of International Law and Politics* 32: Spring (2000).

[10] Friedrich V. Kratochwil, *Rules, Norms, and Decisions: On the Conditions of Practical and Legal Reasoning in International Relations and Domestic Affairs* (Cambridge: Cambridge University Press, 1989).

[11] Notable exceptions to this are the writings of Nicholas Onuf and Friedrich Kratochwil. See Onuf's 'Do Rules Say What They Do? From Ordinary Language to International Law', *Harvard International Law Journal* 26: 2 (1985); and Kratochwil's 'How Do Norms Matter?', in Michael Byers (ed.), *The Role of Law in International Politics: Essays in International Relations and International Law* (Oxford: Oxford University Press, 2000).

[12] See, in particular, Robert Jackson, *The Global Covenant: Human Conduct in a World of States* (Oxford: Oxford University Press, 2000).

4

explained in chapter 2, I see politics as a variegated, multi-dimensional form of human deliberation and action, one that encompasses not just instrumental reason and strategic action, but also forms of reason and action that ordain certain actors with legitimacy, define certain preferences as socially acceptable, and license certain strategies over others. When politics is understood in this way, I come to see international society as more than a 'practical association', as a 'constitutive association' in which debates over who counts as a legitimate actor, over the kinds of purposes that are socially acceptable, and over appropriate strategies, prefigure and frame the rational pursuit of interests. In such a world states create institutions not only as functional solutions to co-operation problems, but also as expressions of prevailing conceptions of legitimate agency and action that serve, in turn, as structuring frameworks for the communicative politics of legitimation. In the modern era politics has given the institution of international law a distinctive form, practice, and content. But international law has also 'fed back' to condition politics. As the other contributors demonstrate, the international legal order shapes politics through its discourse of institutional autonomy, language and practice of justification, multilateral form of legislation, and structure of obligation. Extra-legal politics is thus structurally and substantively different from intra-legal politics.

The 'feedback' effect of law on politics is illustrated by Dino Kritsiotis in his analysis, in chapter 3, of the politico-legal conditions governing the use of force among states. Highlighting the discourse of institutional autonomy that surrounds the contemporary politics of international law, Kritsiotis examines the way in which 'states themselves have come to accept the essential autonomies of "law" and "politics" in their practices'.[13] States have created a legal realm, in which the politics of power and interests is subordinated to the politics of norm-referential argument. Within this realm, law structures politics in a variety of ways, depending both on the nature of the relevant rules and on the 'facts' of the situation. When international law is determinate and commands a high degree of acceptance, it acts, or should act, as a constraint on state action. At the other end of the spectrum, when international law is indeterminate, or when situations arise that were not anticipated when the rules were formulated, international law serves as a discursive medium in which states are able to make, address, and assess claims. To illustrate the 'determinate' end of this spectrum, Kritsiotis examines the

[13] Dino Kritsiotis, chapter 3, this volume, p. 49.

gradual shift from the ambiguous prohibition on war found in the 1928 Kellogg–Briand Pact to the unambiguous prohibition on force enshrined in the UN Charter. The structuring effect of international law at the 'indeterminate' end is illustrated by the 'exceptions' to this prohibition. It is here, Kritsiotis argues, that international law's language and practice of justification becomes crucial, so much so that debates over legal interpretation have come to structure the politics surrounding situations involving the use of force.

Turning from the 'high' politics of the use of force to a pre-eminent 'new issue area', Robyn Eckersley examines in chapter 4 the complex relationship between politics and law in the area of global environmental protection. Focusing on the 1997 negotiations over the Kyoto Protocol of the Framework Convention on Climate Change, as well as subsequent developments in the regime, she enlists a 'critical-constructivist' perspective to shed light on the relationship between international politics and law in the realm of treaty-making. She argues that although politics and law cannot be reduced to one another, they remain mutually enmeshed through the requirement of communicative or procedural fairness and the norms of recognition, reciprocity, and argument that such procedures enable and presuppose. Eckersley holds that such an approach offers both a sociological understanding of the legitimacy of international legal norms and a critical framework that highlights the degree of legitimacy of particular treaty negotiations and helps explain the outcomes for both state and non-state actors. Applied to the climate change case, it illuminates the social 'ambiguity' of international law, the way in which it can discipline powerful actors from a moral point of view while also serving as a tool to legitimate more narrowly conceived national interests. The framework also highlights the tensions facing powerful states, such as the United States, in deciding whether to assert naked power or to uphold the discursive processes of treaty-making as well as the ways in which law can be used by weak and non-state actors to shape expectations and identities.

In chapter 5 Richard Price examines the emergence during the 1990s of a new international legal norm prohibiting the use, transfer, production, and stockpiling of anti-personnel landmines. Marked as it is by broad participation and extremely rapid entry into force, this norm has attained an impressive status compared to the lengthy process taken by many international legal norms to spread and consolidate. This having been said, participation in the legal regime is not yet universal, raising the important question of whether or not the norm has broad enough adherence to qualify as a customary rule of international law, one that would generate obligations even for those states that have not explicitly consented to the treaty. Price carefully illustrates the shortcomings of reigning consent-based approaches to politics of international law, arguing that the insights from constructivist theories of norms are needed to comprehend the movement toward customary legal status. After examining the 'politics of *opinio juris*' in the field of landmines, he examines a number of empirical indicators of compliance, claiming that, contrary to standard approaches, *opinio juris* or empirical compliance should serve as demonstrations that the norm has achieved customary status. It 'may be reasonable to claim customary status for norms when the proscribed practice is sufficiently politicised to significantly raise the threshold for violations, so much so that the burden of proof clearly is reversed in favour of a general rule of non-use'.[14] Price concludes that although the norm has made important strides toward customary status, it probably still falls short of the threshold of an unambiguous customary legal rule. Nevertheless, he shows how the practices of states and non-state actors to enlist and resist the pulls of customary obligation have significantly shaped political practice, particularly the identities, interests, and behaviour of states. Furthermore, he shows that the deployment of distinctive rhetorical and behavioural practices regarding landmines has played a crucial role in constituting political and legal practice.

A distinctive feature of the contemporary international legal order is the progressive 'cosmopolitanisation' of international law, the movement away from a legal system in which states are the sole legal subjects, and in which the domestic is tightly quarantined from the international, toward a transnational legal order that grants legal rights and agency to individuals and erodes the traditional boundary between inside and outside. In chapter 6 Amy Gurowitz goes to the heart of this process by examining the relationship between international human rights law and the politics of migration in Japan. Migrant rights, especially in non-immigrant states such as Japan, provide an important case-study for the impact of international law. Migrants are seeking rights not as citizens but as human beings, and they are often doing so in states without domestic precedent for dealing with non-citizens. The well-established body of international human rights law would thus seem a logical place for migrants and their advocates to look in establishing and reinforcing

---

[14] Richard Price, chapter 5, this volume, pp. 122–3.

arguments for non-citizen rights. Gurowitz shows how the rights enshrined in such law have become increasingly important for migrant rights in Japan, with migrant activists and lawyers using international law in domestic courts to effect change. She argues that although judges rarely find that a policy is illegal under international law, in a number of important cases they have used human rights treaties that Japan is a party to, as well as those to which it is not, to interpret domestic law and the constitution in favour of immigrants. A more comprehensive approach to the relationship between international politics and law than those offered by neorealists and neoliberals, Gurowitz contends, can demonstrate the importance of the legal realm for weak actors fighting 'uphill' battles, and also explain why states highly resistant to integrating migrants find arguments based on international law compelling.

If the relationship between international human rights law and domestic political change is one dimension of the cosmopolitanisation of international law, another is the creation of international judicial institutions for the prosecution of crimes against humanity, genocide, and acts of aggression, the most important of which is the new International Criminal Court (other examples being the ad hoc tribunals for the former Yugoslavia and Rwanda). In chapter 7 David Wippman addresses the relationship between politics and law through an examination of the major issues that divided the United States from the large majority of other states that voted to adopt the Rome Statute of the Court, in particular the role of the Security Council, the powers of the prosecutor, the questions of jurisdiction and state consent, the issue of complementarity, and harmonising of diverse legal systems. While acknowledging the central role that the politics of power and interests played in the Rome negotiations, Wippman explains the influence of international law on particular issues, particularly its distinctive language of justification. On some issues, he contends, the parties' shared understanding of what international law requires foreclosed argument. On many other issues, however, international law was not sufficiently determinate to compel any particular outcome. Even on these issues, though, the parties' arguments, and to some extent their preferences, appear to have been shaped by competing general conceptions of what 'legal' institutions, rules, and arguments should look like, and what role international law and institutions should play in international relations. Importantly, when supporters and critics of the new Court evinced fundamentally divergent conceptions and views on these issues, these were often rooted in the self-identities of the principal actors.

The movement toward the systematic prosecution of individuals for massive violations of international humanitarian law and the laws of war has been matched by a 'new humanitarian interventionism', the equivocatory nature of which has been starkly apparent in the international community's haphazard responses to the wars in the former Yugoslavia. In chapter 8 Nicholas Wheeler confronts the complex interplay between politics and law in this area by examining NATO's targeting policy against the Federal Republic of Yugoslavia during Operation Allied Force. Using the conceptual and theoretical framework advanced in this volume to elaborate Rosalyn Higgins' view of 'law as process',[15] Wheeler shows the limits of the 'law as rules' approach and the value of the proposition that communicative dynamics shape the possibilities of politics. Although the use of force in humanitarian interventions constitutes a hard case for the power of legal norms, he uses NATO's targeting decisions to demonstrate that legal norms inhibit state actions that cannot be legitimated. International legal norms, he contends, are clearly constitutive as well as constraining, with specific legal rules empowering certain actors and disempowering others. Shared logics of argumentation – the fact that when actors resort to legal reasons they employ a distinctive language and practice of justification which both licenses and constrains their actions – shapes politics in significant ways. 'As this examination of NATO's targeting policy shows, even the world's most powerful military alliance recognised the need to justify its actions before the court of domestic and world public opinion. And the fact that Alliance leaders knew that they would be called upon to defend their choice of targets was an inhibiting factor on what could be attacked.'[16]

In chapter 9 the discussion turns to the realm of international political economy, with Antony Anghie exploring the politico-legal practices of the two major international financial institutions, the World Bank and the International Monetary Fund. These organisations, Anghie contends, were created by states through mechanisms of international law, yet they nevertheless represent themselves as autonomous entities that

---

[15] Rosalyn Higgins, *Problems and Process: International Law and How We Use It* (Oxford: Clarendon Press, 1994).
[16] Nicholas Wheeler, chapter 8, this volume, p. 213.

adopt technocratic and objective approaches to the problems they address. Although both the Bank and the Fund are exclusively creations of international law, and unlike states cannot make any claim to preceding international law, they have used their status under international law to isolate themselves from evolving international legal norms. Despite these efforts, Anghie contends, the relative isolation of these organisations from the general concerns of international law has led to questions about their legitimacy. Both organisations have responded to this crisis of legitimacy by deploying concepts such as 'good governance', and a central focus of Anghie's analysis is the politico-legal manoeuvres surrounding such strategies. The good governance strategy has, at one level, enabled the Bank and the Fund to deny that their policies are at odds with international human rights law, and to claim that they are actually busy promoting such law. At another level, though, the crisis of legitimacy and the nature of the two organisations' responses are testimony to the way in which weak actors can appeal to international legal norms to force a redefinition of the social identities and interests of powerful political and economic actors. It is also testimony to the way in which international law works as a site for contests over legitimate agency and action in international relations.

At the intersection of politics and law in international relations lies the vexed question of global governance, and it is on this topic that Wayne Sandholtz and Alec Stone Sweet in chapter 10 conclude the case-study section of the book. Concerned first and foremost with how social and legal norms emerge and evolve, Sandholtz and Stone Sweet advance an ambitious theory of governance, which they define as the process by which systems of rules are produced and modified over time. To explore this process they focus on two different modes of governance: dyadic and triadic. The former refers to 'decentralised' and 'formally anarchic' systems in which the parties to social exchange generate rules among themselves to govern their interactions and resolve disputes. Where the primary mechanisms of rule creation and dispute resolution in such systems are power and persuasion, in triadic systems actors turn to third parties to resolve disputes about rules. Triadic systems are thus more institutionalised, rules become more formalised and organised into hierarchies, dispute resolution becomes more compulsory and binding, and rules emerge to define the procedures for creating new rules. By demonstrating these arguments about modes of governance through case-studies of the dyadic evolution of norms of humanitarian intervention and the development of triadic forms of dispute resolution in the GATT/WTO regime, Sandholtz and Stone Sweet not only show how politics and law are inextricably intertwined, but also how an appreciation of the way in which politics and law interact in different frames of governance breaks down conventional distinctions between the domestic and international political realms.

The perspective on the politics of international law that is advanced in the following chapters may be read as a counterpoint to the 'rationalist' approach elaborated in the 'Legalization and World Politics' special issue of the journal *International Organization*.[17] This collaborative investigation by neoliberal international relations scholars and like-minded international legal theorists probes the apparent tendency toward international regimes of greater 'legalization'. Assuming that states are rational utility-maximisers who create international institutions as functional solutions to co-operation problems, the volume's authors measure a regime's legalisation in terms of the strength of its obligations, the precision of its rules, and whether or not it delegates authority to a third party. The formalistic rationalism of this approach has been criticised by leading constructivists. In the words of Martha Finnemore and Stephen Toope, 'Narrow and stylized frameworks like this one may be useful if they provide conceptual clarity and facilitate operationalization of concepts. However, the empirical applications of legalization . . . suggest the opposite.'[18] They argue that 'Law in this view is constraint only: it has no creative or generative powers in social life. Yet law working in the world constitutes relationships as much as it delimits acceptable behavior.'[19] This book further elaborates this richer view of the politics of international law. It reimagines politics as a socially constitutive form of reason and action, generating multiple 'demands' for institutions. And it sees international law, pre-eminent among these institutions, as politically constitutive, as capable of structuring the exercise of politics through its distinctive discourse of institutional autonomy, language and practice of justification, multilateral form of legislation, and structure of obligation.

Before proceeding, three caveats are needed. First, this is a book about the *politics* of international law, not the 'letter of the law'. It explores how politics conditions international law as an institution, and, most

---

[17] 'Legalization and World Politics', *International Organization* 54: 3 (2000), Special Issue.
[18] Finnemore and Toope, 'Alternatives to "Legalization"', 743–4. See also Jutta Brunnee and Stephen J. Toope, 'International Law and Constructivism: Elements of an Interactional Theory of International Law', *Columbia Journal of Transnational Law* 39: 1 (2000).
[19] Finnemore and Toope, 'Alternatives to "Legalization"', 745.

importantly, how law structures politics. What constitutes the law in particular issue-areas forms part of our analyses, but our purpose is not to provide a survey of international legal doctrine or process. Second, the framework we advance is broadly constructivist, but the way in which this broad constructivism is expressed and articulated varies from one author to another. To use a distinction coined by Ted Hopf, the contributors include both 'critical constructivists', such as Eckersley, and 'conventional constructivists', such as Sandholtz and Stone Sweet.[20] They also include international legal theorists whose ideas fit within a constructivist frame, but who would not generally identify themselves in this way, 'constructivism' being an intellectual approach peculiar to the discipline of International Relations. Finally, I have sought to include 'case-studies' on a broad spectrum of contemporary international issues, but the coverage is not exhaustive. Security (Kritsiotis, Price, and Wheeler), political economy (Anghie, and Sandholtz and Stone Sweet), human rights (Wippman and Gurowitz), environment (Eckersley), and institutional development (Reus-Smit, and Sandholtz and Stone Sweet) are covered. Yet the politics of international law permeates almost all aspects of international society, and of world society as well, and I leave it to others to explore its additional manifestations.

Rethinking international politics and law could never be a self-contained exercise – it inevitably has spillover consequences for how we think about concepts of importance to international relations. In the concluding chapter, I consider the implications of our perspective on the politics of international law for thinking about three concepts: society, power, and ethics. These concepts constitute a central ideational matrix around which many of the principal debates in International Relations revolve, debates that touch issues as central as the scope of sovereign rights, the value of international institutions, and the politics of humanitarian intervention. More than this, though, concepts of society, power, and ethics are deeply entwined with those of politics and law. If politics is defined as a struggle for power, and law as nothing more than an epiphenomenon, then our understandings of society and ethics and international relations will take a different form than if we see politics as a norm-governed activity and law as politically constitutive. Wrapping up our discussion by reflecting on the implications of our perspective for thinking about these concepts thus serves to tie our arguments and

---

[20] Ted Hopf, 'The Promise of Constructivism in International Relations Theory', *International Security* 23: 1 (1998).

insights back to core issues animating the field. My analysis could never be exhaustive, and for reasons of space I concentrate on certain axes of debate and lines of reasoning. Nevertheless, I show how our reconsideration of the politics of international law destabilises dichotomous modes of speaking about the nature of international society, proffered primarily by exponents of the 'English School', reinforces social conceptions of power, and exposes the limitations of international communicative ethics.

# 2    The politics of international law

*Christian Reus-Smit*

In titling this book *The Politics of International Law* I have sought to exploit the double meaning of this phrase. On one reading, it refers to the way in which politics informs, structures, and disciplines the law. This is the reading most prevalent among International Relations scholars, the majority of whom still see international law as an epiphenomenon, a simple reflection of underlying power politics or a functional solution to co-operation problems. On another reading, however, the title conveys the idea of politics *within* law, the idea that law can be constitutive of politics, that politics may take a distinctive form when conducted within the realm of legal reasoning and practice. As explained in the preceding chapter, one of our central purposes is to elucidate these two faces of the politics of international law, to better understand the nature of international politics, how it conditions international law, and the way in which the law 'feeds back' to shape the expression of politics.

This chapter serves two principal tasks. Delivering on my promise in chapter 1, it develops a broad analytical framework for thinking about the mutually constitutive relationship between international politics and law[1] – a framework that asks us to think about the nature of politics in a more expansive way than we have been accustomed to, and to credit law with more structuring power than we have been willing. As noted previously, this framework falls short of a 'theory'. Not dissimilar from John Ruggie's purpose in his celebrated article 'Territoriality and Beyond',[2] my goal is to provide a conceptual 'vocabulary', and to suggest an alternative set of relationships between dimensions of

---

[1] The ideas advanced have been further elaborated in Christian Reus-Smit, 'Politics and International Legal Obligation', *European Journal of International Relations* 9: 4 (2003).
[2] John Gerard Ruggie, 'Territoriality and Beyond: Problematizing Modernity in International Relations', *International Organization* 47: 1 (1993), 144.

international social life, that together will help us 'find our feet' and bring some order to the empirical cases that follow in subsequent chapters. The chapter's second task is to advance an argument about how, historically, liberal politics has shaped the nature of the modern institution of international law, with subsequent chapters taking up the question of law's reciprocal impact on politics.

## Existing approaches

In the preceding chapter I asked three questions that together animate this book: how should we conceptualise international politics and law? How should we understand the relationship between the two? And how does rethinking these concepts help us to understand better important developments in contemporary international relations? Answers to the first two of these questions are legion, but three broad approaches have dominated debate among international relations scholars. The first, which has become a hallmark of realist thought, treats politics as a struggle for material power between sovereign states, and law as either irrelevant or a simple reflection of the prevailing balance of power. The second approach, most closely identified with the rationalist writings of neoliberal institutionalists, defines politics as a strategic game, in which egoistic states seek to maximise their respective interests within existing environmental constraints. International law, from this perspective, is seen as a set of functional rules promulgated to solve co-operation problems under anarchy. The third approach, articulated by constructivist scholars, views politics as a socially constitutive form of action, and law as central to the normative structures that condition the politics of legitimate statehood and rightful action. The following discussion explains each of these approaches, and draws out their principal limitations for understanding the contemporary politics of international law.

### Realism

In the familiar realist image of world politics states are the key actors and are seen as engaged in a continuous struggle with each other to maximise their relative material power. They are portrayed as rational unitary actors principally concerned with survival in an anarchic system, as having 'fixed and uniformly conflictual goals', and as focusing primarily on the distribution of military capabilities.[3] They are conceived as largely

---

[3] Jeffrey Legro and Andrew Moravscik, 'Is Anybody Still a Realist?', *International Security* 24: 2 (1999).

static and unchanging entities with clearly defined national interests that take precedence over the good of international society as a whole. The constant pursuit of power is considered central to explaining state behaviour and the existence of a balance of power is regarded as a necessary condition for international law. In Hans Morgenthau's words, 'Where there is neither a community of interest nor balance of power, there is no international law.'[4] In realist thought international law is thus epiphenomenal: it rests on power but when confronted with the actions of determined states it is weak and ineffectual.

At the very same time, therefore, that realism represents politics and law as separate, it also treats law as mired in, and lacking force without, politics. More particularly, it is regarded as a function of, and serving the political purposes of, powerful states. It is used to justify the actions of such states, but is generally observed by them in the breach. Alfred Zimmern captured this nicely when he observed that international law has at times resembled 'an attorney's mantle artfully displayed on the shoulders of arbitrary power'.[5] Far from separate realms, politics and law are seen as in practice inextricably linked. E. H. Carr argued that law within states was a reflection of the 'policy and interests of the dominant group in a given state at a given period'.[6] Consequently, law could not 'be understood independently of the political foundation on which it rests and of the political interests which it serves'.[7] By implication law is fundamentally political and in relations between states the content of international law is determined by dominant states and will not be upheld when it conflicts with their perceived political interests. It is deployed by these states for their own ends, against subordinate or weaker entities and in this respect cannot be uncoupled from politics. International law is thus not enforceable independently of the will of powerful states, and cannot be regarded, in any compelling sense, as binding.

Because they understand the relationship between politics and law in this way, realists are profoundly sceptical about law providing a viable path to international order. This belief in peace through law, George Kennan argued, 'undoubtedly represents in part an attempt to transpose

---

[4] Hans J. Morgenthau, *Politics Among Nations: The Struggle for Power and Peace*, 6th edn (New York: McGraw-Hill, 1985), p. 296.
[5] Alfred Zimmern, *The League of Nations and the Rule of Law: 1918–1935* (London: Macmillan, 1936), p. 94.
[6] E. H. Carr, *The Twenty Years' Crisis, 1919–1939: An Introduction to the Study of International Relations*, 2nd edn (London: Macmillan, 1946), p. 176.
[7] Carr, *Twenty Years' Crisis*, p. 179.

the Anglo-Saxon concept of individual law into the international field and to make it applicable to governments as it is applicable here at home to individuals'.[8] At best, international law must be considered a form of 'primitive law', akin to that of 'preliterate societies, such as the Australian aborigines and the Yurok of northern California'.[9] What marks it off from the law of the nation-state is its decentralised character, the fact that international law's legislative, adjudicative, and enforcement procedures operate without a central authority. Ignoring altogether the centrality of customary law and *opinio juris*, realists stress that states are only bound by rules to which they have consented, that it is states who judge the fit between the law and their actions, and that it is states who must be relied upon to enforce their own compliance. For Morgenthau, it was 'an essential characteristic of international society, composed of sovereign states, which by definition are the supreme legal authorities within their respective territories, that no such central lawgiving and law-enforcing authority can exist there'.[10]

There are at least three problems inherent in the realist view of international law: it does not adequately address the existence of a growing body of law; it does not offer an account of how law comes to constrain strong states; and it has no account of how weak states and other actors use the law to shape outcomes. If the scope of international law is determined only by the interests of the powerful, it needs to be explained why there is an increasing number of legal instruments, covering issues as diverse as crimes against humanity, human rights, the environment and trade, that often stand in opposition to the self-conceived interests of the strong. How do these instruments come into being and have at least enough force for it to be clear that violation of them will carry significant political costs? At the same time as the body of law is growing it is equally clear that contrary to realist claims strong states are, in important cases, constrained by international law, as NATO was in choosing targets to bomb in its campaign against Serbia.[11] Strong states do not invariably ignore it, and when they choose to deliberately violate it they do so in the knowledge that as well as incurring political costs their actions will have to be justified as 'legal'. As the recent debate about

[8] George F. Kennan. 'Diplomacy in the Modern World', in Robert J. Beck, Anthony Clark Arend, and Robert D. Vander Lugt (eds.), *International Rules: Approaches from International Law and International Relations* (Oxford: Oxford University Press, 1996), p. 102.
[9] Morgenthau, *Politics Among Nations*, p. 295.
[10] Morgenthau, *Politics Among Nations*, p. 296.
[11] See Nicholas Wheeler, chapter 8, this volume.

war with Iraq illustrates, much argument in international relations is precisely over the legal validity of the justifications advanced by states and other actors in defence of their actions. Finally, by focusing attention on the idea that law is an instrument of strong states, realism neglects to investigate the ways in which it is used by the weak to achieve more advantageous outcomes.

## Rationalism

The second major approach to politics and law in international relations is often termed 'rationalism', and finds expression principally in the writings of neoliberal institutionalists. While accepting many of the starting points of structural realism – such as the state as the primary unit of analysis, and the realities of international anarchy – neoliberals are far less dismissive of international law than their realist counterparts. They reimagine politics as a form of utility-maximising strategic action, with states portrayed as rational egoists, seeking the most effective and efficient means available to realise their individual and collective interests. This reimagining opens space for international law, even if it is a relatively circumscribed space. States, as rational actors, recognise that their interests are often best achieved through mutual co-operation. Yet the problems of cheating, insufficient information, and high transaction costs make co-operation difficult to achieve under conditions of anarchy. These problems can be surmounted, however, if states work together to create institutions, defined as 'persistent and connected sets of rules (formal and informal) that prescribe behavioral roles, constrain activity, and shape expectations'.[12] When formally codified, these 'persistent and connected sets of rules' constitute international law, which is understood as a functional, regulatory institution of international society.

Neoliberals long shied away from explicitly discussing international law, preferring to avoid realist ire by using the less provocative language of institutions or 'regimes'. This was matched by a curious lack of engagement with international legal theory. The neoliberal theory of institutional rules drew instead upon rational choice and game theory, garnered principally from the field of micro-economics. Neoliberal thinking about international law was thus veiled behind the discourse of regimes, and to the extent that exploring this phenomenon inspired interdisciplinary bridge-building, it was not toward the discipline of

[12] Robert O. Keohane, *International Institutions and State Power: Essays in International Relations Theory* (Boulder: Westview, 1989), p. 3.

international law. The end of the Cold War, and the attendant talk of a 'new world order', the triumph of liberalism, and the regulatory imperatives of globalisation and fragmentation, did much to overcome this coyness. In fact, over the past decade neoliberals within international relations and international law have been at the forefront of calls for greater engagement between the two disciplines.[13] This interest culminated recently in the 'Legalization and World Politics' special issue of *International Organization*, a collaborative investigation by neoliberal international relations scholars and international legal theorists that probes the apparent tendency toward international regimes of greater legal obligation, precision, and delegated authority.[14]

By opening space for international law and providing a reason for its ever-expanding corpus, neoliberalism moves us well beyond the denials of realism. Yet its understanding of the relationship between politics and law in international relations remains limited.

To begin with, the neoliberal conception of international politics and law cannot account for the historical uniqueness of the modern institution of international law. If institutions are simply functional solutions to co-operation problems under anarchy, one would expect recurring co-operation problems – such as the stabilisation of territorial property rights – to generate recurring institutional practices wherever societies of sovereign states form. But this has not been the case. Historically, different international societies – from Ancient Greece to Absolutist Europe – have evolved different institutional solutions to their co-operation problems, with the modern institution of contractual international law developing only during the nineteenth century.[15] Neoliberals readily admit that explaining the nature and origin of such practices falls outside the purview of rationalist theory.[16]

Second, the rationalist image of states strategically negotiating functional rules captures but one dimension of the contemporary politics of

---

[13] See Kenneth W. Abbott, 'Modern International Relations Theory: A Prospectus for International Lawyers', *Yale Journal of International Law* 14: 2 (1989); Robert O. Keohane, 'International Relations and International Law: Two Optics', *Harvard International Law Journal* 38: 2 (1997); Anne-Marie Slaughter Burley, 'International Law and International Relations Theory: A Dual Agenda', *American Journal of International Law* 87: 2 (1993); Anne-Marie Slaughter, Andrew S. Tulumello, and Stepan Wood, 'International Law and International Relations Theory: A New Generation of Interdisciplinary Scholarship', *American Journal of International Law* 92: 3 (1998).
[14] 'Legalization and World Politics', *International Organization* 54: 3 (2000), Special Issue.
[15] Christian Reus-Smit, *The Moral Purpose of the State: Culture, Social Identity, and Institutional Rationality in International Relations* (Princeton: Princeton University Press, 1999).
[16] Keohane, *International Institutions and State Power*, p. 174.

international law. Ignored almost completely is the way in which international law can serve as a focal point for discursive struggles over legitimate political agency and action, both in the international arena and within the territorial boundaries of sovereign states. When states negotiated the laws of war, or codified the norms comprising the 'International Bill of Rights', they were not just formulating and enshrining a set of rules, they were enacting and proclaiming a particular conception of legitimate statehood and rightful state action. And when the Bush Administration was condemned for its refusal to grant prisoner-of-war status to enemy combatants held at Guantanamo Bay, and the Australian government criticised by the United Nations for its treatment of asylum seekers, these rules became critical resources in the international politics of legitimacy. International law has become a site for the social construction of models of legitimate agency and action, and the models it enshrines have become key justificatory touchstones in the constitutive political struggles of global society.

Third, the idea that politics consists merely of strategic, utility-maximising action, and that law is simply a set of regulatory rules, cannot account for the obligatory force of international law, for the fact that states by and large accept legal rules as binding even in the absence of centralised enforcement mechanisms. The prevailing configuration of states' interests may well explain why states choose to negotiate a legal regime in a particular issue-area, but it cannot explain why legal rules *per se* are considered binding. Their preferred strategy is to attribute obligation to the fact that states have consented to the law, but this merely begs the question of why states regard consent as obligation-inducing,[17] and it leaves customary law, to which states are bound regardless of their consent, completely unexplained.[18] The contributors to the 'Legalization and World Politics' volume try to solve this problem by arguing that the obligatory nature of legalised regimes derives from the legitimacy of the background institution of the international legal system.[19] While this is a promising line of argument, neoliberals have no theoretical resources to explain why states might attach legitimacy to such a system.[20]

---

[17] H. L. A. Hart, *The Concept of Law*, 2nd edn (Oxford: Oxford University Press, 1994), p. 224.
[18] Martha Finnemore and Stephen J. Toope, 'Alternatives to "Legalization": Richer Views of Law and Politics', *International Organization* 55: 3 (2001), 746–7.
[19] Kenneth Abbott, Robert O. Keohane, Andrew Moravscik, Anne-Marie Slaughter, and Duncan Snidal, 'The Concept of Legalization', *International Organization* 54: 3 (2000).
[20] Reus-Smit, 'Politics and International Legal Obligation'.

Finally, although neoliberals have done much to demonstrate the functional imperatives that drive regime formation, their arguments are strongest in issue-areas where it is at least plausible (though perhaps not sustainable) to assume that states have clear, pre-existing material interests, such as national security and economic prosperity and development. These arguments are of declining value, however, when it comes to comprehending the progressive 'cosmopolitanisation' of international law over the past century. Where international law was once the 'law of nations' in their external relations, the residual core of international public law has become increasingly enmeshed within a web of rules governing the rights of individuals and groups, rights that impose correlative obligations on the international community to govern the relationship between states and the peoples that reside within their boundaries. This transformation is difficult to accommodate within a statist, rational-choice framework, as it is driven, in large measure, by normative not material impulses, the catalytic agents are frequently non-state actors not states, and the resulting dilution of national political and legal sovereignty overstretches notions of 'bounded rationality' or 'enlightened self-interest'.

## Constructivism

The idea that politics is simply power or utility-maximising action, and that international law is at worst epiphenomenal and at best a set of functional rules, has been challenged over the past decade by a new wave of constructivist international theory.[21] Often labelled 'the new idealists', constructivists advance three core propositions about the social nature of international relations. First, to the extent that structures shape the behaviour of states and other actors, normative and ideational structures are as important as material structures. Not only does the shared knowledge embedded in such structures determine how actors respond to their material environment, but intersubjective beliefs shape actors' identities and in turn their

---

[21] Emanuel Adler, 'Seizing the Middle Ground: Constructivism in World Politics', *European Journal of International Relations* 3: 3 (1997); Jeff Checkel, 'The Constructivist Turn in International Relations Theory', *World Politics* 50: 2 (1998); Richard Price and Christian Reus-Smit, 'Dangerous Liaisons? Critical International Theory and Constructivism', *European Journal of International Relations* 4: 3 (1998); Ted Hopf, 'The Promise of Constructivism in International Relations Theory', *International Security* 23: 1 (1998); and Vendulka Kubálková, Nicholas Onuf, and Paul Kowert (eds.), *International Relations in a Constructed World* (Armonk, NY: M. E. Sharpe, 1998).

interests.[22] Second, constructivists argue that if you wish to understand the behaviour of states and other actors you need to grasp how their social identities condition their interests and actions. In contrast to realists and rationalists, who explicitly bracket processes of interest formation, constructivists hold that as the social identities of actors vary so too do their interests, with significant implications for how they behave.[23] Furthermore, identities must be seen as social because they are learned – actors are in a constant dialogue with the prevailing norms of legitimate agency that constitute role identities to define their senses of self. Finally, although constructivists emphasise the constitutive power of normative and ideational structures, they stress that these structures only exist because of the routinised practices of knowledgeable social agents, which makes them human artefacts amenable to transformation.[24]

At the heart of constructivist thought is a concern for 'reasons for action'.[25] A reason is both an individual or collective motive (the reason why NATO bombed Serbia) and a justificatory claim (the reason NATO gave for bombing Serbia).[26] Reasons thus have internal and external dimensions, or private and public aspects. Normative and ideational structures are constitutive of actors' reasons in both dimensions: through processes of socialisation they shape actors' definitions of who they are and what they want; and through processes of public justification they frame logics of argument. Thus, European norms governing how 'civilised' states treat their inhabitants and ideas about the

[22] Alexander Wendt, 'Constructing International Politics', *International Security* 20: 1 (1995), 73; Alexander Wendt, *Social Theory of International Politics* (Cambridge: Cambridge University Press, 1999), pp. 92–138; and Alexander Wendt and Raymond Duvall, 'Institutions and International Order', in Ernst-Otto Czempiel and James N. Rosenau (eds.), *Global Changes and Theoretical Challenges: Approaches to World Politics for the 1990s* (Lexington: Lexington Books, 1989), p. 60.

[23] Audie Klotz, *Norms in International Relations: The Struggle Against Apartheid* (Ithaca: Cornell University Press, 1995); and Audie Klotz, 'Norms Reconstituting Interests: Global Racial Equality and US Sanctions Against South Africa', *International Organization* 49: 3 (1995).

[24] Alexander Wendt, 'The Agent Structure Problem in International Relations Theory', *International Organization* 41: 2 (1987).

[25] Friedrich V. Kratochwil, *Rules, Norms, and Decisions: On the Conditions of Practical and Legal Reasoning in International Relations and Domestic Affairs* (Cambridge: Cambridge University Press, 1989).

[26] These two aspects of reasons do not necessarily co-vary. Actors may or may not have different motives for acting than the ones they use to justify their behaviour. They are not unrelated, though. Constructivists have shown how the communicative processes of public justification can, under specific conditions, have a socialising effect on actors' underlying motives. See Thomas Risse, Stephen Ropp, and Kathryn Sikkink (eds.), *The Power of Human Rights: International Norms and Domestic Change* (Cambridge: Cambridge University Press, 1999).

interdependence of security, democracy, and regional stability informed NATO's decision, while international humanitarian norms concerning obligations to prevent genocide and egregious crimes against humanity provided the justificatory framework that NATO used to license the bombing.

Because constructivists are concerned with understanding reasons for action, they focus not just on the so-called 'logic of appropriateness' – on the conformity of action with normative precepts – but also on the 'logic of argumentation', on the way in which norms provide the communicative framework in which actors debate issues of legitimate agency, purpose, and strategy.[27] 'The "logic" of arguing', Friedrich Kratochwil contends, 'requires that our claims satisfy certain criteria, and that means that they cannot be based purely on idiosyncratic grounds. Were this not the case, not only would no one assent to anyone else's decision, but it would be impossible to give a coherent account of the obligatory character of other-regarding choices.'[28]

Contained within these ideas is a view of international politics as both a rule-governed and rule-constitutive form of reason and action, and of international law as a central component of the normative structures that are produced by, and constitutive of, such politics. By broadening the concept of politics to include issues of identity and purpose as well as strategy, by treating rules, norms, and ideas as constitutive, not just constraining, and by stressing the importance of discourse, communication, and socialisation in framing human behaviour, constructivism offers resources for understanding the politics of international law not found in realist and rationalist thought. Currently, however, constructivism suffers from two significant limitations.

To begin with, the constructivist view of politics is poorly articulated, despite the strong implication that it is a form of rule-governed and rule-constitutive action. How does the constructivist view of politics differ from other conceptions? If politics is a form of normative reason and action, how does it differ from other forms of such action? A priest conducting mass is engaged in a normative, rule-governed practice, but does this make it political? Second, although constructivists frequently speak of international law, draw heavily on legal philosophy,

---

[27] Thomas Risse, '"Let's Argue!": Communicative Action in World Politics', *International Organization* 54: 1 (2000); Thomas Risse, 'International Norms and Domestic Change: Arguing and Communicative Behavior in the Human Rights Area', *Politics and Society* 27: 4 (1999).
[28] Kratochwil, *Rules, Norms, and Decisions*, p. 12.

and see international legal theorists as kindred spirits, they are unclear about how social and legal norms differ, about how the international legal system/order should be conceived, and about how that institution conditions politics. Are legal norms distinctive because they are more codified? Is the institution of international law a system of command-like rules backed by sanctions, or something else? If international law is constitutive of politics, how does it have this effect?

## Rethinking politics and the demand for institutions

As the preceding discussion explains, realist and neoliberal approaches are hamstrung by their underlying conceptions of politics and law, conceptions that leave them ill-equipped to comprehend issues as fundamental as the expanding corpus of international law, the obligatory force of that law, the way in which the weak can employ the law as a power resource, the historical uniqueness of the modern international legal order, the role that law plays as a locus for legitimation struggles, and the cosmopolitanisation of international law. Constructivism, I suggest, implies analytically more useful conceptions of international politics and law, but these remain underdeveloped. Rethinking these foundational conceptualisations, and grasping their expression in the modern, liberal international order, is thus essential if we are to reach a more complete understanding of the contemporary politics of international law. In what follows, I expand on the constructivist idea of politics as a socially constituted and constitutive form of deliberation and action, and explain the implications of this expanded understanding for thinking about the 'demand for institutions'.

### The nature of politics

The argument advanced here starts from the assumption – commonsensical to the international relations scholars of the classical period – that politics is a variegated, multi-dimensional form of human deliberation and action, the lifeblood and challenge of which lie at the intersection of these dimensions.[29] To fully comprehend this domain of social life it

---

[29] This argument has been rehearsed in Christian Reus-Smit, 'The Strange Death of Liberal International Theory', *European Journal of International Law* 12: 3 (2001); and elaborated in Reus-Smit, 'Politics and International Legal Obligation'. It also complements arguments recently offered by other scholars who advocate a return to a more classical conception of

is necessary to begin with the nature of political reason or deliberation, as all but the most brute forms of action rest on some type of reasoning and deliberation, however crude or disagreeable we might judge this to be. Political deliberation can be said to integrate four types of reason: *idiographic, purposive, ethical,* and *instrumental.* Idiographic deliberation takes place when actors confront the question 'who am I?' or 'who are we?', and is thus identity-constitutive. Purposive deliberation occurs when they ask 'what do I want?' or 'what do we want?', engaging them in a process of interest or preference formation. Ethical deliberation happens when they address the question of 'how I should act?' or 'how we should act?', situating their purposive and instrumental decisions within the realm of socially sanctioned norms of rightful agency and conduct. Finally, instrumental deliberation – the favoured terrain of realists and rationalists – involves actors confronting two subsets of questions: one strategic-instrumental, the other resource-instrumental. The former asks 'how do I get what I want?' or 'how do we get what we want?', while the latter asks 'what do I need to get what I want?' or 'what do we need to get what we want?'.[30]

These four types of reason, I want to suggest, constitute the key cognitive reference points that frame political deliberation. My crucial point, however, is that political deliberation should ultimately be seen as lying at the difficult intersections between the idiographic, purposive, ethical, and instrumental. That is, politics is a distinctive form of reason because of its *interstitial* quality (see figure 1). Although he used different terminology, this idea of politics is captured in Carr's critical but neglected observation that 'Politics cannot be divorced from power. But the *homo politicus* who pursues nothing but power is as unreal a myth as the *homo economicus* who pursues nothing but gain. Political action must be based on a co-ordination of morality and power.'[31]

If political deliberation is multi-dimensional, so too is political action. Because political action is the behavioural expression of political reason, each aspect of that reason affects the practical expression of politics. Idiographic reason lies behind the practices actors engage in when they seek to articulate, justify, demonstrate, perform, and contest their self-identities through verbal and ritual processes of communicative action.

politics. See, in particular, Robert Jackson, *The Global Covenant: Human Conduct in a World of States* (Oxford: Oxford University Press, 2000).
[30] This is an elaboration of a schema advanced by Ronald Beiner in his *Political Judgement* (London: Methuen, 1983), pp. 129–52.
[31] Carr, *Twenty Years' Crisis,* p. 97.

Idiographic                                    Purposive

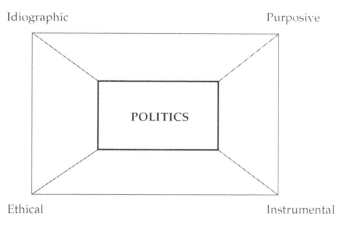

POLITICS

Ethical                                        Instrumental

Figure 1 The interstitial conception of politics

The Washington Summit Communiqué that NATO member states issued on the 50th anniversary of the alliance is a good example of this
form of political action. They declared that 'The North Atlantic Alliance, founded on the principles of democracy, individual liberty and
the rule of law, remains the basis of our collective defence; it embodies
the transatlantic link that binds North America and Europe in a unique
defence and security partnership.'[32] Purposive deliberation encourages
a form of political action in which actors learn, articulate, justify, negotiate, and revise their individual and collective preferences in the context
of other actors' interests, expectations of legitimate conduct, and established societal norms. This type of action was apparent in the agonisingly
slow rise to humanitarian consciousness and commitment of European
states and the United States, in which their initial denials that they had
any fundamental interests in the Balkans were eventually displaced by
a stated humanitarian interest of such importance that it demanded military intervention. Ethical deliberation informs political action in which
actors seek to license their interests and actions in terms of prevailing
norms of legitimate agency and rightful conduct. NATO's statement at
the outset of the bombing campaign against the Federal Republic of
Yugoslavia (FRY) is an example of such political action. 'The crisis in
Kosovo', it reads, 'represents a fundamental challenge to the values of
democracy, human rights and the rule of law, for which NATO has stood

[32] NATO Press Release NAC-S(99)64, 'Washington Summit Communiqué', 24 April 1999,
<www.nato.int/docu/pr/1999/p99-064e.htm>.

26

since its foundation. We are united in our determination to overcome this challenge.'[33] Finally, instrumental deliberation informs a strategic type of political action, the essence of which is the application of available means to achieve individual and collective interests within environmental constraints. When NATO declared that its 'military action against FRY supports the political aims of the international community: a peaceful, multi-ethnic and democratic Kosovo in which all its people can live in security and enjoy universal human rights and freedoms on an equal basis',[34] it was engaging in instrumental political deliberation, and on launching its air campaign it was engaging in strategic political action.

NATO's pronouncements suggest that types of political deliberation and their associated forms of political action stand in a distinctive constitutive relationship. To borrow a phrase from Alexander Wendt, idiographic reason and action 'supervene' upon other political modalities. 'Supervenience', Wendt argues, 'is a nonreductive relationship of dependence, in which properties at one level are fixed or constituted by those at another.'[35] Here this means that deliberation and action around questions of identity pre-structure purposive and ethical deliberation and action, which in turn condition instrumental reasoning and behaviour. In rationalising and justifying their actions, NATO member states explicitly tied their identity as a group 'founded on the principles of democracy, individual liberty and the rule of law' to their 'interest' in meeting 'the challenge' of the 'Kosovo crisis', and their military campaign was presented as an appropriate means to serve such an 'interest'. This is not to suggest, of course, that the process of constitution is unidirectional, even if the posited relationship of supervenience pertains. Through ethical deliberation actors can redefine their interests and even their identities, and instrumental reason and action can reinforce or undermine identities, interests, and ethics depending on experiences of success and failure.

Thinking about politics in the manner outlined above helps us to appreciate more fully the 'political charge' that attends central issues in contemporary international relations, a charge that is occluded by

---

[33] NATO Press Release M-NAC-1(99)51, 'The Situation in and around Kosovo', 12 April 1999, <www.nato.int/docu/1999/p99-051e.htm>.
[34] NATO Press Release M-NAC-1(99)51, 'The Situation in and around Kosovo'.
[35] Alexander Wendt, 'Identity and Structural Change in International Politics', in Yosef Lapid and Friedrich V. Kratochwil (eds.), *The Return of Culture and Identity in IR Theory* (Boulder: Lynne Rienner, 1996), p. 49.

realist and rationalist perspectives. Returning to the Kosovo case, the strategic-instrumental question – how do I (we) get what I (we) want? – and the resource-instrumental question – what do I (we) need to get what I (we) want? – beg a series of deeper identity, purposive, and ethical questions which constitute the heart of the conflict. For NATO, the Serbs, and the Kosovars, the salient issues concerned 'who are we?', 'what do we want?', and 'how should we act?' How these questions were answered constituted Serb and Kosovar nationalisms, split NATO from the United Nations, and provided the discursive context in which secondary instrumental questions were answered. If there had been no debate about these deeper identity, purposive, and ethical issues, and if the parties to the conflict had reached mutually compatible conclusions, the political essence of the Balkans issue would have dissolved. The same can be said of issues such as the 'war against terrorism', the intervention in East Timor, the treatment of refugees, the expansion of the European Union, and the creation of the International Criminal Court. In each of these cases the political resides at the intersection of identity construction, interest formation, ethical debate, and strategic action, and it is the tension between these that marks politics out as a distinctive realm of social action, capable of generating intense passion to the point of violence.

Critics might argue that in concentrating on different modes of political deliberation this understanding of politics ignores other important ingredients of politics, particularly force. The use of physical or moral coercion to achieve political ends is a recurrent feature of both international and domestic social life, and as students of international relations we are conditioned to treat such coercion as the essence of politics. It is crucial to recognise, however, that most applications of coercion or force take place within a framework of political calculation, in which actors seek to reconcile, individually and collectively, issues of identity, purpose, ethics, and strategy. Force is part of the play of politics, but it is generally a secondary part; a calculated means to achieve a given set of political ends. The above perspective, therefore, does not deny the role that force plays in politics. Rather, it concentrates on the deeper political 'rationality' that conditions deployments of force. In this respect, our perspective differs little from that of rationalists, as they too concentrate on the deliberative (or strategic) bases of politics. Realists seem to treat force as more central to politics, defined as the struggle for power. On a closer reading, however, few realists would reduce the struggle for power to the exercise of force; the accumulation of power may permit such exercise, and it may even depend upon it, but political reasons – from survival to aggrandisement – are always more primary.

### The 'demand for institutions'

In 1982 Robert Keohane published a key article in the rationalist tradition of institutional theory, titled 'The Demand for International Regimes'.[36] Setting out to show why states would want to create international institutions, he advanced a 'supply–demand' approach that sees it as rational for states with common interests to create institutions to facilitate co-operation. Institutions aid co-operation by reducing cheating, lowering transaction costs, and increasing information, all of which are necessary if states are to overcome their co-ordination and collaboration problems. We have already seen that when this approach is applied to the modern institution of international law several questions are left unanswered, such as the obligatory force of legal rules, the uniqueness of the modern institution of international law, the role of law in legitimation struggles, and the progressive cosmopolitanisation of international law. Having outlined above a broader conception of politics than that deployed by rationalists, I now wish to suggest how this conception can inform a broader, more holistic understanding of the demand for institutions,[37] an understanding that helps us to better comprehend this question.

Rationalists are correct that instrumental deliberation and action lead actors to pursue institutional arrangements that enable the resolution of specific conflicts and the solution of co-operation and collaboration problems – institutions do indeed lower transaction costs, increase information, and deter cheating, thus facilitating ordered interstate relations. Yet this is not the only demand for institutions. Idiographic deliberation and action prompt the construction of institutions that permit the constitution, stabilisation, and demonstration of legitimate social identities. This is clearly apparent in the institutional orders created after major systemic conflagrations, where the community of states has sought to enshrine notions of legitimate statehood that will ensure international

---

[36] Reprinted as Robert O. Keohane, 'The Demand for International Regimes', in Stephen D. Krasner (ed.), *International Regimes* (Ithaca: Cornell University Press, 1983).

[37] I define institutions here as sets of rules, norms, principles, and decision-making procedures that 'define the meaning and identity of the individual [and actors in general] and the patterns of appropriate economic, political and cultural activity engaged in by those individuals'. See George M. Thomas, John W. Meyer, Francesco Ramirez, and John Boli (eds.), *Institutional Structure: Constituting State, Society, and the Individual* (London: Sage, 1989), p. 12.

peace and stability, with the institutional projects of the Congress of Vienna, the Versailles Peace Conference, and the San Francisco Conference being cases in point. It is also apparent in issue-specific regimes, where the norms and rules, of security, economic, environmental, and human rights institutions coalesce around particular, historically contingent, notions of legitimate statehood that prescribe certain relations between state, society, economy, and nature. Purposive deliberation and action call forth institutions that enable the negotiation and stabilisation of legitimate collective purposes and strategies. In this respect, the norms, rules, and principles that comprise international institutions serve as encoding devices, locations in which the collectively negotiated, socially sanctioned legitimate interests of states – either in particular issue-areas or for the governance of international society in general – are publicly enshrined to serve as orientation points for acceptable political conduct, internationally and, increasingly, domestically. Finally, ethical deliberation and action create reasons for institutions that enable the expression, stabilisation, and pursuit of collectively negotiated, historically contingent moral principles, ideas of justice, and conceptions of fairness. Questions of the right, the good, and the fair constitute a crucial, yet curiously overlooked, dimension of institutional rationality, affecting not only the substantive content of international institutions – from the lofty principles of the United Nations Charter to the existence of foreign aid and human rights regimes – but also the procedural practices of such institutions.[38]

Just as politics ought to be understood as interstitial, institutional rationality should, ideally, be seen in holistic terms. This is for two reasons. First, the politics that generates institutional imperatives cannot be segmented easily into discrete idiographic, purposive, ethical, and instrumental components. When actors create institutions, they are almost always engaged in the simultaneous construction of social identities, definition and validation of individual and collective interests, deliberation on the good and the just, and the strategic pursuit of instrumental objectives. The precise mixture of these political practices will vary from issue to issue, and from one level of institutions to another,

---

[38] Cecilia Albin, *Justice and Fairness in International Negotiation* (Cambridge: Cambridge University Press, 2001); Thomas M. Franck, *Fairness in International Law and Institutions* (Oxford: Clarendon Press, 1995); David Lumsdaine, *Moral Vision in International Politics* (Princeton: Princeton University Press, 1990); Risse, Ropp, and Sikkink, *The Power of Human Rights*; and Nicholas Wheeler, *Saving Strangers: Humanitarian Intervention in International Society* (Oxford: Oxford University Press, 2000).

but the pristine pursuit of strategic interests, devoid of all considerations of legitimate agency and action, is as rare as disinterested codifications of state identities. Second, there has been an overwhelming tendency in the study of international institutions to focus solely on regime rules, on their relationship to state interests, on the constraints they place on states, and on their contribution to order within a particular issue-area. Yet a comprehensive perspective on international institutions must move beyond consideration of the rule content of issue-specific institutions to comprehend the varying form and practice of different institutional arrangements. Only by considering the full spectrum of institutional impulses – from identity construction to instrumental action – can we grasp the totality of institutional formations, their distinctive form, practice, and content.

John Ruggie has shown how the form of the contemporary institution of multilateralism is deeply wedded to the social identity of the modern sovereign states, based as it is on the underlying liberal principle that rules should be equally and reciprocally binding on all legal subjects in all like circumstances.[39] Similarly, the purposive politics that surrounds the codification and institutional pursuit of state interests affects not only the rule content of institutions, but also their procedural practices. Institutional rules instantiate and stabilise the collective interests of states, yet often institutions, such as the Framework Convention on Global Climate Change, are designed procedurally to permit the regime's gradual evolution as ongoing, institutionally structured negotiations lead states to redefine their interests. With regard to the politics of ethics, Cecilia Albin and Thomas Franck have shown how considerations of justice and fairness have conditioned the practices and content of issue-specific institutions.[40] Albin's exhaustive study of the role such considerations play in international negotiations demonstrates their central importance in shaping the negotiations that create new institutions, the procedural rules of those institutions, and the content of their rules. Finally, rationalists have shown how instrumental politics plays an important role in conditioning the content of institutions, the specific rules, norms, and principles they enshrine.

---

[39] John Gerard Ruggie (ed.), *Multilateralism Matters: The Theory and Praxis of an Institutional Form* (New York: Columbia University Press, 1993). Also see Reus-Smit, *The Moral Purpose of the State.*
[40] Albin, *Justice and Fairness*; Franck, *Fairness in International Law.*

## The modern institution of international law

Rationalist approaches to politics and institutional rationality encourage – inadvertently or not – an ahistorical understanding of institutional development. States are ascribed an atemporal, means–ends strategic rationality that they are said to employ to overcome a standard set of co-operation problems that are thought to accompany international anarchy. Because strategic rationality is assumed of all states, and because anarchy is said to generate the same spectrum of co-operation problems whenever it emerges, there is little room for the idea that politics, institutional rationality, and institutional formations might vary historically. The interstitial conception of politics and holistic understanding of institutional rationality outlined above are more sensitive to such variation. The ideals of legitimate statehood that actors conceive and seek to enshrine, the purposes they promote, negotiate, and uphold, the conceptions of justice and fairness they espouse, and the interests they strategically pursue are all historically contingent, and if the preceding argument is correct, so too are institutional formations.[41]

We are concerned here with the implications of this argument for understanding the nature of the modern institution of international law. The following discussion extends ideas that I advanced in *The Moral Purpose of the State*. International societies, I suggested, have deep constitutional structures, which are generated, reproduced, and restructured by the politics of identity that necessarily accompanies the mutual recognition of sovereign statehood. Central to these structures are systemic norms of procedural justice, which license certain forms of rule governance.[42] From the early nineteenth century, a new, distinctly modern constitutional structure evolved in international society, conditioned by the gradual ascendance of political liberalism. This new constitutional structure, and its attendant norm of procedural justice, reshaped the nature of international law, prompting what many have wrongly characterised as a 'positivist' turn. International law came to exhibit certain structural characteristics, as well as distinctive practices and content.

### *The constitutional structure of modern international society*

It is commonplace in international relations theory to distinguish between international systems and societies. The former, emphasised by

---

[41] See Adda Bozeman, *Politics and Culture in International History* (Princeton: Princeton University Press, 1961); and Reus-Smit, *The Moral Purpose of the State*.
[42] Reus-Smit, *The Moral Purpose of the State*, pp. 30–3.

realists, are said to exist 'when two or more states have sufficient contact between them, and have sufficient impact on one another's decisions, to cause them to behave – at least in some measure – as parts of a whole'.[43] The latter, stressed differently by rationalists and constructivists, exist 'when a group of states, conscious of certain common interests and common values, form a society in the sense that they conceive themselves to be bound by a common set of rules in their relations with one another, and share in the working of common institutions'.[44] There is some debate about the precise relationship between these international formations: are there any historical examples of enduring international systems? Do international systems necessarily precede the development of international societies? Can international systems and societies coexist in time and place? While scholars are divided over these issues, they agree on one central point. An international society can be said to exist when states mutually recognise each other's rights to sovereign authority, when sovereignty comes to be based less on states' material capacities to defend their independence than on institutionalised rules, such as non-intervention, non-aggression, and self-determination.[45]

This socially constitutive process of mutual recognition invariably involves the politics of identity. Not all polities are recognised as sovereign by the extant members of an international society. The distribution of sovereign rights has historically been closely related to prevailing ideals of legitimate statehood, and how these ideals are defined, mobilised, and challenged has been central to international politics. Europe's imperial powers went so far as to codify in international law a 'standard of civilisation' that defined which non-European polities would be granted membership of the expanding society of states.[46] First-wave post-colonial states and nationalist movements subsequently turned the liberal ideals underlying this standard against the imperial powers, discrediting imperialism as a fundamental violation of emergent human

---

[43] Hedley Bull, *The Anarchical Society: A Study of Order in World Politics*, 2nd edn (London: Macmillan, 1995), p. 9.

[44] Bull, *The Anarchical Society*, p. 13.

[45] See Barry Buzan, 'From International System to International Society: Structural Realism and Regime Theory Meet the English School', *International Organization* 47: 3 (1993); Alexander Wendt, 'Anarchy is What States Make of It: The Social Construction of Power Politics', *International Organization* 46: 2 (1992); and Robert Jackson, *Quasi-States: Sovereignty, International Relations, and the Third World* (Cambridge: Cambridge University Press, 1990).

[46] Gerrit W. Gong, *The Standard of 'Civilization' in International Society* (Oxford: Clarendon Press, 1984).

rights principles and licensing wholesale decolonisation.[47] Since then we have witnessed the progressive, if controversial, embedding of liberal ideals of legitimate statehood, expressed in everything from the principles of 'good governance' promoted by the World Bank and International Monetary Fund (IMF) to the creation of the International Criminal Court. Far from an aberration, variants of this idiographic politics have marked the development of all historical international societies.

Through the idiographic politics of recognition international societies evolve constitutional structures, defined as 'coherent ensembles of intersubjective beliefs, principles, and norms that perform two functions in ordering international societies: they define what constitutes a legitimate actor, entitled to all the rights and privileges of statehood; and they define the basic parameters of rightful state action'.[48] It is useful to conceive of these structures as comprising three normative components: a hegemonic belief about the moral purpose of the state; an organising principle of sovereignty; and a norm of procedural justice. Sovereignty is usually considered the *grundnorm* of international society, but the politics of recognition means that it is always conjoined, in practice, with a discourse of legitimacy, with a set of arguments about 'good' states and their entitlements. We see this in the anti-liberal, anti-nationalist discourse of the *ancien régime*, as well as in contemporary claims of ascendant liberal states. While such discourses are always contested – as the 'Asian values' critique of universal human rights and the Islamic fundamentalist critique of all things 'Western' attest – in stable international societies they take a hegemonic form, with alternative conceptions of legitimate statehood assuming a counter-hegemonic, oppositional character. The crucial point for our purpose is that different conceptions of the moral purpose of the state generate different norms of procedural justice that, in turn, license distinctive institutional forms of co-operation among states. Absolutist conceptions of legitimate statehood, which attributed monarchical rights to divine will, spawned an authoritative norm of procedural justice that licensed 'naturalist' international law and 'old' diplomacy.[49]

---

[47] Christian Reus-Smit, 'Human Rights and the Social Construction of Sovereignty', *Review of International Studies* 27: 4 (2001).

[48] Reus-Smit, *The Moral Purpose of the State*, p. 30. Also see Daniel Philpott, *Revolutions in Sovereignty: How Ideas Shaped Modern International Relations* (Princeton: Princeton University Press, 2000).

[49] Reus-Smit, *The Moral Purpose of the State*, chapter 5.

International relations scholars are not accustomed to speaking of fundamental changes in relations among states, preferring instead to emphasise continuities and eternal rhythms. When they do speak of epochal transformations, they focus almost exclusively on the advent of sovereign states that accompanied the Peace of Westphalia in 1648. Yet an equally important rupture in international society occurred in the Age of Revolutions (1776–1848). 'From the mid-eighteenth century onward,' Mlada Bukovansky writes, 'the political struggles of European and American aristocrats against the perceived despotism of their monarchs yielded a profound shift in how both leaders and subjects came to view the sources and terms of political authority. Bloodlines and divine sanction began to lose their symbolic power as sources of legitimacy; popular will – however nebulously defined – began its ascent at the ultimate source of legitimate authority.'[50] In time this produced a qualitatively new international society, marked by a distinctive constitutional structure. The moral purpose of the state was increasingly defined in terms of the protection of individuals' rights and the augmentation of their interests. Monarchical sovereignty was displaced by popular sovereignty, and the authoritative norm of procedural justice – which saw the will of God, and by extension that of sovereigns, as the only legitimate source of rules and law – was replaced by a legislative conception. Henceforth, rules would be deemed legitimate only if they were authored by those subject to them (or by their representatives), and if they applied equally to all citizens in all like cases.

Rousseau famously asserted these principles of procedural justice when he wrote that 'Legislative power belongs to the people and belongs to it alone', and that law should treat 'the subjects as a body and actions in the abstract, never one man as an individual, or a particular action'.[51] From the late eighteenth century onward, these ideals came to inform international legal theory, ushering in the 'positive' turn in international law. Rejecting the idea that natural law provided a reliable source of the law of nations, Robert Ward argued that only real, existing treaties, conventions, and customs provided a 'fixed and definite' foundation for such law, as they reflected the consent of states.[52] G. F. von

---

[50] Mlada Bukovansky, *Legitimacy and Power Politics: The American and French Revolutions in International Political Culture* (Princeton: Princeton University Press, 2002), p. 3.
[51] Jean-Jacques Rousseau, 'On Social Contract or Principles of Political Right', in Alan Ritter and Julia Conway Bondanella (eds.), *Rousseau's Political Writings: New Translations, Interpretive Notes, Backgrounds, Commentaries* (New York: Norton, 1988), p. 106.
[52] Robert Ward, *An Enquiry into the Foundations and History of the Law of Nations from the Time of the Greeks to the Age of Grotius, Volume 1* (London: Butterworth, 1795), p. xxxvi.

Martens claimed, similarly, that concrete accords were the only source of legal obligation because they represent the 'mutual *will* of the nations concerned'.[53] Though revolutionary when first articulated, these ideas came to have a deep, constitutive impact on the modern institution of international law, conditioning its form and practice in distinctive ways.

As the preceding discussion indicates, the modern legislative norm of procedural justice incorporates two principles: the principle of self-legislation (that the people or their representatives must define the laws that bind them), and the principle of non-discrimination (that all must be subject to the law equally, and that all cases must be treated similarly). These principles have had a profound and enduring effect on the institutional form of the modern international legal order. They have helped constitute a system with four central characteristics: a discourse of institutional autonomy, a multilateral form of legislation, a distinctive language and practice of justification, and a horizontal structure of obligation.

## *The discourse of institutional autonomy*

The arguments advanced in this chapter suggest that the search for a clearly delineated boundary between the political and the legal in international relations is a problematic exercise.[54] Politics is a form of reason and action that generates multiple institutional imperatives, and because of this, institutional practices such as modern international law are deeply structured and permeated by politics. It is important to remember, however, that institutions are created by political actors as structuring or ordering devices, as mechanisms for framing politics in ways that enshrine predominant notions of legitimate agency, stabilise individual and collective purposes, and facilitate the pursuit of instrumental goals. Politics thus structures and permeates institutions, but institutionalised politics necessarily differs from non-institutionalised politics. Politics in a world without institutions – difficult as it is to imagine – is different to that in a highly institutionalised world.

Recognising that politics has constituted the international legal system, but is in turn transformed by that system, is crucial if we are to comprehend one of the most important features of modern international law – its discourse of institutional autonomy. The fact is that international political actors behave as though the legal realm is separate

---

[53] G. F. von Martens, *Summary of the Law of Nations Founded on the Treaties and Customs of Modern Nations* (Philadelphia: Thomas Bradford, 1795), pp. 47–8.
[54] See Wayne Sandholtz and Alec Stone Sweet, chapter 10, this volume.

from the political. As other contributors demonstrate, in a wide range of contexts political actors have spoken and acted as if at some point in a negotiation, at some stage in a crisis, action moved from the political to the legal realm, a realm in which different types of argument and practice prevail.[55] The nature of these arguments and practices is considered in a subsequent section; what is important here is that a distinctive type of politics has encouraged states and non-state actors to imagine a realm of institutionalised action in which certain 'political' types of behaviour are foreclosed and other 'legal' types are licensed and empowered.

The imagination of such a realm is functionally advantageous, as the habits of mind, modes of discursive engagement, and routinised practices that it engendered have assumed a structural form in modern international society, facilitating order by channelling actors' conduct in distinctive ways. But this instrumental benefit is not sufficient to explain the constitution of such a realm. For that we must return to the modern, legislative norm of procedural justice and its roots in post-absolutist ideals of legitimate statehood. In the Age of Absolutism, politics and law were conjoined in the figure of the sovereign, and the metaphysical precepts of divine and natural law provided theoretical, if not practical, breaks on the abuse of power. The revolutionary rejection of this model of state and political legitimacy demanded new ways of thinking about the relationship between politics and law, resulting in the liberal conception of sovereignty. Under the norm of procedural justice that accompanied this conception, the principle of self-legislation sought to conjoin politics and law in the legislative realm, while the principle of non-discrimination radically separated them in the realm of interpretation and adjudication. Parliament is simultaneously a political and legal realm, but the courts are idealised as a purely legal realm. Spurred on by the general fragmentation of knowledge into discrete disciplines that accompanied modernity, these ideas not only encouraged the view of politics and law as separate domains of human action, but also as separate fields of scholarly enquiry.

Viewed from this perspective, the discourse of institutional autonomy that characterises modern international law is less surprising. Sacral metaphysics were as vital to naturalist international law as they were for municipal law, and their fall provoked a similar crisis of legal authority. As we shall see in the following section, the principle of

[55] See chapters 3, 7, and 8, this volume.

self-legislation eventually conjoined politics and law in the practice of multilateralism. The two have been attenuated, however, in the field of problem or issue definition, and quarantined in the realms of interpretation and adjudication. It matters to international actors whether a problem or issue is defined as political or legal, and while power and self-interest are at play in the politics of definition, the framework of existing legal norms, and the modes of argument that enliven them, discipline that play. Once it has been commonly acknowledged that a problem or issue is legal, in the sense of being governed by a pre-existing set of norms, the narrowly defined politics of power and self-interest in delegitimised and communicative action is empowered. One might ask why actors are drawn to such a legal realm, where the exercise of naked power and self-interest are foreclosed. The answer lies in the politics of both legitimacy and pragmatism. Because international law is a normative order, casting claims in the language of law associates interests and strategies with the norms of international society, conscripting the power of social opinion to one's cause. And because norms are guides to action, defining a problem or issue as legal reduces opportunity costs by invoking standardised, socially sanctioned solutions.

## The multilateral form of legislation

If legislation is the formulation and enactment of legally binding rules (as is commonly defined), then it is as much a part of international life as life within the state. One of the principal activities occupying international actors is the negotiation of new rules to govern their external and internal conduct in a wide range of issue areas. Much of this is informal, involving the gradual accretion of new norms through argument, learning, and repeated practice. These processes are crucially important, as they are the principal means by which customary norms of international law evolve. 'Despite (or because of) their informal origins, rules of customary international law provide substantive content to many areas of international law, as well as the procedural framework within which most rules of international law, including treaty rules, develop, exist and change.'[56] States also engage in more formal modes of legislation, the most common and distinctive being multilateralism.

---

[56] Michael Byers, *Custom, Power and the Power of Rules: International Relations and Customary International Law* (Cambridge: Cambridge University Press, 1999), p. 3.

Again, the contrast with the absolutist period is illuminating. Contrary to suggestions that multilateralism was an inevitable consequence of the rise of a system of sovereign states and the attendant need to stabilise territorial property rights,[57] it was a relatively marginal institutional practice up until the middle of the nineteenth century, after which the number of multilateral treaties greatly multiplied.[58] Bilateralism, integral to the practice of 'old' diplomacy, was the principal mode of co-operation and norm development. The major peace settlements that defined the scope and extension of territorial rights in Europe, principally those of Westphalia and Utrecht, were in essence aggregations of separately negotiated diadic agreements.[59]

It was only with the shift in the terms of legitimacy that accompanied the rise of popular sovereignty and its associated norm of procedural justice that multilateralism became the preferred mode of rule enactment. The principle of self-legislation mandates that those subject to the law should be its author, and the principle of non-discrimination demands reciprocal commitments and equal application. John Ruggie has observed that precisely these principles lie at the heart of multilateralism. 'Multilateralism is an institutional form that coordinates relations among three or more states on the basis of generalised principles of conduct: that is, principles which specify appropriate conduct for a class of actions, without regard to the particularistic interests of the parties or the strategic exigencies that may exist in any specific occurrence.'[60] The centrality of the modern norm of procedural justice to the multilateral mode of international legislation is clearly evident in the current tensions between Washington and the vast majority of other states over new developments in international law, including everything from the ban on anti-personnel landmines to the creation of the International Criminal Court. It is Washington's insistence on special protections and exceptions, and the equal insistence of other states on reciprocally binding rules, that has 'forced' the United States to exit from the new regimes.[61]

---

[57] John Gerard Ruggie, 'Multilateralism: The Anatomy of an Institution', in Ruggie (ed.), *Multilateralism Matters*.
[58] Vaclav Mosteky, *Index of Multilateral Treaties: A Chronological List of Multi-Party International Agreements from the Sixteenth Century through 1963* (Cambridge, MA: Harvard Law School Library, 1965).
[59] Reus-Smit, *The Moral Purpose of the State*, chapter 5.
[60] Ruggie, 'Multilateralism', p. 11.
[61] For an extended discussion of these issues see Christian Reus-Smit, *American Power and World Order* (Cambridge: Polity Press, 2004).

## *The language and practice of justification*

If one of the principal features of the international legal order is its discourse of institutional autonomy, what is it that distinguishes this 'autonomous' institutional realm? The realist answer is that legal systems are distinguished by clear lines of centralised authority and enforcement, both of which are said to be lacking in the international legal order. This view has been widely criticised, however, because it misunderstands the nature of domestic legal systems, in which decentralised modes of interpretation and compliance are crucial, and because it underestimates the sources of authority and modes of enforcement that can evolve in anarchical systems. The rationalist answer – most clearly articulated in the 'Legalization and World Politics' volume – is that a regime of rules and norms becomes legalised when its rules are precise, it imposes strong obligations, and it delegates interpretive authority to third parties.[62] In other words, the legal realm is the realm of formal, enforceable contract. This criterion of demarcation fails, however, when we consider the importance of customary norms to the international legal order.[63] Very often the content of these norms lacks precision, their obligations are strong but not grounded in contract, and they are interpreted and applied not through formal mechanisms of adjudication or arbitration but through social discourse and argument.

As noted earlier, constructivists are unclear about what distinguishes the legal realm from the broader fabric of international social norms. Some deny that there is any meaningful difference, others see legal rules as more specified and codified, while still others emphasise the distinctive nature of legal discourse. Among those who have considered the issue most closely, it is this latter argument that is most widely embraced. Kratochwil, for instance, argues that 'the legal character of rules and norms can be established when we are able to show that these norms are *used* in a distinct fashion in making decisions and in communicating the basis of those choices to a wider audience'.[64] 'This norm-*use* obtains its coherence and characteristic as a distinct phenomenon from a peculiar style of arguing, which is transmitted through the "training" of the practitioners.'[65] It is this view of international law that comes through most prominently in the following chapters. In diverse issue-areas, contributors show that actors enter the realm of international law

[62] 'Legalization and World Politics'.
[63] Finnemore and Toope, 'Alternatives to "Legalization"'.
[64] Kratochwil, *Rules, Norms, and Decisions*, p. 42.
[65] Kratochwil, *Rules, Norms, and Decisions*, p. 211.

when they feel impelled not only to place reasoned argument ahead of coercion but also to engage in a distinctive type of argument in which principles and actions must be justified in terms of established, socially sanctioned, normative precepts.

It is important to recognise here, as Nicholas Wheeler stresses in chapter 8, that international law is a process. Actors assume the existence of a set of socially sanctioned rules, but international law 'lives' in the way in which they reason argumentatively about the form of these rules, what they prescribe or proscribe, what their jurisdictional reach is, what new rules should be enacted, how these relate to established rules, and about whether a certain action or inaction is covered by a given rule. This reasoning is rhetorical in nature. '[L]egal arguments deal with the finding and interpretation of the applicable norms and procedures, and with the presentation of the relevant facts and their evaluations. Both questions turn on the issue of whether a particular interpretation of a fact-pattern is acceptable rather than "true"; consequently strict logic plays a minor role in this process of "finding the law".'[66] Legal reasoning is also analogical. As Kratochwil observes, 'the task of analogies is to establish similarities among different cases or objects in the face of (striking) dissimilarities'.[67] As the following chapters demonstrate, international actors reason with analogies in three different ways. They use analogies to interpret a given rule (rule A was interpreted in a particular way, and given the logic applied, rule B should be interpreted that way as well). They draw similarities between one class of action and another to claim that the former is, or is not, rule-governed (case C was rule-governed, and given its similarities with case D, case D should be rule-governed as well). And they invoke analogies to establish the status of one rule with reference to other rules (rule E has customary status, and since the same levels of assent and dissent are evident in the case of rule F, rule F should be accorded that status as well).

## The structure of obligation

The final distinctive feature of the modern international legal order is its structure of obligation.[68] Rationalists argue that states are obliged to obey international law because they have consented. In Louis Henkin's

---

[66] Kratochwil, *Rules, Norms, and Decisions*, p. 42.
[67] Kratochwil, *Rules, Norms, and Decisions*, p. 223.
[68] The argument advanced in this section is elaborated in Reus-Smit, 'Politics and International Legal Obligation'.

words, '[s]tate consent is the foundation of international law. The principle that law is binding on a state only by its consent remains an axiom of the international political system, an implication of state autonomy.'[69] But while it may be true that consent is a signifier of obligation, we still have to explain why, in the modern international legal order, consent is considered binding. H. L. A. Hart famously observed that a promise could only give rise to obligations if there already exists a rule that states' promises shall be binding, and 'rules presupposed in the very notion of a self-imposed obligation obviously cannot derive *their* obligatory status from a self-imposed obligation to obey them'.[70] In other words, consent is only binding because there exist prior norms, such as *pacta sunt servanda*, which specify that promises shall be binding, and the obligation to observe such primary norms must rest on something other than consent.

The perspective on the politics of international law advanced above brings us a step closer to solving the puzzle of modern international legal obligation. Let us begin with the proposition that actors will only regard a set of rules, and the legal order in which they are embedded, as obligatory if they consider them legitimate. Thomas Franck argues that because the international legal system is decentralised, and lacks the capacity to issue and enforce command-like laws, states will only feel obliged to observe the laws that derive from the system if that system is considered fair. The 'fairness of international law, as of any other legal system, will be judged, first by the degree to which the rules satisfy the participants' expectations of justifiable distribution of costs and benefits, and secondly by the extent to which the rules are made and applied in accordance with what the participants perceive as right process'.[71] This means that if we wish to explain the obligations states feel to observe modern international law, we must ask why they consider its processes fair and legitimate.

While Franck is correct that certain internal characteristics of the international legal system can reinforce a sense of its fairness and legitimacy, the system's legitimacy as a social institution must ultimately be grounded in conceptions of justice and right process that are anterior to those internal characteristics. In Michael Byers' words, 'the basis of obligation is located anterior, not only to the individual rules

---

[69] Louis Henkin, *International Law: Politics and Values* (Dordrecht: Martinus Nijhoff, 1995), p. 27.
[70] Hart, *The Concept of Law*, p. 224.　　[71] Franck, *Fairness in International Law*, p. 7.

of international law, but even to the processes that give rise to those ideas'.[72] By focusing on the constitutional structure of international society, as the bedrock of international legitimacy, we can not only provide an historically grounded account of the legitimacy of the international legal system, and hence legal obligation, but also satisfy Byers' theoretical principle.

As we have seen, the modern conception of legitimate statehood is inherently related to a distinctive systemic norm of procedural justice, one that upholds self-legislation and non-discrimination as guiding principles of rule formulation and application. It is because of these principles, and their relationship to dominant conceptions of legitimate statehood, that consent has become the natural signifier of international legal obligation in the modern world. It is important to recognise, however, that it is just a signifier. Its locutionary force ('I promise') is dependent upon the duty-inducing force of the primary source of obligation, the international legal system's legitimacy, which is in turn dependent upon the prevailing liberal conception of legitimate statehood and attendant norm of procedural justice. Should one doubt this connection, it is worth recalling the structure of international legal obligation that existed in Absolutist Europe. Hugo Grotius wrote that 'Observance of the law of nature and of divine law, or of the law of nations ... is binding upon all kings, *even though they have made no promise.*'[73] In the Christian cosmology of the times, the signifier of obligation was express fealty to the command of God and, by extension, the sovereign. The prevailing systemic norm of procedural justice held that legitimate rules were the commands of those 'who have absolute authority over all the rest without exception',[74] a norm that derived from a dominant understanding of legitimate statehood that enshrined the divine right of kings.

## Conclusion

Philip Allott argues that law 'presupposes a *society* whose structures and systems make possible the mutual conditioning of the public mind and the private mind, and the mutual conditioning of the legal and the

---

[72] Byers, *Custom, Power and the Power of Rules*, p. 7.
[73] Hugo Grotius, *The Law of War and Peace: De Jure Belli ac Pacis Libri Tres* (New York: Bobbs-Merrill, 1925), p. 121, my emphasis.
[74] Jean Bodin, *Six Books of the Commonwealth* (Oxford: Basil Blackwell, 1967), p. 43.

non-legal'.[75] The conceptual and analytical approach outlined above can be read as an elaboration of this insight. It lacks the elegant parsimony of realist and neoliberal understandings of the nature of politics and law in international relations, and because it stresses historically and culturally contingent expressions of practical reason and action, its explanatory insights will travel only with a baggage of qualifications. However, there is much that is obscured by existing approaches. The proposition that international law is simply a codification of the interests of powerful states, or, failing that, nothing more than a functional solution to the co-operation problems of rational egoists, requires us to turn a blind eye to much that is rich, complex, and intriguing about the contemporary politics of international law. The approach advanced here is designed to illuminate this complexity, to help us see how the modern liberal politics has conditioned the institution of international law, and how the distinctive features of that institution shape politics in distinctive ways. We now turn to the reflections of other contributors, whose chapters explore these issues in a wide range of cases, from the use of force and the development of norms against anti-personnel landmines to the International Criminal Court and the nature of governance.

[75] Philip Allott, 'The Concept of International Law', in Michael Byers (ed.), *The Role of Law in International Politics: Essays in International Relations and International Law* (Oxford: Oxford University Press, 2000), p. 70, emphasis in original.

# 3  When states use armed force

*Dino Kritsiotis*[1]

In exploring the state and nature of the relationship between law and politics in the sphere of international relations, it could be said that there is qualified merit in returning to the apparent wisdom of past orthodoxies. In these teachings, separate methodological and professional identities have taken shape – or, to be sure, have been projected – for both international law and politics,[2] and these are perhaps best evidenced in the scholarship of Hans Morgenthau, the high priest of classical realism, who advocated 'upholding the autonomy of the political realm' because of his conviction that the political realist is engaged in a discrete form of human thinking – where interest is defined as power, 'as the economist thinks in terms of interest defined as wealth; *the lawyer, of the conformity of action with legal rules*; the moralist, of the conformity of action with moral principles'.[3] Here, let it be noted, the 'political realm' is the venue for the most intimate forms and tasks of sovereignty, cut distinct from the pedestrian enterprises of international law and its many sub-disciplines as well as with those preoccupied with 'rules' and with quaint statistical synopses of conformity and compliance patterns in state behaviour. In this respect, international law takes on something of a distinctly alien form, removed and remote from the ground realities of sovereign relations: it is caught up in its own methodologies and indulgences, and is divorced from the decisions it aspires to influence. 'The lawyers',

[1] I am indebted to those present at the workshop at the Australian National University for which this chapter was written, and in particular to Grey Fry, Paul Keal, Robert McCorquodale, Thérèse O'Donnell, Chris Reus-Smit, and the readers for Cambridge University Press.
[2] See Martti Koskenniemi, *From Apology to Utopia: The Structure of International Legal Argument* (Helsinki: Finnish Lawyers, 1989), pp. 2–3.
[3] Hans J. Morgenthau, *Politics Among Nations: The Struggle for Power and Peace*, 6th edn (New York: McGraw-Hill, 1985), p. 13 (emphasis added).

Michael Walzer wrote in 1977, 'have constructed a paper world, which fails at crucial points to correspond to the world the rest of us still live in.'[4]

The streamlining of the disciplines of law and politics in this manner seems to have occurred with a consummate and confident ease, and, in terms of general reception, gathered a distinguished tradition of followers. However, we should be aware that it is an approach which has drawn significant and often persuasive criticisms from different quarters in recent times.[5] It is not the intention of this chapter to rehearse these sets of argumentation in all of their respective and fulsome detail. Rather, what it seeks to do is to suggest that, notwithstanding the various critiques it has provoked, this dichotomisation between 'law' and 'politics' does hold a particular relevance when studied in the context of how states utilise international law in their practices relating to the use of force in international relations. Even though states can be classed as political operators, it is the regular resort to legal reasoning and argumentation within their practices that has heralded a phenomenon of international law as a separate realm *within* the political context: the political operators themselves recognise – whether rhetorically or otherwise – law as a distinct system within their own system or sphere of existence, and this chapter is an attempt to investigate how this relationship – or, to be more precise, this series of *relationships* – is configured.

States, then, recognise the autonomous existences and identities of 'law' and 'politics' in their practices, but it is also apparent from these practices that states do not see each of these enterprises as monolithic or unchanging propositions, which is to say that they avoid singular definitions of 'law' and its place within 'politics'. As such, it is not possible to reduce or confine to one formulation the resulting interaction between 'law' and 'politics', and our concern in this chapter is to get at and understand how the changing configurations of the relationships shared between 'law' and 'politics' are framed by changing, prevailing circumstances of both legal and political fact. This is central to the theme of the chapter and, it will be argued, presents an approach that is altogether more coherent and defensible, bringing us much closer

---

[4] Michael Walzer, *Just and Unjust Wars: A Moral Argument with Historical Illustrations*, 3rd edn (New York: Basic Books, 2000), p. xix.

[5] B. S. Chimni, *International Law and World Order: A Critique of Contemporary Approaches* (Newbury Park: Sage, 1993), p. 29. See also, the essay of Andrew Hurrell, 'International Law and the Changing Constitution of International Society', in Michael Byers (ed.), *The Role of Law in International Politics: Essays in International Relations and International Law* (Oxford: Oxford University Press, 2000), p. 327.

to appreciating the 'fascinating complexity' that 'has evolved between international politics and law'.[6] Our findings suggest that states have rejected generalised accounts which seek to equate all law with political action or which seek to hierarchise law and politics in relation to each other.[7]

To understand the full depths of these interactions and their resulting relationships, it is necessary for us to understand the realities and limitations of stereotyping international law as a 'primitive' system of rules awaiting jigsaw-fit applications to specific fact-scenarios, towards 'a more complex understanding of "law" as a sociological phenomenon, of "governance" as a mixed political/legal process of mutual claim making and communication, of "states" as disaggregated social functions in a broad civil society'.[8] We do so even though we remain within our governing conceptual structure – of how law is used and abused, applied and misapplied, interpreted and misinterpreted within the political realm. Such a contention is not of course unique, nor is it confined to occasions where states have used force against other states, but it evidences that, even in terms of the most phenomenal demonstrations of sovereign power, states themselves do not recoil from the institution or processes of legal discourse. Law is not absent or silent from these proceedings – we are now, it would seem, a world apart from statements made at the height of the Cuban Missile Crisis in 1962, that 'the law simply does not deal with such questions of ultimate power – power that comes close to the source of sovereignty'[9] – but it is the nature of its presence within the political realm which awaits to be discovered, and this is done through the series of relationships which we depict and analyse throughout this chapter.

The embrace of argument – specifically international legal argument – has therefore become one of the staple features of state practice on the use of force, so that when states use force against other states, they also *use* international law to define and defend, argue and counter-argue, explain and rationalise their actions. International law is therefore part of an attempt at persuasion, a sort of intellectualised diplomacy if you will, if it is not *the* language of persuasion, and 'justifications and

---

[6] Christian Reus-Smit, Introduction, this volume, p. 4.
[7] See Martin Loughlin, *Sword and Scales: An Examination of the Relationship Between Law and Politics* (Oxford and Portland, OR: Hart, 2000).
[8] David Kennedy, 'The Disciplines of International Law and Policy', *Leiden Journal of International Law* 12: 1 (1999), 27.
[9] See Dean Acheson, 'Remarks before the American Society of International Law', *Proceedings of the American Society of International Law* 57 (1963), 13–14.

judgements'[10] now permeate the so-called realm of politics on all manner of questions relating to coercive action and intervention. Stark examples are commonplace, whether we are examining Operation Provide Comfort in Iraq (1991), or Operation Allied Force against the Federal Republic of Yugoslavia (1999) or even Operation Iraqi Freedom (2003).[11] It is this *use* of international law in these and other episodes that breaks us away from an understanding of international law in exclusive terms as *a system of rules applied to fact-situations*, since it suggests that states have come to regard the law as serving more than just one function, trained on one solitary objective or purpose.

The nature of the relationship at any given point in time, it will be argued, is defined by a whole series of considerations and circumstances, including the legislative history, nature, and ongoing political reassessments of and commitments to a given law. Our first contact with international law comes in the form of a 'rule'; here, international law is at its most pronounced because it is – at least in theoretical terms – clear, it is specific in terms of the behaviour it directs, and there is minimal (if any) opportunity for misinterpretation or for deviation. In order for it to reach this point of precision or common understanding, however, the rule might have to undergo considerable periods of development – of initiation and refinement, reception and reform, and then of further reception by states – before it can be said to gain its optimum legitimacy.[12] We encounter this phenomenon in our discussions in the second part of this chapter, where attentions turn to the protracted legislative background behind and empirical reception of the 'rules' prohibiting war (in the Kellogg–Briand Pact of 1928) and force (in the United Nations Charter of 1945).

The third part takes us to the exceptions for permissible cases of the use of force, where the identities of 'law' and 'politics' as distinct ideas begin to seem a touch superficial, and even to unravel and disintegrate altogether. International law's prohibition of force appears to emerge as a prohibition that exists in name only, because when states use force from time to time – not, it must be said, with sufficient frequency or

---

[10] Walzer, *Just and Unjust Wars*, p. xix. See, further, Thomas M. Franck, *Recourse to Force: State Action Against Threats and Armed Attacks* (Cambridge: Cambridge University Press, 2002).

[11] Christine Gray, *International Law and the Use of Force* (Oxford: Oxford University Press, 2000), p. 19.

[12] Thomas M. Franck, *The Power of Legitimacy Among Nations* (New York: Oxford University Press, 1990).

intent to compromise the Charter's prohibition[13] – the development of justifications for permissible actions questions whether the legal prescription of force is but a benevolent and elaborate duplicity conducted by states before other states, so that legal argument can be rallied to their cause no matter what the circumstance. We soon appreciate that the 'rule' prohibiting force is not an *absolute* rule, against which all contrary actions can be judged.[14] We are here dealing with a *general* rule – that is a rule that admits or is open to exceptions – which appear in the form of justifications for action. It is at this point that the utility of speaking of law as 'rules' is tested, since the justifications either occur as expansions of existing *rights* for action (such as self-defence) or as legal innovations (such as the *right* of humanitarian intervention). International law is here best seen as a discursive exercise, in which states are able to make, address, and assess justifications and it is through this process that international law can develop and store its own 'self-knowledge',[15] working practices, and conditions for regulating international recourses to force. Through their entourages of legal experts, states have crafted precise and at times cunning legal justifications for their actions, so that 'legal styles [as] styles of argument [and] linguistic expression' can be said to 'create worlds' rather than to ' "reflect" them'.[16]

In setting out these reflections, and the concluding thoughts of the fourth and final part of this chapter, it has been necessary to engage certain assumptions on the respective meanings of 'law' and 'politics', at least for the initial part of our discussions. While it has been said that there is no 'essential distinction' between the two,[17] the revelations of state practice suggest that, to a significant extent, states themselves have come to accept the essential autonomies of 'law' and 'politics' in their practices. These autonomies might not only have been affirmed but also enhanced through statements of legal conviction or *opinio juris*

---

[13] See the famous exchange occurring in the pages of the *American Journal of International Law* between Thomas M. Franck, 'Who Killed Article 2(4)? Or: Changing Norms Governing the Use of Force by States', *American Journal of International Law* 64: 4 (1970), and Louis Henkin, 'The Reports of the Death of Article 2(4) are Greatly Exaggerated', *American Journal of International Law* 65: 3 (1971).

[14] See Anne-Marie Slaughter and William Burke-White, 'An International Constitutional Moment', *Harvard International Law Journal* 43: 1 (2002), 1.

[15] Fred Halliday, *Rethinking International Relations* (Basingstoke: Macmillan, 1994), p. 7.

[16] Martti Koskenniemi, 'Letter to the Editors of the Symposium', *American Journal of International Law* 93: 2 (1999), 351, 359.

[17] Martti Koskenniemi, 'Faith, Identity, and the Killing of the Innocent: International Lawyers and Nuclear Weapons', *Leiden Journal of International Law* 10: 1 (1997), 137, 140.

*sive necessitates* of states,[18] which has in turn created a distinct sphere of action and activity for international law: 'law arises in the interaction between ideas (which may be political, philosophical, sociological, or other types of ideas) and practice, [and] becomes itself through specific juridical processes that serve as part of its independent justification'.[19]

## The prohibitions on war and force

### Synopsis

While the problems of defining 'law' and 'politics' persist and will continue to persist, it is now appropriate for us to consider how international law attempts to structure its relationship with political action in matters concerning the use of force in international relations. The historical antecedents to the modern prohibition on the use of force came in the form of the 1919 Covenant of the League of Nations and the 1928 Pact of Paris, which, when taken together, heralded a moment of 'high moral absolutism' in international relations.[20] Questions soon began to proliferate, however, concerning the substantive contribution and fundamental relevance of these treaties:[21] as events unfolded in Europe and further afield, international law came to be regarded as 'something of an epiphenomenon, dependent on power and therefore subject to short-term change at the will of power-applying states'.[22] Perhaps no greater illustration of the crude manipulation – of the mimicry almost – of the institution of international law exists than in the 1939 Ribbentrop–Molotov Pact of Non-Aggression between Germany and the Soviet Union: '[t]heir so-called "pact of non-aggression" was the perfect blueprint *for* aggression'.[23]

This representation of events accords with and exploits the obvious antagonisms believed to be a defining part of the relationship

---

[18] Ian Brownlie, *Principles of Public International Law*, 5th edn (Oxford: Clarendon Press, 1998), p. 7.
[19] Stephen J. Toope, 'Emerging Patterns of Governance and International Law', in Michael Byers (ed.), *The Role of Law in International Politics: Essays in International Relations and International Law* (Oxford: Oxford University Press, 2000), pp. 101–2.
[20] David Thomson, *Europe Since Napoleon* (Harmondsworth: Penguin, 1966), p. 678.
[21] E. H. Carr, *The Twenty Years' Crisis, 1919–1939: An Introduction to the Study of International Relations*, 2nd edn (London: Macmillan, 1946), pp. 170–207.
[22] Michael Byers, *Custom, Power and the Power of Rules: International Relations and Customary International Law* (Cambridge: Cambridge University Press, 1999), p. 22.
[23] Norman Davies, *Europe: A History* (Oxford and New York: Oxford University Press, 1996), p. 997 (emphasis added).

between law and politics: a situation in which sovereign aspirations reign supreme because 'armed force' exists as 'the *ultima ratio* in international politics', whose 'counterpart in the internal sphere is revolution'.[24] However, at the heart of this interpretation lies a generalised assumption about the *nature* of the application of power as an unstoppable force that holds no hostages – international law included – to fortune. Part of this assumption is rooted in the perceived failure of international law to present itself as a countervailing – let alone prevailing – force operating against the excesses of power and political action. Here we have the full embodiment of staid constructions of the relationship – that, without more, the series of textual commands encased in the Covenant and the Pact were as good as an invitation to states to act in a manner of their own choosing because there was no system of sanctions in place for them to fear.[25] The assumption is problematic because it tends to award defining focus to the structural deficiencies of the 'regime' controlling war:[26] the emphasis on structural deficiencies, in essence, becomes a vicarious means for assessing how 'law' and 'politics' contest each other in the regulation of war, typecast as they are as permanent and unrelenting binary opposites. Such an argument can also be viewed as a *non sequitur* to be sure, because 'many treaties and other sources of law provide [for] no sanctions';[27] in any event, in the alternative, it could be argued that these treaties were indeed 'covered by the sanctions of all international law'.[28]

If our focus is broadened, it becomes clear that – from the standpoint of international law – considerable difficulties existed on other fronts aside from the sanctions issue. It should be recalled that the extent of state participation in the League of Nations remained limited – an affliction that the United Nations Charter has been fortunate enough to escape[29] – and its Covenant has been shown to have suffered from certain inadequacies and incoherencies of formulation. This approach

[24] Joachim von Elbe, 'The Evolution of the Concept of the Just War in International Law', *American Journal of International Law* 33: 4 (1939), 684–5.
[25] Louis Henkin, *How Nations Behave: Law and Foreign Policy*, 2nd edn (New York: Columbia University Press, 1979), pp. 88–9.
[26] Francis A. Boyle, 'International Law and the Use of Force: Beyond Regime Theory', in Linda B. Miller and Michael Joseph Smith (eds.), *Ideas and Ideals: Essays on Politics in Honor of Stanley Hoffmann* (Boulder, CO: Westview Press, 1993).
[27] Ian Brownlie, *International Law and the Use of Force by States* (Oxford: Clarendon Press, 1963), p. 83.
[28] Quincy Wright, 'The Meaning of the Pact of Paris', *American Journal of International Law* 27: 1 (1933), 41. See also Franck, *The Power of Legitimacy*, p. 15.
[29] Henkin, *How Nations Behave*, p. 137.

requires us to refine the points of detail on our radar – to see what a particular law said and what it left unsaid, to get a better sense of the berth of interpretative opportunities warranted under the political conditions of the time – as we close in on the full facts and circumstances of each case awaiting assessment. Our concentration on circumstances avoids macro-level characterisations (if this is what we can call them) and the grand theories, insights, and prejudices to which they give rise. The relationship between 'law' and 'politics', once cast as unchanging in view of these stereotypologies, suddenly becomes negotiable and contingent and subject to change and qualification in view of changing sets of circumstances: the limits of 'hard-nosed realism'[30] requires, in the words of Thomas M. Franck, consideration of 'non-coercive factors in understanding the phenomenon of global obligation and rule conformity'.[31] The further we intrude upon these specifics, the more it is that we appreciate the *possibility* that it is the actual formulations of international law – as a complement to the structural deficiences of the system taken as a whole – which also act as frustrators of compliance, perchance *the* frustrator of compliance. Article 10 of the Covenant of the League of Nations, for example, qualified the right of states to go to war, but it became infamous for being 'an abstract provision, which lent itself to more than one interpretation'.[32] Even read alongside other provisions of the Covenant,[33] lawful opportunities still remained for states to assert the right to go to war,[34] so that the problem of compliance assumes a much more complicated dimension than 'hard-nosed realists' would have us believe. This set of arrangements is developed, reformed and made much more transparent in the Charter, and it is to each of these sections of international law's history that we now turn.

## War

Although the Kellogg–Briand Pact, agreed in Paris on 27 August 1928, boasted a greater degree of support than the Covenant of the League of Nations,[35] its formulations – according to which states condemned

---

[30] Franck, *The Power of Legitimacy*, p. 4.     [31] Franck, *The Power of Legitimacy*, p. 16.

[32] Yoram Dinstein, *War, Aggression and Self-Defence*, 3rd edn (New York: Cambridge University Press, 2001), p. 75.

[33] See Brownlie, *International Law and the Use of Force*, p. 62; and Dinstein, *War, Aggression and Self-Defence*, p. 75.

[34] Dinstein, *War, Aggression and Self-Defence*, p. 76.

[35] D. J. Harris, *Cases and Materials on International Law*, 5th edn (London: Sweet and Maxwell, 1998), p. 861. Four states not bound by the Pact – Bolivia, El Salvador, Uruguay,

recourse to 'war' for the 'solution of international controversies' and renounced war 'as an instrument of national policy' – meant that it was a matter of time before the Pact became the chronic entrepôt for a haze of competing and often irreconcilable interpretations. 'War', of course, carried a range of meanings for a range of different purposes,[36] but it was its technical meaning – wars could only commence and end through the formalities of declarations and peace treaties[37] – which surfaced in the vagaries of the interpretative practices of states.

Such practices would come to defeat the objectives of the Pact: 'it is doubtful if the sponsoring governments understood the term "war" in its technical sense since in this case the technical sense would be incongruous in the context of an important multilateral treaty'.[38] Nevertheless, these incongruities rose to special prominence in the official expressions of states, so that – for different reasons – the fundamental concern of the Pact was denied. An example could prove instructive. Following the Japanese gamble to capture by coercive means the Chinese province of Manchuria in September 1931,[39] neither state admitted the existence of a state of war: both states committed themselves to an interpretation of war 'in the technical sense',[40] and since declarations of war had been filed by neither side, a legal state of war did not exist between Japan and China. This seems surprising, counter-intuitive even, but as one of the founding members of the League of Nations, Japan was keen not to have involved itself in an official state of war. For its part, China adopted a path that would lead to the same outcome: to have characterised the situation as one of 'war' would have activated the international laws governing neutral relations between states and this, in turn, would have jeopardised its trade relations – so critical at that time – with the United States. Thus, as has been said of this event, 'hostilities on a considerable scale have been carried on which, for different reasons

and Argentina – were bound by the Saavedra Lamas of 10 October 1933: Brownlie, *International Law and the Use of Force*, pp. 110–11 and a parallel protocol was agreed in February 1929 by the Soviet Union, Estonia, Latvia, Poland, and Romania: *League of Nations Treaty Series* 89, p. 370.
[36] Christopher Greenwood, 'The Concept of War in Modern International Law', *International and Comparative Law Quarterly* 36: 2 (1987), 283.
[37] This is one of the bases on which the definition of war given by Lassa Oppenheim in *Oppenheim's International Law*, volume II, 7th edn (Harlow, Essex: Longman, 1952), that war is a 'contention, i.e. a violent struggle through the application of armed force', is critiqued by Dinstein, *War, Aggression and Self-Defence*, pp. 4–14.
[38] Brownlie, *International Law and the Use of Force*, p. 85.
[39] Westel Woodbury Willoughby, *The Sino-Japanese Controversy and the League of Nations* (Baltimore: Johns Hopkins University Press, 1935).
[40] Brownlie, *International Law and the Use of Force*, p. 85.

on each side, but for reasons which it is not difficult to guess at in the peculiar circumstances of the case, neither party is prepared to recognise as war'.[41]

Attitudes toward this narrow endorsement of 'war' in practice suggest that international law – as has been said of law in general – is no more than 'the output of a political process'.[42] This is to say that the law is somehow devalued – its ambitions abruptly affected – by the machinations of the political process because, through the relentless techniques of interpretation, all forms of behaviour can be defended or justified in legal terms. It has been said that:

> rules are not *automatically* applicable. They need interpretation and interpretation seems subjective. This is not merely a 'practical' difficulty of interpretation. The doctrine of sovereign equality makes it impossible to decide between competing interpretations . . . There is no other basis to make the [interpretative] choice than . . . either by referring to a theory of justice or to the identities of the states involved: one interpretation is better either because it is more just or because it is produced by this, and not that, state. And the former solution is utopian, the latter violates sovereign equality. Both seem purely political.[43]

How else can we describe these passings on the definition of 'war' than as a 'corruption of the rule of law . . . in the narrow chauvinism of diplomats'?[44] It seems impossible to characterise the interpretations of 'war' in the above example as anything other than rank political foibles, defeating the law's career claim to objectivity and to justice. Our 'conceptual matrices' can 'no longer be defended by the texts, facts or histories to which they provided meaning' because they 'were – and are – arenas of political struggle'.[45]

Yet, while the role of political considerations in the process of interpretation is made clear by these remarks, the example in hand serves to reinforce how the separate paradigms of 'law' and 'politics' are used, perpetrated, and reinforced in state practice: both states in our example engaged the formalisms of legal discourse, offering rather precise computations of doctrine at an official level of state action, and doing so for their own private (or, we could say, political)

---

[41] J. L. Brierly, 'International Law and Resort to Armed Force', *Cambridge Law Journal* 4: 3 (1932), 308, 312.

[42] Loughlin, *Sword and Scales*, p. 9.

[43] Koskenniemi, *From Apology to Utopia*, p. 245 (emphasis added).

[44] Martti Koskenniemi, 'The Politics of International Law', *European Journal of International Law* 1: 1/2 (1990), 6–7.

[45] Koskenniemi, 'The Politics of International Law', 31.

reasons.[46] So far, so good. At the same time, however, we should also take note of how the 'political' can itself be constructed by the 'legal': if we take the rationales given for the positions of both states in this episode, the political considerations motivating the acts of interpretation are themselves conceived by reference to legal factors, namely Japan's reputation within an international institution (the League of Nations) and China's concern of neutrality laws disrupting its commercial interactions (with the United States). The fundamental question is thereby raised, as to whether 'legitimising or criticising state behaviour is not a matter of applying formally neutral rules' to specific situations, but 'depends' – or should depend – 'on what one regards as politically right, or just'.[47]

Does this mean that anything can pass as an act of interpretation, that international law is at risk of becoming 'singularly useless as a means for justifying or criticising international behaviour',[48] that '[a]ll law is masked power'?[49] At this juncture, it becomes relevant to assess the degree of determinacy of a given rule, which is itself affected by the histories and sophistication of the political culture (or community?) of that rule. The Kellogg–Briand Pact suffered as a result of the manifold purposes and definitions devoted to 'war' in international law – such as the contexts of neutrality and international humanitarian law, for example – as well as the ambivalent nature of the political commitment to renounce war at that time. In contrast, it is worth recalling that the legal argumentation advanced before the International Court of Justice in the jurisdiction phase of the *Nicaragua Case* brought in April 1984, was *not* framed in terms of the infamous 'Connally Reservation', even though this offered the United States a potential winner of an argument before the Court: the reservation had been appended to the Optional Clause Declaration which the United States had submitted to the Court in 1946. It provided that 'disputes with regard to matters which are essentially within the domestic jurisdiction of the United States of America as *determined by the United States of America*'.[50] In legal terms, could this

---

[46] See Hilary Charlesworth and Christine Chinkin, *The Boundaries of International Law: A Feminist Analysis* (Manchester: Juris Publishing, 2000), p. 30.
[47] Koskenniemi, 'The Politics of International Law', 31.
[48] Koskenneimi, *From Apology to Utopia*, p. 48.
[49] Owen M. Fiss, 'Objectivity and Interpretation', *Stanford Law Review* 34: 4 (1982), 741 (in defining nihilist approaches to legal discourse).
[50] Emphasis added. It should be made clear, however, that the United States has not been alone in making 'domestic jurisdiction' reservations: there are five 'automatic' reservations – those of Liberia, Malawi, Mexico, the Philippines, and the Sudan – that

clause not have been invoked to actualise the exit strategy for the United States from the proceedings before the Court?

In an episode that pointed to the limits of subjective interpretations, Franck has written that this 'failure of the lawyers to use the Connally shield' is 'all the more remarkable' because:

> while the reservation gave the United States a self-judging escape from the Court's jurisdiction, all the other defences left the key jurisdictional decision up to the Court, which rejected every one. Had the US Government simply faced the Court with a 'finding' that the mining of Nicaragua's borders was a 'domestic' matter for the United States, that would have ended the litigation. Instead, the United States went on to lose, not only on the matter of jurisdiction, but eventually also on the merits.[51]

Franck asks: 'What lawyer would want to stand before the fifteen judges of the [International Court of Justice] and argue that the US bombing of Nicaraguan harbours was a domestic matter?'[52] The fact that no lawyer was prepared to put the reservation to the test in this case has been described as 'a tribute to the determinacy of the term "domestic" ' and forms the basis of the following conclusion:

> When a rule is so inelastic that certain legal arguments purporting to be based on it become laughable, the rule may be said to have determinacy. The greater its determinacy, the more legitimacy the rule exhibits and the more it pulls towards compliance. The community expects legitimate obligations to be honoured. To fail to honour them is, in most circumstances, to be seen to act unfairly and anti-systematically. Fortunately, states (like persons) are generally reluctant to incur the opprobrium which such conduct would provoke.[53]

In our assessment of the Manchurian crisis above, we encountered a similar 'tribute to determinacy' in terms of the meaning of war but, on that occasion, we also discovered how this 'tribute' actually produced a perverse and incredulous result – notwithstanding the homage that both of the states involved paid to the formalist incarnation of 'war'.

---

are in force today. See Harris, *Cases and Materials*, p. 1014. For a critique of this practice, see *Norwegian Loans Case*: France v. Norway (1957) *ICJ Reports* 9 (per Judge Lauterpacht) and the *Interhandel Case*: Switzerland v. United States (1959) *ICJ Reports* 6 (per President Klaestad and Judge Spender).

[51] Thomas M. Franck, *Fairness in International Law and Institutions* (Oxford: Clarendon Press, 1995), p. 32.

[52] Franck, *Fairness in International Law and Institutions*, p. 32.

[53] Franck, *Fairness in International Law and Institutions*, pp. 32–3.

The determinacy of a rule is not therefore instrumental; it is not an end unto itself, since other considerations (in this case, how the rules of international law relate to and reinforce one another) have to be factored.[54] In the relations between China and Japan, we were not presented with epic divisions within the relevant 'interpretative community'[55] – both sides had, after all, promoted the same legal position – but, rather, with a potential situation in which the law's irregularities could or would be exploited to service the different political gains and ambitions of the parties involved. What therefore proved 'laughable' was *not* the presentation of unsustainable legal arguments by either side, but, rather, the coincidence of positions in support of differing political ends and agendas: the telling contrivance of the law by virtue of an overt set of highly politicised conditions, actors, and outcomes.

### Force

Aside from a rule's determinacy, therefore, it is also important to consider 'rule coherence', which is to say that '[r]ules, to be perceived as legitimate, must emanate from principles of general application. State behaviour is judged in terms of its effect in reinforcing, undermining, or amending the generalised norms of the system.'[56] Again, it could be said that this notion is a good indicator of the sophistication of a law-making community, because it tells us how far the rules of this community have been made to co-exist, relate with, and reinforce each other.

Before we turn to this issue, it should be said that the modern prohibition on force contained in Article 2(4) of the Charter of the United Nations has fared much better than its predecessor provisions because, as an 'idiot rule', it boasts a 'high level of determinacy' and it 'also makes sense'.[57] This is in part due to the background of the rule, rehearsed to some extent above, but it is also the result of a sharpened commitment on behalf of states and expressed in the preamble to the Charter 'to save succeeding generations from the scourge of war'. Avoiding the shortcomings of the Kellogg–Briand Pact, the Charter places a 'comprehensive'[58] interdiction on 'the threat or use of force against the territorial integrity or political independence of any state, or in any other manner

---

[54] Franck, *Fairness in International Law and Institutions*, p. 41.

[55] Ian Johnstone, 'Treaty Interpretation: The Authority of Interpretative Communities', *Michigan Journal of International Law* 12: 2 (1991), 372.

[56] Franck, *The Power of Legitimacy*, p. 152.  [57] Franck, *The Power of Legitimacy*, p. 75.

[58] Brownlie, *International Law and the Use of Force*, p. 113.

inconsistent with the purposes of the United Nations'. Although, at first blush, with its many twists and turns of phrase, the provision appears to introduce its own interpretative opportunities,[59] it is significant that, but for the rare occasion, states have not chosen to go down the path of exploiting these opportunities, and have instead elected to quantify their actions in terms of exceptions to the rule under international law:

> [i]f a state acts in a way *prima facie* incompatible with a recognised rule, but defends its conduct by appealing to exceptions or justifications contained within the rule itself, then whether or not the state's conduct is in fact justifiable on that basis, the significance of that attribute is to confirm rather than to weaken the rule.[60]

There has thus been a major change of circumstances – in terms of the formulation of the rule itself but also in terms of contemporary political attitudes – which has impacted upon the working of this rule. We know this because when states have attempted to pick apart the composite elements of the rule – an endeavour surely designed to thwart the intended impact of this rule – they have not met with even a modicum of success: the United Kingdom argued before the International Court of Justice in the *Corfu Channel Case* (1949) that its actions in Albanian territorial waters 'threatened neither the territorial integrity nor the political independence of Albania',[61] but the Court was 'not in sympathy' with this restrictive interpretation[62] and, half a century later, Belgium was alone in arguing before the Court that Operation Allied Force was 'an armed humanitarian intervention, compatible with Article 2, paragraph 4, of the Charter, which covers only intervention against the territorial integrity or political independence of a State'.[63]

The room for interpretative manoeuvre within Article 2(4) has thus been curtailed by the very same 'political' interpretations which proved to be the undoing of the Kellogg–Briand Pact. To this set of circumstances, one must then add the relation (or 'coherence') of Article 2(4)

---

[59] See, for example, Derek Bowett, *Self-Defence in International Law* (Manchester: Manchester University Press, 1958), p. 152.

[60] *Nicaragua Case*: Nicaragua v. United States (1986) *ICJ Reports* 14, p. 98.

[61] *Corfu Channel Case* (Pleadings), Vol. III, p. 296.

[62] Harris, *Cases and Materials*, p. 865.

[63] CR 99/15 (translation), Verbatim Record of 10 May 1999, pp. 16–17, <www.icj-cij. org/icjwww/idocket/iyall/iyall_cr/iyall_icr9915_19990510_translation.htm> (although it did also attempt to defend the action in terms of a 'state of necessity'). See also the discussion on the Israeli bombing of the nuclear reactor at Osirak, Iraq in 1981. Anthony D'Amato, 'Israel's Air Strike Upon the Iraqi Nuclear Reactor', *American Journal of International Law* 77: 3 (1983), 585.

to other rules, some of which have enhanced its claim to determinacy. In its 1970 Declaration on Principles of International Law Concerning Friendly Relations and Co-operation Among Nations, the General Assembly proclaimed that 'every state has the duty to refrain from the threat or use of force to violate the existing international boundaries of another state *or as a means of solving international disputes, including territorial disputes and problems concerning frontiers of states*'.[64] Furthermore, and within a few paragraphs of this statement, the General Assembly continued:

> The territory of a state shall not be the object of military occupation resulting from the threat or use of force in contravention of the provisions of the United Nations Charter. *The territory of a state shall not be the object of acquisition by another state resulting from the threat or use of force.* No territorial acquisition resulting from the threat or use of force shall be recognised as legal.[65]

It is difficult to see how these developments are anything other than a consolidation of the rule contained in Article 2(4): there is an invocation of the notion of the 'threat and use of force' and an explicit application of the prohibition to certain fact-situations (such as the acquisition of territory, and, elsewhere in the Declaration, to armed reprisal actions).

Of course, these clear and firm stipulations did not preclude the forcible attempt made by Argentina to acquire control of the Falkland Islands on 2 April 1982 or by Iraq against Kuwait on 2 August 1990 – or from making arguments that could not in any way be reconciled with these provisions of international law.[66] What these legal refinements of the prohibition on force *do* mean, however, is that the prospects for making arguments regarding territorial conquest – and for succeeding in making such arguments – have been considerably narrowed and weakened: even those Latin American states that were sympathetic to the territorial claims of Argentina disavowed its choice of means to

---

[64] United Nations General Assembly Resolution 2625 (XXV), A/RES/2625(XXV), 24 October 1970.
[65] United Nations General Assembly Resolution 2625 (XXV) (emphasis added).
[66] In the Security Council, Argentina argued that its actions constituted 'an act of self-defence in response to the acts of aggression by the United Kingdom' in 'an act which responds to a just Argentine claim': United Nations Security Council, 2346th Mtg., 2 April 1982. For Iraq's territorial claim to Kuwait, see 'Press Release by the Press Office of the Embassy of the Republic of Iraq, London, 12 September 1990', in E. Lauterpacht, C. J. Greenwood, Marc Weller, and Daniel Bethlehem (eds.), *The Kuwait Crisis: Basic Documents,* Cambridge International Documents Series, Vol. 1 (Cambridge: Grotius, 1991), p. 73.

redeem that claim.[67] Furthermore, it has been said that '[v]otes in international bodies show that reactions to the use of force by states are not always dictated by political affinities in disregard of facts and law [since] [s]tates that are friendly to, or are even closely allied with, an accused state have not hesitated to cast their votes against the state when the issues were clear'.[68] When the Security Council was galvanised into action by these events, it adopted Resolution 502 on 3 April 1982, in which it demanded an 'immediate withdrawal of all Argentine forces' from the islands. The same patterns of behaviour are reflected in the practices emanating from Iraq's invasion of Kuwait in August 1990, where a firm line was adopted by the United Nations in general and the Security Council in particular in condemning the actions of Iraq.[69]

A further manifestation of coherence – or normative coincidence – on this point of law occurs in the international law governing belligerent occupation, where the rules and jurisprudential traditions make clear that 'not an atom of sovereignty [invests] in the authority of the occupation'.[70] Article 43 of the 1907 Regulations annexed to the Hague Convention (IV) Respecting the Laws and Customs of War on Land emphasises the '*de facto* nature of the occupant's authority and the respect for the law already in force in the occupied territory' and reflects the principle 'that the military occupation of territory during a war [does] not confer sovereignty upon the occupying power'.[71] The provision deliberately emphasises this point with its statement that the authority of the legitimate power 'having in fact passed into the hands of the occupant':[72] the occupant's authority, the product of an application of force, is factual ('in fact'), it is by that fact made not lawful; the occupation is temporary and not permanent ('passed into the hands'). Furthermore, it could be argued, the high degree of determinacy and coherence this provision shares with the prohibition on force impacts upon the political culture and conscience, and broadens the prospects for it to be treated as

[67] Lawrence Freedman and Virginia Gamba-Stonehouse, *Signals of War: The Falkland Conflict of 1982* (Princeton: Princeton University Press, 1991), p. 150.
[68] Oscar Schachter, *International Law in Theory and Practice* (Dordrecht and Boston: Nijhoff Publishers, 1991), p. 139.
[69] UN Document S/PV.2932, 2 August 1990.
[70] Lassa Oppenheim, 'The Legal Relations Between an Occupying Power and the Inhabitants', *Law Quarterly Review* 33: 4 (1917), 364.
[71] Christopher Greenwood, 'The Administration of Occupied Territory in International Law', in Emma Playfair (ed.), *International Law and the Administration of Occupied Territories: Two Decades of Israeli Occupation of the West Bank and Gaza Strip* (Oxford: Clarendon Press, 1992), p. 244.
[72] *Consolidated Treaty Series* 205 (1907), 227.

'compelling'.[73] As part of that culture, states in general recalled the transgression committed in December 1975 by Indonesia against East Timor a generation after the actual event: it was *not* accepted that, '[e]ven if the initial act of annexation was invalid, the prolonged (and undisturbed) exercise of sovereignty in the territory will finally create prescriptive rights, independently of the original defective title'.[74]

## Exceptions
### General observations

As the opening paragraph of this chapter indicates, those who characterise (or caricature?) law and politics as opposite and contesting forces often proceed from the assumption that international law exists as a series of rules whose stipulations on a given matter are final, authoritative, and conclusive. We have examined this approach from the perspective of states in the context of the 'rules' which have prohibited war and force, and found that it is problematic to speak of 'rules' as a single genre, since not all rules share the same internal properties or political dynamic: the legal and political circumstances of 1928 were altogether different from those prevailing in 1945, in part because the former informed and shaped the latter. In our assessments, though, the prohibitions on war and force have been analysed as *rules* on specific account of their nature and comport: they have been treated as 'rules' in the same sense that we would have spoken of the 'rules' which forbid torture or genocide or the killing of prisoners of war.

However, in the same way that it has proved problematic to fit all 'rules' within the same conceptual template, we should be cautious not to regard all 'laws' as rules, since not all laws are constructed in the form of specific instructions for certain types of action or non-action. When we consider the full remit of other 'laws' on the use of force – the exceptions to the prohibition we have been discussing – we find that, here, international law has in effect designed possibilities for *permissible* uses of force. At this point, we become attracted to other methodological dispensations within international law, such as the policy science school,[75] which emphasises the idea of international law as a normative process and scales back the dichotomisation between 'law' and 'politics'.

---

[73] Franck, *The Power of Legitimacy*, p. 143.
[74] Dinstein, *War, Aggression and Self-Defence*, p. 154.
[75] Myres S. McDougal and Florentino P. Feliciano, *The International Law of War: Transnational Coercion and World Public Order*, revised edn (New Haven: New Haven Press, 1994).

Its teachings profess that international law is emphatically 'not rules';[76] it is 'a continuing process of authoritative decisions' which identifies 'policy alternatives for the future'.[77] Through this conceptualisation, international law is said to be more able to 'contribute to, and cope with, a changing political world'.[78]

This description of law as process seems ill-at-ease with the 'rules' we have just considered, but it does seem to command a greater measure of support when studied in the context of the exceptions to those rules. Such is the case, for example, with the right of self-defence recognised by Article 51 of the Charter of the United Nations: it is described as an 'inherent' right – it is for states to determine in the first instance whether or not they wish to exercise this right – but one that is 'regulated to the extent that it is the business of courts to determine whether, how far, and for how long, that was a necessity to have recourse to it'.[79] Though related, the circumstances operating in the case of exceptions to the prohibition of force therefore yield to different sets of considerations and conditions: our operating legal premise (once a prohibition, now an entitlement or, conceivably, a requirement to *use* force) has changed.

As we move from the rule to its exceptions, we are nevertheless able to contend from the evidence that we continue to operate – to a lesser degree, to be sure – in situations where 'the possibilities for manipulation are limited' because '[w]hether or not people speak in good faith, they cannot say just anything they please'.[80] We discovered this earlier, in the assessments of the Connally Reservation of the United States and the jurisdiction phase of the *Nicaragua Case* (1984). That example taught us that it does *matter* that international law is a 'rigorously formal language' with 'professionally competent and incompetent uses of legal language' because, we learned, '[i]t [is] not possible to say just anything that [comes] to one's mouth and pretend that one [is] making a legal argument'.[81] Those formalities have exhibited themselves once again in

---

[76] Rosalyn Higgins, *Problems and Process: International Law and How We Use It* (Oxford: Clarendon Press, 1994), p. 1.

[77] Rosalyn Higgins, 'Policy Considerations and the International Judicial Process', *International and Comparative Law Quarterly* 17: 1 (1968), 59.

[78] Higgins, *Problems and Process*, p. 3. For a critique of this approach, see Walzer, *Just and Unjust Wars*, p. xix.

[79] Hersch Lauterpacht, *The Function of Law in the International Community* (Oxford: Clarendon Press, 1933), p. 180.

[80] Walzer, *Just and Unjust Wars*, p. 12. Owen Fiss writes of the system 'bounded objectivity'. See Fiss, 'Objectivity and Interpretation', 754.

[81] Koskenniemi, 'Faith, Identity and the Killing of the Innocent', 355.

the reception of Article 2(4) of the Charter where, as we have seen, states have taken a consistent line in discriminating *against* an 'Orwellian interpretation' of its terms,[82] even though, technically, this interpretation was (and remains) open to them. In the same vein, we can say that the advent of legal justifications for the application of force has by no means heralded an era of systematic violations under spurious or unsustainable justifications. Conquest and occupation are today the rarity; they are not the norm: powerful states on the whole do not and as a matter of regularity, as they have done in the past, consume territories in the name of self-defence; they do not engage humanitarian interventions at the slightest of whims or excuses. And, even when such actions occur, it is imperative for us to remember that states do not 'finish up [as] judges in their own cause', as there are 'a variety of important decision-makers other than courts, who can pronounce on the validity of claims advanced'.[83]

### Self-defence

When we consider the mechanics of the law of self-defence in greater detail, it soon becomes apparent that the decision as to whether or not to exercise the right of self-defence resides, first and foremost, with any state that believes that it has been (or, for some,[84] is about to become) the victim of an 'armed attack'. This approach, at least, informed the position of the International Court of Justice in the *Nicaragua Case* (1986), when it concluded in the context of the right of collective self-defence that it is 'the state which is the victim of an armed attack which must form and declare the view that it has been so attacked'.[85] In order to safeguard the right of collective self-defence from admitting a 'vicarious defence by champions'[86] (the concern of Sir Robert Y. Jennings in his dissenting opinion) the Court also proclaimed that reliance on collective self-defence did not 'remove the need' for the occurrence of an armed attack and, indeed, provided that 'the requirement of a request by a state which is the victim of the alleged attack is additional to the requirement that such a state should have declared itself to have been attacked'.[87]

---

[82] Oscar Schachter, 'The Legality of Pro-Democratic Invasion', *American Journal of International Law* 78: 3 (1984).

[83] Higgins, *Problems and Process*, pp. 247–8.   [84] Higgins, *Problems and Process*, p. 242.

[85] Nicaragua v. United States (1986), p. 104 (paragraph 195).

[86] Nicaragua v. United States (1986), p. 555 (per Sir Robert Y. Jennings).

[87] Nicaragua v. United States (1986), p. 105 (paragraph 199).

The idea preserved by these statements is that the right of self-defence does indeed *inhere* in states for it is they who are entitled to make the first call as to whether to activate the right of self-defence. In this respect, it can be said that the law affords some latitude and discretion to states as to when to exercise their right of self-defence. However, in the dictum cited, the Court uses the word 'alleged attack' which serves to reinforce the point that the right of self-defence is not an *absolute* right: it is, rather, regulated through the application of legal principles and responses forthcoming from 'international scrutiny' and from 'community judgment'.[88] To assist us in this cause, the Court attempted to articulate an objective meaning of the term 'armed attack' in a famous paragraph in the *Nicaragua Case* (1986),[89] but these parameters have found little favour in state practice[90] as well as in the opinions of scholars.[91] Contrary to the findings of the Court, states have often asserted more liberal interpretations of the notion of 'armed attack'– not all of which have been unsuccessful. Indeed, one critical reflection concludes that, through their actions, states are capable of – and have in fact been involved in – 'subverting important legal categories' from matters relating to the use of force to international criminal law.[92]

That states form their own interpretations and make legal claims before other states and international institutions is not, in and of itself, a new feature of international relations. Nor is it an innovative development in questions pertaining to the use of force.[93] We have witnessed such practices on previous occasions – ranging from Israel's action to 'self-defend' its nationals at Entebbe in July 1976 to the claim made by the United States that it had been the victim of an 'armed attack' in September 2001 – and it is contended that these laws are designed for states to make claims and counter-claims as the result of situations in which they find themselves and which could not have been predicted at

---

[88] Oscar Schachter, 'Self-Defense and the Rule of Law', *American Journal of International Law* 83: 2 (1989), 263. See also, Schachter, *International Law*, p. 139.
[89] Nicaragua v. United States, pp. 103–4 (paragraph 195).
[90] Dinstein, *War, Aggression and Self-Defence*, p. 218.
[91] Higgins, *Problems and Process*, p. 251; and Christopher Greenwood, 'The International Court of Justice and the Use of Force', in Vaughan Lowe and Malgosia Fitzmaurice (eds.), *Fifty Years of the International Court of Justice: Essays in Honour of Sir Robert Jennings* (Cambridge: Cambridge University Press, 1996), pp. 380–1.
[92] Antonio Cassese, 'Terrorism is Also Disrupting Some Crucial Legal Categories of International Law', *European Journal of International Law* 12: 5 (2001), 993.
[93] Rosalyn Higgins, *The Development of International Law Through the Political Organs of the United Nations* (London: Oxford University Press, 1963), p. xx.

the time Article 51 was authored. It has been argued, with some degree of persuasion, that:

> These controversial issues indicate that the rules of self-defence fall far short of a code of conduct that would provide precise 'hard law' for many cases likely to arise. Even though governments have a stake in securing clarity as to what is permitted and forbidden, there are obvious limits to achieving that objective. General formulas accepted as law are subject to continuing interpretation and, therefore, to fresh arguments as to what the law should be. Concrete situations create new perceptions and 'accomplished facts'.[94]

Lest it be considered that this approach transforms the law into a subservience of the powerful, it must also be said that while it remains for individual states to make their respective claims in the first instance, there is no guarantee that these will be favourably received by other states and by international institutions. Hence the reference, in the above citation, to the process of 'continuing interpretation' – a process that the United States submitted to in December 1986 when it claimed that it was acting in self-defence against Libya for a series of state-sponsored acts of terrorism perpetrated on American targets.[95] Here, by virtue of its application of armed force, the United States was testing the boundaries of its right of self-defence in international law, a factor that would not register large in any of the orthodox transcriptions of (and supposed enmities between) 'law' and 'politics' announced earlier. On that occasion, the United States did not garner the wholehearted support of states – which it would have clearly desired – though the episode does provide a neat contrast to the changed attitudes and responses that greeted the use of force by the United States against Iraq in June 1993 for its role in the foiled assassination attempt on former President George H.W. Bush.[96] Then again, even at that moment, we are drawn back to the dichotomy between 'law' and 'politics' in that the *nature* of this support for the use of force was not quantified: it matters a great deal as to whether support is expressed in political or legal terms. As one commentator has noted with respect to the 1993 action, it was only the Russian Federation and

---

[94] Schachter, 'Self-Defense and the Rule of Law', 267.
[95] Christopher Greenwood, 'International Law and the United States Air Operation Against Libya', *West Virginia Law Review* 89: 4 (1987).
[96] W. Michael Reisman, 'The Raid on Baghdad: Some Reflections on its Lawfulness and Implications', *European Journal of International Law* 5: 1 (1994), and Luigi Condorelli, 'A propos de l'attaque américaine contre l'Iraq du 26 juin 1993', *European Journal of International Law* 5: 1 (1994).

the United Kingdom which 'offered express support' for the '*legal* argument' advanced by the United States on that occasion.[97] For the action to have constituted a precedent with long-term legal ramifications, 'a more coherent, legal endorsement from the strike's political advocates [would have needed] to be forthcoming' if this was the case.[98]

At one and the same time, these events supply the normative context for events which have followed in the form of Operation Infinite Reach of August 1998 (the United States' action against the Sudan and Afghanistan)[99] and Operation Enduring Freedom of October 2001 (the coalition action against Afghanistan).[100] From that normative context, we can extract elements of both a legal and political significance. The legal significance derives from the fact that, in all of these cases, the United States developed detailed lines of legal argument elaborating its right of self-defence rather than a right of armed reprisal action.[101] For international law, this amounts to a classic expression of legal conviction, or *opinio juris sive necessitates*, of the United States on its understanding of the scope of its right of self-defence. The political significance has involved a growing sensitisation of states and institutions to a changing set of security challenges that have presented the root and foundation for possible legal change. For example, the international support for Operation Enduring Freedom was unprecedented – perhaps as unprecedented as the unique facts that preceded the use of force against Afghanistan in October 2001 – and has demonstrated the persuasive nature of the case of the United States and the United Kingdom in framing their response as a measure of collective self-defence. In Resolutions 1368 (12 September 2001) and 1373 (28 September 2001), the Security Council

[97] Gray, *International Law and the Use of Force*, p. 117.
[98] Dino Kritsiotis, 'The Legality of the 1993 US Missile Strike on Iraq and the Right of Self-Defence in International Law', *International and Comparative Law Quarterly* 45: 1 (1996), 175.
[99] Ruth Wedgwood, 'Responding to Terrorism: The Strikes Against bin Laden', *Yale Journal of International Law* 24: 2 (1999); and Leah Campbell, 'Defending Against Terrorism: A Legal Analysis of the Decision to Strike Sudan and Afghanistan', *Tulane Law Review* 74: 3 (2000), 1089.
[100] Sean D. Murphy, 'Terrorism and the Concept of "Armed Attack" in Article 51 of the UN Charter', *Harvard International Law Journal* 43: 1 (2002) 41; Eric P. J. Myjer and Nigel D. White, 'The Twin Towers Attack: An Unlimited Right to Self-Defence?', *Journal of Conflict and Security Law* 7: 1 (2002), 6–9; and Nico J. Schrijver, 'Responding to International Terrorism: Moving the Frontiers of International Law for "Enduring Freedom"?', *Netherlands International Law Review* 48: 3 (2001), 280–6.
[101] Abstinence from invoking a right of armed reprisals accords with the legal position stated in General Assembly Resolution 2625 (1970): see above, note 64. See, further, William O'Brien, 'Reprisals, Deterrence and Self-Defence in Counterterror Operations', *Virginia Journal of International Law* 30: 2 (1990).

affirmed this position, in a move that we can regard as both political (in terms of its support) and legal (in terms of its very precise invocations of the language of self-defence). In this, the Security Council was not alone: NATO, too, acted immediately to lend a supportive hand[102] and the foreign ministers of the Organisation of American States resolved that:

> these terrorist attacks against the United States of America are attacks against all American states and that in accordance with all the relevant provisions of the Inter-American Treaty of Reciprocal Assistance (Rio Treaty) and the principle of continental solidarity, all States Parties to the Rio Treaty shall provide effective reciprocal assistance to address such attacks and the threat of any similar attacks against any American state, and to maintain the peace and security of the continent.[103]

This dialogue of interpretations (and, when they occur, counter-interpretations) has proved critical and necessary to the worth and relevance of international law in the contemporary world, so that the right of self-defence emerges as a method by which states frame and communicate the merits of their ca(u)se for action:

> [P]ragmatic resolution from the conundrum posed in a 'hard case' requires application of a rule of reasonableness. The strict application of Article 51 [of the United Nations Charter] *is* reasonable, in almost all cases. An exception may be made, however, where effective government has ceased to exist in the place where the danger to lives has arisen. In that event, though, other normative practice also becomes relevant.[104]

So, when states (powerful or otherwise) use force and then make claims on the basis of self-defence under Article 51, they are only doing so pursuant to a particular provision of the Charter, but also as part of the *system* intended by the Charter, which has 'far outstripped the Kellogg Treaty in shaping state conduct after World War II, precisely because it is not a static system of norms but provides a living, growing and above all discursive system for applying [its] rules on a reasoned, principled, case-by-case basis'.[105]

---

[102] Statement of NATO Secretary-General Lord Geoffrey Robertson, 2 October 2001, <www.nato.int/docu/speech/2001/s011002a.htm>.
[103] Terrorist Threat to the Americas, Res. 1, Twenty-Fourth Meeting of Consultation of Ministers of Foreign Affairs Acting as Organ of Consultation in Application of the Inter-American Treaty of Reciprocal Assistance, OEA/Ser.F/II.24, RC.24/RES.1/01 (21 September 2001).
[104] Franck, *Fairness in International Law*, p. 272.
[105] Franck, *Fairness in International Law*, p. 260.

### Humanitarian intervention

Thus far, we have concerned ourselves with an established or existing *right* to use force and with questions relating to the scope and interpretation of the right of self-defence under international law. However, the matter assumes other complexities when we turn to the issue of law-creation and the attempt to introduce new justifications for the use of force under international law. The most prominent example of this phenomenon in recent times relates to the case of humanitarian intervention, a right that is not mentioned in the United Nations Charter, but which has been asserted in the legal claims of states after the Cold War: the ECOWAS (Economic Community of West African States) intervention in Liberia (1990), Operation Provide Comfort in northern Iraq (1991), and the NATO intervention over Kosovo (1999).

At first sight, each of these cases would appear to bode ill for the relevance of international law and its impact on the processes of political decision-making within the intervening states: the absence of a conventional basis and authorisation from the Security Council in accordance with its enforcement powers under Chapter VII of the Charter stopped none of these interventions from taking place in a series of apparent violations of the Charter's prohibition on the use of force. One reading of these events would placate them as unmistakable representations of the 'hegemonial approach to international relations', an approach which 'involves maximising the occasions when the powerful actor will obtain "legal approval" for its actions and minimising the occasions when such an approach may be conspicuously withheld'.[106] Indeed, the very notion of humanitarian intervention has been castigated as 'a practice only available to strong states or other states acting alongside the powerful'.[107] These perceptions do, of course, possess an ancient and understandable base, but a distinction does need to be drawn between the disregarding of law and those *prima facie* attempts to introduce normative change which do, on occasion, succeed: 'what matters is not so much the number of states participating in [the law's] creation and

---

[106] Ian Brownlie, 'International Law at the Fiftieth Anniversary of the United Nations: General Course on Public International Law', *Hague Recueil* 255 (1995–I), 49.
[107] Supplementary Memorandum Submitted by Professor Ian Brownlie CBE, QC in House of Commons Foreign Affairs Committee, *Fourth Report: Kosovo*, volume 2: *Minutes of Evidence and Appendices* (2000), p. 240.

the length of period within which that change takes place, as the relative importance, in any particular sphere, of states inaugurating the change'.[108]

It is this emphasis on the *inauguration* of change that carries certain appeal: it suggests that not all bids (if this is indeed an accurate description of what occurs) to introduce normative change are successful, that there is more to the picture than an initial move made by a state (or a collection of states) to engineer a change in the law. To be sure, equitable considerations also guide this line of thinking, in that, in a decentralised system, all normative change must start somewhere, and to start making distinctions between state actors in view of their respective power bases is to court inequalities of treatment in some form or other. What is required is a firm sense of how states respond to acts of 'inauguration': the International Court of Justice kicked this element into touch in the *Nicaragua Case* (1986) when it said: '[r]eliance by a state on a novel right or an unprecedented exception to the principle might, *if shared in principle by other states*, tend towards a modification of customary international law'.[109] The italicised portion of this statement speaks the language of prioritisation – that, beyond attempts at inauguration, indicators of change ultimately rest with states and it is here that the rule of recognition for the legal regulation of force (as it is elsewhere in international law) is located.

As part of this process, the Court made clear that a condition precedent for normative change was that state practice would need to be accompanied by statements of legal conviction: in the view of the Court, 'statements of international policy' would just not do.[110] The Court reflected upon this issue in the context of United States practice on 'grounds for intervening in the affairs of a foreign state for reasons connected with . . . the domestic policies of that country, its ideology, the level of its armaments, or the direction of its foreign policy'.[111] The Court is here revealing its own affinity to distinguishing between 'law' and 'politics',[112] a theme that transcends other aspects of its ruling. For example, it had earlier acknowledged the position of the United States on the adoption of General Assembly Resolution 2131 (XX) of 1965 – which was regarded as

---

[108] Hersch Lauterpacht, 'Sovereignty Over Submarine Areas', *British Yearbook of International Law* 27 (1950), 394.
[109] Nicaragua v. United States (1986), p. 109 (paragraph 207).   [110] Ibid.   [111] Ibid.
[112] See also the approach of Lord Browne-Wilkinson in Regina v. Bow Street Metropolitan Stipendiary Magistrate, ex parte Pinochet Ugarte (No. 3) [1999] 2 All ER 97, 101j–102b.

'only a statement of political intention and not a formulation of law'[113] – before it proceeded to attach weight to the United States' position on General Assembly Resolution 2625 (XXV). And later on, the Court took note of justifications 'advanced solely in a political context' which, it said, were 'naturally not for the Court to appraise [because these] were not advanced as legal arguments'.[114]

What the Court is in effect doing in these statements is recognising that states can and do project themselves on separate trajectories at one and the same time: a political path in which the *reasons* for an intervention exist and its legal parallel, where the *grounds* or official justifications for an action are articulated, and that these trajectories may or may not coincide. As if to shore up this position, the Court referred to the justifications offered by the United States for its action in Nicaragua 'on the legal plane',[115] and was quite categorical in stating that it was *not* entitled 'to ascribe to states legal views which they do not themselves formulate'.[116] The point to be made here is that the Court is not just providing us with a sample of its methodological preferences, but it is also making a statement on how it understands the behaviour of states when it comes to making and assessing claims relating to the use of force. We are, as a result, presented with a bifurcation of legal and political action, and this, in turn, informs the considerations that are relevant – and those which are irrelevant – at the *official level of state action*.[117] Within this analysis, we are forced to question whether weight should be attached at all to 'genuine cases of intervention', taken to mean those 'undertaken with humanitarian intent' and not just 'humanitarian pretensions'.[118] This is the business of piercing the veil of the formal representations of states, which sits at odds with the treatment of other claims under the laws on the use of force. Christine Chinkin, for example, has written that a state's 'motive for accepting or rejecting a plea of collective self-defence is irrelevant to the legality of its actions'.[119] The same, it should be argued, applies for humanitarian intervention, where the essence of the claims made and received on the official level of state

[113] Nicaragua v. United States (1986), p. 107 (paragraph 203).
[114] Nicaragua v. United States (1986), p. 134 (paragraph 266).
[115] Nicaragua v. United States (1986), p. 109 (paragraph 208).
[116] Nicaragua v. United States (1986), p. 134 (paragraph 266).
[117] Dino Kritsiotis, 'The Legal Travails of Kind-Hearted Gunmen', *Modern Law Review* 62: 6 (1999), 943.
[118] Noam Chomsky, *The New Military Humanism: Lessons from Kosovo* (Monroe, ME: Common Courage Press, 1999), p. 80.
[119] Christine Chinkin, *Third Parties in International Law* (Oxford: Clarendon Press, 1993), p. 318.

action is limited to one of overt and not covert meaning – neither is it one of overt or covert explanation.[120]

Even operating on the assumption that humanitarian intervention is now accommodated under international law – as a proposition of international custom – that development should not be taken to mean that political considerations have been removed from the spectrum of state behaviour and that international law provides a conclusive and definitive response to all cases of humanitarian catastrophe. Quite the contrary. As has been intimated above, the degree of latitude afforded to political action depends on the nature of the legal proposition under consideration: in 'the theoretical and traditional understanding' of humanitarian intervention under international law, it

> has been framed as a *right* of states and not as an *obligation* requiring action. Inherent in the very conception of a right is an element of selectivity in the exercise of that right. This is in keeping with the right-holder's sovereign discretion to decide whether or not to exercise the right in question and commit its armed forces to foreign territories and explains why it is the right *of* – rather than the right *to* – humanitarian intervention that has taken hold in practice as well as legal scholarship.[121]

To be sure, it would be too ambitious and radical a proposition to set down an *obligation* to use force in all cases of humanitarian catastrophe, and one of the chief attractions of a *right* of humanitarian intervention is that it builds a necessary and certain flexibility into the decision-making process, a process that is and remains decidedly political precisely because it awards states a discretion to decide whether or not to exercise the so-called 'right' of intervention. A legal *right* of humanitarian intervention provides vital room for a political assessment of whether or not to intervene – and, in reaching their ultimate decision, intervening states need to take account of numerous considerations, such as the viability of an operation, the extent of public and political support, as well as the availability and viability of other courses of action open to them.

That discretion, however, does not operate wholly outside legal scrutiny: what it suggests is that states are entitled to make *prima facie* claims on the basis of such a right, but that they carry the evidential

---

[120] Martin Hollis, 'Say It With Flowers', in James Tully (ed.), *Meaning and Context: Quentin Skinner and his Critics* (Cambridge: Polity, 1988), p. 136.
[121] Dino Kritsiotis, 'Reappraising Policy Objections to Humanitarian Intervention', *Michigan Journal of International Law* 19: 4 (1998), 1027.

burden to explain and to justify why it is that the exercise of that right should be regarded as lawful or permissible in a given case. If humanitarian intervention is accepted in principle, actions undertaken in its name will not automatically incur the wrath of states (as is the case with, say, armed reprisal actions), any more than they will lead to an automatic acceptance by the audience of states. The critical matter is the displacement of the evidential burden: '[w]hether a claim invoking any given norm is made in good faith or abusively will *always* require contextual analysis by appropriate decision-makers – by the Security Council, by the International Court of Justice, by various international bodies'.[122]

## Collective security

Part of the concern underpinning criticisms of humanitarian intervention relate to the selective nature of its application[123] – hence the call to routinise such actions within the framework of the Charter and its system of collective security. That system has its base in Chapter VII of the Charter, which awards the Security Council considerable enforcement powers in order to discharge its 'primary responsibility' for the maintenance of international peace and security under Article 24 of the Charter. From the start, this organisation of power at the international level and in an institutionalised form constituted a core element in the design of a global system of collective security, and 'fitted into the "impersonal perspectives of the law" rather more than it conformed to the realities of political interests and power'.[124] This interpretation is assisted by the Charter's provision for 'a more complex institutional mechanism' than that devised for the League of Nations,[125] and, of course, by the undeniable advances that had been made at around the same time in the substantive laws regulating force (which have formed an earlier part of our discussions). As things came to pass, it seemed that the Charter repaid the 'faith in the ultimate assertion of reason in the relations of man [from which] conceptions like the League of Nations and collective security must be regarded as manifestations of a permanent and ever recurring purpose, and their eclipse must be regarded as temporary and transient'.[126]

---

[122] Higgins, *Problems and Process*, p. 247.
[123] Kritsiotis, 'Reappraising Policy Objections', 1026–34.
[124] Schachter, *International Law*, p. 389.
[125] Schachter, *International Law*, pp. 389–90. See also Nigel D. White, *Keeping the Peace: The United Nations and the Maintenance of International Peace and Security*, 2nd edn (Manchester: Manchester University Press, 1997), p. 3.
[126] Hersch Lauterpacht, 'Neutrality and Collective Security', *Politica* 2: 6 (1936), 154.

This impressive set of arrangements within Chapter VII of the Charter is apt to mislead – but it should not mislead us all of the time. To read Chapter VII as a decisive triumph for the de-politicisation of decision-making on questions of collective security, is to fail in a rather fundamental way to appreciate the very nature of how the Security Council was intended to act or function from situation to situation. The Council is, after all, a *political* organ of the United Nations, so that its decisions are bound to reflect the particularised sets of circumstances and preferences that prevail at any given point in time, whether because of available resources, present political commitment, and so on. To this extent, it can and should be questioned whether its members really do 'function collegially, rather as the prince-electors of the Holy Roman Empire' and 'not merely [as] a meeting of sovereign states'.[127] The truth of the matter is that, after more than four decades of the Cold War in which its activities were freeze-framed and despite considerable changes that have occurred within its practices,[128] the Council is still in the initial phases of developing its own political identity and corporate persona. Succeeding in this challenge will have important and long-term implications for its own legitimacy or perceived legitimacy.[129]

In the period since the Security Council has begun to find its feet, we have nevertheless witnessed how the politicised nature of its operations has asserted itself in spectacular fashion at various pressure points – all of which have occurred within the legal framework set down by the Charter. Upon closer examination, we realise that the enforcement powers of the Council in Chapter VII are contingent upon the occurrence of a threat to the peace, breach of the peace, or act of aggression,[130] and that some of the Council's findings have been said (or seen) to stretch the meanings of these vital terms to breaking-point. One can think here of Resolution 748 (1992) of March 1992, adopted under Chapter VII of the Charter, in which the Council determined that 'the failure by [Libya] to demonstrate by its concrete actions its renunciation of terrorism and in particular its continued failure to respond fully and effectively to the requests in Resolution 731 (1992) constitute[d] a threat to international peace and security'. We are, it would seem, on familiar terrain with politicised appreciations of legal terminologies, precisely because

---

[127] Franck, *Fairness in International Law*, p. 285.    [128] White, *Keeping the Peace*, p. 7.
[129] David D. Caron, 'The Legitimacy of the Collective Authority of the Security Council', *American Journal of International Law* 87: 4 (1993), 554.
[130] Article 39 of the United Nations Charter.

a Security Council resolution was used as the vehicle for realising the objectives and demands of the United States and the United Kingdom: 'law' and 'politics' asserted their presence and their antagonisms in popular impressions, but did so this time within the changed context of an institutional setting.

Such impressions of and refrains concerning the episode were heard several times over, and, it can be speculated, will still be heard for years to come. At their base, we find that the 'law' is constructed as a series of propositions (or rules) with objective meaning, freed from all forms of political interference, trespass, manipulation. Yet, as the foregoing assessments advise, we need to return to the importance of *circumstance* in each given case, because it cannot be taken for granted that, in that setting, the 'law' was framed as a determinate rule, let alone one of an objective or singularly identifiable meaning. It is of course true that the authors of the Charter (and Chapter VII in particular) used 'language clearly intended to evoke images of inter-state conflict',[131] but the real thrust of Chapter VII is to confer a broad *discretion* on the Security Council – a magnificent latitude in which political considerations can and do and should make their presence felt. This discretion is obvious from reading the Charter; it is no less apparent from the drafting history of the relevant provisions as well.[132]

While the nature of the Council's discretion is not in doubt, the manner in which this discretion is exercised – and not exercised – carries significance for the coherence (or 'integrity')[133] and acceptability of the system as a whole. The trend is not to notice this when the Security Council performs on par with expectations – as was the case during the Gulf Crisis of 1990–1 – because, here, the Council responds in a way that seems worthy of its intended purpose and responsibilities. Greater notice is, however, taken when the Security Council performs below expectations made of it – the Rwandan genocide of 1994 is a case in point as is the crisis over Kosovo in 1999 – or where it exceeds those expectations by acting in an adventurous or innovative manner, as it did when it established international criminal tribunals for the former Yugoslavia

---

[131] Tom J. Farer and Felice Gaer, 'The UN and Human Rights: At the End of the Beginning', in Adam Roberts and Benedict Kingsbury (eds.), *United Nations, Divided World: The UN's Roles in International Relations*, 2nd edn (Oxford: Clarendon Press, 1993), p. 245.
[132] Jochen Abr. Frowein and Nico Krisch, 'Article 39', in Bruno Simma (ed.), *The Charter of the United Nations: A Commentary*, 2nd edn (Oxford and New York: Oxford University Press, 2002), pp. 719–26.
[133] See Ronald Dworkin, *Law's Empire* (Cambridge, MA: Belknap Press, 1986), pp. 176 ff.

in 1993 or for Rwanda in 1994.[134] These decisions, all taken pursuant to a discretion provided for in law, are all politicised to greater or lesser degrees and the challenge that we face (or should face) as a result of these practices is to examine whether the Council's enforcement powers were used or withheld on principled grounds, whether they can be defended according to agreed criteria and considerations.

Where the Security Council has not redeemed general expectations, that challenge has manifested itself in an acute form because states have responded to what they have seen as overtly political decisions of the Security Council – decisions not taken on principled or relevant or reasonable grounds – with actions of their own, actions that suggest considerable angst with the deficiencies and deficits within the existing institutional structure. This phenomenon is experienced more and more, and it is one that surfaced in the jurisprudence of the International Court of Justice in the *Corfu Channel Case* (1949), where the Court determined that it could

> only regard the alleged right of intervention as the manifestation of a policy of force, such as has, in the past, given rise to most serious abuses and such as cannot, *whatever be the present defects in international organisation*, find a place in international law.[135]

The import of this statement is that, irrespective of the 'defects in international organisation' – and, one could add with some confidence given the tenor of the Court's judgment, the reasons for those defects – states cannot adopt their own initiatives or policies that precipitate coercive methods of dispute resolution. Yet, if this was the way of the Court in 1949, it has proved not to be the way of state practice then or since. In his dissent in the *Nicaragua Case* (1986), Jennings presented the alternative view, when he said that the system of collective security had 'never come into effect':

> Therefore, an essential element in the Charter design is totally missing. In this situation, it seems dangerous to define unnecessarily strictly the conditions for lawful self-defence, so as to leave a large area where both a forcible response to force is forbidden, and yet the United Nations employment of force, which was intended to fill that gap, is absent.[136]

While these words were conceived during the Cold War, it could be suggested that their logic carries forth to contemporary situations where

---

[134] See Danesh Sarooshi, 'The Powers of the United Nations International Criminal Tribunals', *Max Planck Yearbook of United Nations Law* 2 (1998), 141.
[135] *Corfu Channel Case* (Merits): United Kingdom v. Albania (1949) *ICJ Reports* 4, p. 35.
[136] Nicaragua v. United States (1986), p. 544.

the politics of Council life produces the same crippling effects as those experienced during the Cold War. The difference is that the entrenched ideological politics of the Cold War period has now been replaced by politics of other varieties, whether this be in the form of historical ties or loyalties based on ethnic or religious identities or on economic interests or on policy strategies, shown most powerfully in the months preceding Operation Allied Force in 1999 or Operation Iraqi Freedom in 2003. Such political overtures impact adversely upon the 'coherence' of the Security Council record, because the expectations are that 'conceptually alike cases will be treated alike'.[137] We know that the practice has fallen below this standard – and below expectations – if one takes a brief look at the cases on humanitarian intervention: compare the interventions in Liberia (1990), northern Iraq (1991) and southern Iraq (1992), and Kosovo (1999) where the Security Council did not authorise action, with those interventions, such as Somalia (1992), Rwanda (1994), and Zaire (1996), where it did. The same can be said for the pro-democratic intervention in Sierra Leone (1998) – again, not authorised by the Security Council – as contrasted with the authorisation provided for the use of force in identical factual circumstances in Haiti (1994).

States have chosen to *react* to these discrepancies with evident determination: they have not purchased the apparent line of the International Court of Justice in 1949, that the 'present defects of international organisation' must be accepted and left as and where they are found. Their actions, stemming from or anticipating the political vortexes in New York, have gained considerable ground in capitals all over the world, from Washington, DC to London, Abuja to Accra, Berlin to Paris. And the unauthorised interventions which have ensued have not been treated as automatic violations of the law but as possible promoters of new legal arrangements that, should conditions so dictate, co-exist alongside the Charter. We can intimate as much from the words of United Nations Secretary-General Kofi Annan, who asked most poignantly and profoundly in the wake of Operation Allied Force over the Kosovo crisis: '[o]n the one hand, is it legitimate for a regional organisation to use force without a [United Nations] mandate? On the other, is it permissible to let gross and systematic violations of human rights, with grave humanitarian consequences, continue unchecked?'[138]

---

[137] Franck, *The Power of Legitimacy*, p. 143.
[138] Kofi Annan, 'Two Concepts of Sovereignty', *The Economist* (18–24 September 1999), 81.

These reflections are not meant to suggest that the laws on the use of force have become a free-for-all when the Security Council proves divided or inactive on a given matter. The road to the realisation of an apparent right of humanitarian intervention has not come easy,[139] and, for some critics, it has not even come at all. Moreover, there are instances where states in general have not been as accepting or as receptive to certain typologies of claim, as in the cases of Operation Desert Fox of December 1998 and Operation Iraqi Freedom of March 2003. On both these occasions, the United States and the United Kingdom proclaimed that their actions were authorised by the Security Council in order to enforce the disarmament obligations imposed on Iraq by Resolution 687 (1991) at the end of the 1990–1 Gulf Conflict.[140] Yet, these episodes exposed significant degrees of criticism and dissent and seemed to match the position stated by one expert commentator, that there is 'no entitlement in the hands of individual members of the United Nations to enforce prior Security Council resolutions by the use of force'.[141]

Be this as it may, the lesson emanating from all of these episodes is that undue acts of the politicisation of Security Council business come – and will inexorably come – with their consequences, and that sometimes these consequences will be of legal significance as they could open up certain rights of action for states to use force without the authorisation of the Council. Prime Minister Tony Blair of the United Kingdom hinted at the future scope for such actions in state practice in remarks made during preparations for Operation Iraqi Freedom, when he advised the House of Commons that 'we cannot have a situation in which there is a material breach [of Security Council resolutions] recognised by everybody and yet action [in the Security Council] is *unreasonably blocked*'.[142] Clearly, as we have discussed, that does not mean to say that any action undertaken by the United Kingdom – or any other state for that matter – without explicit authorisation of the Council will be deemed permissible or acceptable in law; what it does highlight, however, is the increasing potential for further unauthorised actions in the event of further crises

---

[139] Nicholas J. Wheeler, *Saving Strangers: Humanitarian Intervention in International Society* (Oxford: Oxford University Press, 2000).

[140] On Operation Desert Fox, see UN Document S/1998/1181 (16 December 1998) (United States) and UN Document S/PV.2955 (16 December 1998), at 6 (United Kingdom). For the justifications for Operation Iraqi Freedom, see UN Document S/2003/351 (21 March 2003) (United States) and UN Document S/2003/350 (21 March 2003) (United Kingdom).

[141] Higgins, *Problems and Process*, p. 259.

[142] Liaison Committee of the House of Commons, United Kingdom:<www.publications.parliament.uk/pa/cm200203/cmselect/cmliaisn/334-i/3012103.htm>, (21 January 2003), p. 14 (emphasis added).

of confidence in the Security Council – that is, when its deliberations are 'not likely to be as productive as [they] should be'.[143]

## Conclusion

It has been the central claim of this chapter that orthodox teachings of the relationship between 'law' and 'politics' have adopted generalised understandings of each of these terms, presenting each of them in something of a monolithic and, at times, an unchanging light. The result is that the 'relationship' that emerges is itself represented in generalised terms, in which politics and law either become synonymous entities or in which a hierarchical order is established between them. We have sought to break from these traditions of thinking, and to demonstrate that 'law' comes in all forms and varieties and cannot be used in the generic sense of 'rules' if any meaningful grasp is to be had on the so-called relationship that exists with the political world. A recent invitation issued by James Crawford to 'recast the tradition of realism itself in more realistic, that is to say in more comprehensive and representative, terms'[144] has underscored this need to embrace nuance and detail – to try to come to closer terms with the particulars before estimations are made of the 'relationship' between 'law' and 'politics'.

Our excursus has taken place in the field of the use of force, where we have seen the lessons of the orthodox teachings – of the dichotomisation between 'law' and 'politics' – taken up in the jurisprudence and in the practice of states themselves. That, in turn, has led to criticism that 'normative jurisprudence' has acquired its own 'unreality' because of 'its total neglect of the role of law in sustaining relations of power and its descent into uninteresting exegesis and apologia for legal technique'.[145] Yet, the observations made here have attempted to demonstrate how, over significant periods of time, normative advances have indeed been made in relation to the use of force in international law and practice.

The relationships – and there are indeed relationships – which ensue between law and politics are forged according to the prevailing circumstances. Attempting to configure these relationships is no mean task, but we have seen the function of law as both a constraining factor but also as

[143] Liaison Committee of the House of Commons, p. 14.
[144] James Crawford, 'Foreword', in Michael Byers (ed.), *Custom, Power and the Power of Rules: International Relations and Customary International Law* (Cambridge: Cambridge University Press, 1999), p. x.
[145] Costas Douzinas, *The End of Human Rights* (Oxford: Hart, 2000), p. 7.

a vital discursive medium.[146] The prohibition on force exemplifies the law's attempt at restraining state action but, even then, we must be modest and realistic in admitting that '[i]t is no more possible to demonstrate "proximate causation" [of law on the ultimate decision taken] than in any other human process'.[147] We must content ourselves that the rule in question has achieved the highest level of determinacy and political acceptability because, from then on, '[t]he weight and consequence of legal advice in the final decision... are, and must remain, unknowable'.[148] In terms of the exceptions to the use of force, we have adverted to the value of international law as a communicative device,[149] helping frame the various claims which states wish to make to other states and institutions in defence of their coercive actions under international law.

---

[146] Abram Chayes, *The Cuban Missile Crisis* (New York: Oxford University Press, 1974), p. 7.
[147] Chayes, *The Cuban Missile Crisis*, p. 5.     [148] Ibid.
[149] Dino Kritsiotis, 'The Power of International Law as Language', *California Western Law Review* 34: 2 (1998).

## 4    Soft law, hard politics, and the Climate Change Treaty

*Robyn Eckersley*[1]

This chapter offers a critical constructivist interpretation of the legislative phase of international politics and international public law manifest in the treaty-making process. Drawing in particular on the critical theory of Jürgen Habermas and the constructivism of Alexander Wendt, I seek to show how treaty-making is shaped and constrained, on the one hand by the deeper constitutional structure and associated norms of international society and, on the other hand, by the particular roles, interests, and identities of those state and non-state actors involved in the rule-making process.[2]

Central to the contributions in this volume is the idea that assumptions made about the nature of politics (including the nature of political community) circumscribe understandings of law, while particular kinds of legal order, in turn, shape and constrain the political understandings and practices of social agents. The central problem with neorealist and neoliberal institutionalist approaches is that they not only tend to reduce law to politics but also tend to employ an unduly limited understanding of politics (which is typically reduced to the play of power and/or national interests). Critical constructivists, in contrast, proceed on the basis of a broader conception of politics that encompasses not only questions of material capability and utility but also questions of morality/justice and identity. Moreover, critical constructivists understand the relationship between law and politics as mutually constitutive

[1] I am grateful to Peter Christoff, Bill Hare, Mat Paterson, and especially Christian Reus-Smit for valuable critical feedback on earlier drafts of this chapter. I also thank Gerry Nagzdam for research assistance.
[2] See Richard Price and Christian Reus-Smit, 'Dangerous Liaisons?: Critical International Theory and Constructivism', *European Journal of International Relations* 4: 3 (1998), for an analysis of the sympathies between constructivism and critical theory.

and mutually enmeshed. Indeed, this mutual enmeshment of law and politics makes the delineation of any clear practical boundary almost impossible, despite the fact that boundaries are routinely invoked by political actors for justificatory or regulatory purposes.

Using the climate change negotiations as a case study, and focusing in particular on the contrasting roles played by the United States and the European Union (EU) in the negotiations, I highlight this mutual enmeshment of law and politics by exploring the constitutive tensions between the regulative ideals of treaty law and the actual production of treaty law. Such an approach offers both a sociological understanding of the legitimacy of international legal norms as well as a critical framework that enables an evaluation of the *degree* of legitimacy of particular treaty negotiations and outcomes from the perspective of both state *and* non-state actors.

Mainstream approaches to treaty-making take the distribution of material capabilities and/or interests of states in the context of a fixed structure and logic of international anarchy as a sufficient explanation of treaty processes and outcomes. This chapter argues that these power-based and interest-based understandings of treaty-making are inadequate and that their understanding of the modes of interaction by states under conditions of anarchy is too limited. Power-based and interest-based understandings do not attend to the significance of regulative ideals and the necessary argumentative and normative dimensions of the 'legislative moment' in international politics. Moreover, while the structure of international society is anarchic, in the sense that there is no world government to enforce international legal norms, I argue that it is too limiting to assume that there is only one mode or rationality of interaction among states under anarchy (i.e., Hobbesian and Lockean respectively). Instead I suggest that understanding state interaction in international society as multicultural rather than unicultural provides the crucial context for understanding why it is that particular states (as well as particular coalitions of state and non-state actors) are likely to relate to others as enemies, rivals, or friends, and why particular agreements are likely to be struck, or come unstuck. That is, different historically specific 'cultures of relating' provide the context for understanding the sorts of interaction (i.e. non-cooperation, coercion, bargaining and/or moral argument) that are likely to prevail *within and across* different groupings of actors in the formal and informal discursive processes of treaty-making.

Now it might be argued that the climate change negotiations pose an especially hard case for those who seek to resist both the neorealist and neoliberal institutionalist understandings of international politics and law. After all, the negotiations have been characterised by intense political disagreement and self-interested bargaining by states to protect economic and strategic interests, the assertion by the US of its position as a great power, and general delay in terms of concrete outcomes. However, I show that it is possible to criticise these mainstream explanations as unnecessarily reductionist without denying the obvious significance of power and interests, especially the role of the US in the negotiations, and without denying the importance of the sway of domestic factors *vis-à-vis* discursive argument in international meetings in shaping outcomes. I therefore launch my defence of critical constructivism by posing some hard questions for neorealists and neoliberal institutionalists arising out of the climate change negotiations. I then seek to show how critical constructivism – in its sensitivity to the role of both state and non-state actors in treaty negotiations, and its openness to the play of not only power and interest but also morality and identity – is able to provide a more rounded understanding of the climate change negotiations than mainstream rationalist approaches. In the course of this defence, I respond to some of the typical criticisms levelled against the idealism of critical constructivism.

## The climate change negotiations: some hard questions for neorealists and neoliberals

The international climate change negotiations provide an especially graphic illustration of the multifaceted challenges that typically confront attempts to develop common political norms and global environmental regulations. At issue are debates over a highly technical science, different climatic vulnerability and different costs of adaptation and capacities to respond on the part of different states, intense debates over the rules of adjustment and burden sharing, and fundamental normative disagreements over environment and development priorities. Moreover, any serious and concerted effort to reduce greenhouse gas emissions necessarily entails measures that strike at the heart of the domestic policies of states, including energy, industry, transport, infrastructure development, taxation, and pricing policy. For many states, any attempt to regulate such 'domestic' matters is tantamount to an infringement of their sovereignty. Nonetheless, against these enormous odds, a principled agreement to reduce greenhouse gas emissions has been reached by a majority of states, and developed countries have agreed to take the first practical steps to reduce emissions.

The basic objective of the United Nations Framework Convention on Climate Change (UNFCCC), which opened for signature in 1992 at the Earth Summit in Rio de Janeiro, is for the parties to achieve 'stabilization of greenhouse gas concentrations in the atmosphere at a level that would prevent dangerous anthropogenic interference with the climate system' (Article 2) and within a timeframe sufficient to protect ecosystems, food production, and economic development. Moreover, the Convention established basic principles of equitable burden sharing in Article 3, the most significant being that the parties should protect the climate system 'in accordance with their common but differentiated responsibilities'; that developed countries should take the lead in combating climate change; and that full consideration should be given to the specific needs and special circumstances of developing countries, especially those that are particularly vulnerable to the impacts of climate change.

However, the most substantive provision in Article 4 merely required the parties to 'adopt national policies and take corresponding measures on the mitigation of climate change' (4[29][a]), leaving considerable discretion as to when and how. At the Earth Summit in 1992, many environmental non-governmental organisations (NGOs) were highly critical of the 'soft' legal form in which the commitments were expressed. The notable absence of any binding timetable or targets for greenhouse gas emissions reductions in the 1992 document – an absence largely attributable to then US President George Bush senior – was widely seen as a *failure* of commitment.[3] Nonetheless, the UNFCCC established an institutional framework that provided the norms and principles that would guide future negotiations. By the time of the Kyoto meeting in 1997, 167 states and the European Union were parties to the Convention.[4]

Moreover, at the third conference of the parties (COP3) at Kyoto the negotiations had reached a point where the developed countries were able to agree to both timetables and differentiated targets, in accordance with the basic principles laid down at Rio. Essentially, in the Kyoto Protocol the developed countries agreed to reduce their aggregate

---

[3] See Gareth Porter, Janet Welsh Brown, and Pamela S. Chasek, *Global Environmental Politics*, 3rd edn (Boulder, CO: Westview Press, 2000), p. 117.
[4] Sebastian Oberthur and Hermann E. Ott, *The Kyoto Protocol: International Climate Policy for the 21st Century* (Berlin: Springer-Verlag, 1999), p. 33.

levels of greenhouse gas emissions below 1990 levels by an average of 5.2 per cent by the staggered time period 2008–12. The US negotiators, under pressure particularly from the EU, moved from their initial negotiating position of stabilisation to a target of a 7 per cent reduction in emissions, while the EU agreed to an 8 per cent reduction. Only three OECD countries (Norway, Iceland, and Australia) were allowed an increase in emissions. No commitments were required of developing countries at that stage of the negotiations, consistent with the principle of the UNFCCC that developed countries take the lead.

The Protocol also set down a set of 'flexibility mechanisms' designed to enable developed countries to reduce their particular reduction targets at least cost. In particular, targets can be met individually or jointly ('joint implementation') by developed countries, accumulated carbon credits can be traded with parties who are unable to reach their targets, and the establishment of a Clean Development Mechanism allows for emission reduction credits resulting from projects undertaken in developing countries. Provision was also allowed for the use of carbon sinks (i.e., carbon sequestration schemes, such as forests). However, the details of exactly how and to what extent states were free to use these mechanisms to achieve their targets were left open at Kyoto and eventually became part of what was to prove a highly fraught agenda at the COP6 at The Hague, where a major stand-off between the US and EU produced a breakdown in the negotiations. However, despite the formal reneging by the US of its Kyoto commitments in March 2001, most of the contentious details were finally resolved by the remaining parties in the compromise reached at the resumed COP6 meeting in Bonn in July 2001, where the rules concerning sinks and compliance were made more flexible (and the use of nuclear power was ruled out as a means of offsetting emissions). This agreement was put into binding legal form at COP7 in Marrakesh in November 2001.

The new concessions mainly worked to the benefit of the so-called umbrella group (an alliance formed in Kyoto between the US, Canada, New Zealand, and Australia, on the one hand, and Russia, Ukraine, Khazakstan, Norway, and Iceland, on the other, to pursue the idea of joint implementation). Many environmental NGOs have been mistrustful of the so-called flexibility mechanisms and sink provisions on the grounds that they carried the potential for developed countries to 'trade' or 'plant' their way out of their Kyoto obligations without taking any significant steps to reduce emissions at source in their domestic economies. The Kyoto targets are also well below what is required to achieve the basic UNFCCC objective of a stabilisation of greenhouse gas concentrations in the atmosphere to safe levels. However, these targets must be understood as but the first step in a dynamic process of emissions reduction, with a second round of negotiations over new commitments expected to start by 2005 (and to include developing countries). The Protocol has therefore succeeded in setting up a framework for ongoing action, and much will depend on whether much more stringent targets can be set for future commitment periods.

Nonetheless, the Bonn agreement has been widely hailed as a diplomatic breakthrough, all the more so because of the non-cooperative stance of the US. The Kyoto Protocol and the action plan concluded at Bonn provide the first concrete steps towards the technological and social revolution that is needed over the next 50 years to wean the world economy from fossil fuel dependence. Although the threshold for the Protocol to enter into force is high, it is likely to be cleared. Article 25 provides that the Protocol shall come into force once 55 parties to the UNFCCC ratify it, and the ratifying states together represent at least 55 per cent of the total CO2 emissions in 1990 stemming from industrialised countries. One hundred states had already ratified by the end of 2002 (with Canada's eventual ratification in December 2002 marking the 100th). The US and Australia are the only OECD countries who have not ratified. Russia's ratification would enable the second hurdle to be cleared and the Protocol to enter into force. It is expected that Russia will eventually ratify since it carries surplus emissions capacity resulting from economic downturn and it stands to gain a windfall for these so-called 'hot-air' accounts.

Nonetheless, in view of the enormous challenges confronting this first step towards moving away from fossil fuel energy sources, and in view of the way in which the climate change negotiations have unfolded, it might still be tempting to fall back on the assumptions and explanatory framework of the neorealist framework of international politics and law. The most salient feature of these negotiations from a neorealist perspective would be the rejection by the United States in March 2001 of the emissions reduction commitments it made at the signing of the Kyoto Protocol in 1997. For neorealists, the content of international law is determined by the most powerful states and the law will not be upheld if it conflicts with their material and strategic interests. The US was able to assert itself as the world's biggest economic and military power – responsible for roughly one-quarter of global greenhouse gas emissions – by refusing to co-operate in the negotiations when they conflicted with US economic and strategic interests, without fear of any effective material sanctions from 'weaker' states, thereby putting at risk the entire multilateral effort to reach an agreement over emissions reductions. Indeed, President George W. Bush might be said to have walked out of a traditional realist textbook in his unashamed declaration that agreeing to implement the US Kyoto emissions reduction targets did not suit the economic interests of the US, irrespective of whatever common benefits emissions reductions might bring. Despite the last-minute rescue of the negotiations at the COP held in Bonn in July 2001, non-cooperation on the part of the US continues to jeopardise ratification of the Kyoto Protocol, while some of the concessions granted to members of the umbrella group on matters such as carbon sinks and the so-called flexibility mechanisms threaten to undermine the basic purpose of the UNFCCC and the Protocol. In short, a neorealist would consider the treaty essentially doomed or severely compromised on account of non-cooperation by the world's most powerful state.

Neoliberal institutionalists, in contrast, would analyse the problem in functional terms as a major 'collective action' failure on the grounds that the incentive structures created by the climate regime were not sufficient to induce co-operation of the single biggest greenhouse gas emitter. Neoliberal institutionalists typically determine whether a state will be a leader, a bystander, or a laggard on the basis of relative ecological vulnerability and abatement costs.[5] So, for example, if abatement costs are too high, then states are unlikely to co-operate in environmental treaties. That is, irrespective of three changes of president (from George Bush senior, to Bill Clinton, to George Bush junior), the fundamental reliance of the US economy on fossil fuels meant that agreeing to binding commitments towards emissions reductions was always going to be an unlikely prospect. In short, the climate change regime conflicted with US 'interests'.

---

[5] Detlef Sprinz and Tapani Vaahtoranta, 'The Interest-based Explanation of International Environmental Policy', *International Organization* 48: 1 (1994); Hugh Ward, 'Game Theory and the Politics of Global Warming: The State of Play and Beyond', *Political Studies* 44: 5 (1996); Porter, Welsh Brown, and Chasek, *Global Environmental Politics*; Yasuko Kawashima, 'A Comparative Analysis of the Decision-making Processes of Developed Countries toward $CO_2$ Emissions Reduction Targets', *International Environmental Affairs* 9: 2 (1997); and Detlef F. Sprinz and Martin Weiss, 'Domestic Politics and Global Climate Policy', in Urs Luterbacher and Detlef F. Sprinz (eds.), *International Relations and Global Climate Change* (Cambridge, MA: MIT Press, 2001).

In view of the foregoing analyses, the climate change regime negotiations might appear to pose an easy case for neorealists and neoliberals and an especially hard case for critical constructivists. However, these cursory analyses tell only part of the climate change story while also obscuring a number of weaknesses in the neorealists' and neoliberal institutionalists' analysis. Moreover, the highly contingent character of the negotiations is such that the force of the neorealist understanding of law and politics can be found to wax and wane at different points (for example, waxing at Rio in 1992 in the light of the 'soft' character of the commitments extracted by the US, waning at Kyoto in 1997 when these commitments 'hardened', waxing at The Hague in 2000 when the negotiations broke down, waning at Bonn when the negotiations were rescued despite the absence of the US, and waning as the number of ratifications of the Protocol increase). This precarious neorealist hold on the changing fortunes of the treaty suggests some fundamental limitations in the neorealist analysis. Here I shall single out for attention two questions to which neorealists do not have easy answers. First, why did the US move from its negotiating position of stabilisation of emissions to agree to a 7 per cent cut at Kyoto in 1997 and drop its insistence that developing countries should also commit themselves to emissions reductions when neither of these agreements suited its strategic and domestic economic interests? Second, given that moving away from a fossil fuel economy was always going to be a central objective of the Climate Change Treaty, why did the US bother to remain part of the negotiations until as late as March 2001, given that the commitment to negotiate binding targets and timetables was made as early as COP1 in Berlin in 1995?

Now neorealists would probably declare that it was in the 'strategic interests' of the US to sign the UNFCCC in 1992 and remain in the negotiations in order to shape them in ways that suited its strategic interests. When the legal text threatened to 'harden' in ways that were inimical to US material interests, it walked away. Yet the acceptance by the US negotiators under George Bush senior of the principled commitments (or 'soft legal norms') in the UNFCCC in 1992 on the assumption that only binding legal norms are consequential would seem a particularly naïve strategy given the role such principles typically play in guiding and disciplining subsequent negotiations (which is also borne out in this case-study). In other words, it assumes that the US would be able to engage effectively in subterfuge either in orchestrating 'non-decisions' or in getting other states to agree to legal norms that would undermine the principles of the UNFCCC or the targets in the Protocol – something the US was clearly unable to do at Kyoto in 1997 and at The Hague in 2000.[6] As it turned out, the US shifted its position substantially at Kyoto, although such a move did raise questions as to how the commitments could be carried through domestically. That is, during the period of the Clinton Administration, the then Republican-dominated US Senate – sensitive to the concerns of coal-producing states in the US – had passed by consensus the Byrd–Hagel resolution making any action by the US legislature conditional on developing states also taking action.[7] Nonetheless, the very fact that the US executive agreed to shift its position at Kyoto despite a hostile Senate resolution cannot be explained as mere strategic power play. Rather, it must be understood in the light of developing countries holding fast to the principle of common but differentiated responsibilities elaborated in the UNFCCC. Admittedly, President Clinton signed the Protocol on the basis of a voluntary commitment by Argentina to accept voluntary emissions targets.[8] However, it was clear at COP3 that the vast majority of developing countries were opposed to making any commitments (voluntary or otherwise) in the first commitment period. Moreover, while the action plan agreed at the Bonn meeting did increase the possibility that some OECD countries (such as Australia) might be able to minimise taking emissions reduction measures by relying on carbon sinks, the agreement nonetheless represented a breakthrough insofar as the parties firmed their resolve to continue the treaty process and undertake binding commitments *in the absence of the US*. All OECD countries, except the US and Australia, have now ratified the Protocol.

Turning to the neoliberal explanation, it might be argued that the details of the incentive structures created by the climate change regime were not sufficient to motivate the US to join, since joining would generate economic losses. The EU, on the other hand, as the 'green leader' of the negotiations, stood to gain because it was not only vulnerable to the impacts of climate change (like most countries) but (unlike most countries) it had already geared its economy towards a more energy-efficient future relative to other states and stood to reap the economic benefits

[6] Michael Grubb and Farhana Yamin, 'Climatic Collapse at the Hague: What Happened, Why, and Where Do We Go From Here?', *International Affairs* 77: 2 (2001).
[7] Peter Newell, 'Who "CoPed" Out in Kyoto: An Assessment of the Third Conference of the Parties to the Framework Convention on Climate Change', *Environmental Politics* 7: 2 (1998), 154.
[8] Michael Lisowski, 'Playing the Two-Level Game: US President Bush's Decision to Repudiate the Kyoto Protocol', *Environmental Politics* 11: 4 (2002), 111.

of being one of the first movers in 'ecological modernisation'. Indeed, these points were exploited in the negotiations by the umbrella group, which sought to tarnish the green reputation of the EU by pointing out that its relatively good emissions record has been achieved by coincidental rather than deliberate developments. In particular, the closure of many East German industries following German reunification and the restructuring of the British energy industry, gave Germany and Britain relatively impressive emissions reduction records.[9]

For neoliberal institutionalists, that the US chose to become involved, and remain in the negotiations until as late as 2001 may be explained in terms of the US's concern to shape the UNFCCC and the Protocol (and any subsequent action plans) in a way that gave it maximum flexibility in meeting its targets. The soft-law character of the UNFCCC commitments is not considered significant because, in game-theoretic terms, 'play is still in the pre-game phase',[10] meaning that the 'real action' (i.e., the hard bargaining about who pays) has not begun. When the 'real game' began, the US made trade-offs at Kyoto that it was unable to fulfil. According to Robert Putnam's two-level game analysis, the inability of the US to ratify the Kyoto commitments is a case of 'involuntary defection'.[11] George Bush junior simply turned this into a voluntary defection. Yet these neoliberal responses to the two questions only go part of the way to explaining the negotiation processes and outcomes to date. While neoliberalism provides a more plausible explanation than neorealism of the treaty negotiations and outcomes, it nonetheless remains limited since it assumes that state interests remained fixed during the negotiating process and that the regime negotiations and outcomes merely provide incentives that change behaviour, not fundamental interests and identities/social roles. Yet American interests have not been uniform throughout the negotiations and the US has, on occasion, shifted its position in the face of the negotiations (as at Kyoto in 1997). In any event, it is too early to judge whether the withdrawal of the US has in fact led to a 'collective action failure'. Indeed, the entry into force of the Protocol is now imminent, with Russia on the brink of ratification. While it is premature to make any final pronouncements about the success (or otherwise) of the negotiations it is nonetheless possible to offer

---

[9] Oberthur and Ott, *The Kyoto Protocol*, p. 16.

[10] Ward, 'Game Theory and the Politics of Global Warming', 861.

[11] Robert Putnam, 'Diplomacy and Domestic Politics: The Logic of Two-Level Games', *International Organization* 42: 3 (1988), 440, reprinted in Peter B. Evans, Harold K. Jacobson, and Robert D. Putnam (eds.), *International Bargaining and Domestic Politics: Double-Edged Diplomacy* (Berkeley: University of California Press, 1993).

some reflections on the relationship between politics and law in relation to what has been over a decade of negotiations. As we shall see, this entails building upon but also reframing the rationalist emphasis on power and interests by drawing attention to the issues of identity, morality, and legitimacy that are typically neglected in the rationalist analyses.

## Critical constructivism explained and defended

A critical constructivist understanding of international politics and law begins with an understanding of the constitutional structure of treaty-making, which constitutes states as juridically recognised entities and structures the norms of recognition and procedural justice that apply in the processes of treaty-making. The regulative ideals embedded in this constitutional structure are essentially contractual in that the creation of mutually binding norms and rules follows procedures that are intended to enable common understandings between states to emerge by means of free, not forced, consent. Practical discourse (which includes both strategic bargaining and moral argument) is thus essential to the effectiveness and legitimacy of international treaties. Whereas democratic states are accountable to their societies by a relatively dense set of understandings and obligations that serve to limit state power, the relationships *between* the state actors formally involved in international treaty-making and international, civil society are relatively thinner and more tenuous. The identities and interests of states are therefore likely to be shaped to a considerable degree by domestic factors (an argument that liberals tend to emphasise), *but* states are nonetheless *also* enmeshed in and shaped by regional, international, and global social structures and processes, such as the state system and global capitalism. Moreover, as we shall see, these types of international enmeshment vary from state to state in ways that influence the modes of interaction (for example, moral deliberation, bargaining, coercion, and non-cooperation) pursued by states in particular negotiations.

While states are not obliged to participate in treaty-making, if they do participate (and, there are significant *social* pressures to participate), the ideals of communicative justice at the international level require that they be formally respected as juridically equal in the negotiations. Indeed, the principle of equal sovereign rights of member states cannot ultimately be realised by states withdrawing and completely isolating themselves from international politics. To safeguard their sovereign rights, states must enter into, and seek to shape, the international conversation – essentially, practice their 'rights of membership' on the world stage by attending treaty negotiations. This is why, for example, norms such as avoiding deception, avoiding violence, and keeping promises, which includes complying in good faith with treaty responsibilities, are generally observed even when observance may be inconvenient or costly or when parties have the power to ignore the rules. These norms, as Friedrich Kratochwil points out,[12] are *constitutive* of international society. Observance of treaties is not simply a case of enlightened self-interest or deferred gratification of self-interest (as neoliberals suggest); rather, it is fundamental to the continued mutual recognition of states as members of an international society.

Neorealists (and neo-Marxists) might respond to this very idealised account of international treaty-making by pointing to the obvious gap between ideals and practices, particularly the practices of powerful states such as the US. My response to this criticism is to accept, on the one hand, that these liberal regulative ideals are indeed frequently distorted by discrepancies in the negotiating power and capacities of different states, but to insist, on the other hand, that these regulative ideals are not thereby rendered irrelevant. Rather, the regulative ideals remain a *constitutive element* of all treaty negotiations insofar as they continue to inform shared understandings about the norms of recognition, the norms of procedural justice, and the *legitimacy* of outcomes. Moreover, these constitutive ideals may be transformed over time by the practices of agents. As we shall see, the 'critical' dimension of critical constructivism regards as significant the increasing involvement of non-state actors in the treaty-making process – an involvement that has introduced a challenge to the state-centric character of treaty-making, both in terms of the actual negotiations and the regulative ideals. Such an involvement may, over time, possibly lead to more inclusive norms of communicative justice in treaty-making.

## The critical dimension and the question of legitimacy

Habermas' recent analysis of the relationship between law and politics provides the most extended analysis of the constitutive tensions between the regulative ideals and practices of law-making while also

---

[12] Friedrich V. Kratochwil, *Rules, Norms, and Decisions: On the Conditions of Practical and Legal Reasoning in International Relations and Domestic Affairs* (Cambridge: Cambridge University Press, 1989), p. 71.

providing a critical dimension that transcends the state-centric, contractual regulative ideal of international treaty-making and holds out a more inclusive and rational ideal of political communication. For Habermas, in modern times, law has a dual character: it provides the substantive and formal rules to stabilise, integrate, and regulate society as well as the procedural requirements to ensure the legitimacy of those regulations. The rationality and legitimacy of legal norms are derived from the mutual respect accorded to the argumentative rules, roles, and contexts that define the discussion leading to the creation of legal norms. Although Habermas has directed his study to the democratic legitimation of state legal systems, his reconstruction of law and politics contains significant insights that can be enlisted to illuminate the international legal order.

The first insight concerns his understanding of the unavoidable tensions between law-making ideals and practices. For Habermas, 'law has a legitimating force only so long as it can function as a resource for justice'.[13] This is not a wishful normative claim but rather a quasi-empirical claim, reconstructed from the implicit presuppositions of communicative action, most notably, the implicit orientation of actors towards resolving practical disagreements by reaching mutual understanding by means of discursive argument. While in practice there is typically a gap between 'facts' and 'norms', between the actual production of positive law and its animating rationale, for neorealists merely to expose the obvious lack of fit between the legislative ideals and the practice of treaty-making in order to argue that the ideals are weak or irrelevant is to misunderstand the way in which regulative ideals work. That is, all communication is implicitly *oriented* towards reaching mutual understanding by means of reasoned argument rather than coercion or bribery, even if such understanding is not *actually* reached. Such an ideal thus remains a constitutive element of every act of communication. Even in highly distorted communicative settings parties can still feel obliged to explain themselves to others by giving reasons for their preferred positions if they are to persuade others of the acceptability of their arguments or simply to be recognised as legitimate participants. Success in such argumentation is a function, *inter alia*, of the degree of trust, truthfulness, and respect between the parties and whether parties have the capacity to perform the promises they undertake (the latter was something that the US clearly lacked during its negotiations at Kyoto).

---

[13] Jürgen Habermas, *Between Facts and Norms: Contributions to a Discourse Theory of Law and Democracy*, translated by W. Rehg (Cambridge: Polity, 1996), p. 145.

However, it is not only brute power but also practical exigencies that create an enduring tension between the idealised presuppositions embedded in communication and the practical exigencies of real-world communication. Procedural shortcuts (decision rules, time limits, delegated authority, limited rights of representation, and so on) are always necessary for efficacious decision-making. However, these shortcuts cannot be taken too far because *too many* shortcuts can render the resulting decisions increasingly contingent and unstable.[14] In this respect, Habermas' communicative ideal serves not as a blueprint but rather as a critical vantage-point that provides a basis for evaluating the 'degree of distortion' of particular communicative contexts, while also accepting that all real communicative contexts are at best asymptotic approximations to the ideal. Far from removing power and practical exigencies from the equation, Habermas' regulative ideal enables us to observe the many ways in which the presence of brute power and the pressure of practical exigencies can each distort or short-circuit unrestricted communication. *Yet it also explains how power can be disciplined by moral argument.* In the climate change negotiations, we can find examples of both the unilateral assertion of brute power in disregard of the norms of communicative justice as well as the disciplining of brute power via the enlistment of discursively agreed norms and principles.

While some observers have considered the discourse ethic to be fundamentally at odds with the processes of regime formation between sovereign states in international relations,[15] Habermas' recent discourse theory of law points out that even in this thinnest of common life-worlds where bargaining usually predominates, moral discourses can still be incorporated into rule-making procedures, and, indirectly, into the modes of argument employed by the parties. That is, even in those circumstances where strategic bargaining looms large, the legitimacy of any resulting compromise agreement still turns on the *fairness of the bargaining conditions*. In this context, the discourse principle – normally oriented towards consensus – must be brought to bear indirectly, through fair procedures which regulate the bargaining.[16] Moreover, bargaining often relies, in the first instance, on prior understandings about particular facets of the world (such as scientific understandings) that are not

---

[14] Jürgen Haacke, 'Theory and Praxis in International Relations: Habermas, Self-Reflection, Rational Argument', *Millennium* 25: 2 (1996), 286.
[15] For example, Haacke, 'Theory and Praxis in International Relations'; and Andrew Linklater, *The Transformation of Political Community: Ethical Foundations of the Post-Westphalian Era* (Cambridge: Polity Press, 1998).
[16] Habermas, *Between Facts and Norms*, pp. 166–7.

value-neutral, often uncertain, and typically contestable. Establishing the parameters of such understanding for the purposes of bargaining invariably takes the discussion beyond the boundaries of instrumental rationality,[17] and requires a hermeneutic explication of world-views and self-understandings on the part of claimants. It is noteworthy that Habermas considers ecological questions to 'push beyond contested interests and values and engage the participants in a process of self-understanding by which they become reflectively aware of the deeper consonances (*Ubereinstimmungen*) in a common form of life'.[18]

A related insight arising out of critical theory's attention to discursive processes concerns the relationship between the formal processes of law-making and the informal processes of political opinion formation in the public sphere. For Habermas, political will formation (i.e., law-making) and political opinion formation are mutually informing processes that are shaped by a complex web of political actors, both state *and* non-state. We can see this on the international stage,[19] even though the formal lines of accountability and responsibility between the officially recognised state treaty negotiators and domestic and global civil society remain weak and ill-defined. That is, these lines of accountability and responsibility can still be found to work in diffuse and indirect ways. While states are the only juridically recognised entities in the treaty-making process, in practice they are by no means the sole instigators, authors, subjects, and enforcers of international law, a recognition that calls for a less state-centric framework for understanding the relationship between international law and international society. Indeed, treaty-making has increasingly become a major arena for discursive battles about the future shape of international society for both state and non-state actors.

Clearly, power and self-interest remain crucial to any critical constructivist understanding of treaty-making. However, unlike neorealism and neoliberalism, critical constructivism is also sensitive to the sway of moral argument while providing a critical framework for historicising and evaluating the legitimacy of particular negotiations and outcomes. However, Habermas' reconstructive theory does not seek to understand *why* it is that power, interests, and/or moral arguments come to prevail at different times. To understand the orientation of particular actors to negotiations, and their preparedness to respond to different types of

---

[17] Habermas, *Between Facts and Norms*, p. 160.
[18] Habermas, *Between Facts and Norms*, p. 165.
[19] Jürgen Habermas, *The Inclusion of the Other: Studies in Political Theory*, ed. C. Cronin and P. De Greiff (Cambridge, MA: MIT Press, 1998), p. 177.

argument in efforts to negotiate common norms, it is also necessary to explore the ways in which history, tradition, social roles, ideology, and practical precedents shape the dialogue and provide the context for those arguments that come to prevail.[20]

## *The constructivist dimension and the question of identity*

Earlier, we noted that states are enmeshed in different international social structures in varying degrees, and that these types of enmeshment influence the modes of interaction (for example, coercion, bargaining, or moral argument) pursued by states in treaty negotiations. Wendt's analysis of the different 'cultures of anarchy' in the international community is especially pertinent in this regard since it explores the sociological phenomenon of relating to others in the context of historical relationships that have helped to produce different social roles and corresponding 'cultures of relating'. In the case-study we will see how such an understanding sheds considerable light on the different social roles played by the EU and the US in the climate change negotiations.

Neorealists and neoliberals assume that the anarchic character of international society is such that states will always behave in mistrustful and/or instrumental ways. Against these assumptions, Wendt has argued that just as different social structures can produce different social roles and identities, and different modes of relating, so too can different 'cultures of anarchy' produce different state roles and relationships. For example, Wendt shows how states may relate to other states as enemy, rival, or friend and these roles correspond to three different 'cultures' of international politics – Hobbesian, Lockean, and Kantian (these are identified by Wendt as 'salient' logics and therefore need not be taken as exhaustive). Moreover, these different cultures of anarchy explain why states, when they inhabit certain roles, conform to certain behaviours. That is, when they relate to other states as enemies they are only likely to 'co-operate' with others when implicitly or explicitly coerced; when they relate as rivals they tend to comply mostly out of self-interest; and when they relate as friends they comply principally because of shared and 'internalised' understandings. Below, I explain how special considerations apply to powerful states; that is, when they relate to other states in their role of 'world leader' they are more likely to set an example by conforming to multilateral norms (both procedural and substantive)

[20] Kratochwil, *Rules, Norms, and Decisions*, p. 33.

than when they relate to other states simply in their capacity as a 'great power' (where they can act unilaterally and with impunity). We might also expect that moral reasoning might, potentially at least, play a bigger role than instrumental reasoning in political communication between 'friends', given the greater depth of association and shared understandings, although this point is not explored by Wendt. It is also quite possible, however, that pragmatic reasoning would continue to occur in relation to the minutiae of agreements, albeit against a larger background of shared moral/ethical understandings.

Wendt makes it clear that the existence of a Kantian culture of relating among sovereign states need not necessarily imply that there are not important differences and disagreements among states; rather it simply means that states mostly relate to each other as friends rather than rivals or enemies. Here 'friendship' is understood as a 'role structure' whereby disputes are settled without war or threat of war *and* mutual aid is provided to members in the face of external threat.[21] This relationship of friendship is said to be more enduring than the relationship between allies, which is more contingent and precarious.[22] Friendship is based on a shared knowledge and history of the other's peaceful intentions. In such circumstances, co-operation cannot be reduced to material self-interest but can only be understood in terms of the mutual *internalisation* of shared norms. That is, the conception and welfare of the 'self' is taken to include others in the community.[23] However, this identification with the other is rarely total since actors, including state leaders, typically have multiple identities[24] and this is especially so for the leaders of hegemonic states, as we shall see. We can therefore expect contestation and some resistance to surface among members over shared understandings, including debates about free-riding and burden-sharing in any negotiations over common problems. Although Wendt restricts his analysis of the 'culture of friendship' to collective security communities, we might expect members of a 'Kantian security team' (such as the EU) to find it easier to reach agreement about other common problems, such as environmental problems. Moreover, we would expect the extent to which this might occur to be partly a function of the depth of mutual understanding between negotiators and the openness of the discursive processes *within* the community.

---

[21] Alexander Wendt, *Social Theory of International Politics* (Cambridge: Cambridge University Press, 1999), pp. 298–9.
[22] Wendt, *Social Theory of International Politics*, p. 299.
[23] Wendt, *Social Theory of International Politics*, p. 306.     [24] Ibid.

According to Wendt, at this juncture, the international behaviour of states is mostly Lockean (rather than Hobbesian) but with increasing Kantian dimensions.[25] This can partly explain why neoliberal institutionalism has become the dominant framework for analysing environmental regimes, while also historicising this dominance and suggesting new directions for political research. Indeed, Wendt's framework can be usefully applied to all three cultures of anarchy in ways that historicise the insights of both neorealists and neoliberals.

Moreover, the general constructivist focus on roles, identities, and associated modes of relating can be refined and applied in relation to dominant states such as the US, which is enmeshed in international social structures in unique and contradictory ways. Traditionally, theorists of international relations have assumed that hegemony is simply a function of economic and military material capability, which is understood to determine the degree to which a dominant state can control or influence other states and therefore govern or otherwise hold sway over the system.[26] However, Bruce Cronin has drawn an illuminating distinction between a 'powerful state' (defined simply in terms of material capabilities) and a 'hegemon' (defined in terms of international leadership, understood as a *social* property rather than something that arises merely from superior material capability). A hegemonic state is a state that is able to shape the international order according to norms and rules that mostly suit its interests but which are defended and more or less accepted by others as universal in conception. However, in assuming a leadership role in such an order, a hegemonic state is also bound to conform to such norms and rules in order to set an example and uphold the legitimacy of the order, even when they conflict with its short-term interests. That is, while leadership provides greater influence over multilateral norms and rules, it also brings with it a greater responsibility to conform to these generalised rules of conduct.[27] Such social pressures create 'role strain' between a dominant state's position as powerful state (where it has the capabilities to act unilaterally and appease domestic social forces and interests) and its role as a hegemonic state (where there are social expectations that it will conform to generalised rules of conduct, which suit its longer-term interests in maintaining a stable and legitimate international order). Cronin has called this tension

[25] Wendt, *Social Theory of International Politics*, p. 43.
[26] Bruce Cronin, 'The Paradox of Hegemony: America's Ambiguous Relationship with the United Nations', *European Journal of International Relations* 7: 1 (2001), 106.
[27] Cronin, 'The Paradox of Hegemony', 110–12.

*97*

'the paradox of hegemony', which he argues helps to explain why dominant states often engage in inconsistent behaviour (i.e., swinging from unilateral and multilateral action) in different settings.

### An integrated critical constructivist framework

The insights of Habermas and Wendt (supplemented by Cronin) are complementary and can be usefully combined into an integrated critical constructivist framework that provides a more rounded understanding of the climate change negotiations than either neorealists or neoliberal institutionalists can offer. Habermas offers both a sociological understanding of the legitimacy of treaty negotiations, including the tensions between ideals and practices and the requirements of public justification, as well as a critical framework that enables an evaluation of the *degree* of legitimacy of particular negotiations and outcomes from the perspective of both state *and* non-state actors. This suggests that we should look not only to state behaviour but also to the reasons provided by particular states as well as the *reactions* of other states and global civil society if we are to fully understand the status and sway of legal norms. Wendt's analysis helps to give this understanding historical specificity by suggesting that the international community should be understood as made up of many different constellations of states with different 'cultures' and modes of relating to 'the other'. This suggests that we need to look at historical patterns of engagement of different states and the associated social roles and forms of interaction before we can understand whether moral arguments (that is, generalisable claims that are acceptable to differently situated parties) are likely to gain any purchase *vis-à-vis* bargaining, coercion, or non-cooperation in particular negotiations.

## A closer look at the climate change negotiations

To those who might insist that the climate change negotiations can only be understood in terms of power and/or interest, critical constructivists would point to the ways in which power and interests have been *framed and disciplined by moral argument in the negotiations*. As we have seen, critical constructivists understand so-called 'real-world politics' as typically combining these different modes of interaction, with the consequence that the distinctiveness of any one of these different modes should not be over-emphasised at the expense of understanding the various ways in which they may act upon and qualify each other.[28] Of particular interest here is the way in which the *form* of the UNFCCC, initially at least, had helped to facilitate a temporal and analytical separation between the negotiation of basic norms and principles in the framework document and the subsequent negotiation of binding commitments and more detailed rules (such as the Kyoto Protocol) in subsequent conferences of the parties (COPs). Indeed, the Protocol itself required further specification on many contentious matters, specification that the parties were unable to achieve at the COP6 at The Hague but were able to mostly resolve at the Bonn meeting. The degree to which the negotiating parties (particularly the greener states but also many developing states) continued to refer back to the agreed foundation principles in the UNFCCC provides significant evidence of their enduring normative force and legitimacy in the face of attempts to undermine them in the subsequent and more testing negotiations over the details of binding commitments and detailed rules. The core environmental justice principle of 'common but differentiated responsibility' and the related principle that the developed countries should take the lead are fundamentally moral norms – a point that is often ignored in the more cynical analyses of the hard-headed politics of adjustment and burden-sharing that have subsequently taken place, where selfish haggling has predominated and it is therefore presumed that moral arguments have lost their relevance. Yet moral norms remained a fundamental backdrop for the negotiations; they framed and set limits to the more selfish politics of haggling over burden-sharing and adjustment, and they help to explain why certain arguments (including many put forward by countries, such as the US, with a strong fossil fuel dependency) were ruled out. Indeed, there are few better ways of demonstrating the influence of moral norms than when they are agreed to despite the strenuous, self-serving lobbying of powerful states.[29] The attempt by US negotiators at Kyoto to seek greater developing country involvement was effectively rejected because it was outside the basic principles and objectives of the UNFCCC.

For all the shortcomings of the climate change regime, then, it nonetheless demonstrates – contra neorealists – that treaties are not

[28] Ian Hurd, 'Legitimacy and Authority in International Politics', *International Organization* 53: 2 (Spring 1999); and Thomas Risse, ' "Let's Argue!": Communicative Action in World Politics', *International Organization* 54: 1 (2000), 3.
[29] Audie Klotz, *Norms in International Relations: The Struggle Against Apartheid* (Ithaca: Cornell University Press, 1995); and Richard Price, 'Moral Norms in World Politics', *Pacifica Review* 9: 1 (1997).

always *just* a tool for the powerful. While the persuasive force of moral argument is always precarious in the face of the force of brute military and economic power, both weak and strong states need to respect the prevailing norms of communicative justice if they are to be *recognised* as legitimate members of the international society of states. This insight applies with equal force to the US as a hegemonic state, whose role as world leader had created expectations that it will set an example and conform to the generalised norms that it has played a major role in creating under the first Bush Administration. The refusal by particular states to submit to the discursive processes and outcomes of treaty-making can attract strong social censure by both state *and* non-state actors. Moreover, we can expect such censure to be especially strong in relation to hegemonic states. As we have seen, for hegemons, with greater influence over the creation of common norms comes greater responsibility *towards* the international community and greater expectations *by* the international community that such norms will be respected.

In this respect, the Kyoto negotiations are insightful since Clinton's negotiators squarely confronted this paradox of hegemony. Internationally, the US had committed itself to the principles of the UNFCCC and the Berlin mandate that developed states should take the lead and agree to binding targets, yet in response to domestic political pressures it came to the negotiations proposing arguments that were contrary to those agreements. However, these arguments were rejected at the negotiations. At Kyoto at least, the US negotiators chose to resolve this paradox by succumbing to international pressure to respect the prior understanding. Accordingly, it negotiated a compromise (by trading developing country involvement for greater flexibility in meeting its commitments). Enlisting Cronin's analysis, we can say that in this instance the US chose to protect its reputation as a hegemonic leader and uphold the basic rules and norms of multilateralism, rather than exert itself as a great power (by 'walking away'). Those who occupy the role of world leader must act as role models.

However, since the Kyoto meeting, emissions growth in the US had made it increasingly difficult for the US to comply with its Kyoto target of a 7 per cent reduction without incurring heavy economic costs.[30] President Bush junior chose to resolve the paradox of hegemony

[30] According to Christiaan Vrolijk, 'Introduction and Overview', *International Affairs* 77: 2 (2001), 256, US emissions are now around 13 per cent above 1990 levels.

by asserting the US's role as a great power by adopting a unilateral posture *vis-à-vis* the negotiations. Unlike great leaders, great powers do not act as role models; they merely assert their will. However, contrary to what neorealists might suggest, *this was not inevitable* in the sense that there were no other plausible options facing the US. Bush's posture cannot simply be deduced from material capabilities or 'objective interests' but rather must be understood in terms of the particular ideological proclivities of the new Administration. It was not the US Senate that prompted a *sudden* reversal in US foreign policy in 2001, since this opposition had been a constant for many years prior to Bush's repudiation.[31] In any event, public opinion in the US at the time of the repudiation was in *favour* of ratification.[32] Moreover, the costs of meeting the Kyoto targets can be drastically reduced by carefully tailored domestic energy policies that harness cost-effective energy improvements and 'double dividends' from shifting the burden of taxation.[33] Rather, it was President Bush's new National Energy Policy, which unashamedly promoted the further rapid exploitation of oil and gas reserves, that made the repudiation necessary, and it has been argued that the basis for this policy was mostly politically manufactured rather than 'objective'.[34]

Moreover, the unilateral posture has come at a heavy price insofar as it has attracted considerable condemnation not only from many parties to the negotiations but also from US civil society and global civil society. The weight of shared international understandings and expectations of legitimate conduct, stemming from the treaty negotiations (and associated debates within civil society), seems to be clearly *against* the US (and Australia) on this issue.

This social censure also highlights the links between political opinion and political will formation insofar as the role of NGOs and civil society are increasingly significant to the processes of *legitimation* in international negotiations. Indeed, the climate change negotiations have also been 'at the forefront of attempts to open up international negotiations to NGO participation'.[35] NGOs, ranging from environmental NGOs,

---

[31] Lisowski, 'Playing the Two-Level Game', 102.

[32] An ABC News poll released on 17 April 2001 revealed that 61 per cent of Americans supported ratification of the Kyoto Protocol. See Lisowski, 'Playing the Two-Level Game', 114.

[33] Michael Grubb and Joanna Depledge, 'The Seven Myths of Kyoto', *Climate Policy* 1: 2 (2001), 271.

[34] See, for example, Bill McKibben, 'Some Like it Hot', *New York Review of Books* 48: 11 (5 July 2001) and Lisowski, 'Playing the Two-Level Game', 101–19.

[35] Peter Newell, *Climate for Change: Non-State Actors and the Global Politics of the Greenhouse* (Cambridge: Cambridge University Press, 2000), p. 137.

corporations, the media, scientists, policy think tanks, and international organisations, have played a crucial role in identifying and publicising the problem (or downplaying it), developing policy-relevant knowledge, research and political agenda-setting, negotiating policies and rules (sometimes as members of official delegations), monitoring and implementation.[36] Moreover, official sessions and selected events at the negotiations are now broadcast live not only to TV screens in the official conference building but also worldwide on the internet, creating high public visibility and high expectations. NGOs have made full use of modern communications technology such as the internet and mobile phones to stay in touch with relevant delegates and negotiating texts in the formal conference and the reaction of constituents elsewhere in the world. From the perspective of the formal negotiators, the world has been – literally – watching, a fact that can sometimes have a chastening effect on the formal negotiators.[37] At the same time, however, the use of such technologies has put many state and non-state delegates from developing countries at a considerable disadvantage.

In *reducing* politics to brute power or strategic calculation, both neo-realists and neoliberals have overlooked the significance of the discursive processes of opinion and will formation in world politics and underestimated the importance of NGOs, both 'green' and 'grey', in shaping the expectations, behaviour, and identities of states in international negotiations – including their preparedness to co-operate in international fora.

These limitations are highlighted when we shift attention to the contrasting role of the EU in the climate change negotiations. While it is certainly true that the EU was much better placed – in terms of socio-economic and institutional capacity – than the US and other members of the umbrella group to make moves on emissions reductions, to reduce its role to an instrumental calculator is to overlook the significance of its self-understanding as a green leader seeking to further the cause of *global* emissions abatement. For example, the EU played an influential role at Kyoto in extracting stronger commitments from the US while at The Hague it steadfastly refused to concede to many of the US demands on the grounds that they would undermine the environmental objectives of the Protocol (in this it was strongly backed by many

---

[36] See Newell, *Climate for Change.*
[37] See Oberthur and Ott, *The Kyoto Protocol*, pp. 83–4.

environmental NGOs). Moreover, this green identity of the EU at The Hague was not simply a function of the presence of green party delegates from France and Germany in the EU's negotiation team but also must be understood in the context of the deeper legacy of environmental movement activity and green party formation in Europe over the previous three to four decades coupled with the development of a more progressive business community (relative to the US) that is prepared to take a longer-term view of the economic benefits of a less fossil fuel dependent economy. That is, the relatively greener identity of the members of the EU (particularly states such as Germany and the Netherlands) cannot be understood without exploring the role and influence of NGOs and green parties in domestic and regional EU politics, its shared history of ecological problems, and the emerging understanding about the longer-term ecological and economic benefits of eco-efficiency and 'ecological modernisation'. This identity of the EU contrasts starkly with that of the US, which (particularly under George Bush junior) is driven by US fossil fuel interests and short-term economic horizons. The relationship between states in the EU might be said to provide the closest example of a 'Kantian culture' on Wendt's analysis, whereby states see themselves, in certain respects at least, as part of a *team* based on shared understandings, concerns, histories, and institutional legacies. This does not mean that there were not important differences among community members; however, it does provide a more co-operative framework for resolving these differences. In the climate change negotiations, the EU resolved many of its own benefit and burden-sharing conflicts through its united 'bubble proposal', which set an overall EU target but allowed differential targets within the EU to account for differing economic circumstances and costs of adjustment among member states. Nonetheless, the EU's identity as a green leader sought not only to promote the good of the European region but also a more general notion of collective well-being – an identity that cannot simply be explained in terms of the national interests of the member states.

However, that the EU members tended to spend more time talking among themselves than to other states in the climate change negotiations is testimony to the demands of reaching a regional consensus among the members. Ironically, the relatively greener identity of the EU and its preoccupation with its internal communicative processes may also have precluded the EU (both as a unit and also in terms of individual members) from engaging more extensively with countries *outside* the EU (other than the US), particularly developing countries, which might have been able to play a more constructive role in the negotiations had they been afforded a better opportunity to be involved.

For critical constructivists, the shared ideas in any political community form a *social structure*, which may be reproduced over time by coercion, self-interest, and/or legitimacy. In this respect, the discursive processes (which includes the influence of green and grey NGOs) within the EU may be contrasted with those operating in the federal structure of the US. At the national level, the US fossil fuel lobby vastly outweighs the environment lobby in terms of money, power, and strategic influence, and it has played a significant role in shaping public expectations, opinion, and American lifestyles and identity around, for example, a car and freeway culture. In particular, the fossil fuel lobby proved to be a major force behind the Byrd–Hagel resolution and it launched a US$13 million advertising campaign after the resolution in the lead-up to the Kyoto meeting warning Americans of the economic costs of implementing the mooted Protocol.[38] More significantly, George W. Bush's abrupt decision in 2001 to repudiate America's Kyoto commitments (which represented a retraction of election campaign promises) has also been attributed in no small measure to the political influence of the oil, coal, and gas interests in the US.[39] Against this background, the main policy objective of the US – 'flexibility' – suited what Michael Grubb has called 'the confluence of political interests and economic ideology' in the US.[40] Whereas participation in the international climate change negotiations has further enhanced the identities of the members of the EU as good regional *and* international citizens (at least *relatively* speaking – there are no ideal green states), the negotiations have had no such effect on the US. Rather, the unilateralist posture of the current US Administration has been overwhelmingly shaped by powerful domestic economic interests and arguments that happen to suit a Republican ideological framework that is largely resistant to alternative environmental discourses, including the 'win–win' discourse of 'ecological modernisation'.

---

[38] Oberthur and Ott, *The Kyoto Protocol*, p. 72.   [39] McKibben, 'Some Like it Hot'.
[40] Michael Grubb, with Christiaan Vrolijk and Duncan Brack, *The Kyoto Protocol: A Guide and Assessment* (London: Royal Institute of International Affairs and Earthscan, 1999), p. 112.

## Conclusion

The climate change case-study supports the critical constructivist claim that not only are politics and law mutually enmeshed, so too are strategic bargaining and moral reasoning. Moreover, it demonstrates that treaty-making is possible without a hegemon, that the identities and interests of states can be shaped by both domestic and transnational discursive practices, and that NGOs are increasingly significant to any understanding of the discursive processes and legitimacy of multilateral agreements. Moreover, critical constructivism provides a rational reconstruction of the discursive and procedural requirements for a legitimate legal order in a modern, pluralistic world that goes beyond the dominant state-centric requirements of procedural justice. After all, legitimacy is always a question of degree. Given that the political community affected by global warming is far more extensive than the society of states, then critical constructivists would consider the ideals and practices of treaty-making to be *more* legitimate if they were to rest on an inclusive, cosmopolitan regulative ideal that is more commensurate with the global reach of the problem confronted. Yet critical constructivism is also able to shed sociological light on the enduring tensions between the prevailing communicative ideals and the actual production of positive law. And in directing attention to the importance of history, culture, and social roles/identities, it can shed light on the preparedness of different parties to respond to different kinds of argument in the actual production of treaties.

Finally, critical constructivism is able to draw attention to the social ambiguity of existing international law (both soft and hard) in the way it can sometimes be used to discipline powerful actors from a moral point of view while also serving as a tool to legitimate more narrowly conceived national interests on the part of more powerful states. As we have seen, soft legal norms can play a crucial role in legitimising and delegitimising particular claims and behaviour, irrespective of whether they find refinement in specific rules, practical achievements, and compliance standards. If there is a political lesson to be had from these insights, it is that even existing international law ought not to be entirely dismissed as a vehicle for progressive social change.

# 5    Emerging customary norms and anti-personnel landmines

*Richard Price*[1]

A new international legal norm rapidly emerged in the 1990s prohibiting the use, transfer, production, and stockpiling of anti-personnel (AP) landmines. Marked as it has been by broad participation and extremely rapid entry into force, this norm has attained impressive status compared to the lengthy process taken by many international legal norms – especially those governing warfare – to spread and consolidate. Yet, participation in the legal regime is not universal, raising the question of whether or not the norm has broad enough adherence to qualify as a customary rule of international law. A ruling of such status by a court – say in a civil case by a victim seeking damages from AP landmine use, analogous to recent rulings on cases of torture – would mark a critical benchmark in the consolidation and application of the norm. Such a determination would mean that the AP landmine norm is held to generate legal obligations even for non-state actors and those states that have not signalled their explicit consent to the treaty.

In this chapter I undertake two main tasks. First, I examine whether the AP landmine norm would qualify as a rule of customary law, and in doing so I contribute to this volume's critique of realist and neoliberal accounts of international law. I examine the customary status of the AP landmine taboo by illuminating the shortcomings of consent-based approaches to international legal and political theory, and show how incorporating insights from constructivist international relations scholarship can enrich our understanding of the emergence of customary legal norms. So equipped, I demonstrate some important strides this norm

[1] I wish to thank J. Marshall Beier, Anita Krajnc, Abdullah Mojadeddi, Sandra Rein, and Michael Griesdorf for their invaluable research assistance as participants in the Mines Action Research Program, funded by the Department of Foreign Affairs and International Trade, Canada, from which some of the material for this chapter was drawn.

has made towards customary status, though I conclude that at present the norm would likely fall short of the threshold of an unambiguous customary legal rule before a court.

In the process of this assessment I endeavour to accomplish a second task central to this volume: namely, illuminating how politics and law have interacted to produce the current state of affairs regarding AP landmines. I examine the effects that a concern with customary law has had on the politics of the use of force, and show how the practices of states and non-state actors to both capture and resist the pulls of customary legal obligation have importantly shaped political practice regarding AP landmines. In this way, the case-study of the customary legal status of landmines serves as a window to critically examine the relationship between international politics and international law.

## Custom, consent, and constructivism

How do we know an international legal norm when we see one? The existence of treaty law that commands widespread adherence provides the most obvious demonstration. This follows from the predominant conception of consent as the basis of international law, as famously stated by the Permanent Court of International Justice in the *Lotus Case* of 1927.[2] According to this view of international law, a state is legally bound only by those rules to which it grants its explicit consent, which usually occurs as treaty ratification. International legal scholars and jurists, however, have long recognised that other sources of law exist, including more informal sources such as custom. There is more or less a consensus among international legal scholars and jurists that establishing customary obligations upon states involves demonstrating two requirements: general state practice – widespread norm-conforming behaviour – and *opinio juris* – the belief by states that the practice is undertaken as an obligation of international law. There is, however, controversy about how to measure these features and which of them is more important. Moreover, the very notion of international custom making claims of obligation upon states sits uneasily with the theory of consent that has been a predominant basis of both state practice and scholarship of international law. It is difficult to reconcile consent with custom since the former is premised upon an individualistic and voluntaristic ontological conception of the international system of states, whereas

---

[2] The Lotus Case, *PCIJ Reports 1927*, Series A, No. 9, p. 18.

the latter presupposes a communitarian ontology of international society. Similar to the weakness of neoliberal accounts of law identified in the introduction of this volume, the result for consent theory has been a persistent set of paradoxes as to how custom could be said to develop and exist at all. Above all, there is the chronological paradox that *'opinio juris* is a prerequisite for customary law, but in order to produce *opinio juris*, state officials must be convinced that the law already exists'.[3] How could customary norms ever develop with such a conception of law?

Michael Byers, among others, has usefully identified a number of these difficulties, and in an attempt to overcome them has sought to integrate insights from international relations scholarship into conceptualisations of international law. Byers recognises that:

> States either support, are ambivalent towards, or oppose potential, emerging or existing customary rules and usually behave accordingly. Anything a State does or says, or fails to do or say, therefore has the potential to be considered legally relevant, and thus to contribute to the development, maintenance or change of a rule of customary international law.[4]

It is in precisely this spirit that numerous avenues for deducing customary norms are identified in this chapter. However, Byers' own integration of international relations theory into customary international law is limited to a conception of norms emphasised by the neoliberal institutionalist school. While these efforts are fruitful, they do not exhaust the contributions of international relations research on norms. Indeed, they are subject to the same limitations as the convincingly critiqued neoliberal conception of norms in international relations, since both have a conception of norms (or law) that is premised upon an individualist ontology usually driven by a materialist conception of state interests. While this theoretical account captures some of the phenomena of norms and law, it leaves out numerous dimensions also – above all, the ways in which not only norms but state interests themselves are socially constructed, the importance of non-state actors in creating and

---

[3] Susan Benesch, Glenn McGrory, Cristina Rodriguez, and Robert Sloane, 'International Customary Law and Antipersonnel Landmines: Emergence of a New Customary Norm', in International Campaign to Ban Landmines (hereafter ICBL), *Landmine Monitor Report 1999: Toward a Mine-Free World* (New York: Human Rights Watch, 1999), p. 1025, <www.icbl.org/lm/1999/>.
[4] Michael Byers, *Custom, Power and the Power of Rules: International Relations and Customary International Law* (Cambridge: Cambridge University Press, 1999), p. 19.

reinforcing law, the importance of identity in constituting norms, and the intersubjective bases for norms.

Byers has noted that customary law is constantly evolving as the relevant actors, whether states or ordinary individuals, continually engage in legally relevant behaviour: 'They are, in this sense, both creators and subjects of the law.'[5] However, since Byers explicitly adopts the assumptions of state interests and consent, he does not pursue the full implications of the latter point. To provide a full picture of the status of norms we need to attend to a recursive examination of the effect of social norms upon the agents as evidence for the existence and status of the norm. While customary law appears vexing to consent-based approaches because it rests at the nexus of individualist and communitarian ontologies, social constructivism specifically seeks to provide a bridge between agents and structures and thus provides a natural home for elucidating the nature of customary norms.[6]

## Constitutive norms and customary law

A major contribution of constructivism inheres in the insight that norms do not merely constrain already existing states from pursuing their exogenous interests, but they also constitute actors and interests. Conceiving of norms as constitutive of the practices of war has important implications for understanding customary international law, including the emerging norm prohibiting the use of anti-personnel landmines. During the 1990s the rapid mobilisation of an international campaign to ban AP landmines led to a treaty of international law, the Landmines Convention of 1997. With 150 signatories and 141 ratifications, the question has arisen: is there already a customary norm prohibiting the use of AP landmines, such that even states which have not become party to the Convention are legally obliged not to use them?[7] To what degree do even non-party states evince elements of obligation, and how has this come about?

The traditional requirements of customary law would direct us to identify, along with behaviour, whether states indicated a belief that the

---

[5] Byers, *Custom, Power and the Power of Rules*, p. 5.
[6] On the bridge-building quality of constructivism see Emanuel Adler, 'Seizing the Middle Ground: Constructivism in World Politics', *European Journal of International Relations* 3: 3 (1997); and Richard Price and Christian Reus-Smit, 'Dangerous Liaisons?: Critical International Theory and Constructivism', *European Journal of International Relations* 4: 3 (1998).
[7] Benesch et al., 'International Customary Law'.

practice of not using AP landmines is required by law (*opinio juris*). Other pathways, however, have proved crucial for the incurring of obligations, particularly the social pressures of identity. At a crucial phase of the campaign in 1997, Japan and Australia felt obliged to join the momentum and support the landmine ban not so much because either believed that all AP landmine use was an illegal act of the state, as would be required of a criterion of *opinio juris*. Rather, both these countries adopted pro-ban policies – in spite of opposition from their defence ministries and key allies like the US – because their leaders evidently felt it intolerable to be left outside the club of responsible international citizens once they judged that the balance had tipped such that resistance signalled outlier status.[8] That is, key states were socialised into an emerging norm not out of domestically driven assessments of how well the norm served their own national interests (as per neoliberal theories of international relations or consent-based theories of law), but rather by communitarian pressures of emulation and identity. Moreover, it was after such commitments that states could then come to view their use of AP landmines as required by law, hence the norm had become in this sense 'already illegal'.

Two points are important here. First, we could note that if we take into account these constitutive processes, the chronological paradox that bedevils consent-based theories of law dissolves. Second, we can see how this emergent legal rule has the effect of helping define what constitutes a law-abiding member in good standing of the international community. In other words, we can identify how *a concern with emergent elements of obligatory force shapes who state actors are and what they want*. In this way the multilateral force of treaty law imparts a communitarian quality to international politics.

Beyond the legal obligations that pro-ban states have incurred for themselves, is the AP landmines taboo universal enough to make claims upon those states that have not indicated their embrace of the norm? An understanding that norms have not just regulative but also permissive effects helps us appreciate that the taken-for-granted use of AP landmines in uncontroversial fashion for much of the twentieth century has in fact constituted a permissive norm of warfare: it was a universally shared norm that the use of AP landmines was an acceptable practice. The movement banning AP landmines and the resulting Landmines Convention prohibiting their use, however, has unsettled that norm.

---

[8] See Richard Price, 'Reversing the Gun Sights: Transnational Civil Society Targets Land Mines', *International Organization* 52: 3 (1998).

This still leaves unanswered, however, the question of whether a new prohibitionary norm can be said to have emerged in its place. This issue was addressed in the *Nuclear Weapons Case* Advisory Opinion delivered by the International Court of Justice (ICJ) in 1996. There the court advised that there was not

> any principle or rule of international law which would make the legality of the threat or use of nuclear weapons or of any other weapons dependent on a specific authorization. State practice shows that the illegality of the use of certain weapons as such does not result from an absence of authorization but, on the contrary, is formulated in terms of prohibition.[9]

On the other hand, the court later drew upon the tradition of international humanitarian law encapsulated in the Marten's clause to argue that 'States do not have unlimited freedom of choice of means in the weapons they use', concluding that the use of nuclear weapons would scarcely be reconcilable with respect for the requirements of law applicable in armed conflict.[10] In other words, even as it denied the doctrine that restrictions upon states can be presumed, the ICJ placed those very restrictions upon the conduct of all states. What conclusions on this issue are we to draw from the *Nuclear Weapons Case* at the ICJ?

Among several relevant considerations[11] we could note there is a crucial potential difference between the nuclear weapons case and possible future cases of customary law involving such controversial practices as the use of AP landmines or child soldiers. Absence of authorisation would not necessarily imply the lack of a prohibition if the conduct in question contravened some other fundamental source of law, such as customary law or *jus cogens*. In the case of AP landmines, in the absence of treaty obligation there is not a legal vacuum, but rather a well-established tradition of customary norms of warfare that provide the grounds for the contention that the use of AP landmines would violate existing customary norms of war. Three central concepts in the just war tradition – military necessity, unnecessary suffering/superfluous injury, and non-combatant immunity/discrimination – have been put forth as grounds for arguing that the use of AP landmines is already illegal under

---

[9] *Legality of the Threat or Use of Nuclear Weapons*, Advisory Opinion, *ICJ Report 1996* 226, para 52 (8 July).
[10] *Legality of the Threat or Use of Nuclear Weapons*, para 78.
[11] See Richard Price, *Anti-Personnel Landmines and Customary International Law*, Report (Ottawa: Canadian Department of Foreign Affairs and International Trade, 2000).

international law.[12] I will not rehearse those arguments in detail here, but just note that these norms of customary international law of war provide the positive legal grounds for advancing the claim that the use of AP landmines would be already illegal as a violation of customary international law. Thus, while the ICJ in the *Nuclear Weapons Case* Advisory Opinion argued that any use of nuclear weapons was *likely* to be illegal since it would likely violate the customary norm against using indiscriminate weapons, it could not definitively rule on the issue since it was an advisory opinion for a *hypothetical* case. Any future case seeking to condemn the use of landmines as illegal, then, could well meet with a favourable ruling *on this dimension* if the case was carefully chosen to constitute an obviously indiscriminate use of an indiscriminate weapon that violated the customary laws of war.

This tack is also important to keep in mind given state positions like that of India, which has opposed a general prohibition by maintaining that the use of AP landmines in discriminate and responsible ways should not be subject to prohibition.[13] By so arguing, India has raised the threshold of its own acceptable behaviour and trapped itself into a position whereby it has implicitly accepted a legal obligation to prevent indiscriminate (civilian) casualties from its use of AP landmines, thereby living up to the obligations of landmine use stipulated in the Convention on Conventional Weapons (CCW). Thus, countries like India that have sought legitimacy for their efforts to resist an emerging obligatory norm on AP landmines have been able to do so only by reinforcing the constitutive and customary norms of warfare and humanitarian law, and it is those very norms which lend support to an emerging customary norm against the use of AP landmines. In this way, state concern with potentially emerging obligations of law has important effects on the politics of the use of force. The very attempt to formally resist customary obligations is done on the terrain of legal discourse; that is, by referring to other legal obligations. By not reverting to a more avowedly political discourse the legitimate place of law in the use of force is reaffirmed. Thus, even as some states seek to resist the more thoroughgoing obligatory force of custom, the obligatory force of treaty commitments – and

[12] Human Rights Watch and Physicians for Social Responsibility, *Landmines: A Deadly Legacy* (New York: Human Rights Watch, 1993), pp. 274–5; and International Committee of the Red Cross, 'Banning Anti-Personnel Mines: The Ottawa Treaty Explained' (Geneva: ICRC, 1998).
[13] J. Marshall Beier, 'Anti-Personnel Landmines and Customary Law: The Case of India', unpublished manuscript (Toronto: York University, 2000).

the liberal modernist regime of multilateral international law – is reinforced.

## The politics of *opinio juris*

As mentioned above, the notion that states can be bound legally by customary norms traditionally has required some combination of a demonstration of general state practice and *opinio juris*. However, among both scholars conceptualising international law and jurists applying it, there is debate as to how to interpret these constituent features of customary international law, how to apply them, and how to weigh their relative importance. Without detailing the various positions, we can note that this indeterminancy of the sources of customary law means that there is some inherent unpredictability as to how any given court could rule on non-obvious cases like the customary status of the AP landmines ban.

Some judgements in cases of international law have veered towards a somewhat demanding criterion that universal or uniform practice of states and clear *opinio juris* are necessary to establish custom.[14] In other cases, however, such as torture, less demanding criteria have been applied. American and British courts among others have ruled that customary law exists primarily due to *opinio juris* even in the face of state practice which widely violates the norm.[15] In such cases it has been argued and ruled that *opinio juris* is more important than practice; that is, a rule need not be universally followed, just widely defended to establish international customary law. The legal treatment of torture in the *Filartiga* and *Pinochet* cases reflects this standard. No one argues that torture does not occur, and indeed with some frequency, yet the prohibition against torture still has been accepted by states and by courts as a norm of customary international law (and even as a more fundamental norm of *jus cogens*).

This conceptualisation of custom that emphasises *opinio juris* over behaviour usefully captures the fact that states often agree to a regulative norm more fully in rhetoric than in practice. It is also compatible with an insight from international relations scholars who have argued that a

---

[14] See The Lotus Case, *PCIJ Reports 1927*, Series A, No. 10.
[15] See *Filartiga v. Pena-Irala*, United States Court of Appeals, Second Circuit, 630 F. 2nd 876 (1980), at 882, 884; *Regina v. Bow Street Metropolitan Stipendiary Magistrate, ex parte Pinochet Ugarte* (No.3) [1999] 2 WLR 827 (opinion of Lord Browne-Wilkinson) [hereafter *Pinochet III*].

key feature of norms is that they are, to a point, counterfactually valid. That is, norms may be said to exist and persist even in the face of violations.[16] As a result, state practice and belief in the general validity of the norm can diverge in any given situation without necessarily denying the subsequent persistence and influence of the norm. At some point too much divergence by too many states would indeed extinguish the norm, but the point is that any norm, like the domestic legal norm proscribing murder, can tolerate some level of disconfirming practice without disappearing and without relinquishing the validity of its claim of obligation. Thus, since virtually all norms are violated to some degree, what matters most from the perspective of identifying settled social norms is the extent to which there is general acceptance of the central validity claims of the norms.[17]

When extreme circumstances are invoked to justify a departure, or when attempts are made to conceal violations, violations are less harmful to the overall persistence of a norm and the norm can be said to be more robust, than situations in which norms are violated more as a matter of course. Important here is the intersubjective phenomenon that the transgressor feels compelled to justify (or deny) the violation because of mutually shared expectations that such behaviour is normally unacceptable and requires defence to reconfirm the status of the violator as a legitimate member of international society. This stage in the development of a norm marks the potential transition of a practice from being understood as residing solely in a domain of power politics – where the domestically driven security interests of states are ontologically primitive – to a realm where communitarian expectations of obligation are increasingly accorded prominence. A concern with reasons for action results in the deployment of legal discourse, which helps transform the character of politics towards a more holistic international society with a broader array of legitimated actors (like judges). An emergent international legal rule induces states to engage in practices they would not otherwise perform. This is not to ignore that at the same time resistant states try to wrestle the issue of AP landmines away from the

---

[16] John Ruggie and Friedrich Kratochwil, 'International Organization: A State of the Art on the Art of the State', *International Organization* 40: 4 (1986); and Friedrich V. Kratochwil, *Rules, Norms, and Decisions: On the Conditions of Practical and Legal Reasoning in International Relations and Domestic Affairs* (Cambridge: Cambridge University Press, 1989).
[17] Mervyn Frost, *Ethics in International Relations: A Constitutive Theory* (Cambridge: Cambridge University Press, 1996), p. 105.

non-state actors who instigated the ban and the states who joined as allies in the ban movement.[18]

Under such a doctrine of customary law, the norm could be said to exist if states generally cease to defend the use of mines, even before they actually stop using them.[19] Even if the empirical evidence would tend towards supporting a general ruling of the existence of *opinio juris* so conceived, two provisos would have to be taken into account to establish a general rule of customary international law. First, scholarship and rulings on *opinio juris* have generally held that the *opinio juris* of any 'specially affected states' must accord with the norm for it to be valid as a customary rule.[20]

Second, it has been argued that a new rule of customary law does not incur a legal obligation for any state that counts as a 'persistent objector' to an emerging new rule of customary international law. According to this requirement, a 'persistent objector' state which actively and persistently objects to an emerging customary rule of law is not to be held legally bound by it. This idea stems in good part from the ruling of the ICJ in the *Anglo-Norwegian Fisheries Case*, wherein the court decided that the rule advocated by Britain for jurisdiction of the seas was inapplicable as Norway had always opposed it.[21]

### Opinio juris *and AP landmines*

What would be the status of the AP landmines taboo according to the above conceptualisation of *opinio juris*? If one were to compare extant *opinio juris* regarding AP landmines with rulings by courts on the existence of other customary legal rules, the results would be mixed; there are some grounds to suggest that a positive ruling could be made by a court finding the AP landmines taboo is a customary rule of international law, but there are other grounds which point towards the likelihood that a court would reach a negative ruling.

Regarding the former, if one compares the evidence of custom deemed sufficient for the findings of a customary rule against torture in the *Filartiga Case* of 1980 or of a rule against aggression and intervention by the ICJ in the *Nicaragua Case*, the case of AP landmines compares very favourably. However, there is an important unfavourable comparison with the customary norm prohibiting torture; namely, that the AP

---

[18] See Price, 'Reversing the Gun Sights'.
[19] Benesch et al., 'International Customary Law'.
[20] North Sea Continental Shelf Cases, *ICJ Reports 1969*, p. 93.
[21] Fisheries Case, *ICJ Reports 1951*, p. 131.

landmines taboo is not embraced with the same degree of rhetorical universality as the torture taboo. This is not insignificant, since Frederic Kirgis has suggested that the reason there has been inconsistency by the ICJ among others in the standards used to determine customary status is that in practice a sliding scale seems to operate in determinations of customary law. As he put it:

> On the sliding scale, very frequent, consistent state practice establishes a customary rule without much (or any) affirmative showing of an *opinio juris*, so long as it is not negated by evidence of non-normative intent. As the frequency and consistency of the practice decline in any series of cases, a stronger showing of *opinio juris* is required. At the other end of the scale, a clearly demonstrated *opinio juris* establishes a customary rule without much (or any) affirmative showing that governments are consistently behaving in accordance with the asserted rule.[22]

How would the mines taboo measure up to such a scale? In terms of treaty participation support for the landmines taboo is very widespread. Support is even more widespread if we consider more general sources of state rhetoric, since many states who are not parties to the Landmines Convention have nonetheless expressed varying degrees of support for the norm in a variety of official statements. The existence of a widely if not universally embraced legal rule has clearly shaped the rhetorical practices of states. Prominent non-parties such as the United States, Russia, Turkey, India, and China have all in various ways expressed support in principle for the eventual elimination of AP landmines. The United States in rhetoric has repeatedly supported the norm; indeed President Clinton was the first head of state to call for a ban on AP landmines. While the US has sought throughout the process various exceptions to the comprehensive AP ban, US policy made explicit the US intention to 'aggressively pursue an international agreement to ban the use, stockpiling, production, and transfer of AP landmines'.[23] China, although it has opposed the Landmines Convention, has declared that 'China is not opposed to the objective of prohibiting APLs in a phased approach, but cannot agree to any immediate total ban.'[24] Even those who

---

[22] Frederic Kirgis, Jr, 'Custom on a Sliding Scale', *American Journal of International Law* 81: 1 (1987), 149.

[23] 'Presidential Decision Directive 48', <www.pub.whitehouse.gov/uri- . . . oma.eop.gov. us/1997/5/16/16.text.1>, accessed 9 June 2000.

[24] Sha Zukang, 'Chinese Comments on the Issue of APL: Excerpts of a Speech Given by Sha Zukang, Ambassador of the PRC for Disarmament Affairs, June 1997', *Beijing Review* (5–11 January 1998), 19–20.

have actively continued to use AP mines have declared their rhetorical support for a ban, including Angola and Russia. 'Russia wholeheartedly supports the effort and struggle of worldwide joint-efforts to quickly solve the landmine problem and is prepared to do all that is required of it to achieve this goal. At the same time, however, we cannot immediately join the Convention.'[25] Similarly, India has stated that it 'remains committed to the objective of a non-discriminatory, universal and global ban on anti-personnel mines through a phased process that addresses the legitimate defence requirements of States, while at the same time, ameliorating the humanitarian crises that have resulted from irresponsible transfer and indiscriminate use of landmines'.[26] Even Sri Lanka, which in a 1997 preparatory meeting for a ban treaty was one of only four states to openly declare a continued need to use AP landmines, has simultaneously voted in favour of numerous UN resolutions mentioned above, as well as made statements that 'measures were needed to ban the manufacture, stockpiling, transfer and use of indiscriminate landmines, sooner than later'.[27] Similarly, although Egypt has sharply resisted the ban, Egyptian officials have stated that Egypt 'associate[s] ourselves with the humanitarian aspects as well as with the need for a total ban on APLs'.[28]

When actors have been directly accused of using landmines, some situations parallel that of Sri Lanka, where neither the government nor the Tamil Tigers have attempted to conceal the fact of their ongoing use of AP landmines.[29] There has developed, however, a pattern of sensitivity to the norm and patterns of clandestine use or denial that represent a very significant change from the period before the late 1990s when the movement to ban landmines gained prominence. While fifteen countries were accused of using mines in 2001, for example, only six acknowledged such use. Typical is the case of Turkey which denied

---

[25] Vladimir Kuznetsov, 'The Ottawa Process & Russia's Position', *Krasnaya Zvezda* (27 November 1997), p. 3, as in *What The Papers Say* (28 November 1997), p. 37.
[26] Statement by Satyabrata Pal, Acting Permanent Representative of India, at United Nations Disarmament Conference, Geneva, 27 June 2000, p. 4.
[27] UN Document, Press Release GA/DIS/3096 (11 November 1997).
[28] 'Explanation of Vote by Ambassador Dr. Mahmoud Darem on the Resolution on Anti Personnel Landmines', internal Egyptian government document, The Permanent Mission of Egypt to the United Nations, 1998.
[29] In addition to Sri Lanka, *Landmine Monitor* reports that from March 2001 to mid-2002 Russia, Burma (Myanmar), India and Pakistan acknowledged the use of landmines. ICBL, *Landmine Monitor Report 2002: Toward a Mine-Free World* (New York: Human Rights Watch, 2002), <www.icbl.org/lm/2002/>, accessed 11 March 2003.

such accusations in 1998 and instead stated that:

> Turkey associates itself with the fundamental humanitarian consider-
> ations which have motivated the mentors of the Ottawa process. We
> welcome the Convention's entry-into-force . . . We do not exclude our
> signing of the Ottawa Convention in the future, when our security
> concerns have been comprehensively and satisfactorily addressed.[30]

Angola similarly refused to acknowledge accusations of continued use,
while accusing UNITA of such behaviour, until it could no longer deny
such use in 2001. Georgia too conforms to the pattern of denying or con-
cealing proscribed behaviour; the official response to allegations of use
mostly has been silence. And even an exception to this general silence
confirms the pattern: a statement from one official from the Ministry
of Defence noted, 'Those mines and ammunition we use at present are
military secrets. Landmines have their importance and let us leave it in
secret.'[31] Similarly, a Georgian Defence Ministry official told Landmine
Monitor that Georgian armed forces laid anti-personnel mines in several passes bordering Abkhazia in 2001, though the Georgian Foreign
Ministry has denied any use of anti-personnel mines.[32] Anita Krajnc has
found that 'Egypt is secretive when confronted about its use of APLs
within its territories. For example, when asked by the UN assessment
mission in February 2000 about its use of APLs, the Egyptian government chose not to discuss the topic.'[33]

A most prominent use of AP landmines in recent years has occurred
in Chechnya, both by the Russian military and Chechen rebels. Prominent Russian decision-makers in general have refrained from justifying
their use of AP landmines; the preferred rhetorical stance has been one

---

[30] 'Turkey's Explanation of Vote on the Draft Resolution Entitled: Convention on the
Prohibition of the Use, Stockpiling, Production and Transfer of Anti-Personnel Mines and
on Their Destruction', A/C.1/53/L.33, 4 November 1998.
[31] Vacho Jgrenaya, 'Peaceful Caucasus: Toward a Future Without Landmines', Regional
Landmine Conference, Tbilisi, Georgia, 5–7 December 1999, in ICBL, *Landmine Monitor Report 2000: Toward a Mine-Free World* (New York: Human Rights Watch, 2000),
<www.icbl.org/lm/2000/report/LMWeb-24.php3#P18173_2403557>, 10 August 2000. In
response to Russian mining of Georgia's border in its conflict with the Chechens, the
Department for the Protection of the State Border of Georgia has stated officially that
it is 'considering the possibility of mining the Chechen stretch of the Russian–Georgian
border'. See Aleksandr Igorev and Georgiy Dvali, 'Minefields Will Separate Russia from
Georgia', Moscow Kommersant in Russian, FBIS Reports (12 April 2000), p. 3.
[32] ICBL, *Landmine Monitor Report 2002*.
[33] Anita Krajnc, 'Anti-Personnel Landmines and Customary Law: The Case of Egypt',
unpublished manuscript (University of Toronto, 2000), pp. 4–5.

of silence. Lower-level officials, however, have explained their use of mines along Chechen stretches of the border with Georgia: 'We have decided not to disclose precisely what kind of mines we will lay or on which stretches of the border and how. We do not want to leak any information that the rebels could make use of. Because the lives of our soldiers are at stake. And General Manilov has also recommended that we do not go into detail.'[34] It is significant to note that while states like Turkey and Russia made general justifications of their continued need for AP landmines when pressed to join the treaty, no high officials in official pronouncements explicitly defended the specific allegations, or even admitted such use. Clearly, states can no longer simply regard the use of AP landmines as normal and uncontroversial behaviour by international standards. The rhetorical response even of most violator states to allegations of use contributes to the sense of aberration of the use of AP landmines, rather than normalising such behaviour and establishing a contrary permissive rule sanctioning the use of these weapons as an acceptable routine for all states.

Most of the key states whose participation in the Landmines Convention is routinely regarded as crucial for universalising the status of the norm – above all the United States, Russia, and China – have expressed support in principle for the ban by arguing that they support an *eventual* ban, when a variety of circumstances have been met. Comparably, in the *Nuclear Weapons Case*, the ICJ held that the commitment of the nuclear powers under the Nuclear Non-Proliferation Treaty (NPT) to *eventually* eliminate their arsenals was not adequate evidence of *opinio juris*. A similar position of expressing support in principle for an eventual ban is one adopted by many states who have not acceded to the Landmines Convention, and more states support a ban on nuclear weapons than on AP landmines. Thus, according to the measure of support in principle for an eventual ban, the AP landmines case does not compare favourably to the opinion in the *Nuclear Weapons Case* in terms of simply adding up the numbers to determine what number of states constitutes an adequate threshold of a customary norm.

Still, we must note that all such temporising language is not always the mere hypocritical subterfuge realists would be quick to point out in cases like Russia, which has flouted the ban in practice while officially maintaining that it too would eventually join.[35] Rather, engaging in such

---

[34] Igorev and Dvali, 'Minefields Will Separate Russia', p. 3.
[35] Geoffrey York, 'Russia Flouts Land-Mine Vow', *Globe and Mail* (4 June 2001).

legal discourse can mark a crucial step in the process of legal obligation imparting its influence on the identities and purposes of states. Turkey, for one, having initially adopted the rhetorical stance of supporting the ban when conditions permitted, committed itself in April of 2001 to adopt the mine ban treaty along with Greece,[36] which will leave the US as the sole member of NATO not to have joined the pact.

We saw above that assessments of customary legal status must ascertain whether any 'specially affected states' reject the rule. There are good reasons to reject the applicability and importance of the doctrine of 'specially affected states' to the emergence of a customary norm prohibiting AP landmines. The foundational doctrine of the sovereign and legal equality of states, a cornerstone of international law, is not to be overridden lightly. To be sure, it must be noted that there sometimes may be good political reasons for the doctrine to keep reins on the political relevance of international law, and act as a counterweight to the egalitarian multilateralism of custom that would confer upon Monaco the same international legal weight as China. As such, moments of the potential application of the doctrine represent the transitional nexus between a modernist politics and law of consent, and a more deeply communitarian politics and law of a globalised international society that empowers not only smaller states but non-state actors as well (judges and courts applying law, and non-governmental organisations surveying state performance).

Thus the doctrine of 'specially affected states' represents a legal tightrope stretched across different conceptions of world politics. Too easily applied as a convenient political substitute for conferring greater legal weight upon great powers over lesser states, it would corrode the legitimacy of law. Not applied, it would risk incurring the dismissal of law by great powers. In the *Nuclear Weapons Case* the ICJ opined that the international community was 'profoundly divided' on the issue of whether non-recourse to nuclear weapons constitutes expression of *opinio juris*, despite the fact that the vast majority of states argue for a prohibition (significantly more states than have supported a ban on landmines).

That is, power politics powerfully intruded upon the avowed impartial character of law in the ICJ opinion: clearly, all states were not regarded as equally subject to and productive of customary law. To go further in declaring a prohibition on nuclear weapons in the face of great

---

[36] Elif Unal, 'Turkey, Greece Agree to Clear Landmines', *Reuters* Newswire (6 April 2001).

power opposition was seen by the justices of the court as going too far in risking the relevance of international law. In short, while a deepening international society is a necessary condition for justices to be empowered to render an opinion on the issue of nuclear weapons, these agents act knowing full well the grip states have on one end of the tightrope they must walk.

While the customary status of nuclear weapons use hinged crucially on this political doctrine, its applicability seems more dubious in the case of AP landmines. If any states were to be regarded in a meaningful sense as 'specially affected', it would be those with enormous landmine problems, and among these states the majority practice has been to endorse the ban. The ten countries with the highest number of landmine casualties include Afghanistan, Angola, Bosnia-Herzegovina, Cambodia, Croatia, Eritrea, Iraq [Kurdistan], Mozambique, Somalia, and Sudan, while Egypt is often cited as probably the most mine-infested country.[37] Out of this list, eight have ratified or acceded to the treaty.[38] Only Egypt, Somalia, and Iraq have neither signed nor ratified the treaty. The criteria applied in the *North Sea Continental Shelf Cases* implies that the standard of 'specially affected' states requires that practice among those states be 'extensive' and 'virtually uniform'. In the case of mines, agreement on the prohibition among mines-affected states is certainly extensive, though it would not unequivocally meet a criterion of 'virtually uniform'.[39]

In sum, the level of *opinio juris* in favour of banning AP landmines is very substantial. The rhetorical practice of states already parallels the case of torture, where violations generally are carried out surreptitiously, accusations are denied, and allegations are made of adversaries engaging in the dubious practice. We saw above the argument that a customary norm could be said to exist if states generally cease to defend the use of mines, even before they actually stop using them. The empirical evidence of the case of AP landmines already largely conforms to this requirement. However, the *opinio juris* is not as universal and

---

[37] United States Office of Humanitarian Demining Programs, *Hidden Killers, 1998: The Global Landmine Crisis* (Washington, DC: US Department of State, 1998).

[38] Interestingly, while in power, the Taliban in Afghanistan (one of the most mine-infested countries in the world), endorsed the prohibition, though it could not join the treaty since the regime was not recognised by the international community. On 30 July 2002, the Transnational Islamic State of Afghanistan acceded to the Landmine Convention.

[39] Of this group, Angola continued to use AP landmines despite its signing the treaty, though its violations appear to have ceased since its ratification of the treaty.

virtually unquestioned as the renunciations of other customary norms such as those prohibiting torture or genocide. The occasional and tepid rhetorical support in principle for an eventual ban by some states such as India and Egypt is so tempered with qualifications that it would be difficult to sustain an argument that they provide adequate expression of clear *opinio juris* in favour of the contemporary content of the norm. Moreover, numerous states such as Pakistan, Iran, Iraq, North and South Korea, Cuba, Israel, Libya, and Syria among others have maintained a clear opposition to a comprehensive ban, far more states than would dare to publicly maintain such rhetorical challenges to norms prohibiting torture, apartheid, or genocide. As a result, an assessment of state practice becomes vital in determining where the AP landmines norm lies on the sliding scale of *opinio juris* and practice, and in the struggle between different forms of politics and law.

## Empirical indicators of behavioural compliance pulls

A premise of this chapter is that integrating insights from constructivist international relations scholarship with legal conceptualisations of customary international law will enrich the ability to discern the status of international norms in ambiguous situations, and overcome some of the difficulties that issue from positivist conceptions of norms. In particular, there are a number of dimensions of empirical normative effects that plausibly can establish the existence of customary international norms. In the legal debates over the requirements of custom it has been argued by some, as seen above, that *opinio juris* ought to be the primary consideration and actual state behaviour a secondary consideration. The present section examines the contrary: namely, the view that states may exhibit the influence of international norms, and thus embody the existence of the socialising pressures of international law, without explicitly granting their conscious consent. To use the sliding scale, it could be contended that either *opinio juris* or behaviour can provide a demonstration of the existence of customary international norms. This is not to argue that any demonstration of behavioural effects that display any degree of sensitivity to a norm should be considered enough to plausibly establish a universal claim of obligation. It is here that Kirgis' suggestion of the sliding scale between practice and *opinio juris* is particularly helpful. It is a contention of this chapter, however, that it may be reasonable to claim customary status for norms when the proscribed practice is sufficiently politicised to significantly raise the threshold for violations, so much so that the burden of proof clearly is reversed in favour of a general rule of non-use.[40] The latter consideration incorporates into customary international law the insights from international relations that prohibitionary norms may exert significant socialising influence – and thus demonstrate internalised manifestations of a pull of obligation – in ways other than explicit legal consent, and that norms may have ontological status even in the face of violations. This marks one of this volume's contributions insofar as we are equipped to identify further ways in which international law affects state practice and how customary obligations can develop in the first place, taking into account a fuller range of idiographic, purposive, ethical, and instrumental reasons for action.

Conversely, this standard would seem to imply that in many circumstances states would have to *both* violate a norm in practice *and* reject it as a matter of *opinio juris* to qualify as a persistent objector to an emergent customary norm. Even if we accept the validity of the persistent objector doctrine, to qualify as a persistent objector to a new rule a state would have to manifestly and continuously reject the norm from its inception.[41] Moreover, Byers argues that 'If the objecting State is serious about its objection, the principle of reciprocity requires that it continue to deal with other States on the basis of the old rule (or absence thereof) even if those other States are not doing the same in respect of it. If it does not, it may effectively have abandoned its position of persistent objection.'[42] Significantly, requiring the objecting state to meet this criterion in relations with other states does offer a given state a consent-based way out of an emerging customary norm, *but only by reversing the burden of proof in favour of a communitarian presumption of obligation.* Here again we encounter a crucial transitional nexus of a norm from consent to custom, and of the delivery of its associated practice from the domain of one kind of politics into another occasioned by the concern for law.

Several developments among non-treaty parties have exhibited this kind of behaviour. In 1999 Turkey reached an agreement with Bulgaria on the 'non-use of antipersonnel mines and their removal and/or destruction from their common border', arguing 'that by signing this

[40] It is to be noted that this formulation runs against the ICJ's repeated position that practice by itself is insufficient to establish customary law. See Byers, *Custom, Power and the Power of Rules*, p. 130.

[41] Not all accept the validity of the persistent objector doctrine. See Jonathan Charney, 'The Persistent Objector Rule and the Development of Customary International Law', *British Yearbook of International Law* 56 (1985).

[42] Byers, *Custom, Power and the Power of Rules*, p. 104.

agreement the two countries have proved their determination to contribute to the ongoing efforts of the international community aimed at the total elimination of this inhuman weapon'.[43] This agreement means that Turkey has not consistently maintained practices that establish a contrary rule that permits the unquestioned use of AP landmines. Such behaviour would seem to fall short of the kind of opposition noted by Byers as necessary to establish persistent objector status.

Recognition of such phenomena has a further and farreaching implication; namely, that a state that would not qualify as a persistent objector to an emerging customary norm could be held to have obligations to that norm even before the norm has general customary status. This would be the case so long as the evidence of *opinio juris* or behavioural indicators render it implausible for the state to contend that it does not recognise the normative pulls of obligation of the emerging custom that it has incurred for itself, even if it does not explicitly recognise that all states are to be bound. It is such pulls of obligation at such moments that constitute the crucial development process of customary norms, and in the absence of recognising them it is impossible to account for the development of customary law. The practical implication is the possibility that, much like treaty law, a court could rule that some states could be held to customary obligations, while others might not. This doctrinal revision merely follows the logic of the reversal of burden of proof already embodied in existing notions of the persistent objector, but in a way that captures the transition of norm emergence from the preserve of individual consenting states to a constitutive systemic property.

So reformulated, assessing the status of the norm proscribing AP landmines involves empirical examinations of the following considerations: Is there a change in general state practice from the use of mines as routine, widespread, normal, and uncontroversial to politicised, exceptional, aberrant, and abhorrent? Have there been shifts in the elements of use above even among hold-out states? Has the threshold for use been raised to exceptional circumstances for the general practice of states? What is the legal significance of reserving the right to use a dubious weapon? At what level of decision-making are decisions to employ AP landmines made? Do changes in military training and doctrine reflect acceptance of the norm?

[43] Turkey, Ministry of Foreign Affairs, Information Department, 'Joint Statement of the Minister of Foreign Affairs of the Republic of Turkey HE Mr. Ismail Cem and the Minister of Foreign Affairs of the Republic of Bulgaria HE Ms. Nadezhda Mihailova', 22 March 1999, <www.mfa.gov.tr/grupb/bc/bcc99/march/02.htm>, accessed 13 August 2000.

## Use

From the onset of the Landmine Convention in December 1997 to March 1999 it appears likely that there was AP landmine use in thirteen countries, with unconfirmed allegations of use in six other countries.[44] While the *Landmine Monitor Report 1999* reported that 'nowhere in the world in 1998 and 1999 were mines being laid on a very large scale and sustained basis',[45] military operations in Chechnya and Kosovo altered that assessment the following year, and mines were reported to have been employed in twenty conflicts by eleven states and thirty non-state groups from May 1999 to mid-2000. From May 2001 to mid-2002, those numbers dropped to nine states and use by opposition groups in fourteen countries. Further:

> Mine use has halted, at least temporarily, in several countries where it has been most widespread in recent years: Angola (no use since the April 2002 peace agreement); Eritrea and Ethiopia (no use since the end of the border conflict in June 2000); and Sri Lanka (no use since a cease-fire in December 2001). Also, in contrast to the previous reporting period, *Landmine Monitor* has not recorded new mine use by the governments of DR Congo, Israel, and Kyrgyzstan, nor by rebels based in Angola, FYR Macedonia, Senegal, Sri Lanka, and Uganda.[46]

Those gains were offset to some extent by the massive laying of mines by India and Pakistan along their border in late December 2001.

To what extent has the norm changed standard military practice? Is there less use of AP landmines than before the rise of the norm? This would appear to be the case, given that it is estimated that between 2.5 million and 4 million mines were being planted annually in the 1980s and mid-1990s, and far less in recent years.[47] Still, just over a dozen non-signatory states have used mines from 1997 to 2002, including Burma (Myanmar), Eritrea, Georgia, India, Israel, Kyrgyzstan, Nepal, Pakistan, Russia, Somalia, Sri Lanka, Turkey, Uzbekistan, and FR Yugoslavia. In addition, scores of rebel groups have used landmines in this period. The emerging norm has thus not appeared to change the behaviour of the above non-signatories, though the use of mines by Georgia would mark the end of its moratorium on the use of landmines since 1996.

---

[44] ICBL, *Landmine Monitor Report 1999*, p. 4.
[45] ICBL, *Landmine Monitor Report 1999*, p. 3.
[46] ICBL, *Landmine Monitor Report 2002*, <www.icbl.org/lm/2002/findings.html>, accessed 11 March 2003.
[47] ICBL, *Landmine Monitor Report 1999*, p. 3.

What effect has the treaty had on signatories or states parties? The only state party confirmed to have used landmines is Angola, though subsequent to the peace agreement ending its civil war in 2002 it ratified the treaty and has not used AP mines. There have been allegations of use by other state parties,[48] and Russia deployed mines inside Tajikistan, a treaty party.[49] States that have signed but not ratified the treaty and who have probably used mines include Burundi, Ethiopia, Senegal, and Guinea-Bissau. This is a very small percentage of the 146 states who have signed the treaty, but as many of them do not face conflict the key question is whether there are cases of governments experiencing conflicts that have refrained from using landmines? Included in this group of states would be the Philippines, Indonesia, Colombia, Algeria, and the United States.

US behaviour clearly has been affected by the emerging norm, at least under the Clinton Administration:

> There has been no reported use of antipersonnel mines by US armed forces since 1991 in the Gulf War. The US has banned the use of non-self-destruct antipersonnel mines since May 1996, except for the defense of Korea until 2006 (or beyond if alternatives are not available). Under current policy, the government will prohibit the use of 'pure' self-destructing antipersonnel mines (ADAM and PDM) globally in 2003, again except for Korea until 2006. Under current policy, the use of antipersonnel mines in mixed systems is not geographically or time restricted, but could be ended in 2006 if suitable alternatives are identified and fielded. Antipersonnel mines were not employed by US air or ground forces in Yugoslavia during Operation Allied Force from March 24 to June 10, 1999.[50]

US behaviour has exhibited powerful compliance pulls for a very nascent norm. With the exception of forces travelling uniquely to Korea, the US ceased to offer practical training involving the use of both non-self-destructing and self-destructing AP landmines.[51] Similarly, in June 1998 the Joint Chiefs of Staff directed all their services to begin

---

[48] Sudan, Rwanda, Zimbabwe, and Uganda in the conflict in the DR of Congo, where mines have been used but it has been impossible to verify by whom.
[49] ICBL, *Landmine Monitor Report 2001: Toward a Mine-Free World* (New York: Human Rights Watch, 2001), <www.icbl.org/lm/2001/findings/>, accessed 14 March 2003.
[50] Human Rights Watch, 'Clinton's Landmine Legacy', *Human Rights Watch Reports* 12: 3 (June 2000), <www.hrw.org/reports/2000/uslm/>.
[51] Memorandum for SEE Distribution; Subject: Commandant's Training Policy for Non-Self Destructing Anti-Personnel Landmine, 26 April 1999, <www.wood.army.mil/CTSC/TRADOC%20NSD-APL.htm>, accessed 29 April 2000. See also Office of the Undersecretary of Defense for Policy, 'Report to the Secretary of Defense on the Status

development of tactics and service doctrine which eliminated the need to rely on landmines in anticipation of a 'future and likely prompt international agreement to ban all APL'.[52] While the International Campaign to Ban Landmines claimed that 'There were no instances of use of antipersonnel mines by the United States or coalition forces' during the 2001–2 fighting in Afghanistan, Byers has claimed that 'Canadian soldiers operating in Afghanistan were ordered by their American commander to lay mines around their camp. When they refused to do so, US soldiers – who were not subject to the same restrictions – laid the mines for them.'[53] Still, even if such circumscribed use is confirmed, it appears that the use of AP mines has become politicised enough that reversion to standard AP landmine use would require decisions made at the highest political levels. In addition, it is not yet clear if the alleged US use in Afghanistan entailed the placing of new US mines or rather involved making use of previously planted mines for its base through the selective demining of an already existing minefield; nor has the US declared that it used mines. The use of new mines and an explicit proclamation that it has done so would amount to far more of a full-frontal assault on the mines taboo than taking advantage of mines laid in previous conflicts, or the current stance which has been to remain silent on the matter. In short, the actual practice of the United States with regard to the use of AP landmines exhibits surprisingly powerful evidence of emerging concern with community standards of obligation. Given the hostility of the George W. Bush Administration to multilateral treaties, however, this sensitivity to the norm could well meet the same fate in the short term as a number of other prominent emerging multilateral norms and institutions – namely, outright rejection or violation. Still, the fact that the US did not use AP landmines in its 2003 war against Iraq suggests at the least that the threshold continues to forestall their use as routine.

In the meantime, the US does reserve the right to use AP landmines, as do numerous other states. Does reserving the right to use the weapon constitute adequate legal rejection of a prohibitionary norm, or does it in

of DoD's Implementation of the US Policy on Anti-Personnel Landmines', May 1997, <www.defenselink.mil:80/pubs/landmines/>, accessed 7 April 2000.
[52] United States Department of the Army Information Paper, 'PDD-64: Anti-Personnel Landmines: Expanding Upon and Strengthening the US APL Policy', 8 July 1998, cited in Michael Griesdorf, 'An Alternative Methodology for Constructivism: Measuring the American Adherence to an AP Landmine Ban', unpublished report (Toronto, July 2000), p. 18.
[53] See ICBL, *Landmine Monitor Report 2002*, <www.icbl.org/lm/2002/findings.html>; Michael Byers, 'The Laws of War, US-Style', *London Review of Books* 25: 4 (20 February 2003), 5, <www.lrb.co.uk/v25/n04/print/byer01_.html>, accessed 20 February 2003.

fact demonstrate a presumption of an obligation not to use the weapon? On this issue in the *Nuclear Weapons Case*, the ICJ advised that the emergence of a customary rule was hampered by tensions between a nascent *opinio juris* and strong adherence to policy of deterrence by nuclear-weapon states, by which they reserve the right to use nuclear weapons in certain circumstances. The ICJ opined that the *policy* of deterrence – reserving the right to use – implied the absence of a belief in a legal obligation. It should be noted, however, that it is eminently tenable to argue to the contrary (as did dissenting judges in this case), and to contend that the powerful history of non-use of nuclear weapons is evidence of an entrenched custom. Conceptually, it is necessary to take this into account for it is only by appreciating these processes of how nascent norms emerge and operate that we can understand how customary norms develop, and thus how they come to exist at all. The alternative is defining such phenomena out of existence by a consent-based approach to law, which simply leaves us with no way to account for the development of customary law and leaves us mired in the paradoxes of consent-based theories.

Still, we are left with the question of when a norm (identified sociologically) is a *legal* norm. The practical argument being made here is that it is the process of jurists' decisions that marks a key transition to customary law. Politically, the very delivery of such a question into the hands of non-state actors – judges – itself indicates a deepening and variegated international society away from an account of international life as an anarchy among states. The legal-theoretical underpinning for such a decision argued here is that an adequate demonstration of a legal obligation can occur upon empirical identification that the threshold has been raised enough that the burden of proof is reversed, from a presumption that the weapon will be used to a presumption that it will not be used, and the concomitant expectation of extraordinary justifications for departures and changes in behavioural practices such as those noted above. While such behaviours are not indicated in cases such as Russia, India, Pakistan, or Yugoslavia, they are evident for the United States, Georgia, and Turkey. Such a reversal of the burden of proof marks the transition of this practice of warfare from an ontologically individualist concern to a communitarian one, and as such testifies to a key effect of a multilateral regime of international law.

This section has examined the extent to which, in addition to or regardless of the extent of explicit consent of states in terms of *opinio juris*, there are significant enough empirical manifestations of behavioural compliance pulls towards the norm even among rhetorically resistant states that the argument of persistent objector status for those states would fail. On the basis of the above findings, few states examined in this study could be said to qualify as persistent objectors to an emerging norm proscribing the use of AP landmines. It was noted above that the prescriptive status of the AP landmines ban is supported in principle or in terms of the evidence of practice even by non-party states – the United States, China, Russia, and other major non-signatories have all indicated some degrees of support for an eventual ban on AP landmines. This is important for a determination of customary law, since only those states who could qualify as 'persistent objectors' could potentially claim exemption from a new rule of customary law should one be determined to exist. On this score, the opposition by many non-signatory states is ambiguous at best, and seems to fall short of the requirement that they unambiguously and persistently reject the norm. Moreover, the failure of a state to unambiguously qualify as a persistent objector to a nascent norm means that the state in question is in important respects participating in normative and legal change. Being so constitutive of the process of law-making, it is thus not able plausibly to claim it can opt out of those ties that make up international society.

Still, the persistent objector rule has generally been understood to apply to situations where a norm has already emerged. In this sense denying such status to certain states would be premature and meaningless without demonstrating that the general customary legal status of the norm has in fact been attained. That is, unless the concept of customary law is reformulated in such a way (as suggested above) that states could be legally held to evidence of their own internalised obligations even before a general customary status has been definitively established. With such a reformulation, the chronological paradox that bedevils legal approaches to custom dissolves. Depending upon the sources used for custom and the relative weight given to them, the behavioural evidence and *opinio juris* in some respects can be interpreted as quite favourable towards a judgement of customary status, but unfavourable in others. In terms of the sliding scale argument considered in this chapter to determine the likelihood of a judgement of customary status, the indicators are clearly sliding towards such status, and fairly rapidly, but without yet having unambiguously arrived.

## Conclusions

This chapter has examined the customary legal status of the norm prohibiting the use of AP landmines to illustrate the relationship between contemporary international politics and international law. It was found that: there is without question substantial *opinio juris* supporting the norm, though it is not universal; a court could very well rule that the use of AP landmines violates fundamental rules of international society; the practice and rhetoric of all but a few states would fall short of persistent objector status. These together indicate a profound influence of the nascent legal rule prohibiting the use of AP landmines.

This state of the use of force can only be understood in terms of a profound concern by states and non-state actors for reasons of action as occasioned by international law. Alternative realist arguments pointing to the alleged lack of utility of landmines must not only dismiss the utility ascribed to them by various powerful actors (particularly states who reject the norm), but fail to appreciate the norm-constituting processes by which assessments of utility come to be so politically contested.[54] These practices in turn affect the form of international law. To prevent the structural empowerment of non-state actors – here, judges – being put in a position to successfully apply customary law against them in courts, some states have made recourse to a legal discourse of consent. Thus numerous states which have sought to avoid contributing towards the emerging customary status of the norm have done so in ways that entrench international treaty law. If custom becomes decreasingly important as a source of law in international politics, it may be because treaty law has become more, not less, entrenched, and the communitarian obligations of international society deepened.

[54] See Price, 'Reversing the Gun Sights'.

# 6 International law, politics, and migrant rights

*Amy Gurowitz*[1]

Migrants to Japan have historically received few legal protections under domestic law. Without domestic resources to draw on when fighting discrimination, foreigners and their advocates have drawn extensively, and successfully, on a wide range of international social and legal norms. Specifically, three interrelated types of international norms and laws have been important. First, general, diffuse, non-codified social norms about what it means to be a modern state have been critical in shaping arguments about immigration and immigrant rights. Second, international legal norms, largely written into conventions signed by Japan, have had a direct impact by causing government changes in domestic laws to comply with international legal obligations. Finally, international law has had an indirect, or less direct, impact when lawyers and judges have used various unratified conventions, declarations, and acts of international organisations to interpret domestic law in favour of migrants, even when they do not actually find a practice illegal based on international law.

These three types of international legal and social norms have been critical in extending rights to two groups of foreigners in Japan. Most of the Koreans now living in Japan immigrated, or were forced to immigrate, after the 1910 Japanese annexation of Korea. Koreans were then made citizens, but after the Second World War they were classified as aliens and stripped of their Japanese citizenship. Until the 1965 peace

[1] Original research for this project was supported by an SSRC-MacArthur Peace and Security in a Changing World Fellowship, with additional travel support from the Cornell University Graduate School and Peace Studies Program, and conducted while visiting the Institute of Social Science at Tokyo University. Comments on earlier versions from Saori Katada and Peter Katzenstein were extremely helpful. I am grateful for comments from reviewers and the editor, Chris Reus-Smit. Parts of this research are also published in *World Politics* 51: 3 (1999).

treaty between Korea and Japan, Koreans lived in a state of limbo with no official status and with few remedies for discrimination against them. For most, even the 1965 treaty did little to change their situation despite granting many of them permanent residency.

Since the Second World War, Japan's general approach to immigrants has been to avoid them if at all possible, and to maintain a policy of non-integration when exclusion is impossible. Immigration and integration, it is thought, will compromise the ideal of the homogeneous nation. Nonetheless, in addition to a significant population of ethnic Koreans, Japan has experienced nearly a quarter-century of migration. After a late start in the importation of labour, the first stage of post-war labour migration to Japan began in the late 1970s and lasted until around 1986. This phase was characterised by the migration of large numbers of female workers from Thailand, the Philippines, South Korea, and Taiwan. The second stage, beginning in the mid-1980s, saw a shift towards male undocumented labour from South and Southeast Asia, China, South Korea, and Iran. The third stage is marked by the 1990 reform of Japan's immigration laws which opened a number of 'side doors' to low-skilled labour under the guise of reuniting ethnic Japanese from Latin America (*Nikkeijin*) with their country of origin, bringing in trainees, and allowing foreign students to work up to twenty hours per week.

In this chapter I ask three primary questions about migrants rights. What rights have been extended to foreigners in Japan? What role have international social and legal norms played in the extension of these rights? Why have actors pushing for migrant rights found reference to these norms beneficial? An examination of the impact of international legal and social norms on the rights of foreigners illuminates three shortcomings of existing rationalist approaches to international law and domestic politics pointed out by Christian Reus-Smit in chapter 2. First, realists offer no account of how weak actors use international law to shape outcomes.[2] Japan as a weak state did so in the late nineteenth century, and weak actors within Japan do so today. As I will argue, actors within Japan are successful in their use of these norms because of the politics of international law in Japan. Second, neoliberal approaches to international law beg the question of why states attach legitimacy to the international legal system. Japan has historically attached significant legitimacy to the institution of international law, not because it sees it as an inherent good, but because it is seen as a necessary system to work

---

[2] Christian Reus-Smit, chapter 2, this volume, pp. 15–18.

within to be a legitimate member of international society. Finally, rationalist approaches are blind to the ways in which international law has structured discourse and practice between actors both internationally and domestically. As Reus-Smit points out, international law is a site for the social construction of models of legitimate statehood and rightful state action.[3]

In this chapter I will first place the study of international legal and social norms in Japan in the context of debates over internationalisation. I will indicate how the impact of international standards has to be understood in this larger context by briefly discussing the first type of international norm – diffuse, non-codified social norms about what it means to be a modern, developed state – and then turning to the focus of the chapter – the direct and indirect impact of international legal norms. I will conclude with a discussion of the importance and limitations of legal and social norms as a means to the end of greater rights and integration for foreigners.

## Internationalisation

The importance of international social and legal norms in Japan cannot be understood outside of the general context, and historical significance, of 'the perennial theme' of internationalisation.[4] This theme began in 1853 when US Commodore Matthew Perry, at the behest of the Western powers, arrived in Japan with the mission to open and civilise the country. Between 1853 and 1858 treaties were negotiated between Japan and Western states, and Western consuls were sent to Japan. As with other states the West deemed uncivilised, the treaties were unequal, and forced on Japan to the benefit of the Western states.

When the Tokugawa Empire fell in 1868 the Meiji government announced 'that the goal of the whole nation should be to restore the glory of Japan in the eyes of all nations, that the iniquitous aspects of the treaties the Bakufu had concluded with the West would be revised, but that foreign relations should be conducted in accordance with the law of nations'.[5] Japanese intellectuals adopted the distinction between East and West from Europeans whose authority derived from their

---

[3] Reus-Smit, chapter 2, p. 20.
[4] Herbert Passin, 'Overview: The Internationalization of Japan – Some Reflections', in Hiroshi Mannari and Harumi Befu (eds.), *The Challenge of Japan's Internationalization: Organization and Culture* (Hyogo, Japan: Kwansei Gakuin University, 1983), p. 16.
[5] Hidemi Suganami, 'Japan's Entry into International Society', in Hedley Bull and Adam Watson (eds.), *The Expansion of International Society* (Oxford: Clarendon Press, 1984), p. 191.

imperialist power and, according to Victor Koschmann, began to narrate their own history in terms of European assumptions.[6]

Yasuaki Onuma, a leading Japanese legal scholar, argues that after Japan was forced to enter international society, it tried to master modern international law, seeking survival and equal status among the European powers.[7] After the Meiji restoration, maintaining independence was the foremost concern of the government because of the fear that if Japan was not sufficiently strong militarily and economically it might be colonised. During the negotiation of the unequal treaties the Western powers had argued that extraterritoriality was necessary in order to protect Westerners from the 'primitive' Japanese legal system, and now international law was seen as a way to overturn the treaties.[8] Adoption of international law, quite explicitly the law of *civilised* nations, was also seen as a way to demonstrate that Japan was itself civilised.[9]

The use of international law in this period was part of a larger move to 'internationalise', meaning essentially to modernise and Westernise.[10] Herbert Passin argues that today internationalisation can be seen on at least four levels: nationally, in Japan's participation in international society; organisationally, in adjustment of Japanese organisations; culturally, in the adaptation of Japanese culture to international interdependence; and individually, at the level of popular culture.[11] He argues that internationalisation involves 'being in step with the world, *sekai-nami'* where 'the world' refers to the Western industrialised states.[12] The term internationalisation (*kokusaika*) became

See also Gerrit W. Gong, *The Standard of 'Civilization' in International Society* (Oxford: Clarendon Press, 1984), p. 181, on the transition to rule of law.

[6] J. Victor Koschmann, 'Asianism's Ambivalent Legacy', in Peter J. Katzenstein and Takashi Shiraishi (eds.), *Network Power: Japan and Asia* (Ithaca: Cornell University Press, 1997), p. 84.

[7] Yasuaki Onuma, 'Japanese International Law in the Prewar Period – Perspectives on the Teaching and Research of International Law in Prewar Japan', *The Japanese Annual of International Law* 29 (1986), 23.

[8] Kenneth L. Port, 'The Japanese International Law "Revolution": International Human Rights Law and its Impact in Japan', *Stanford Journal of International Law* 28: 1 (1991), 146.

[9] Onuma, 'Japanese International Law', 29; and Suganami, 'Japan's Entry into International Society', 192.

[10] Gong notes that the terms modernisation, Westernisation, and civilisation were all used during the Meiji era. Gong, *The Standard of 'Civilization'*, p. 164.

[11] Passin, 'Overview', p. 20. On internationalisation see also Glenn D. Hook and Michael A. Weiner (eds.), *The Internationalization of Japan* (London: Routledge, 1992); and Hiroshi Mannari and Harumi Befu (eds.), *The Challenge of Japan's Internationalization: Organization and Culture* (Hyogo, Japan: Kwansei Gakuin University, 1983).

[12] Passin, 'Overview', p. 21. See also Ogata Sadako, 'Interdependence and Internationalization', in Hook and Weiner (eds.), *The Internationalization of Japan*, p. 64. It should be

widely used in the 1970s and 1980s, and is used to refer to such diverse things as learning English, travelling internationally, keeping up with other advanced industrial states and the latest high technology, and fully participating in international institutions.[13] While Japan has a long history of questioning its role in the world, and its position *vis-à-vis* the major powers and the West, this debate reignited around the late 1970s and early 1980s, especially once Japan's role as a major economic power became clear. Glenn Hook and Michael Weiner argue that the salience of the theme of internationalisation in this period can be seen from former Prime Minister Yasuhiro Nakasone's 1980 pledge to transform Japan into an international state.[14] Whereas historical debates about internationalisation involved catching up, contemporary debates have more to do with the idea that economic power brings with it new responsibilities that extend beyond the purely economic realm.[15]

The government has pursued a number of diverse policies to meet the demands of internationalisation including developing closer links with European states and regional institutions[16] and, more recently, becoming increasingly involved in aid to Eastern Europe. Ezra Vogel points out that internationally minded Japanese have begun to envision their country taking a leadership role by assisting developing countries and championing their causes at international meetings, an idea reflected within the Ministry of Foreign Affairs.[17] The government has also increased its role in the Asian region. One of the clearest shifts in Japan's international involvement, and one with direct bearing on issues of

noted though that internationalisation does not only mean Westernisation. There have historically been strong counter-arguments in Japan for Asianisation, and today Japan is trying to become more integrated in the Asian region. I am grateful to Saori Katada for stressing this point.

[13] Myron Weiner, 'Opposing Visions: Migration and Citizenship Policies in Japan and the United States', in Myron Weiner and Tadashi Hanami (eds.), *Temporary Workers or Future Citizens? Japanese and US Migration Policies* (New York: New York University Press, 1998), p. 9. Weiner argues that internationalisation did not mean the incorporation of foreigners into Japanese society. While this was clearly not the intent, I argue that the idea of a closed, ethnically homogeneous society has been called into question by the idea of internationalisation, and that the two issues are now intimately linked in domestic debates.

[14] Glenn D. Hook and Michael A. Weiner, 'Introduction', in Hook and Weiner (eds.), *The Internationalization of Japan*, p. 1.

[15] Ogata, 'Interdependence and Internationalization', p. 64, note 49.

[16] Dennis T. Yasutomo, 'The Politicization of Japan's "Post-Cold War" Multilateral Diplomacy', in Gerald L. Curtis (ed.), *Japan's Foreign Policy After the Cold War: Coping With Change* (New York: M. E. Sharpe, 1993), p. 330.

[17] Ezra F. Vogel, 'Pax Nipponica?', *Foreign Affairs* 64: 4 (1986), 756; and author interview with Haruka Okumura, Human Rights Division, Ministry of Foreign Affairs, 10 February 1997.

immigrants, is its participation in UN human rights machinery, and the UN in general.[18] Yasuhiro Ueki argues that Japan's attitude towards the UN has been ambivalent and pragmatic, but that economic success is undermining this and creating expectations in and out of Japan for more global responsibility.[19]

This intense pressure to internationalise, which has come from the outside largely in the form of demands on Japan's economy, but has been translated within Japan into a much more general call to be more open and modern socially and culturally, has had critical implications for immigrants and for the use of international legal and social norms in Japan.[20] Activists within and outside of the government have linked the issue of immigration and migrant rights to this larger debate over internationalisation and have used this linkage to set the terms of the discussion over foreigners. Diffuse and non-codified social norms about being a modern state have mattered and have set the stage for more specific legal norms to have an impact. There is a feeling among many in Japan that it is against international norms, in the sense of being 'abnormal', that Japan seeks to remain closed to immigrants. While it is true that Japan lags behind other industrialised states both in sheer numbers of foreigners and in its treatment of them, there are no written, codified norms indicating that states should let immigrants in and generally become more accepting of them (although there are many codified norms specifying more narrow treatment of them).

The debate over immigration has largely taken place along the lines of 'to internationalise or not' and has occurred in the context of increased international and domestic pressure on the Japanese government to internationalise. In general, supporters of immigrant rights and more extensive migrant worker programs argue that:

- as one of the most advanced industrialised countries Japan has a responsibility to accept immigrants, especially from developing countries;

[18] Japan has also been actively seeking a seat on the UN Security Council, and has been engaged in much debate over participation in international peacekeeping missions.
[19] Yasuhiro Ueki, 'Japan's UN Diplomacy: Sources of Passivism and Activism', in Gerald Curtis (ed.), *Japan's Foreign Policy After the Cold War*, p. 347.
[20] For a more extensive discussion of the relationship between internationalisation and debates about foreigners see Amy Gurowitz, 'Mobilizing International Norms: Domestic Actors, Immigrants, and the State', unpublished manuscript, 2003.

- Japan should become more internationalised and accepting immigrants and refugees will express a commitment to internationalisation;
- Japan must shed its image as an ethnocentric society;
- Japan has a low birth rate and therefore needs more workers.[21]

Opponents, on the other hand, tend to argue that:

- the economic benefits of migrant worker programmes in Europe have been outweighed by the enormous social costs and this should serve as an example for Japan;
- diversity is a cause of social disintegration;
- technological innovation can continue to absorb demand for labour;
- Japan should increase aid to improve living standards in developing states, not import labour creating a dual labour market;
- Japan is overpopulated and migrant workers might become permanent.[22]

Interestingly, the two sides of the debate use the terms *sakoku* (keep them out at all costs) and *kaikoku* (open the doors, at least to some degree). Both words are taken from the mid-nineteenth-century debates over whether Japan should remain in feudal isolation or open its borders in order to catch up with the West.[23]

Acceptance of at least some immigration and respect for the rights of those immigrants in Japan is seen as one of the key symbols of internationalisation, and the problem of discrimination, previously focused on Burakumin, Ainu, and Koreans, is now being made more internationally visible as it encompasses migrant workers.[24] Haruo Shimada, a leading economist and specialist on immigration to Japan, argues that the foreign worker issue is

> likely to call into question Japan's position in the world community. It is undeniable that Japan has forged ahead of the world, and even of the other industrialized countries, in terms of economic and income opportunities, and yet it still protects its homogeneity on the human level, and plainly gives the outside world the impression that it is a closed society.[25]

---

[21] Masami Sekine, 'Guest Worker Policies in Japan', *Migration* September (1991), 60.
[22] Sekine, 'Guest Worker Policies in Japan', 60.
[23] Takashi Oka, *Prying Open the Door: Foreign Workers in Japan* (Washington, DC: Carnegie Endowment for International Peace, 1994), p. 4.
[24] Hook and Weiner, 'Introduction', p. 2.
[25] Haruo Shimada, *Japan's 'Guest Workers'* (Tokyo: University of Tokyo Press, 1994), p. 202.

He goes so far as to say that

> the future of the Japanese economy and society, the nation's position in the world, and its international reputation will very largely depend on whether or not it adopts [policies for accepting foreign workers] and how effectively it is able to implement them. In this sense Japan's response to the foreign worker problem is a litmus test of the kind of nation it seeks to become.[26]

The connection between debates over internationalisation and those over immigration can be seen most directly at the local governmental level. Katherine Pak, in an extensive study of the differences between national and local responses to foreigners in Japan, argues that local actors commonly invoke an ideal of internationalisation that envisions a transformation of domestic social relations and reconciliation of Japan with Asia. She argues that the challenge to the status quo is coming from the local context because of local autonomy movements and long-standing patterns of delegating social policy within Japan. In addition, there has been a rise in the number of international sections in local governments. As a result, says Pak, 'combinations of locally based NGOs and local governments are slowly but steadily constructing a policy of accommodation in response to the realities of Japan's *de facto* emergence as a destination of international migrant flows'.[27] According to the Japanese press, many municipalities have begun to treat foreigners like other residents, not even giving regard to legality or illegality,[28] and Pak finds that position papers in Kawasaki and Hamamatsu are 'laden with radical language which promises to protect the human rights of' foreign nationals.[29]

## International legal norms

The foregoing discussion highlighted how activists have linked internationalisation with immigrant issues to shape the debate and to challenge the idea that a state as powerful as Japan can reasonably cling to ideals

---

[26] Shimada, *Japan's 'Guest Workers'*, p. viii. Sellek and Weiner also refer to this as a 'litmus test'. Yoko Sellek and Michael A. Weiner, 'Migrant Workers: The Japanese Case in International Perspective', in Hook and Weiner (eds.), *The Internationalization of Japan*, p. 205.
[27] Katherine Tegtmeyer Pak, 'Immigration Politics in Japan: Differences in Issue Articulation across Levels of Government and Society', American Political Science Association Convention, Chicago, 1995, p. 21.
[28] *Migrant News*, 3, December (1996).    [29] Pak, 'Immigration Politics in Japan', p. 22.

of a homogeneous society. The broader context of internationalisation is also directly related to the impact of international legal norms on foreigners in Japan. International law has legitimacy and therefore power, especially in this context of internationalisation. As Japan struggles to be seen as a legitimate state, complying with international law is seen as one representation of that legitimacy. International law is therefore a tool for activists, but it is a tool that is useful because it is perceived as a benchmark of legitimacy.

As noted earlier, with little domestic recourse for discrimination and rights abuses, international standards became potentially critical for foreigners in Japan. But prior to 1979 Japan had ratified only two international human rights agreements. In 1973, on the 25th anniversary of the Universal Declaration on Human Rights, seventeen non-governmental organisations (NGOs) launched an appeal to the government to take immediate action on ratification of international human rights conventions. They made further appeals in 1974, 1976, and 1977, each on International Human Rights Day.[30] NGOs like the Japanese Civil Liberties Union (JCLU) lobbied vociferously for ratification of the International Covenant on Civil and Political Rights,[31] and groups like the National Women's Committee of the UN, Amnesty International, the Tokyo Bar Association, and the Asian Human Rights Centre[32] protested by attempting to embarrass the government through comparisons of its ratification record to that of other states, and arguments that failure to ratify would 'seriously damage the Japanese image as a peace-seeking nation that pledges to give first priority in her policy and diplomacy to the high ideals enshrined in the United Nations Charter'.[33] During major debates about ratification in the Diet, Minister of Foreign Affairs Sunao Sonoda spoke about the developing international environment in which the salience of human rights was increasing, and stressed the need to ratify the covenants in order to pursue diplomacy on an equal basis with other states.[34]

---

[30] Saito Yasuhiko, 'Japan and Human Rights Covenants', *Human Rights Law Journal* 2: 1–2 (1981), 88–90.
[31] Article 27 of the Covenant is one of the most important articles in an international covenant for minorities. While it applies to national minorities (who are generally citizens), it is often used in court cases involving immigrants.
[32] Yasuhiko, 'Japan and Human Rights Covenants', 89.
[33] Yasuhiko, 'Japan and Human Rights Covenants', 91. Yasuhiko was the chair for NGO meetings making these arguments to the government.
[34] Yasuhiko, 'Japan and Human Rights Covenants', 94.

Under this pressure to internationalise, in 1979 the government ratified both the International Covenant on Civil and Political Rights (ICCPR) and the International Covenant on Economic, Social, and Cultural Rights (ICESCR), in 1982 the Refugee Convention, in 1985 the Convention on the Elimination of all Forms of Discrimination Against Women (CEDAW), and finally, in 1995 the Convention on the Elimination of Racial Discrimination (CERD).[35]

As I will discuss in detail below, Japanese lawyers, activists, and government officials have attributed the various improvements in policy towards Korean-Japanese, as well as other minorities in Japan, in large part to these ratifications. Treaties have the force of law in Japan, and are generally regarded as taking precedent over statute, but being subordinate to the constitution.[36] Therefore ratification of treaties requires, and has resulted in, extensive change in domestic law. Changes in domestic law as a result of ratification have largely occurred through the legislature, although the courts have also enforced Japan's treaty commitments. Japanese courts tend to be quite conservative and are reluctant to deal with arguments based on international law, in part because they are relatively unfamiliar with it and in part because of the relationship between the universal nature of international law, and the view within Japan that the country is unique in the international system.[37] While international law is rarely successful in courts *directly* (i.e., courts do not tend to find that a domestic practice is illegal based on international law), treaties not ratified, a treaty that the state cannot be a party to (for example a European treaty), a UN declaration, and other acts of international organisations have been a very, if not the most, effective route to judicial change in many human rights-related issues.[38]

[35] CERD is one of the most widely ratified human rights conventions in the world. Japan ratified it only after the US did, something not lost on human rights observers in Japan. Interviews at the International Movement Against all Forms of Discrimination and Racism (IMADR) in Tokyo, 11 February 1997.
[36] See Constitution of Japan, Article 98 (2). Yuji Iwasawa, 'The Domestic Impact of Acts of International Organizations Relating to Human Rights', Draft Paper, Second Trilateral Symposium, Swiss Hotel Atlanta, 24–26 March 1996, p. 2.
[37] Author interviews with Professor Yuji Iwasawa, University of Tokyo, 17 February 1997, and Yasushi Higashizawa, 18 February 1997. On universalism versus uniqueness, see Peter J. Katzenstein, *Cultural Norms and National Security: Police and Military in Postwar Japan* (Ithaca: Cornell University Press, 1996), p. 177; and Peter J. Katzenstein and Yutaka Tsujinaka, *Defending the Japanese State: Structures, Norms and the Political Responses to Terrorism and Violent Social Protest in the 1970s and 1980s*, Cornell East Asia Series 53 (Ithaca: East Asia Program, Cornell University, 1991).
[38] Information on the role of law in Japan, and on current trends, was gathered from author interviews with Yuichi Kaido, Attorney, 15 February 1997; Higashizawa, 18 February 1997;

The impact of Japan's international legal obligations is in part due to the internationalisation of lawyers in Japan. Lawyers have become internationalised insofar as there is an increasing awareness of, and education about, international law. One prominent international law professor points out that student interest in international law has increased dramatically over the last fifteen years.[39] The growing interest in international law began, and is strongest, in the human rights arena. The Japan Federation of Bar Associations (JFBA) began extensive research into international norms around 1984–5 and now has a practical manual for lawyers on the ICCPR and other covenants that interprets the covenants, and discusses cases from around the world that have made use of them (including cases from other countries and UN Human Rights Committee decisions).[40] In addition, the JFBA has begun organising symposiums on human rights during their regular meetings, and during their 1996 meeting 600 lawyers attended.[41] Government ministries have also begun consulting with international lawyers during the last few years.[42]

The results of this recent turn to international law have been significant. Most important changes for foreigners in Japan have occurred as a result of either the direct impact of international law through the legislature or courts, or its indirect impact in the courts. The next two sections outline the specific changes that have occurred.

## *The results of treaty law and customary international law*[43]

Before 1982 Koreans were excluded from the national pension plan but in 1982, in connection with Japan's ratification of the Convention Relating to the Status of Refugees, the nationality restrictions were eliminated. Prior to this revision a Korean brought a lawsuit against the Social Insurance Agency to be paid an old age pension because he had been persuaded to join even though it was known that he was Korean. The

Susumu Yamagami, Director of Adjudication Division, Immigration Bureau, Ministry of Justice, 16 February 1997; Iwasawa, 17 February 1997; and IMADR, 11 February 1997, as well as from the writings cited by Yuji Iwasawa.

[39] Author interview with Tadashi Hanami, Sophia University, 14 February 1997.

[40] Japan Federation of Bar Associations, *Utilizing International Human Rights Covenants in the Courtroom* (Hotei ni ikaso kokusai jinken kinyuko) (Tokyo: Japan Federation of Bar Associations, 1996).

[41] Author interview with Higashizawa, 18 February 1997.

[42] Author interview with Kaido, 15 February 1997.

[43] Many of the cases cited here are also discussed in Amy Gurowitz, 'Mobilizing International Norms: Domestic Actors, Immigrants, and the Japanese State', *World Politics* 51: 3 (1999).

plaintiff argued that the refusal to pay him went against the constitution as well as Article 9 of the ICESCR. A district court rejected this by arguing that Article 9 was not self-executing but the High Court reversed the decision in 1983 and used human rights treaties in its interpretation. The government now recognises that 'everyone' in Article 25 refers to aliens as well as nationals.[44]

In 1985 Japan ratified the CEDAW and as a result revised its nationality law so that not only children born to Japanese fathers, but also those born to Japanese mothers, are now considered Japanese nationals. All children previously born to Japanese mothers can acquire Japanese nationality by simply declaring their intention to do so before their twentieth birthday.

The requirement to carry documentation has been a continual thorn in the side of permanent foreign residents in Japan. In 1993 the UN Human Rights Committee concluded that making it a penal offence for aliens to fail to carry documentation at all times, a requirement that does not apply to Japanese nationals, is against the ICCPR. While the government did not fully comply with this finding, it did make the documentation the size of a credit card and the Diet adopted a resolution asking the police not to abuse the power to demand presentation of the certificate.[45]

In 1982 Japan revised its law regarding deportation of aliens to conform with requirements of the international covenants and, in order to comply with the refugee convention, made some improvements to its re-entry system for immigrants. Prior to 1982 permission was required for each re-entry and that permission expired in under one year. This was revised in 1982 to allow Koreans multiple re-entry permits and to extend their stays for up to two years. Yet many still faced hardship if they wished to study abroad or work overseas. In 1991 the law was further changed to extend the time allowed outside of Japan.[46]

In 1979, upon ratification of the covenants, the government acknowledged that it would need to change its national health insurance laws to cover aliens. It made changes in 1982, in conjunction with ratification of the refugee convention, to include refugees, and finally in 1986 eliminated the nationality requirement from the health insurance

---

[44] Certain protections such as livelihood protection apply to Koreans, but not to short-term migrants or illegal aliens. See Yuji Iwasawa, 'The Impact of International Law on Japanese Law: Revolution or Accommodation', SJD Dissertation (University of Virginia, 1996), p. 156.

[45] Yuji Iwasawa, *International Law and Human Rights in Japanese Law* (Oxford: Clarendon Press, 1998), pp. 158–9.

[46] Iwasawa, *International Law and Human Rights*, pp. 144 and 149.

scheme.[47] Similarly, to conform to its obligations under the refugee convention, in 1982 Japan removed nationality requirements from the Child Dependency Allowance Law, the Special Child Dependency Allowance Law, and the Child Allowance Law.[48] In an additional smaller change, the Tokyo Appeals Court has concluded that the requirement that defendants pay the expense of interpreters in court is in violation of the ICCPR.[49]

Finally, in what a *New York Times* front page article referred to as the case that may one day be seen as Japan's Rosa Parks, a Brazilian living in Japan brought a discrimination suit against a jewellery store owner and won based on CERD.[50] Ana Bortz, a Brazilian journalist living in Japan, was refused service in a jewellery store because of her nationality. In October 1999 a district court judge ruled that Bortz had suffered discrimination and ordered compensation. The court found that although the government was obligated by its 1996 ratification of CERD to legislate against all forms of racial discrimination, it had failed to do so. In the absence of such legislation, the court argued, the convention would serve as a standard for judging discrimination. This was the first case in Japanese history ruling on discrimination between two private individuals.[51]

There have also been a number of cases in which plaintiffs have tried, but failed, to use international treaties or customary law to support their cases. Some Koreans have started claiming in court that they retain Japanese nationality and that the move to deny them their nationality was a violation of the Universal Declaration of Human Rights which provides that no one should arbitrarily be deprived of her/his nationality. The courts have not yet accepted this argument. But interestingly, judges have stated that the reason is not that domestic law takes precedent over international law, but that the right not to be deprived of nationality is not yet an established customary international law.[52] In 1990 the Ministry of Human Welfare issued instructions that the Livelihood Protection Law should apply only to aliens who had lost their Japanese

---

[47] Iwasawa, *International Law and Human Rights*, p. 170.
[48] Iwasawa, *International Law and Human Rights*, p. 174.
[49] Author interview with Higashizawa, 18 February 1997.
[50] Howard W. French, ' "Japanese Only" Policy Takes Body Blow in Court', *New York Times* (15 November 1999).
[51] Keiko Yamanaka, 'Contesting Immigrant Rights in Japan', *World On the Move* 6: 2 (2000), 9.
[52] Yuji Iwasawa, 'Legal Treatment of Koreans in Japan: The Impact of International Human Rights Law on Japanese Law', *Human Rights Quarterly* 8: 2 (1986), 146, note 68.

nationality under the Peace Treaty, but should not apply to undocumented or short-term immigrants. An undocumented immigrant and a foreign student challenged the order arguing that it ran counter to Article 9 of the ICESCR. The court found for the government, arguing that the article was not directly applicable.[53]

Finally, additional changes have been made to social policies that, while they cannot be directly linked to international legal norms, have occurred following, or in conjunction with, the changes noted above. In Japan, twenty-five years of affiliation with the national pension plan is required for eligibility, although foreign workers must still pay mandatory fees. In 1994 the law was amended enabling foreigner workers to receive a lump sum payment upon application within two months of departure from Japan. Housing also shows some signs of improving. In June 1994, the Osaka District Court laid down a critical decision ordering a landlord to pay damages to a Korean resident who he discriminated against on the basis of nationality.[54] Finally, in 1991 the Ministry of Health and Welfare (MOHW) ruled that foreigners with a visa status of one year or more could join the national health plan. This has since been further expanded and over-stayers and short-term migrants can now join.[55]

### *Indirect impact*

As previously stated, international law has an indirect, or less direct, impact when lawyers and judges use various unratified conventions, declarations, and acts of international organisations to interpret domestic law in favour of migrants, even when they do not actually find a practice illegal based on international law. Interestingly, lawyers and judges have used international norms and laws that Japan is not directly subject to, either because they are European laws or because Japan is not party to a particular convention, to interpret domestic laws. These may be considered codified norms that are laws applicable to some countries, but not to Japan. This form of legal argumentation, relatively new in Japan and due largely to the internationalisation of the legal profession, has resulted in a number of critical changes for foreigners.

[53] Iwasawa, *International Law and Human Rights*, p. 169.
[54] Tadashi Hanami, 'Japanese Policies on the Rights and Benefits Granted to Foreign Workers, Residents, Refugees and Illegals', in Myron Weiner and Tadashi Hanami (eds.), *Temporary Workers or Future Citizens? Japanese and US Migration Policies* (New York: New York University Press, 1998), p. 233.
[55] Author interview with Higashizawa, 18 February 1997.

Argumentation relying on international laws to which Japan is not subject shows the legitimacy of international law as a form of reasoned argument. Adoption of laws to which Japan is not subject takes place not for legal reasons *per se*, but because those laws have a legitimacy by virtue of their legal status. As Reus-Smit points out, these actors are engaged 'in a distinctive type of argument in which principles and actions must be justified in terms of established, socially-sanctioned, normative precepts'.[56]

Article 900 of the civil code states that illegitimate children receive half of the inheritance of children born to married parents. In 1990 a child born out of wedlock brought a suit arguing that this policy was unconstitutional and invoking the CEDAW, the Universal Declaration on Human Rights, the UN Convention on the Rights of the Child, the ICCPR, and a 1972 Economic and Social Council resolution on the status of the unmarried mother. The Tokyo High Court dismissed the claim without reason in 1991. But in 1993, in what Yuji Iwasawa refers to as 'an epoch making decision' in which 'the Tokyo High Court took an initiative to change society with the support of international human rights law', another challenge was brought against Article 900 invoking the above conventions as well as an additional provision of the children's convention and a general comment of the Human Rights Committee (with the latter offered as the authoritative interpretation of the ICCPR). The court held that the article was unconstitutional on the grounds of unreasonable discrimination and used international human rights law as an aid in interpreting the constitution.[57]

Naturalisation is technically not overly difficult in Japan (although it is very discretionary), but in the past most Korean-Japanese have not tried to naturalise because of the government policy requiring that applicants assimilate into Japanese society and 'recommending' that Koreans take Japanese names.[58] This 'recommendation' is clearly not in the spirit of Article 27 of the ICCPR, and in 1982 when a former Vietnamese citizen wanted to restore his Vietnamese name in court the judges allowed it arguing that 'in view of the present reality that the society increasingly has become mobile and internationalized . . . this Court believes that the selection of one's name . . . should be allowed'.[59] In 1985 the

---

[56] Reus-Smit, chapter 2, p. 41, this volume.
[57] Iwasawa, 'The Domestic Impact', p. 13.
[58] Annual naturalisation rates are extremely low, less than 1 per cent of the Korean population. See Iwasawa, 'The Impact of International Law', p. 128.
[59] Quoted in Iwasawa, 'The Impact of International Law', p. 130.

law was changed so that Japanese nationals married to foreigners could take the foreign name. This was a profound change in the sense that being Japanese is no longer necessarily equated with having a Japanese name.[60]

While courts have generally rejected arguments based on the Universal Declaration of Human Rights, arguing that it is not legally binding, the Supreme Court has used the Declaration as an aid in interpreting the constitution. Under Article 14 of the constitution 'all nationals [*kokumin*] are equal under the law and there shall be no discrimination in political, economic, or social relations because of race, creed, sex, social status or family origins'. The term *kokumin* is a source of historic dispute. After the Second World War, the Supreme Commander for the Allied Powers wrote a draft constitution in which he used the term 'all natural persons', not 'all nationals'. The final Japanese version changed the wording to *kokumin*, literally 'all of the people' but understood to mean all Japanese nationals.[61] In the early post-war period the courts have interpreted the human rights provisions of the constitution as applying to nationals, not aliens. But in 1964, much earlier than most of the other changes relevant for aliens, the Supreme Court found that while Article 14 is technically directed at nationals, it must apply in spirit to foreigners in light of the fact that Article 7 of the Universal Declaration provides that all are equal before the law without any discrimination.[62]

Fingerprinting of aliens is one of the most criticised practices of the Japanese government's treatment of foreigners. Since 1980 many resident aliens have refused to be fingerprinted, claiming that the practice violates their human rights as stated in the constitution as well as the ICCPR's clauses on degrading treatment, discrimination, and due process. The Tokyo District Court in principle acknowledged arguments about the ICCPR, but argued that fingerprinting did not violate the constitution because there was sufficient cause for the practice and that it was not clear from the *travaux préparatoires* of the covenant what is meant by degrading treatment.[63] Nonetheless, in 1982 the

---

[60] Iwasawa, 'The Impact of International Law', p. 129.
[61] Koseki Shoichi, 'Japanizing the Constitution', *Japan Quarterly* 35: 3 (1988), 234–40.
[62] Iwasawa, *International Law and Human Rights*, p. 85.
[63] *Travaux préparatoires* refers to the legal process of tracing the proceedings leading up to a law, treaty or convention when the meaning is unclear from the text of the law. The process is intended to try and root out the spirit or intention of a law.

Alien Registration Law was revised raising the age limit for fingerprint-ing to sixteen, and increasing the interval between fingerprintings (but at the same time increasing the fine for non-compliance). In 1985 the law was changed again when, in the face of international and domestic protests, the method used was altered. Finally, after countless adjust-ments in the face of international, Korean, and domestic protest, finger-printing was eliminated for permanent residents in 1993, removing one of the most despised immigration control procedures of the Japanese government.[64] Following this change an Osaka High Court, in ordering compensation for a plaintiff arrested for refusing to be fingerprinted and forced to do so, cited the international covenants on degrading treatment and the Vienna Convention on the interpretation of treaties. To interpret the covenants the court referred to general comments of the Human Rights Committee, a decision of the European Commission on Human Rights, and a judgement of the European Court of Human Rights.[65]

Yasushi Higashizawa, a lawyer working on foreigners' rights in Japan, cites a number of cases where international covenants were cited by lawyers to back up their cases and interpret international law but where the impact of these references is unclear. Higashizawa argues that many lawyers cite them, but without details, thus making it easy for courts to reject them. He and the Japan Federation of Bar Associations are pushing lawyers to make better use of international resources. For example, in one case a Filipina over-stayer had a child with a Japanese national. They planned to marry but he died. The woman and child stayed in Japan, but were not allowed to join the insurance plan because the Ministry of Health and Welfare had ruled that only foreigners legally in Japan for a year or more were eligible for the national health plan. In late 1995 the Tokyo District Court rejected the woman's claim saying that it was up to government discretion whether to include foreigners in the plan. Higashizawa argues that the attorneys for the case did not place suffi-cient emphasis on the ICCPR and ICESCR. Since 1996 the government has addressed the problem of foreign undocumented women having children with Japanese men who do not marry them. The Immigration Bureau has now said that generally speaking the woman should get special permission to remain in Japan legally.[66]

[64] Iwasawa, 'The Impact of International Law', p. 144.
[65] Author interview with Higashizawa, 18 February 1997, and Iwasawa, 17 February 1997.
[66] Author interview with Higashizawa, 18 February 1997.

## Conclusion: the importance and limitations of legal versus social norms

The story of Japan, international legal norms, and migrants, is really two interwoven stories, both with implications for the politics of international law. The first story is about a state adopting international laws to be seen as a legitimate state. Even this story has two phases for Japan. Earlier in its history Japan adopted international laws, and modelled its own domestic law after the legal structure of powerful states, to become a legitimate power. The government used the institution of international law to appear like the European powers, and to be able to play the game of power politics in the role of the powerful, not the role of the victim. But after the 1970s Japan the more powerful state also needed international law to be seen as a legitimate state. And now the symbol of legitimacy was not power *per se*, but whether it adopted international laws to govern its domestic human rights policies. Japan ratified a variety of international conventions because without having done so it appeared aberrant, unlike the legitimate club of states to which it aspired. These ratifications in turn had a profound impact on domestic laws addressing foreigners in Japan. In short, in both time periods, the international community offered up a model of legitimate statehood that involved adopting international standards, and Japan took it on.

But the second story has been the focus of this chapter. What have the implications of international laws been for migrants in Japan? In many ways they have been highly significant. As Lawrence Repeta argues, with the adoption of the human rights covenants (and I would argue other international instruments), human rights activists have 'gained a tool of coherent legal structure sanctioned by the UN and many nations viewed by Japan as the most advanced'.[67] In the context of concern over internationalisation and reputation, the usefulness of this tool should not be downplayed and it is difficult to account for improvement in policies towards foreigners without the contextual background of Japan's international identity and the international standards.

It matters in particular that these international standards are *laws*. David Martin[68] argues that between 1945 and the 1970s UN

---

[67] Lawrence Repeta, 'The International Covenant on Civil and Political Rights and Human Rights Law in Japan', *Law in Japan* 20 (1987), 3.
[68] David A. Martin, 'Effects of International Law on Migration Policy and Practice: The Uses of Hypocrisy', *International Migration Review* 23: 3 (1989).

pronouncements on human rights were routine and were not widely expected to have any real impact on government practice. Nonetheless, these legal norms can now be invoked in NGO claims against governments, sometimes lending support to those claims.[69] Before the development of international human rights instruments, opponents of government practice might have been able to argue that a particular policy was a 'bad idea', but they now have more powerful weapons: government practice is not only bad, but 'violates international law'.[70] These laws 'transform the NGO from a busybody unjustifiably poking its nose into someone else's business into a steward of agreed international principles, simply asking questions or pressing points it has a right to care about'.[71] Similarly, Ellen Lutz and Kathryn Sikkink argue that law has an important expressive function. It formally restates social values and communicates norms. In the case of Latin America they point out that legalisation increased the number of pathways available to those seeking to raise human rights by increasing the number of venues in which human rights issues could be raised.[72] The Japanese case is similar in that international law has opened a new avenue for those in Japan seeking to overcome discrimination.

International law has been critical even though law in Japan is thought to have weak sanctions and despite the fact that social norms are thought to be more important for social change. Legal norms are thought to affirm social consensus and to be effective when social control breaks down.[73] But law in Japan provides a route for foreigners to seek remedies that are otherwise largely unavailable. There is no social consensus favouring migrant rights, nor are there many social norms in their favour. Law may not be the first-choice remedy in Japan, but it is often the most effective for foreigners. As John Haley[74] points out, despite weak sanctions, law establishes a legitimate norm of principle. Once there are

---

[69] It should be noted that reference to international norms does not necessarily lend legitimacy to NGO claims. If the government in question views international norms as irrelevant or, as in the case of Malaysia, as tools of Western hegemony, reference to these norms may be detrimental.

[70] Martin, 'Effects of International Law', 554. I would argue that the same logic can be used when norms that are not codified in law are involved, although the impact may certainly be greater if there is a legal basis for the argument.

[71] Martin, 'Effects of International Law', 554.

[72] Ellen L. Lutz and Kathryn Sikkink, 'International Human Rights Law and Practice in Latin America', *International Organization* 54: 3 (2000), 657–8.

[73] Katzenstein, *Cultural Norms and National Security*, pp. 43–4.

[74] John Owen Haley, *Authority Without Power* (New York: Oxford University Press, 1991), p. 186.

public expressions of law violations they must be addressed. That said, without the sort of continued change in social norms discussed in the beginning of this chapter, brought about in part by many everyday people in Japan seeing  their country as 'abnormal' with regard to foreigners, the impact on foreigners will be limited.

# 7    The International Criminal Court

*David Wippman*[1]

In July 1998, after years of preparatory work and five weeks of intensive negotiations, 120 states voted in Rome to approve a treaty intended to establish the first permanent International Criminal Court (ICC). Less than three years later, with a speed that surprised even the treaty's proponents, the treaty surpassed the sixty ratifications needed to bring it into force. The United States, joined by only six other states, voted against the treaty, and continues to search for ways to limit the new court's reach, even though almost all of the United States' closest allies have ratified the treaty or are moving towards ratification.

This outcome was not pre-ordained. The United States, under President Clinton, was predisposed to support efforts at creating an international criminal court. Such a court was consistent with the Clinton Administration's overall attitude towards human rights and accountability for human rights abuses, and with US support for the Yugoslavia and Rwanda war crimes tribunals. In 1994, the International Law Commission (ILC) produced a draft statute for the International Court, the culmination of years of work undertaken at the request of the United Nations General Assembly. This draft statute, which included a 'gatekeeper' role for the United Nations Security Council, helped trigger an official commitment from the Clinton Administration to support in principle the ICC project.

The ILC draft attracted numerous comments and criticisms from states and non-governmental organisations (NGOs) alike. These

[1] The author would like to thank Jeffrey Dunoff, Steven Ratner, Jane Stromseth, Robert Summers, the participants in Alan Sykes' and Jack Goldsmith's international law colloquium at the University of Chicago Law School, and the participants in Andrew Guzman's International Law Workshop at Berkeley's Boalt Hall School of Law for helpful comments on an earlier draft of this chapter.

comments and criticisms were reflected in the draft consolidated text that formed the basis for the 1998 Rome negotiations, but which left open all of the important and contested issues. As the negotiations in Rome began, the United States had reason to believe that its views would attract enough votes to produce a treaty the United States could support, if not ratify. But when the Rome negotiations ended, the United States felt compelled to vote against the treaty, joined only by China, Iraq, Israel, Libya, Qatar, and Yemen.[2]

It may be possible to explain this outcome largely in terms of traditional accounts of state pursuit of material interests, along the lines of conventional realist analyses of international law and politics. But such an explanation would be unsatisfactory in several important respects. For realists, international law and legal institutions such as the ICC are created by powerful states to further their political purposes. In this case, the largest and most powerful states – the United States, China, India, and to some extent Russia – all opposed the treaty adopted in Rome.

More importantly, the entire enterprise of creating the ICC does not fit comfortably within the realist framework. States wishing to maximise their freedom of action internally and internationally in general have an interest in insulating their conduct from any authoritative external review and assessment. Even if such assessments cannot be enforced in the conventional sense, a decision by a respected international tribunal that a state's action (undertaken by nationals acting in accordance with official policy) is illegal, or worse, criminal, threatens to undermine international and domestic support for the action at issue. From this standpoint, it is not surprising that the Nuremberg, Yugoslavia, and Rwanda tribunals were all imposed on particular states by other states whose own actions would not be subject to scrutiny. But the Rome treaty potentially subjects nationals from all states to scrutiny and possible criminal prosecution. An interest-based analysis can account for this outcome, but only in part.

Similarly, a neoliberal institutionalist analysis, which sees states as rational actors in pursuit of efficient means to realise individual and collective interests, captures only part of what transpired at Rome. To some extent, the Rome treaty was motivated by a desire to solve

---

[2] The final vote in Rome was unrecorded. As a result, there is some uncertainty as to precisely which states joined the United States and Israel in voting against the treaty. The states mentioned in the text are the ones most often named in news reports of the outcome.

collective action problems and to reduce the transaction costs inherent in establishing ad hoc tribunals. But the Rome treaty was driven even more fundamentally by a desire on the part of many participants in the negotiations to develop and stabilise norms of legitimate behaviour by states and non-state actors. As suggested by Christian Reus-Smit in chapter 2, rationalist analysis works best in areas where states can plausibly be seen to have clear, pre-existing material interests; it does not work well in explaining the creation of institutions such as the ICC that are driven in significant part by normative as well as material impulses.

A more complete understanding of what transpired in Rome requires consideration of the 'reasons for action' of the various actors involved, including both states and NGOs. In particular, it requires consideration of how actors' interests and identities interacted to produce positions on particular contested issues. Further, it requires consideration of the context of the negotiations, which drove actors to frame their positions in ways compatible with the overall enterprise of creating a quintessentially legal institution.

This chapter attempts to explain the outcome in Rome by examining the arguments made by the United States and other countries on the key contested issues, and the role of law and politics in the formulation and resolution of those arguments. If politics is understood broadly, to encompass, as suggested by Reus-Smit, purposive and identity-constitutive forms of reason and action as well as those based on material interests, then the outcome in Rome was determined by politics. This was necessarily so, since international law (whether considered as a body of rules or a process of decision-making) does not provide clear answers to the key contested issues. Whether to confine the court's initial jurisdiction to genocide, war crimes, and crimes against humanity (the eventual majority position) or to include such other crimes as drug trafficking, aircraft hijacking, and terrorism, whether to require Security Council authorisation for the initiation of investigations and prosecutions or to confer that power in addition on an independent prosecutor and on the individual state parties, whether to adopt a broad jurisdictional scheme or a narrow one – are all questions of institutional design that are not susceptible to resolution through simple application of pre-existing legal principles.

But it is incomplete, both theoretically and descriptively, to say that law did not control the contested issues at Rome. Many issues were not contested precisely because they were viewed by the Rome delegates as largely if not wholly controlled by pre-existing law. Moreover, even the contested issues were not negotiated in a vacuum. The parties to the Rome negotiations understood that they were creating a legal institution – a criminal court with a defined jurisdiction over specified crimes and with formal procedures for the initiation and conduct of investigations, the indictment and trial of alleged offenders, and the sentencing and incarceration of those convicted. This effort took place against – and could only make sense within – the larger context of existing international law and institutions. Because international law has its own 'language of justification', much of the negotiations in Rome took the form of legal arguments. These arguments were deployed in support of the interests of the particular actors making the arguments, but the process of invoking and pursuing legal argumentation in turn helped shape the range of possibilities viewed as permissible and the content of the final agreement in particular and distinctive ways. Moreover, these legal arguments were also shaped by competing general conceptions of what legal institutions and rules should look like and what role international law and institutions should play in international affairs. In turn, those competing general conceptions were shaped by the actors' conceptions of their interests and their identities.

In this sense, law and politics were inseparable at Rome; each shaped the other. The forms of argumentation, though, were distinct. Legal arguments took the form of claims about what international law requires or should require as a legal system. They enabled actors to press positions through nominally disinterested invocation of accepted principles agreed to in other contexts and in advance of the Rome negotiations. By contrast, political arguments took the form of claims about what would or would not advance the interests of particular actors. They did not appeal to previously agreed-upon principles. Both kinds of arguments were often made simultaneously. For example, arguments on whether the court should exercise jurisdiction over nationals of states that did not ratify the treaty creating the court sometimes relied on explicit appeals to political interests (for example, powerful states, particularly the United States, will not support or accept a court with jurisdiction over non-party nationals) and sometimes on equally explicit appeals to what international law does or does not permit (for example, treaties cannot bind non-party states).

The two kinds of argument were seen as different in nature, with varying applicability depending on the issue and the determinacy of existing law with respect to that issue. From the standpoint of the participants, legal arguments on some issues held the potential, at least in theory, to be dispositive. The US contention that the Rome treaty could not bind non-party states was one such argument. Delegates to the Rome conference did not dispute the existence or validity of the legal rule relied on by the United States; rather, they denied the accuracy of the US premise that the court's exercise of jurisdiction over non-party nationals would amount to binding non-party states to treaty obligations they had not accepted. Implicitly, it was generally accepted that if the US premise were valid, the legal rule governing non-party states would control even if contrary in this instance to the preferences of most states. By contrast, arguments about the proper relationship between the court and the UN Security Council were understood to be predominantly political, with no argument inherently dispositive and everything at least potentially open to bargaining.

On some issues, legal arguments joined political arguments as possibly persuasive but not controlling. For example, many delegates urged that the definition of crimes to be included within the court's jurisdiction track existing international law as closely as possible, for reasons of clarity, consistency, and efficiency, values important to most legal systems. In addition, many participants in the negotiations favoured or opposed proposed articles on the basis of their perceived fit with particular conceptions of the role of international law and international legal institutions in promoting a particular vision of international order. Thus, an expansive jurisdiction for the court has been supported as necessary to an effective criminal court and attacked as a form of judicial overreaching; similarly, the United States has variously been urged to support the proposed court as a means to bolster international law generally or to oppose it as an intrusion on sovereign decision-making inappropriate for a still primitive international legal order.

In an effort to assess the role of and relationship between law and politics in the ICC negotiations, this chapter examines the major issues dividing the United States from the large majority of states that voted to adopt the ICC statute. In particular, the chapter examines the arguments made with respect to the role of the Security Council in referring cases to the court, the scope of the court's jurisdiction, and the function of complementarity, as well as the identity and interests of those making the arguments. The chapter also examines the systemic arguments made for and against US support for the ICC.

This review of the Rome negotiations supports the view articulated by Reus-Smit that politics is driven by normative as well as material concerns, and that law is both a product of – and constitutive of – this multifaceted politics. In the context of the ICC, the arguments of both supporters and critics of the proposed new court evinced a combination of normative, material, and identity-based concerns. Ultimately, those concerns reflected fundamentally divergent conceptions of the role of international law and legal institutions in international relations, with court supporters generally seeing international law as a means to constrain national politics and advance a human rights-oriented conception of international society, and critics expressing scepticism about both the efficacy and desirability of using international law in that way.

## Law, politics, and persuasion in the ICC negotiations

The structure of the arguments in Rome was determined in part by the law-making nature of the enterprise in which the participants were engaged. It was also determined by the identity of the actors participating in the negotiations, and the way in which they went about defining their interests.

### Legal argumentation

The delegates in Rome came to hammer out a treaty that would create a court with a defined structure, composition, and powers, identify proscribed behaviour and the circumstances under which the court could adjudicate that behaviour, and establish obligations on state parties to support the work of the institution. The participants viewed the treaty as a means to constrain the behaviour of individuals and governments, and to co-ordinate the response of state parties to particular crimes.

In most essential respects, the form and content of the Rome statute closely resemble those of national law. The rules are general in application, forward-looking, internally consistent, and capable of being fulfilled. They are designed to operate within, and only make sense in, a larger legal context of established background norms (for example, that treaties are to be performed). In short, the rules of the ICC treaty look much like the rules establishing domestic criminal courts and conferring on them jurisdiction over specific crimes. More broadly, the participants viewed the Rome process as legitimate,[3] and the assembled states as

---

[3] Not all states viewed all aspects of the Rome process as legitimate, however. The United States, for example, objected strongly to the rush to judgement that characterised the conference's final hours. See William Lietzau, 'International Criminal Law After Rome: Concerns from a US Military Perspective', *Law and Contemporary Problems* 64: 1 (2001), 130.

competent to establish binding rules, at least to the extent that in doing so they were acting within the limits on their law-making authority established by pre-existing international law.

The participants also understood, of course, that the process of establishing rules in Rome was a political process. But the participants correctly viewed law and politics as encompassing distinct modes of argumentation. The distinction relates to law and politics as ideal types. International law, like domestic law, emerges through politics and changes as a result of politics. But at least in theory, law and politics differ; once established, the former is to be applied by reference to its own internal logic, and not in response to powerful interests or in furtherance of the personal preferences of those expected to apply the law. As Paul Kahn observes, '[o]nce the legal rules are set, outcomes should not depend on the relative power of the disputants. To identify the operation of political power within an institution of law is to discover a "defect", a site at which reform must be pursued if the values of law are to be maintained.'[4] In other words, law in idealised form is not strategic; outcomes are supposed to depend not on the struggle of individual and group preferences, but on the application of rules and doctrine to facts. Thus, for lawyers and judges confronted with a problem or dispute, the relevant questions are: Is there a governing legal rule? Are there applicable exceptions? What outcome do doctrine and precedent direct? Seen this way, law is supposed both to limit and to justify subsequent political action, until the law itself is changed through political processes.

Partly because law in application is not supposed to be strategic, law is commonly (though not always correctly) associated with the public interest rather than with the narrow, private interests of particular actors. Indeed, the perceived legitimacy of law, which is part of what gives law its power to shape behaviour, whether nationally or internationally, rests on this association.

By contrast, politics in this dichotomy is considered a purely strategic domain. Power and interests determine outcomes. For political actors, the relevant questions are: What do I want? How can I best attain my goals or maximise my interests? Politics is therefore associated with the private interest; at the international level, it is associated with the particular interests of individual states rather than the larger good of the international community.

---

[4] Paul W. Kahn, 'American Hegemony and International Law: Speaking Law to Power: Popular Sovereignty, Human Rights, and the New International Order', *Chicago Journal of International Law* 1: 1 (2000), 1.

Of course, this distinction between law and politics is oversimplified and open to criticism on numerous grounds. As suggested earlier, politics permeates law, so much so that various schools of critical theory deny that any distinction between the two is meaningful. From this standpoint, law is simply another form of politics. Law-making is viewed as an opportunity for the powerful to establish rules to further their own interests. The application of legal rules is likewise viewed as political. However precise legal rules appear, they can never be wholly determinate; thus, their application will always require choices between defensible alternative interpretations concerning which rules apply to a given situation and what those rules require. Because such choices are not dictated by law, they are inescapably political.

Nonetheless, the distinction between law and politics sketched out above regularly structures and suffuses law-making negotiations of the sort conducted in Rome. This may seem ironic, since at the moment of law-making, and in particular at the moment of institutional design embodied in the creation of a court, the clash between the competing conceptions of law and politics described above is more apparent than real. Even those holding to a conventional view of the opposition of law and politics would concede that politics (understood as the pursuit of interests by individuals and groups) does play – and within limits should play – a central role in the processes by which law is made. The extent to which the interplay of competing interests produces law that reflects a larger community interest is, and will remain, hotly contested, as will the possibility for the subsequent neutral application of legal rules once made, but the centrality of politics in law-making is a given.

At the same time, it would be a mistake to conclude that law-making and the creation of legal institutions is only about interest group politics. The establishment of new legal rules and judicial bodies does not take place in a vacuum, where everything is up for bargaining and all outcomes are controlled by the distribution of power among the protagonists. Instead, law-making takes place against a backdrop of existing legal norms and institutions, which condition and limit the range of options viewed by the participants in the process as possible, and which simultaneously shape the process itself. Such background influences may take many forms, from constitutional constraints (for example, no *ex post facto* legislation) to shared notions of what legal institutions ought to look like (for example, a separation of the functions of prosecution and adjudication).

Because of the values associated with law, and because of the legal context within which law-making negotiations take place, participants in law-making tend to view some kinds of reasoning and argumentation as valid and appropriate, as persuasive, and others not. There is pressure to frame interests in legal terms, to argue that a provision should be adopted or rejected because it is mandated by, or violative of, existing international law, that it strengthens or weakens international law, or that it furthers community rather than individual state interests. This in turn feeds back into the position the party is seeking to advance. To take just one example, the United States argued forcefully, as explained more fully below, that it would violate the law of treaties to extend the court's jurisdiction to the nationals of non-party states. This legal argument was designed to advance a perceived US interest (avoidance of the prosecution of US military personnel carrying out official policy) but was necessarily framed more broadly than advancement of that interest actually required.

In Rome, where many of the delegates were lawyers (many of the decision-makers in national governments were also lawyers), legal argument dominated most issues; even when law manifestly could not dictate a particular resolution, ideas about law shaped the arguments raised. Many of the disputes in Rome related to disagreements over the proper function of legal institutions; other disputes related to concerns that the court's statute in application would fail to uphold the ideal of law as a body of rules made by legitimate authority and neutrally applied. Conversely, attacks on opposing positions commonly alleged that those positions were 'political', understood as a synonym for self-interested, or that they jeopardised the independence essential to any legitimate court. Thus, the United States expressed fear that vesting broad power in the court's prosecutor would lead to 'politicised' prosecutions, understood as prosecutions based not on impartial application of the court's rules but instead on the preferred outcomes of particular actors. Similarly, the United States worried that the exercise of jurisdiction over nationals of non-parties would amount to 'judicial overreaching', that is, that the court would exercise power not legitimately conferred upon it by those with the authority to do so. Conversely, other states feared that exempting some states from the rules applicable to others would be to 'politicise' the law in a different way, to violate the legal principle that like should be treated alike.

Of course, as noted earlier, many of the delegates in Rome consciously wanted to use the law-making process as a way to constrain and shape politics. Their goal was to limit the future discretion of individual states by obligating them to support prosecutions under specified circumstances, and by shifting decision-making authority from national government officials to judges and prosecutors independent of any state or particular group of states. More broadly, their goal was to shape what governments will in the future consider acceptable behaviour. This effort (which is continuing) is political but also legal; it is an attempt to achieve political goals through law. It builds on existing international law and legal institutions, including most notably the international criminal tribunals for Yugoslavia and Rwanda. More broadly, at least for liberal Western states and their NGO allies, it reflects a conscious attempt to expand the reach and impact of human rights and humanitarian law generally.

## Actors, interests, and identity

Some countries have clearly opted to identify themselves, both at home and internationally, as champions or at least supporters of this new 'human security' agenda. For these states, support for a 'strong' ICC was attractive to their domestic publics and consistent with their self-image. Most, such as Canada, are developed Western states, but others, such as Senegal, are in the developing world. These states have varying motivations for their stances but most relate to their own conception of their identity and role in international affairs as well as to more traditionally defined conceptions of national interest.

Collectively, the states pressing hard for an independent court with broad jurisdictional authority were known as the 'like-minded states'. Most were European, but many came from other regions. These states regularly caucused and co-ordinated their positions, strongly supported by most of the 300 or so NGOs present in Rome.

Canada was at the forefront of the like-minded. For Canada, this role was in keeping with its traditional posture as a leading supporter of the United Nations in its peace and human rights activities. Canada has long played an active role in UN peacekeeping and other humanitarian endeavours disproportionate to its geopolitical weight. By doing so, Canada has simultaneously reaffirmed its identity as a human rights-oriented liberal democracy, and positioned itself to exercise diplomatic influence it might not otherwise command. Under the activist leadership of its liberal Foreign Minister, Lloyd Axworthy, Canada played a particularly aggressive role in promoting the ICC.

The core of support for the ICC came from Europe. Some European states, the Nordic states in particular, have long positioned themselves as champions of the human rights agenda. Indeed, most of the European states have chosen to identify themselves with this agenda to one degree or another. These states maintain strong human rights standards in their own national law, but are also accustomed to external supervision and even adjudication of their human rights practices, through the European Court of Human Rights. The process of European integration has forced all of these states to accept to a considerable degree the pooling of their sovereignty in the institutions of the European Union, and they are therefore less sensitive than countries such as the United States to claims that institutions such as the ICC represent a sacrifice of national decision-making authority. Some European states have additional and more particularised reasons for identifying themselves as ICC supporters. Germany, for example, seeks continually to reconfirm its modern liberal (and anti-Nazi) identity; not surprisingly, it was Germany which championed universal jurisdiction, the broadest of the jurisdictional schemes considered in Rome. Moreover, most of these states have relatively little reason to fear that the court they were supporting would adjudicate crimes of their own nationals, since most rarely use armed force, and when they do, it is almost always as peacekeepers under UN or other international organisation auspices. For them, the ICC was an opportunity to confirm their liberal credentials, contribute to international peace and security, and, perhaps, to distinguish themselves from and even place a modest check on the unilateralist stance and actions of the United States.

For France and the United Kingdom, however, the situation was more complicated. Both have interests as permanent members of the Security Council that pulled them closer to the US position. France, which has often intervened militarily in Africa, and which conceives of itself as still having great power interests, had other reasons for scepticism concerning some elements of the like-minded position. The United Kingdom, which also has occasion to intervene militarily in Africa and elsewhere, and which prides itself on a special relationship with the United States, had its own reasons to gravitate towards some of the US arguments in the course of the negotiations. But in the end, France and the United Kingdom yielded to the pull of European solidarity.

States from other regions also joined the like-minded camp, for various reasons. Senegal, for example, has sought in recent years to distinguish itself from its African neighbours by expressing early and strong support for international humanitarian law and endeavours. South Africa has similarly and more credibly sought to position itself as a regional leader committed to the development of international law and institutions, in part by parlaying the international reputation and credibility of Nelson Mandela into a larger role on the world stage. A number of governments in Latin America, seeking to reinforce to both domestic and international audiences their transition from authoritarian rule and an era of human rights abuses to liberal democracy and respect for human rights, also actively supported the creation of a strong ICC.

Other states had reasons to be hostile to the entire enterprise. Most of the Arab world, with the notable exception of Egypt, whose national, Cherif Bassiouni, chaired the drafting committee in Rome, was quietly hostile to the idea of the ICC. These states have authoritarian regimes and a record of human rights violations; they feared that the ICC would be used as a tool of Western interests and that their nationals and government officials might some day be subject to ICC investigation and prosecution. But at the same time, many Arab states hoped that the court's statute could be drawn in such a way as to minimise the risk to themselves, while affording an opportunity for attacking Israeli occupation practices. Most Asian states were also sceptical of the ICC. China, which has long been hostile to external supervision of its human rights record, and which does not wish to dilute its power as a permanent member of the Security Council, joined the United States in voting against the statute. India and Pakistan, both of which have reason to fear the court's exercise of jurisdiction in their mutual conflict, also do not support the court, nor did many other governments with execrable human rights records, in Asia and elsewhere.

For the United States, the ICC represented both an opportunity and a risk. The United States fully subscribes to the notions of human dignity inherent in the assertion of international criminal jurisdiction over genocide, crimes against humanity, and war crimes. Moreover, the United States conceives of itself as a nation dedicated to the rule of law, both at home and abroad.

At the same time, the United States generally resists surrendering ultimate decision-making authority to international tribunals and institutions. This is not, or not only, simple exceptionalism, a refusal to play by the rules that apply to everyone else, as it is often construed by critics of the US position. As Kahn points out, the US conception of its own identity and history is involved. The United States as a nation is 'deeply committed to its myth of popular sovereignty'.[5] Americans believe 'that unless an assertion of government authority can be traced to an act of popular sovereignty, it is illegitimate'.[6] When Congressional and other ICC critics complain that 'this Court strikes at the heart of sovereignty',[7] they are not spouting empty rhetoric; instead, at some level, they are appealing to deeply held conceptions of national identity and the proper relationship between law and self-government.

By contrast, international human rights law, and the ICC in particular, reject the primacy of popular sovereignty rooted in national communities.[8] For ICC supporters, especially the legion of human rights groups present in Rome, the ultimate goal is to overcome national politics through claims of right asserted on behalf of individuals and against states and other individuals. To achieve this goal, proponents of a 'strong' court sought to abandon the state consent model of traditional international law, to universalise the scope of the court's authority, and to provide for enforcement, in short, to mimic effective national legal systems.

This approach presented a threat both to US conceptions of sovereignty and to US interests as the sole remaining superpower and the most influential member of the UN Security Council. The US regularly has close to 200,000 troops deployed abroad, far more than any other country. US military capabilities allow it to project power, and to use coercion in support of policy goals, in ways that no other country can emulate. Because of its unique status and global role, the United States attracts criticism and envy. Ultimately, the United States feared that the court might be used as a tool to constrain US freedom of action involving the use of force.[9]

At the same time, the United States has long provided the lion's share of the support – financial, political, logistical, and even military – for the Yugoslavia and Rwanda tribunals. The United States has done so both because it values accountability and because it sees accountability as a way to marginalise extremists and foster regional stability. For the United States, the challenge in Rome was to achieve an agreement

---

[5] Kahn, 'American Hegemony and International Law', 3.
[6] Kahn, 'American Hegemony and International Law', 3.
[7] Senator Rod Grams, 'Is a UN International Criminal Court in the US National Interest?', Statement at the Hearing before the Subcommittee on International Operations of the Committee on Foreign Relations, United States Senate, 105th Congress, 2nd Session (23 July 1998), p. 8.
[8] See Kahn, 'American Hegemony and International Law', 9–11.
[9] Lietzau, 'International Criminal Law After Rome', 126.

that would permit international prosecutions of gross human rights and humanitarian law violations without constraining US freedom of action.

The United States might well have achieved such an agreement under the configuration of actors and interests that existed in 1994, at the time of the International Law Commission's draft statute. It might still have reached an acceptable agreement in 1998, had it proved more nimble in the negotiations.[10] But the United States was out of synch with the rapidly evolving sentiment in Rome and during the months leading up to it. The growing success of the Yugoslavia and Rwanda war crimes tribunals, and the mobilisation of human rights organisations and other civil society groups on behalf of efforts to combat atrocities through law, worked a dramatic shift in the post-1994 attitude of governments towards the ICC.

The effect of this shift in attitudes was magnified in the Rome negotiations by the extraordinary organisation and skill displayed by many of the hundreds of participating NGOs. These organisations lobbied tirelessly for their conception of a strong ICC, both among the delegations in Rome and in national capitals. They saw themselves, far more even than the most staunch like-minded state, as the guardians of the international public interest. They prepared countless position papers, summarised and disseminated information on the proceedings, offered advice to and even served as members of official delegations, and publicised and criticised any state proposals that threatened to undermine their conception of the court.

When the dust finally settled at Rome, the United States and other major powers were left on the sidelines. As discussed below, the arguments raised in the process were framed in the language of justification peculiar to the international law-making setting, and reflected the identities of the parties as well as their interests.

## Legal and political claims

As the negotiations in Rome began, some aspects of the court's statute were viewed by the delegates as largely predetermined by existing law. For the most part, these aspects related to due process rights of the

---

[10] See Ruth Wedgwood, 'Fiddling in Rome: America and the International Criminal Court', *Foreign Affairs* 77: 6 (1998), 20–4; and Ruth Wedgwood, 'Courting Disaster: The US Takes a Stand', *Foreign Service Journal* 77: 3 (2000), 34.

accused (for example, the rights to be informed of the charges, to a public hearing, to examine witnesses, to counsel, and to an appeal, and prohibitions on *ex post facto* application of law and double jeopardy). While there was significant disagreement over the form these protections should take (reflecting in part differences between common law and civil law systems), the necessity of protections based on established human rights norms was not at issue. Many other features of the court were viewed as largely technical, and modelled on other tribunals (for example, the functions of the registry or the process for selecting judges).

Efforts to depart significantly from widely shared perceptions of existing law, though relatively few, generally occasioned considerable controversy. Arab states, for example, argued vigorously, and ultimately successfully, for inclusion in the definition of war crimes of a provision criminalising 'the transfer, directly or indirectly, by the Occupying Power of parts of its own civilian population into the territory it occupies'. This provision, clearly aimed at Israeli West Bank settlement policy, arguably diverges from pre-existing treaty and customary law, and was sharply criticised on that basis.[11] Its acceptance reflected the desire of a majority of the delegates to garner Arab support for the treaty and is a relatively clear instance in which politics in the conventional sense trumped legal argument.

For the most part, however, disagreements at the Rome conference centred on issues with regard to which existing international law was viewed as neither determinate nor controlling. In particular, sharp differences emerged among delegations concerning the scope of the court's jurisdiction and the 'trigger mechanism' for the exercise of that jurisdiction (that is, the means by which crimes within the court's jurisdiction would be referred to it for prosecution). Similar differences emerged over the scope of the prosecutor's authority, the definition of crimes, the role of the Security Council, the method for amending the court's statute, and numerous lesser issues. The negotiations were complicated by the fact that most of these issues were closely interrelated; from the standpoint of any given actor, gains on one issue might permit concessions on others. By the same token, '[s]tates were reluctant to agree to

---

[11] In post-Rome meetings of the Preparatory Commission, an informal understanding emerged that the provision should not be interpreted as a departure from existing law. This understanding was included in the Finalised Draft Text of the Elements of Crimes, PCNICC/2000/1/Add. 2 (New York: United Nations, 2 November 2000), a supplement to the Rome treaty.

compromises on specific issues without knowing how the entire package would emerge'.[12]

Underlying the differences on specific issues were differences on systemic questions: How should national security and national interest be ascertained and defined – broadly (to encompass the strengthening of international law and institutions) or narrowly (to focus on the possible constraints international law and institutions pose)? How should international legal institutions relate to international political institutions and to individual states? Which issues should be resolved through legal process and which through diplomacy?

## The role of the UN Security Council

The United States entered the Rome negotiations with the view that the UN Security Council was the appropriate body to refer cases to the proposed court for investigation and prosecution. For much of the period leading up to Rome, this position commanded the support of all five permanent members of the Security Council. For them, this proposal had the obvious advantage of precluding prosecutions any one of them viewed as unacceptable. But for that very reason, most states, strongly encouraged by most NGOs, vigorously opposed the proposal. Although international law had little to do with either the positions taken on this issue or the outcome, both sides in the debate framed the issue in legal terms.

Like-minded governments and NGOs attacked the US position as an unwarranted interference with the independence of the court and its prosecutor. In their view, the US approach would 'politicise' the court in a way that would not be accepted in any effective national legal system. As a practical matter, they feared that individual permanent members of the Security Council would use the veto to block prosecution of their own nationals and the nationals of their allies, noting that for most of the past fifty years, many of the world's most prominent war criminals, from Pol Pot to Laurent Kabila, had 'sheltering patrons among the Permanent Five'.[13] Many non-aligned states, led by India, strongly opposed any role for the Security Council, viewing it as a Western-dominated forum in

---

[12] Philippe Kirsch and John T. Holmes, 'The Rome Conference on an International Criminal Court: The Negotiating Process', *American Journal of International Law* 93: 1 (1999), 4.

[13] Lawrence Weschler, 'Exceptional Cases in Rome: The United States and the Struggle for an ICC', in Sarah B. Sewall and Carl Kaysen (eds.), *The United States and the International Criminal Court: National Security and International Law* (Lanham, MD: Rowman & Littlefield, 2000), p. 92.

which they exercised little or no influence. They argued that reliance on the Security Council as the exclusive trigger mechanism for exercise of the court's jurisdiction ran counter to the principle of sovereign equality, by conferring special privileges on a handful of states. Thus, most states favoured a system in which individual state parties could refer cases to the prosecutor for investigation and possible prosecution.

The United States noted that the Security Council was the body entrusted by the UN Charter with the primary responsibility for promoting international peace and security, and that international criminal prosecutions might impede the Council's effort to negotiate a political resolution to a conflict. As the United States pointed out, peace sometimes requires cutting deals with individuals who might properly be treated as war criminals. Accordingly, the United States contended that decisions on which situations should be referred to the court for prosecution should rest with the Security Council.

Most delegates found the US legal argument unconvincing. It was obvious to all that nothing in the Charter *requires* that the Security Council decide which cases or situations should be referred for international criminal prosecution, and the inference from the Council's UN Charter-conferred role in maintaining international peace was too tenuous to carry much weight. It was also obvious, however, that international law did not *preclude* a court reliant solely on Security Council referrals (the Yugoslavia and the Rwanda tribunals were both set up that way).

Given the inconclusiveness of the legal arguments, the issue boiled down to voting strength. Opponents of Security Council primacy had the advantage of numbers, but the united opposition of the permanent members of the Security Council (the 'P5') might well have proved insurmountable: even the strongest supporters of an 'independent' court would have had little hope for the success of an international institution opposed by all the permanent members of the Security Council.

The issue was ultimately resolved by compromise, but it was a compromise made possible only by the defection of the United Kingdom from the P5 position. In one of the preparatory meetings preceding the Rome negotiations, the United Kingdom reversed its earlier support for the exclusivity of Security Council referrals. In making this shift, the UK was attempting to give effect to the new 'ethical foreign policy' proclaimed by Prime Minister Tony Blair and his recently elected Labour Party. The UK was also responding to pressure from other European states to support the EU's first 'post-Bosnia try at a common foreign and security policy'.[14] By joining the other 'like-minded governments' in support of a 'strong' court, the UK may also have helped mute sharp public criticism of the Blair government's role in arming mercenaries assisting the elected government of Sierra Leone. For the United Kingdom, then, the pull of its human-rights image and European solidarity overcame its P5 and Anglo-American interests.

The UK's defection left France isolated among the European states, and put pressure on it to join the UK in abandoning the P5 position. France was initially reluctant to accept a diminished role for the Security Council (in which France, of course, may exercise a veto), a reluctance the more understandable given France's history of intervention in former African colonies. For France, the solution was to negotiate a right to opt out of the court's jurisdiction over war crimes for a period of seven years.

With the British and French shifts, and with Russia wavering, the stage was set for a compromise that favoured the like-minded position. Under a proposal drafted by Singapore, the Security Council could require the court to defer an investigation or prosecution for renewable twelve-month periods, provided none of the permanent members vetoed such an action. This proposal addressed in significant part the concern that a court acting wholly independently of the Security Council might interfere with the latter's efforts to resolve a conflict, but of course did nothing to address the underlying concern of the United States, China, and others that the court might prosecute their nationals. Nonetheless, the proposal attracted such broad support that the United States felt compelled to signal its willingness to accept the 'Singapore option'. With that issue resolved, the focus of debate shifted to other issues.

### *The* proprio motu *prosecutor*

The 1994 ILC draft provided that only the Security Council or individual states party to the court's statute (or in the case of genocide, party to the Genocide Convention), could trigger the court's exercise of jurisdiction over a covered crime. By authorising the prosecutor to initiate investigations and prosecutions *proprio motu*, that is, on his or her own authority, the drafters of the Rome treaty dramatically transformed the ILC vision of the court. States have been notoriously reluctant to utilise existing state complaint procedures to bring other states in front of treaty bodies on human rights charges; prosecutors are unlikely to exhibit any such

[14] Wedgwood, 'Fiddling in Rome', 21.

reluctance. States must consider the diplomatic and political repercussions of referring situations for prosecution; they must also consider the likelihood of retaliatory complaints. Prosecutors are largely free of such constraints, though even prosecutors must consider the possible implications of alienating powerful states whose political or financial support is essential to the viability of the court.

The NGO community, almost unanimously convinced that an independent prosecutor was essential to a strong and effective court, launched a vigorous campaign to enhance the prosecutor's authority. They argued, and eventually convinced the like-minded group, that both the Security Council and individual states would employ inappropriate political criteria in determining which situations to refer to the court. The permanent members of the Council would use the veto to protect themselves and their allies; individual states would be reluctant to act at all, or would do so only against political opponents. The result would be selective justice and the discrediting of the court as a legal institution. They pointed out that the prosecutor of the two existing war crimes tribunals had *proprio motu* powers, and urged that the ICC prosecutor be given the same.

Opponents of the *proprio motu* prosecutor also argued for the primacy of law over politics, even though they reached the opposite conclusion on the prosecutor's role. The United States in particular warned that the prosecutor, despite various checks on his or her authority built into the statute, would ultimately be unaccountable to any executive or legislative authority. This gave rise, in more colourful terms, to the fear of a 'global Ken Starr', or as some suggested, 'an overzealous or politically motivated prosecutor targeting, unfairly or in bad faith, highly sensitive political situations'.[15] Further, the United States suggested that the prosecutor would be overwhelmed by complaints from thousands of victims and hundreds of NGOs, and that he or she would have to set priorities, disappointing many and giving rise to concerns of politicisation.[16] To the extent that the prosecutor chose to act independently of states and the Security Council, he or she would lack the support necessary for effective prosecutions.

The disagreement reflected both a divergence of interests and a related divergence in conceptions about the appropriate role of international

---

[15] Silvia A. Fernández de Gurmendi, 'The Role of the International Prosecutor', in Roy S. Lee (ed.), *The International Criminal Court: The Making of the Rome Statute* (The Hague and London: Kluwer Law International, 1999), p. 181.
[16] Fernández de Gurmendi, 'The Role of the International Prosecutor', p. 181.

law and institutions. The like-minded group wanted to give the prosecutor authority comparable to that exercised by national prosecutors in liberal democratic states. The United States thought such authority only made sense in the context of effective national legal systems, in which the prosecutor could be supervised by a higher executive authority and ultimately held accountable to a legislature and a larger body politic. The like-minded states responded that the safeguards in the statute, including the provisions for the selection and supervision of the prosecutor by a pre-trial chamber of the court, and those relating to the authority of the state parties to remove a prosecutor for malfeasance, rendered the risk of politicised prosecutions acceptable.

Of course, in traditional national interest terms, the risk of politicised prosecutions was substantially lower for most if not all of the like-minded states than it was for the United States. The United States is a far more likely target for complaint than the like-minded states most strongly supporting the independent prosecutor. In the end, however, the US position was largely rejected.

### Jurisdiction and state consent

Under the ILC 1994 draft statute, states could ratify the treaty creating the court without necessarily accepting its jurisdiction over particular offences; moreover, consent of both the territorial state and the custodial state was necessary for the court to exercise its jurisdiction, except in cases of Security Council referral. This approach was criticised in ensuing negotiations on the ground that it would render the court incapable of pursuing most international crimes in the absence of a Security Council referral. More broadly, it was viewed as incompatible with the notion of an effective and legitimate court which could operate in the international interest, free of political control or manipulation. From the outset, many states expressed concern that the ILC approach 'would set aside the interests of the international community – which could not be reduced to the sum total of the States forming part of it – and would prevent the court from playing its role as the guardian of the international public order'.[17]

Germany led an effort to abandon state consent altogether and to adopt universal jurisdiction as the standard. The Germans argued that

---

[17] Report of the Ad Hoc Committee on the Establishment of An International Criminal Court, reprinted in Cherif Bassiouni (compiler), *The Statute of the International Criminal Court: A Documentary History* (Ardsley, NY: Transnational Publishers, 1998), p. 631.

existing international law, most notably the Geneva Conventions, conferred on all states not only the right but the obligation to prosecute individuals responsible for genocide, crimes against humanity, and war crimes. In their view, the power held by states individually should also be held by the court as the embodiment of the state parties' collective prosecutorial authority; put another way, the Germans and others argued that states may do together whatever any one of them can do individually. If adopted, the German proposal would have permitted the court to prosecute genocide, crimes against humanity, war crimes, and, eventually, aggression, wherever committed and without regard to the nationality of the accused.

Most states were not prepared to move quite so far away from a state-consent model. The United States insisted that the state of the accused's nationality should have to consent to any prosecution, at least with respect to states that did not ratify the treaty. This position, if it had prevailed, would have barred any prosecution of US nationals, but would likewise have barred any prosecution of other non-party states' nationals absent their government's consent or a Security Council referral. For most states, this position was a non-starter; it would gut the goal of a court able to prosecute serious crimes even in cases of Security Council deadlock.

As the negotiations proceeded, most states settled on a variant of an earlier South Korean proposal: the court could exercise its jurisdiction if *either* the territorial state *or* the state of the accused's nationality consented. The United States insisted that the consent of *both* states should be required. For the United States, this was a make-or-break issue. At the conference, Ambassador David Scheffer, head of the US delegation, warned other delegates that if the United States did not prevail on this point, it would have to consider 'actively opposing' the court.

The United States openly acknowledged its underlying concerns, but attempted to frame them in a way that would resonate with states committed to what they saw as the international public interest. The United States reminded other delegations that it is the only country with the capacity to project substantial military power anywhere in the world at short notice, and that it is and will be called upon to do so to stop precisely the kinds of atrocities the court is designed to adjudicate. At the same time, because it is the sole remaining superpower, and because it occasionally uses force to protect its interests and the interests of its allies, the United States presents an attractive target to many states. Exposing the United States to the risk of unwarranted and politicised prosecutions before an international tribunal might constrain the United States from carrying out precisely the kinds of humanitarian and peace-keeping missions that the countries most strongly supporting the ICC presumably wanted. Further, the United States pointed out that a court operating without at least tacit US support would find it difficult to command the perceived legitimacy and the financial, intelligence, and logistical support necessary for effective operation.

The influence of these explicitly political arguments was modest. Many delegates, especially among the like-minded, very much wanted US support for the court and worried that US opposition would gravely undermine it. But they viewed the price of US support as simply too high. Moreover, few states were much impressed with arguments pertaining to the special position of the United States, since many felt their own soldiers would be as much at risk as those of the United States. And some states, especially those in the developing world, were openly hostile to what they saw as unjustified US exceptionalism.

Recognising the limited appeal of its exceptionalist claims, the United States emphasised a legal argument that, if accepted, should have decided the issue, but which, if accepted, carried some risk to US law enforcement interests in other contexts.[18] Specifically, the United States contended that treaty-based attempts to confer jurisdiction over the nationals of non-party states violated a well-established rule of international law, codified in the Vienna Convention on treaties, that treaties bind only the parties to them. In responding to this argument, no state challenged the general proposition that treaties do not bind non-parties. This starting point was taken as a given. Instead, disagreement centred on whether this uncontested rule could properly be applied in this case. Proponents of the court denied that the treaty purported to bind non-consenting states. Strictly speaking, they were correct: non-parties are not subject to the obligations imposed on parties; they do not, for example, have any duty to co-operate with the court by providing requested information or surrendering suspects for prosecution.

How, then, can the treaty confer the authority on the court to prosecute nationals of non-party states if those states are not bound by the treaty? The answer turns on differing views as to the source of the court's jurisdiction. Proponents of the treaty argue that under existing international law, the states on whose territory the crime is committed have the

[18] See Michael P. Scharf, 'The ICC's Jurisdiction over the Nationals of Non-Party States: A Critique of the US Position', *Law and Contemporary Problems* 64: 1 (2001), 103.

authority to prosecute it themselves *and* they have the authority to delegate their right to prosecute to an international tribunal by ratifying the treaty creating it or by consenting ad hoc to its exercise of jurisdiction. Ambassador Scheffer conceded that 'a state may delegate its territorial jurisdiction to another state in particular cases with the consent of the state of nationality of the defendants', but argued that 'there seem to be no precedents for delegating territorial jurisdiction to another state when the defendant is a national of a third state in the absence of consent by that state of nationality'.[19]

Treaty supporters rejected this argument, noting that many states, including the United States, are parties to treaties on terrorism, torture, hijacking, and similar crimes that confer jurisdiction on state parties without regard to whether the state of the accused's nationality consents. As Scheffer observes, however, it does not automatically follow that because states can confer jurisdiction on each other, they can do so on an international tribunal. As a practical matter, states (especially powerful states) might be comfortable with one form of delegation and not the other, since the bilateral negotiations between states possible in the former instance are not possible in the latter. As Lt. Col. William Lietzau, a member of the US delegation in Rome, has observed, when a state accepts a delegation of authority to prosecute, it 'must accept responsibility for the exercise of jurisdiction, and may ultimately be held accountable for it' by other states.[20] That check on the exercise of delegated authority is largely absent in an international tribunal, which operates outside the realm of ongoing diplomatic and political interaction that characterises the relations between states.

In essence, then, the dispute was framed as a disagreement over competing legal values. For the United States, the dominant value was accountability, without which the exercise of judicial power is illegitimate. For the like-minded group and their supporters, the dominant values were independence and impartiality. Each side claimed the legal high ground.

Whatever the ultimate merits of the US delegation argument, it did not appear to sway any votes. Given the legalistic nature of the entire enterprise of creating the court, it seems likely that the issue of jurisdiction over nationals of non-party states would never even have arisen

---

[19] David Scheffer, 'International Criminal Court: The Challenge of Jurisdiction', Address to the Annual Meeting of the American Society of International Law, 26 March 1999, <www.state.gov/www/policy_remarks/1999/990326_scheffer_icc.html>.
[20] Lietzau, 'International Criminal Law After Rome', 135.

had it been clearly impermissible under existing international law. But as things stood, the legal argument advanced by the United States was simply too uncertain to be persuasive, much less controlling. The outcome therefore mirrored the outcome on the closely related issue of the role of the Security Council, for essentially the same reasons.

## Complementarity and its limits

Proponents of the Rome treaty frequently point to the numerous safeguards it contains to prevent the politicised prosecutions the United States has warned against. Foremost among these is complementarity, the requirement that the ICC defer to national court investigations and prosecutions. To protect the lone US soldier or peacekeeper wrongly accused of a war crime, the United States need only investigate the accusation itself, in good faith.

But the real issue is not the isolated soldier wrongly accused, or even the aberrant soldier who runs amok and commits a massacre. Rather, as Lietzau points out, '[t]he concern is use of the court as a tool for influencing US foreign policy by holding at risk those who implement that policy'.[21] This concern exists despite complementarity because complementarity does not protect a state that engages in a particular action (for example, a military strike against a particular target) that the state reasonably believes is legitimate under international humanitarian law but that the court or the prosecutor believes is not legitimate.

Any military conflict of significant magnitude is likely to generate instances in which observers after the fact disagree on the propriety of a particular target, the necessity of a particular use of force, the legal status of a particular weapon, or the proportionality of a particular action. As Professor Ruth Wedgwood has observed, the United States trains its military personnel to be 'forward leaning', to anticipate threats and to respond 'when they perceive a hostile act or a demonstration of hostile intent'.[22] But what the United States views as a necessary and proportionate use of force, others might view as aggression or war crimes. Similarly, reasonable observers may disagree on the legitimacy of particular targets. In Kosovo, for example, the United States used air strikes to disable the Serbian electrical grid, on the theory that it supported Serbia's integrated air defences. Some critics saw this as an unjustified attack on

[21] Lietzau, 'International Criminal Law After Rome', 136.
[22] Ruth Wedgwood, 'Speech Three: Improve the International Criminal Court', in Alton Frye (ed.), *Toward an International Criminal Court?: Three Options Presented as Presidential Speeches* (New York: Council on Foreign Relations, 1999), p. 67.

protected civilian infrastructure. In these and similar cases, the United States could not meet the requirements of complementarity. It could not investigate or prosecute in good faith because it would not consider the action at issue to be a violation of the applicable law, even if proven.

From the standpoint of the United States, the problem is not simply that an individual soldier might be exposed to prosecution as a result, or even that his or her superiors might be. The problem is that the threat or initiation of such prosecutions might constrain future US decision-making concerning both the circumstances and the manner in which the United States uses military power.

This concern is reflected in the compromise proposal on jurisdiction floated by the United States in the final weeks of the conference. The United States suggested then that conduct which the state involved is prepared to acknowledge as 'official' should be excluded from the court's jurisdiction. Since few states would be prepared to describe a massacre or other atrocity as 'official' action, this modification would not preclude prosecution of the deliberate atrocities the court is supposed to address. But it would prevent prosecutions of soldiers or their superiors over what Wedgwood describes as 'good faith differences in military doctrine'.[23]

The US effort to exclude 'official actions' from the scope of the Court's effective jurisdiction reflects the philosophy that has consistently animated US positions since the United States first announced its support for the ICC project in 1995. The United States views the ICC as an institution that should exercise coercive authority over individuals, but not states. To the extent it exercises such authority over states, even indirectly by holding nationals accountable for official actions, it usurps authority that should be left to political institutions such as the UN Security Council. Other states, however, were only too happy to shift decision-making authority away from the political institution of the Security Council to what they saw as the relatively apolitical institution of the court.

The United States might nonetheless have prevailed with its official action proposal had it come considerably earlier in the negotiations. As it was, however, the US proposal was too little, too late. Once again, most states objected to 'widening the net' in a way that would let governments less scrupulous about characterising particular actions as official preclude prosecutions of potential indictees.

[23] Wedgwood, 'Speech Three', pp. 67–8.

By design, complementarity places primary responsibility for the prosecution of atrocities on national legal systems. This is simultaneously a recognition of the limits – political, financial, and logistical – of an international tribunal and a means to bolster its influence and effectiveness. No one thinks the ICC can prosecute more than a tiny fraction of the crimes that will fall within its jurisdiction. But the prospect of an ICC prosecution may induce national courts to undertake such prosecutions themselves. To the extent that this occurs, international law, as embodied in the ICC statute, will further a political goal – an increase in national court prosecutions – through the mechanism of domestic law. Many signatories to the ICC treaty have already modified their domestic law (including, in some cases, their constitutions) to ensure that they can undertake prosecutions of the offences covered by the court's statute.

For the United States, complementarity was an important step in the right direction of striking an appropriate balance between international and national legal systems. But for reasons considered more fully below, it did not go far enough.

### Systemic arguments

As noted earlier, the United States entered the Rome negotiations committed to the goal of establishing an international criminal court. But the US differed with most other states on the appropriate role of international criminal law and an international criminal court in a decentralised international legal order.

### The nature of international law and legal institutions

Critics of the ICC, in the US Congress and elsewhere, often adopt a quasi-realist approach to international law and institutions. John Bolton, former Assistant Secretary of State for International Organization Affairs in the Bush Administration, and Under-Secretary of State in the current Bush Administration, argues that equating international law with national law 'is naive, often irrelevant to the reality of international relations, and in many instances simply dangerous. It mistakes the language of law for the underlying concepts and structures that actually permit legal systems to function, and it seriously misapprehends what "law" can realistically do in the international system.'[24] Bolton goes on to argue that '"law" is a system of rules that regulates relations among

---

[24] John Bolton, 'Speech Two: Reject and Oppose the International Criminal Court', in Frye (ed.), *Toward an International Criminal Court?*, p. 41.

176

individuals and associations, and between them and sources of legitimate coercive authority that can enforce compliance with the rules'. For Bolton, 'real law in a free society' requires a framework 'that defines government authority and thus limits it, preventing arbitrary power'; it also requires 'political accountability through democratic popular controls over the creation, interpretation, and enforcement of the laws' as prerequisites for 'three key structures: authoritative and identifiable sources of the law for resolving conflicts and disputes; methods and procedures for declaring and changing the law; and the mechanisms of law interpretation, enforcement, execution, and compliance'. In Bolton's view, '[i]n international law, essentially none of this exists'. As a consequence, he views the proposed court as an unaccountable and undemocratic institution likely to act in a politicised way and to infringe on US sovereignty.[25]

Moreover, Bolton contends that the court should not (and cannot) have 'sufficient authority in the real world' to carry out its mission of deterring atrocities through international justice. In his view, 'it would be a grave error to try to transform matters of international power into matters of law'. Among other things, he notes the danger (also cited by the US delegation in Rome) that opportunistic invocations of the court's jurisdiction could impede efforts to resolve protracted conflicts through negotiated settlements entailing amnesty for perpetrators of crimes within the court's jurisdiction.

Bolton's argument conflates several points, which for analytical purposes should be kept separate. The argument that international law is not really law because it lacks the structures of national legal systems and cannot be enforced amounts to the standard critique of international law as law. But as H. L. A. Hart, among others, has shown, this critique is misplaced in several important respects. First, the presence or absence of the institutions commonly associated with domestic legal systems – a legislature, courts with compulsory jurisdiction, and centrally organised sanctions – cannot determine whether a particular system of rules constitutes law. Even in national legal systems, courts and legislatures are created by and derive their authority from law; accordingly, the presence or absence of bodies resembling domestic legislatures and courts cannot itself be the hallmark of law.

Second, the Austinian view that law may be reduced to orders backed by threats is too simplistic. As Hart has suggested, orders backed by threats may be issued by anyone with the power to do so, but no one

---

[25] Bolton, 'Speech Two', p. 41.

would consider the orders of a gunman to amount to law. Moreover, even in national legal systems, we do not automatically deny the title of law to rules that cannot effectively be enforced by centralised sanctions (for example, constitutional law).

Third, though the differences between international and municipal law that Bolton alludes to are real and substantially affect the form and evolution of international law, nonetheless, states and other international actors routinely speak of international legal rules as obligatory; experience pressure to conform to those rules and criticise those who deviate from them; and in cases of breach, deny not the validity of the rules but the appropriate interpretation of the rules and the underlying facts. For Hart, this perception of international law as law by those operating within the system is the best evidence that the title of law is in fact warranted, even if it lacks important features common to national legal systems.[26]

Certainly, the delegates to the Rome conference all assumed that they were working within a legal system to create a legal institution – a court – that would apply binding law regulating the conduct of individuals. That the law at issue did not emerge through a classic legislative process, and would depend on the at best uncertain co-operation of states for its enforcement, did not dissuade them from considering the creation of the ICC to be a law-based enterprise.

Bolton's concerns about accountability have less to do with whether international law is law than with its proper function in the international system. In this regard, Bolton has two principal points. First, he fears that the court itself (and the prosecutor in particular) will not be subject to the checks and balances of a national legal system, thus giving rise to politicised prosecutions. Proponents of the court claim that the court and prosecutor are accountable to the Assembly of State Parties, as much or more than courts and prosecutors in national legal systems are accountable to the larger body politic. Whether the Assembly of State Parties will in fact exercise adequate supervision over the court remains to be seen. Experience with the existing war crimes tribunals suggests that there is relatively little risk that the court will run amok. Moreover, if the present ratification trends continue, Western, liberal rule-of-law-states will hold the balance of power in the Assembly of State Parties, with control over the selection, retention, and discipline of the prosecutor.

[26] H. L. A. Hart, *The Concept of Law* (Oxford: Clarendon Press, 1961), p. 209.

As a general matter, however, it is simply harder for many in the United States to place confidence in an independent international institution operating outside of the direct control of an interested body politic than it is for Europeans (who deal with similar institutions within the EU on a daily basis) and others. Moreover, the United States has more to lose from the possible constraining effects of the court than do any of the like-minded states. So for the United States, both identity and interest align to raise questions about accountability and about the limited ability of the United States to influence an independent ICC.

Second, and more important, Bolton and others fear that the ICC represents a dangerous attempt to substitute law for politics in international affairs. In this view, the important decisions regarding the response to the kinds of political crises that give rise to genocide, crimes against humanity, and war crimes will be and must be political. Policy-makers both within and outside of the affected states will have to determine the optimum balance between peace and justice on a case-by-case basis. Whether to grant an amnesty as the price of a peace accord, to rely on a truth commission, or to prosecute offenders are questions that require political answers, which cannot reasonably be determined in advance or entrusted to the discretion of a court with a mandate to prosecute offenders regardless of other considerations.

For the United States, creation of the ICC in its present form represents a deliberate (if minor) shift in the architecture of international society. It transfers coercive authority, even if only slightly, from powerful states and the UN Security Council to an international tribunal which is not really suited to exercise such authority.

Of course, supporters of the ICC have a sharply different vision of the court's proper place. In their view, the purpose of the court is precisely to substitute the rule of law for what they see as the failure of politics. Left to their own devices, states rarely prosecute those responsible for atrocities. The Security Council has established several ad hoc tribunals, but ignored countless other conflicts where tribunals could have been established with equal justification. Where Bolton and others see in the ICC a likelihood of politicised prosecutions, supporters see an opportunity to overcome the barriers to justice posed by politics, understood as the short-term self-interest of states. For court proponents, ad hoc decisions to forgo prosecutions are generally illegitimate, extorted by criminals as the price for surrendering power or ending bloodshed.

Some court supporters acknowledge that, in at least some cases, an insistence on proceeding with prosecutions may prolong a civil war or other conflict. They urge trust in the discretion of the prosecutor regarding which cases to pursue as preferable to trust in the self-interest of states and domestic political elites. On balance, they maintain, a strong international criminal court will help deter the kinds of violence that give rise to the need for consideration of amnesties in the first place.

These competing views of the role of international law and institutions rest on largely untestable assumptions about their likely effectiveness in a system with no single, governing political authority. At the same time, these apparently conflicting views partly overlap. What critics fear is a distorted mirror image of what proponents seek. Both believe that the court has the potential to constrain politics. In other words, both believe that the court can lead governments and individuals to take decisions they would not otherwise make.

Experience with the International Criminal Tribunal for Former Yugoslavia suggests that the ICC will on occasion pursue indictments, evidence, and prosecutions in situations and in ways that may discomfit many of the governments that ratify the ICC statute. As the ICTY's registrar has observed, '[i]f a prosecutor suspects that a crime within his jurisdiction was committed, he must investigate, and, if a case presents itself, he must prosecute'.[27] This is, of course, an overstatement. All prosecutors must exercise prosecutorial discretion in choosing which cases to pursue, and this is especially true of international prosecutors who face serious resource constraints. But the larger point made by the registrar is accurate; the prosecutor's decisions are, or should be, based on legal and institutional criteria that differ at least in significant part from those that national government policy-makers are likely to apply. Thus, international tribunals may pursue indictments when at least some governments fear that doing so will impede peace negotiations or hamper other objectives; they may demand information that governments prefer to keep confidential; and they may publicise failures of co-operation and financial support. Senior ICTY officers frequently press friendly and unfriendly governments for greater support, and while the Office of the Prosecutor took national government concerns into account in deciding, for example, whether and when to indict Slobodan Milosevic, such decisions are ultimately outside the control of the states creating the court. Once established, the institution takes on a life of its own as a legal and political actor.

---

[27] ICTY Press Release, Address by the Registrar of the ICTY, Mr Hans Holthuis, to the Plenary of the Preparatory Commission of the International Criminal Court During its Seventh Session (6 March 2001).

Admittedly, states have responses available to them if they are un-happy with the functioning of the institution they have created. They can, for example, reduce or withhold financial support, logistical assis-tance, intelligence, and other forms of co-operation. But such responses tend to be partial and inconsistent, since different states will have dif-ferent views about the operations of the court.

Overall, the ICC can be expected in at least some instances to pursue cases in which UN politics, left to run their ordinary course, would not yield international prosecutions. Despite much discussion of interna-tional criminal tribunals for Iraq, Cambodia, and Indonesia, opposition from various states, including France, Russia, and China, has so far pre-vented the establishment of such tribunals. The ICC will make it much easier to pursue prosecutions in such cases. Indeed, for many states, rat-ification of the ICC statute may serve as a pre-commitment device. By obligating themselves to support prosecutions now, without reference to any specific country or situation, states can surmount political obstacles that might preclude them from supporting an ad hoc tribunal in partic-ular cases in the future. They will have a ready answer to present to other governments, and to domestic interest groups, who when the time comes might view the prosecutions as unfriendly acts. Thus, by ratifying the ICC statute, governments may lay the groundwork for prosecutions they view as desirable at a greatly reduced political price.

The flipside of this coin, of course, is that prosecutions may also take place in situations that some of those states in the future will regret. This fear is particularly acute for powerful states likely to engage in military interventions abroad, and for states already engaged in – or likely to engage in – internal conflicts in which respect for humanitarian law is rare. Whether this concern is likely to preclude ratification depends on a state's understanding of its own national interest.

## International law and national interest

The ICC has generated a vigorous debate in the United States over how to define the national interest. This debate turns largely on differing perceptions of what the ICC is likely to accomplish. But it also turns, at least in part, on competing perceptions of the role of the United States in international affairs, and the nature and function of international law and institutions.

US critics of the court view it as an institution designed in significant part to place constraints on the exercise of US military power. In their view, US military predominance will increasingly induce adversaries to seek out non-military means of undermining US power, and the court offers one such means. In the worst-case scenario, they fear it will not deter the Slobodan Milosevics and Saddam Husseins of the world from initiating wars or encouraging atrocities, but will constrain United States decision-making on the use of force.[28]

Proponents offer a fourfold response. First, they argue that the United States is unlikely to allow the relatively slight risk of an ICC prosecution to deter it from using force when US interests otherwise require it. They note that the United States used force in Kosovo, even though the International Criminal Tribunal for the Former Yugoslavia had jurisdiction over any war crimes committed there.

Second, they argue that the court will further US interests, narrowly conceived. By deterring gross abuses in the first place, the court will foster domestic and regional stability in war-torn areas, and thus alleviate the need for the United States to employ force in conflicts such as those in Bosnia, Kosovo, and Somalia. When the United States is called upon to respond to such conflicts with force, its ability to generate multilateral support for the actions it undertakes, both initially and in the peacebuilding stage, will be greatly enhanced if the United States is perceived by other states to be operating within a legitimate international legal and political framework.

Third, they argue that the US position on the ICC undermines US interests in building support for international norms and institutions, which disproportionately benefit the United States. As Abram Chayes and Anne-Marie Slaughter observe, all the critical elements of the global economy, including trade, foreign investment, international funds transfers, telecommunications and more, depend on a complex and generally respected international legal framework; similarly, efforts to combat drug trafficking, terrorism, weapons proliferation, and related threats to US national security rely in significant part on international co-operation facilitated by international law.[29] US pursuit of objectives in these and other areas requires the co-operation of other states. By its refusal to support the ICC, the United States undermines support for international law and institutions generally.

[28] See Lietzau, 'International Criminal Law After Rome', 126–9.
[29] Abram Chayes and Anne-Marie Slaughter, 'The ICC and the Future of the Global Legal System', in Sewall and Kaysen (eds.), *The United States and the International Criminal Court*, p. 237.

Fourth, they argue that by opposing its friends and allies on the ICC, the United States undermines its own capacity to lead. As William Nash puts it:

> US absence from the court would be a supremely isolating act. It will underscore US ambivalence about joining in collective efforts and institutions to enhance security, an attitude that, however reasonably presented, weakens the claim of the United States to international leadership. Other nations increasingly question the intentions of a leading power that appears willing to lead exclusively on its own terms. The United States loses leverage and credibility by fueling impressions that its cooperation in international politics requires an exemption from the rules.[30]

In particular, US leadership may be undermined on issues of international security, where multilateral support is becoming ever more important. As internal conflicts proliferate and interstate conflicts dwindle, the utility of traditional military force declines. With growing frequency, the United States relies on non-military measures to achieve objectives requiring coercion. Such measures, which include trade sanctions, flight bans, and restriction on loans from multilateral lending institutions, require the support of other states to be effective. Even when the United States does use force, it usually seeks to work through coalitions to share the burdens, especially for peacekeeping and other non-traditional military interventions. The US isolation on the ICC, which is seen by other states as part of a pattern of US exceptionalism, may hinder US efforts to build support for future foreign policy initiatives.

The force of these arguments is difficult to assess. The United States surely will not allow the threat of an ICC prosecution to prevent it from using force when vital interests are at stake. But the possibility of prosecution may operate more subtly to affect US decisions on military doctrine, stationing of troops, and other matters. The United States might, for example, prefer to base troops in countries that are not party to the ICC, to minimise the risk that soldiers indicted for crimes committed elsewhere might be surrendered to the court. Moreover, the mere possibility of an ICC prosecution of US personnel may offer grounds to oppose peacekeeping and humanitarian missions, particularly for those inclined to oppose them on other grounds. Indeed, the United States has

---

[30] William L. Nash, 'The ICC and the Deployment of US Armed Forces', in Sewall and Kaysen (eds.), *The United States and the International Criminal Court*, p. 162.

already vetoed a resolution extending the mandate for the UN peace-keeping mission in Bosnia, in an effort to compel other states to grant UN peacekeepers immunity from ICC prosecutions.[31]

Arguments about deterrence tend to be even more equivocal. The evidence is inconclusive, turning more on anecdote and intuition than on any careful empirical analysis. Still, it is at least plausible that the ICC will have some deterrent effect; from that standpoint, support for the ICC may further, even if only modestly, important US interests.

The effects of the US stance on the ICC on US leadership capacity are also uncertain. Certainly, the participants in the Rome negotiations, including members of the US delegation, pointed to the perception of US exceptionalism as an impediment to US efforts to lead. Indeed, some delegates appeared to oppose many US proposals simply because they were made by the United States. This reaction, exacerbated by the US rejection of the Kyoto treaty on global warming, by the US position in the landmines treaty negotiations, and by similar instances of perceived US exceptionalism, clearly poses a problem for the United States. But it is difficult to know how serious the problem is, or how exactly the United States should seek to address it.

While resentment of the United States may hinder US efforts to generate support for its positions on some issues, it is unclear whether US leadership on core security issues will be significantly impaired. Resentment of the United States did not prevent the United States from assembling the original Gulf War coalition. Similarly, the US position on the ICC does not seem to have had any measurable influence on US leadership in Kosovo or Afghanistan. But perceptions of US exceptionalism may well have undermined more recent US efforts to generate support for its decision to disarm Iraq by force.

In any event, the problem may to some extent be unavoidable. US military, economic, and political predominance is certain to generate some resentment, whether or not the United States seeks special treatment in international fora. To the extent that US exceptionalism in treaty negotiations and international fora exacerbates the problem, the appropriate solution is not so obvious as critics of the US position on the ICC seem to believe. In some instances, obdurate insistence on its position may lead other states to proceed without the United States and yield a worse result from the US perspective than the United States could have achieved

---

[31] In a compromise, Security Council Resolution 1422, adopted in the summer of 2002, requests the ICC to defer for one year (with the possibility of renewal), any ICC investigations of the acts of UN peacekeepers who are nationals of non-party states.

by exhibiting a greater willingness to accommodate other states' views. The ICC is one such case: the United States might well have achieved a better outcome by exhibiting greater flexibility early in the negotiations.

But this stems in part from the unusual character of the ICC treaty. It applies to the nationals of non-party states. As a result, the possibility that the ICC will adversely affect US decision-making exists even though the United States is not a party to the treaty; indeed, the potential impact on non-parties may be greater than on parties, who can opt out of the court's jurisdiction over war crimes for seven years, and who can opt out of amendments adding new crimes to the court's jurisdiction.

Most treaties do not present the same kind of challenge as the ICC. When the United States refused to ratify the Ottawa landmines treaty, for example, it did not face the prospect of being indirectly bound through legal rules governing the conduct of its nationals. As a legal matter, the United States remains free to use anti-personnel landmines in Korea and elsewhere.[32] While the outcome of the landmines negotiations placed pressure on the United States to modify its policies, the United States could, by refusing to ratify, insulate itself from the direct effects of the treaty.

In other cases, the US refusal to accommodate other states in treaty negotiations may ultimately yield outcomes more closely in line with US interests than a treaty reached through concessions to the majority. The US refusal to accept majority preferences in the negotiation of the law of the sea treaty resulted, years later, in modifications to that treaty favourable to the United States.

As a general matter, the United States does have an interest in avoiding repetitions of the outcomes of the landmines and ICC negotiations. It does not want to encourage other states to work around it in multilateral fora. At the same time, the United States does not want to purchase a purely nominal leadership at the cost of going along with treaty provisions it finds problematic, nor does it want to suggest that there are no costs to proceeding over US objections. Some in the Bush Administration and in Congress think the solution is to oppose the ICC with such vigour that the court is crippled at birth, thus demonstrating the folly of proceeding without the United States.[33] In keeping with this approach,

---

[32] Because US allies are bound by the convention, however, the United States faces practical and political constraints on the use of landmines in combined operations.

[33] The American Service Members Protection Act, adopted in August 2002, precludes any US government co-operation with the ICC, prohibits military aid to states that ratify the ICC statute, with exceptions for NATO members and 'major non-NATO allies',

the United States launched a campaign to secure bilateral 'Article 98' agreements precluding the parties from surrendering each other's nationals to the court. As of March 2003, the United States had entered into such agreements with twenty-four states.

This approach, which the Clinton Administration opposed, seems sure to backfire. Instead, the United States needs to balance its treaty-specific concerns with more general concerns over its ability to lead; more specifically, it needs to factor the systemic issues into its decision-making process more fully and explicitly than it has in the past, even if the result of that altered calculus varies from case to case.

A good example is the recently completed Optional Protocol to the Convention on the Rights of the Child on Involvement of Children in Armed Conflict.[34] The evolving international consensus was that states should not allow anyone under eighteen to join the armed forces or to participate in hostilities. The United States has long set seventeen as the age for recruitment and has resisted formally excluding seventeen-year-olds from hostilities, for reasons having to do with recruitment practices in high schools and force readiness requirements. When the US position encountered broad resistance from other negotiating states, the United States, having learned from the landmines and ICC negotiations, moved in a timely way to offer a compromise: exclude those under eighteen from participation in hostilities but permit recruitment of seventeen-year-olds. This compromise yielded an agreement that the United States could join, even though it meant changing an important US military practice in order to conform to an international human rights instrument. It also meant that the United States could preserve its larger interests in fostering multilateral co-operation and strengthening its human rights credentials.

## Conclusion

The United States conceives of itself, in Madeleine Albright's words, as the 'indispensable nation'. By virtue of its political, military, and economic pre-eminence, the United States can, does, and should assume

and restricts US participation in UN peacekeeping operations. But the Act includes broad presidential waiver provisions.
[34] Optional Protocol on the Involvement of Children in Armed Conflict, UN Doc. A/54/L.84 (New York: United Nations, May 2000). The following discussion of the child soldiers issue draws in significant part from Eric Schwartz, 'The United States and the International Criminal Court: The Case for Dextrous Multilateralism', *University of Chicago Journal of International Law* 4: 223 (2003).

unique global responsibilities. US participation, and sometimes US leadership, is often essential to the management of global problems. As a result, the United States tends to assume that it should receive unique accommodations in multilateral treaty negotiations when its interests suggest a course of action at variance with the preferences of its allies. On many important issues, such as the Kyoto Protocol, the United States appears ready to continue to forge its own path, even if doing so alienates many of its friends.

This approach has its advantages, and may be unavoidable when US interests diverge too sharply from those of other states. It also has its limitations. While other states cannot simply work around the United States on issues such as global warming, they can work around the United States in other areas, and the more the United States is seen externally as an overbearing or unreliable partner, the more other states are likely to try to work around it.

In Rome, the delegates effectively legislated for all states, even non-consenting states, by establishing legal rules applicable to all persons, including nationals of non-parties. The lack of a central legislature has long been central to the critique of international law as law. The quasi-legislative process adopted in Rome partly answers that critique, but at the cost of alienating the powerful states with the most to lose from the emergence of such a process. For the United States in particular, Rome represents a relatively unusual form of international law-making, in which other states, acting without US consent, can fashion an international institution and international legal rules that could constrain US power.

US critics objected to the Rome process, and to the landmines convention process before it, in part because they proceeded on the basis of one state, one vote. Formally, at least, this approach to international law-making adheres to the principle of sovereign equality. So long as states can exclude themselves from the application of the treaty by the simple act of withholding ratification, they have little reason to complain. But when the treaty effectively governs the actions of non-party states, whether through application to their nationals or through the generation of customary international law, the situation changes. Issues of representation arise that are not amenable to a one-state, one-vote formula.

For some, the simple majoritarianism of the Rome process was illegitimate. It represents an effort to shift some decision-making on peace and security issues from the Security Council, where membership and veto power rest on recognition of historical power differentials, to a forum in which the United States, though highly influential, ultimately casts just one of the many votes to be counted. In some fora, in Europe in particular, states are experimenting with qualified majorities. In the absence of a qualified majority voting process, negotiations such as those in Rome will continue to pose a problem for the United States and others with interests that diverge from majority positions. In such situations, the United States would do well to look to the child soldier negotiations as a model.

Rather than pursue an aggressive unilateralism, it should work hard to generate compromise solutions. In the context of the ICC, this means that the United States should adopt a 'good neighbour' policy. It should not oppose the institution, as it is now doing, but should continue to pursue its interests by contributing to ongoing discussions, in keeping with the prior Administration's policy. The United States may be affected significantly by the resolution of still outstanding issues, most notably the definition of the crime of aggression. Active opposition would only exacerbate perceptions of US exceptionalism, and spur heightened efforts to work around the United States on the ICC and on other issues. Instead, consistent with its own history of support for international criminal prosecutions, the United States should carve out a role for itself as a principled but reasonable observer of the court, ready to support it as appropriate, and ready to oppose any inappropriate exercise of jurisdiction, if necessary.

# 8    The Kosovo bombing campaign

*Nicholas J. Wheeler*[1]

In the period between March and June 1999, the North Atlantic Treaty Organisation (NATO) waged a bombing campaign against the Federal Republic of Yugoslavia (FRY). The war began with the suppression of air defence systems followed by attacks against police, military, and paramilitary forces in Kosovo and southern Serbia responsible for the ethnic cleansing of Kosovar Albanians. When this failed to bring Slobodan Milosevic to the bargaining table, NATO escalated the air campaign to strategic targets inside Yugoslavia, including the targeting of dual-use civilian infrastructure. This aroused considerable opposition from human rights NGOs, and sections of public opinion in NATO countries, especially Germany, Italy, and Greece. The Alliance was accused of placing civilians at unnecessary risk, and of violating that body of international humanitarian law pertaining to the protection of non-combatants in armed conflict (hereafter IHL or the laws of war). The Yugoslav government claimed that the bombing killed 2,000 civilians, but most commentators accept the conclusion of a detailed investigation by Human Rights Watch (HRW) that put the figure nearer 500.[2]

NATO's compliance with the laws of war represents an important case for exploring how far law influences the conduct of military operations. Recent studies by theorists in the disciplines of international relations and international law have identified a significant role for legal rules in

[1] This chapter benefited considerably from the comments of the contributors to the workshop on the politics of international law held at the Australian National University, Canberra, November 2000. I would like to thank Alex Bellamy, Michael Byers, Anne Harris, Andrew Linklater, Chris Reus-Smit, Gerry Simpson, and Paul Keal for their comments on earlier versions of this chapter.
[2] Human Rights Watch, 'Civilian Deaths in the NATO Air Campaign', <www.hrw.org/reports/2000/nato/>, accessed 11 January 2000.

inhibiting the exercise of power.[3] However, this research has stopped short of examining military security issues, especially in relation to the use of force.[4] This has allowed the realist claim to stand that law only exerts an influence in relation to secondary or peripheral issues in foreign policy decision-making, and that it is dispensed with if it impinges on the use of force. The realist position is developed more fully below, but I contend that it ignores the importance of justification: states seek to defend their actions by reference to shared rules and norms. Realism acknowledges this use of language but considers that actors can always find a rationale to cover their actions. But language is not infinitely malleable, and governments are often constrained from acting if they cannot find a plausible justification. This notion of law as a constraining factor in policy-making does not imply any physical or material restraint on state action; rather, the idea of constraint employed in this chapter is derived from a constructivist understanding of how actors are embedded within a normative context structured by rules.

A bold attempt to systematically explore the constraining power of law in foreign policy decision-making was Abram Chayes' pathbreaking study of the Cuban missile crisis. What makes this work important is that in focusing on the hard case of nuclear crisis decision-making, Chayes chose an issue where realism would predict that law played only a minor factor in the deliberations of policy-makers. This was the view of Dean Acheson who, as a member of the Executive Committee that President John F. Kennedy set up to manage the stand-off with the Soviet Union, was present at all the key meetings. He reflected after the crisis that, 'The power, position and prestige of the United States had been challenged by another state; and law does not deal with such questions of ultimate power.'[5] As the State Department's legal adviser during the crisis, Chayes was well placed to support or challenge this judgement. His book, published twelve years after the crisis, rejected Acheson's dismissal of the role played by legal factors. Chayes argued that 'the

---

[3] Friedrich V. Kratochwil, *Rules, Norms, and Decisions: On the Conditions of Practical and Legal Reasoning in International Relations and Domestic Affairs* (Cambridge: Cambridge University Press, 1989); Michael Byers, *Custom, Power and the Power of Rules: International Relations and Customary International Law* (Cambridge: Cambridge University Press, 1999); and Stephen J. Toope, 'Emerging Patterns of Governance and International Law', in Michael Byers (ed.), *The Role of Law in International Politics: Essays in International Relations and International Law* (Oxford: Oxford University Press, 2000).
[4] Gerry Simpson, 'The Situation on the International Legal Front: The Power of Rules and the Rule of Power', *European Journal of International Law* 11: 2 (2000), p. 457.
[5] Quoted in Abram Chayes, *The Cuban Missile Crisis* (New York: Oxford University Press, 1974), p. 1.

men responsible for decision did not ignore legal considerations' and that they 'played a part in defining and shaping [the] possibilities'.[6] This chapter assesses how far this conclusion applies to the conduct of NATO's bombing campaign against Yugoslavia. The Alliance was not confronted with an issue of state survival, but its decision to use force did place NATO military personnel at risk, and it exposed civilians in the FRY to considerable danger. What has to be investigated is how far the protection of civilians shaped NATO's targeting policy, and whether there are examples of the Alliance not hitting certain targets because of concerns that this could not be justified under the laws of war.

In focusing on the role of legal factors in NATO's target selection, this chapter rejects the contention that there is an authentic interpretation of the law that state behaviour can be judged against. As I show in the next section, this is the fallacy that underpins what Rosalyn Higgins calls the 'law as rules' approach. This purports to separate law and politics into neat compartments. In keeping with the theme of this volume, I argue that law and politics are mutually constitutive. Once this view is accepted, it becomes easier to disarm the realist criticism that law is merely a rationalisation of state policy, since this assumes that law is a fixed category. There is no single correct way of applying the law in particular cases because it is open to different interpretations, each of which is plausible in its own terms. This problem of legal indeterminacy is well illustrated in the Kosovo case by the different positions taken by NATO on the one hand and the human rights NGOs Amnesty International (AI) and HRW on the other. What makes this dispute so fascinating is that there was agreement on the legal rules that should be applied, but disagreement over the correct application of the rules. How should such controversies be resolved? And how far should we look to politics rather than law to understand why one interpretation is privileged over another? In highlighting these questions, it is important to remember that it was only possible to have a conversation between NATO and its critics because each side shared a common normative language that constituted the givens of the legal discourse.

## Law as rules or process?

The problem of law's indeterminate character does not arise for those who view law as a system of rules that judges apply in particular cases.

---

[6] Chayes, *The Cuban Missile Crisis*, pp. 100–1.

The task of adjudication is to find the appropriate rule and apply it.[7] The assumption underlying this conception of law is that it should be quarantined from the political realm. Judges who allow political or ethical considerations to enter into their legal determinations are failing to exercise their proper function of applying the law. Judges Fitzmaurice and Spender classically articulated this view of international law as an autonomous domain of study in their opinion on the South West Africa cases in 1962. They wrote:

> We are not unmindful of, nor are we insensible to, the various considerations of a non-judicial character, social, humanitarian and other ... but these are matters for the political rather than for the legal arena. They cannot be allowed to deflect us from our duty of reaching a conclusion strictly on the basis of what we believe to be the correct legal view.[8]

Fitzmaurice and Spender are not denying that all legal decisions have political consequences, but they are arguing that these should not be based on particular value choices. Instead, they should be based on judges applying past legal decisions to current cases. Viewing international law as the application of the 'correct legal view' is open to the charge that this makes it unresponsive to changing progressivist values in global society. Higgins argues that existing rules should not be applied regardless of changing normative contexts, and that the relevance of previous cases should be decided in such a way as to promote the moral purposes of international society.[9] Higgins is strongly influenced by the conception of law as a process pioneered in the 1950s and 1960s by Myres McDougal and the so-called 'New Haven' school of policy science. This approach is well encapsulated in the following passage by McDougal, quoted by former State Department legal adviser Abraham D. Sofaer, a strong advocate of this way of thinking when in office:

> It is no more feasible or desirable to attempt to define aggression 'once and for all' than it is so to define any other legal term or concept of international or municipal law. For observers with full awareness of the factors realistically affecting decision, the task of 'defining aggression' is not inappropriately conceived as one of searching for a precise, certain, and final verbal formula that would abolish the discretion of decision-makers and dictate specific decisions. It is rather, in broad

---

[7] Rosalyn Higgins, *Problems and Process: International Law and How We Use it* (Oxford: Clarendon Press, 1994), p. 3.
[8] Quoted in Higgins, *Problems and Process*, p. 4.
[9] Higgins, *Problems and Process*, pp. 4–6.

outline, that of presenting to the focus of attention of the various officials who must reach a decision about the lawfulness or unlawfulness
of coercion, the different variable factors and policies, that in differing
contexts and under community perspectives, rationally bear upon their
decisions; of indicating the interrelations of these factors and context.[10]

The claim of the New Haven school is that the meaning of legal concepts
is open to deliberation in the light of changing world order values. More
specifically, the task of decision-makers is to apply interpretations of the
law that strengthen the value of human dignity which McDougal and
his supporters identify as the standard against which legal decisions
should be made.

A basic criticism of the New Haven school is that it makes law so
flexible that it becomes whatever the policy-maker wants.[11] This is the
standard realist criticism of international law; a tool of convenience employed by policy-makers when it serves their interests and quickly for-
gotten when it challenges them. Realists accept that states find it politically useful to advance a legal justification for their actions, but they
would agree with Sir Arthur Watts, a former legal adviser to the UK
Foreign and Commonwealth Office, that all governments need to do is
'advance a legal justification for their conduct which is not demonstrably
rubbish. Thereafter, political factors can take over, and the international
acceptability or otherwise of a State's conduct can be determined by
considerations of international policy rather than international law.'[12]
Policy-makers view law as just another instrument in the foreign policy
toolbox, and what they look for from their legal advisers are rational-
isations that will enable them to advance a case even when breaching
the existing law. Stephen Krasner depicts this lip service that states pay
to legal rules as 'organised hypocrisy'.[13] Legal factors enter into the
decision-making process but only as instrumental maxims.

Higgins is unimpressed with the realist contention that legal argument is merely post-hoc rationalisation. She argues that, 'Such a comment merely presupposes that there is a "real" international law that
all men of good faith can recognize – that is, rules that can be neutrally

---

[10] Quoted in Abraham D. Sofaer, 'International Law and Kosovo', *Stanford Journal of International Law* 36: 1 (2000), pp. 10–11.
[11] Kratochwil, *Rules, Norms, and Decisions*, pp. 193–200 and Friedrich V. Kratochwil, 'How Do Norms Matter?', in Byers (ed.), *The Role of Law in International Politics*, p. 41.
[12] Arthur Watts, 'The Importance of International Law', in Byers (ed.), *The Role of Law in International Politics*, p. 8.
[13] Stephen D. Krasner, *Sovereignty: Organized Hypocrisy* (Princeton: Princeton University Press, 1999).

applied, regardless of circumstance and context.'[14] Instead, decision-makers are faced with making choices between competing legal claims, each of which could, depending on context, be valid. At the same time, Higgins is keen to emphasise that viewing law as process rather than rules does not mean that every policy position can be justified by reference to the law. She writes: 'There is no escaping the duty that each and every one of us has to test the validity of legal claims. We will each know which are intellectually supportable and which are not.'[15] The law is not infinitely elastic because choices must be made in the light of past decisions, and that 'core predictability that is essential if law is to perform its functions in society'.[16]

A good illustration of what is at stake in the debate over law as rules or process is provided by NATO's decision to go to war against Yugoslavia. For advocates of a rules-based approach, NATO clearly breached specific UN Charter provisions governing the use of force. This action, they would argue, is not 'intellectually supportable' under any conceivable interpretation of international law. From the perspective of law as process the picture looks very different. NATO's use of force was not legal if tested strictly against the specific rules of Article 2(4) and Article 51. However, viewed in terms of the wider moral purposes of the Charter and international law, and taking into account the factual circumstances of the case (the crimes against humanity committed by Serb forces in Kosovo and existing Security Council resolutions), a different verdict emerges. This is the argument of Sofaer who considers that none of the individual factors that could be cited in support of the use of force carries enough weight by itself, but taken together, the action was 'reasonable in the light of the Charter's provisions and purposes'.[17] What is noteworthy about this passage is the way Sofaer uses the language of 'reasonable' and not legal. This begs the question whether this justification is a valid legal claim. Sofaer denies that he is interpreting the law to fit the needs of policy-makers, but it is apparent that his rationale for Kosovo supports the promotion of liberal values and purposes. Little wonder then that Friedrich Kratochwil argues that the New Haven approach is 'in constant danger of becoming just an apology for the policies and preferences of the most powerful'.[18] In a decentralised legal order,

---

[14] Higgins, *Problems and Process*, p. 7.    [15] Ibid.
[16] Higgins, *Problems and Process*, p. 8.
[17] Sofaer, 'International Law and Kosovo', p. 15.
[18] Kratochwil, 'How Do Norms Matter?', p. 42.

each state is free to interpret the law depending upon the interests and values it has at stake. But the brake on this process – and the one referred to by Higgins above – is that if a government wants to be a legitimate participant in the legal discourse, it has to justify its positions in terms of shared standards of legal reasoning. NATO might have failed to win the legal argument over Kosovo, but it certainly recognised the need to justify its conduct in terms of the existing normative framework of international law.

As Christian Reus-Smit argues in chapter 2, once policy-makers take on the burden of legal justification, they enter into a distinctive language and practice of justification in which actions must be justified in terms of established, codified normative precepts. As Quentin Skinner has shown, the range of legitimating arguments that any actor can invoke is limited by the prevailing normative context. Crucially, the agent 'cannot hope to stretch the application of the existing principles indefinitely; correspondingly, [the agent] can only hope to legitimate a restricted range of actions . . . any course of action is inhibited from occurring if it cannot be legitimated'.[19] States are not under any compulsion to offer legal justifications, and it is always open to the powerful to give up legal argument for the exercise of brute force. However, there are very few instances of states openly claiming to be violating international law; instead, governments seek to give an explanation of their actions in terms of its rules and principles. The fidelity that states pay to the law, even when privately they know they are breaking it, reflects the acceptance of legal rules as binding. Lawyers like Louis Henkin, Higgins, and Thomas Franck explain this obligatory character of the law in terms of reciprocity: states refrain from openly violating the law, even though there might be a short-term interest in doing so, because they do not want to jeopardise the structure of international legal obligations.[20]

Even if we agree with Higgins and the constructivists that the language of legal reasoning sets definite limits to what can be justified as lawful, the indeterminacy of this language still leaves considerable space for disagreement, and hence room for political manoeuvre. States can agree on the relevant principles but disagree on what this means

---

[19] Quentin Skinner, 'Some Problems in the Analysis of Political Thought and Action', in James Tully (ed.), *Meaning and Context: Quentin Skinner and his Critics* (Cambridge: Polity Press, 1988), p. 117.
[20] Louis Henkin, *How Nations Behave: Law and Foreign Policy*, 2nd edn (New York: Columbia University Press, 1979), p. 45; Higgins, *Problems and Process*, p. 16; and Thomas M. Franck, *The Power of Legitimacy Among Nations* (New York: Oxford University Press, 1990).

in terms of their application; they can contest the relevant legal principles to be applied; argue over the applicability of particular rules to specific situations; and dispute whether exceptions to these rules can legitimately be invoked. Can law, then, provide any basis for adjudicating between conflicting claims? For advocates of Critical Legal Studies (CLS), the answer is no because the law is contradictory at the level of both rules and the higher-level principles that might be thought to provide a basis for resolving legal disagreements.[21] Consequently, the only basis for deciding disputes is the application of political principles that are disputed. Martti Koskenniemi is a leading advocate of this position in his writings on international law. He considers that:

> Our inherited ideal of a World Order based on the Rule of Law thinly hides from sight the fact that social conflict must still be solved by political means and that even though there may exist a common legal rhetoric among international lawyers, that rhetoric must, *for reasons internal to the ideal itself*, rely on essentially contested – political – principles to justify outcomes to international disputes.[22]

What defines the approach of scholars like Koskenniemi is that there is no rational basis for adjudicating between different legal claims or the principles that underpin them.

This argument is rejected by Higgins who denies that we are only left with politics when deciding between competing claims. She argues contra CLS that there is the 'prospect of rationally choosing' between conflicting legal positions, and that choices remain legal if they are made by authoritative decision-makers relying on 'past decisions, and with available choices being made on the basis of community interests and for the promotion of common values'.[23] This is an appealing response to the radical indeterminacy thesis of CLS, but it places too much faith in common interests as a solution. Gerry Simpson illustrates this problem in relation to Kosovo. On the one hand, NATO's legal justifications rely on the common interest in defending the human rights values enshrined in the UN Charter and customary international law. But those who oppose NATO's action as illegal invoke the common interest in upholding the rules of non-intervention and non-use of force. As Simpson points out, 'One response to the "social complexity" of this dispute would be

---

[21] Kratochwil, 'How Do Norms Matter?', p. 43; and Martti Koskenniemi, 'The Politics of International Law', *European Journal of International Law* 1: 1/2 (1990).
[22] Koskenniemi, 'The Politics of International Law', p. 7.
[23] Higgins, *Problems and Process*, p. 9.

a decision in support of humanitarian intervention. Another might insist on the sanctity of borders. These are legitimate responses but how should we decide which is to be preferred? What higher level interests could possibly prove decisive?'[24] For Koskenniemi, the only way of deciding between these different positions is an appeal to political preferences, but once this move is conceded, what is left of the autonomy of the law?

With regard to NATO's recourse to force, the dispute arises over how to decide between conflicting legal principles – human rights or state sovereignty? In the case of NATO's conduct of the war, the controversy is not over the appropriate legal rules to apply. Instead, disagreement arises over the interpretation of the rules in relation to specific targeting decisions.

## 'Operation Allied Force': a model of civilian protection in war?

Appearing before the Senate Armed Services Committee on 14 October 1999, US Secretary of Defense, William S. Cohen, and General Henry H. Shelton, Chairman of the Joint Chiefs of Staff, described the Kosovo campaign as 'the most precise and lowest-collateral damage air campaign in history'.[25] 'Collateral damage' is a euphemism for the unintended but foreseeable deaths of civilians killed as a consequence of attacks against legitimate military targets. The phrase was born during the Vietnam War to disguise the horror of the civilian carnage wreaked by the US military. Nevertheless, compared to past conflicts, Kosovo was a very clean war in terms of the deaths of non-combatants. There were two essential features of this conflict that helped produce this outcome. The first was technological. A significant number of the munitions were precision guided or 'smart bombs' (35 per cent compared to 8 per cent in the US-led war against Iraq in 1991) and the unprecedented accuracy of these weapons significantly reduced collateral damage. The extent of involvement by military lawyers in the targeting process was the second factor militating against civilian casualties. Compared to the Vietnam War when the lawyers had been excluded from military

---

[24] Simpson, 'The Situation on the International Legal Front', p. 463.
[25] William S. Cohen and Henry H. Shelton, Joint Statement on 'Kosovo After-Action Review', Hearings of Senate Armed Services Committee, 14 October 1999, p. 1.

decisions, this was a striking change in military practice.[26] The increased role of lawyers in the US targeting process had been foreshadowed in the war against Iraq. A decade later, with Kosovo, this process, as Michael Ignatieff points out, was fully complete with lawyers 'integrated into every phase of the air campaign . . . [contributing] assessments of the standard Geneva Convention questions for each target: was the objective military; were the means selected proportional to the objective; and what were the risks of damage to civilians'.[27] The conviction that the Alliance exercised considerable care in its choice of targets led NATO press spokesman Jamie Shea to opine that:

> The principle of discrimination [often referred to as the proportionality rule] is one of the most fundamental components of the law of armed conflict . . . There is absolutely no question that is exactly what NATO is doing; it is distinguishing between civilian and military objectives and in fact I would argue . . . that you cannot find another armed conflict in the history of modern warfare where there has been more discipline and care taken to comply with the laws of war and to make that distinction than in the targeting exercise of the NATO Alliance.[28]

The Alliance's 'discipline and care' in targeting did not prevent some terrible mistakes: the attack against the train which tragically appeared on the Grdelica railroad bridge just after the pilot released his bomb; the killing of seventy-three Albanians when a NATO pilot mistook military trucks for the convoy of tractors that was hit near Djakovica; the bombing of the Chinese embassy on 5 May which NATO planners had incorrectly identified as a military storage facility; and the hitting of the market place and hospital in Nis killing fifteen people two days later. Under the 1977 Additional Protocol I to the 1949 Geneva Convention (hereafter Protocol 1), states are not legally responsible for mistakes provided that military commanders believe themselves to be attacking legitimate military targets, and these strikes are not indiscriminate ones.[29]

---

[26] Michael Ignatieff, *Virtual War: Kosovo and Beyond* (London: Chatto and Windus, 2000), p. 197.
[27] Ignatieff, *Virtual War*, pp. 197–8.
[28] Quoted in Amnesty International, 'NATO/Federal Republic of Yugoslavia: "Collateral Damage" or Unlawful Killings? Violations of the Laws of War by NATO during Operation Allied Force', June 2000, <www.web.amnesty.org/ai.nsf/index/Eur700182000>, accessed on 7 April 2001.
[29] Peter Rowe, 'Memorandum', *Foreign Affairs Committee*, Fourth Report, Kosovo, 23 May 2000, p. 357. Most NATO members have signed this agreement (the exceptions are France, Turkey, and the US). Given the centrality of the latter to Operation Allied Force, applying

Even if political and military officials cannot be held individually responsible for mistakes, should NATO's claim be accepted that it did everything it could to spare civilians from harm? The highest political body of the Alliance, the North Atlantic Council (NAC), approved three phases of targeting. Phase 1 was the suppression of Serb air defence and command and control systems, and the campaign opened with attacks against this target set. Phase 2 included targets in Kosovo and the FRY that supported the ethnic cleansing by police, paramilitary, and military units. These targets included bridges, arms production centres, and military bases, all essential to denying the Serbs the capacity to hurt the Kosovars. Phase 3 was strikes against 'strategic' targets in the FRY. NATO Secretary-General Javier Solana and the Supreme Allied Commander Europe (SACEUR) General Wesley Clark were authorised by the NAC to decide when to move to Phase 2, and this occurred on 29 March 1999. A decision to move to Phase 3 was never formally put to the NAC because of fears that this would create considerable political unease among some member states. Instead, the rest of the campaign fell into what NATO called 'Phase 2-plus'.[30] This was characterised by tactical strikes against military forces in Kosovo, and an increasing emphasis on strategic strikes against targets in the FRY designed to coerce the Milosevic regime into accepting NATO's political demands. As the campaign of denial failed to blunt Serb ethnic cleansing, NATO attacked key aspects of the regime's power base, including a whole range of dual-purpose facilities like power transmission stations, oil refineries, and factories that were alleged to have important military applications. It was the selection of these targets that posed the greatest risk to Serb civilians.[31]

The best argument that can be made in support of NATO being inhibited by legal concerns relates to the targets struck in the opening weeks of the campaign. NATO's graduated strategy of escalation has been strongly criticised by Lt. General Michael C. Short who was the commander of the air campaign during the operation. In testimony to the US Senate Armed Services Committee in October 1999, Short asserted

Protocol 1 might seem a little moot. However, the US has stated that it accepts the relevant standards in the treaty relating to the definition of legitimate military targets.

[30] Ivo H. Daalder and Michael E. O'Hanlon, *Winning Ugly: NATO's War to Save Kosovo* (Washington, DC: Brookings Institution, 2000), p. 118.

[31] For a compelling moral critique of targeting dual-purpose facilities essential to civilian life, see Henry Shue, 'Bombing to Rescue? NATO's 1999 Bombing of Serbia', in Deen K. Chatterjee and Don E. Scheid (eds.), *Ethics and Foreign Intervention* (Cambridge: Cambridge University Press, 2003).

that the key to winning the campaign was not destroying the Yugoslav 3rd army in Kosovo, but the application of decisive force against the centre of power in Belgrade:

> I'd have gone for the head of the snake on the first night. I'd have turned the lights out the first night, I'd have dropped the bridges across the Danube, I'd hit five or six political, military headquarters in downtown Belgrade. Milosevic and his cronies would have waked up [sic] the first morning asking what the hell was going on.[32]

General Klaus Naumann, Chair of NATO's Military Committee, in testimony before the UK House of Commons Defence Committee, expressed strong doubts as to the wisdom of such a strategy in terms of alliance cohesion. He also pointed out that it would have been 'more or less indiscriminate'.[33] Short recognised the absolute legal prohibition against attacking civilians or purely civilian targets, but argued that it was permissible to attack economic assets that contributed to the Serb military machine. This belief reflects US Air Force doctrine that distinguishes between deliberately attacking civilians and striking legitimate dual-purpose targets that will serve to undermine civilian morale.[34] It was the harmful consequences of this strategy for Serb civilians and Alliance solidarity that worried Naumann. According to an interview he gave to the Channel Four documentary 'War in Europe' in February 2000, he recalled a conversation with Solana regarding SACEUR's request to attack the police headquarters and the Ministry of the Interior in downtown Belgrade. Naumann recollected, 'When we saw that some 500 or 600 meters away from the Serb Ministry of the Interior there's a hospital in Belgrade. And when we saw this, I said, "If we hit by sheer accident this hospital, then the war is over".'[35] As is evident from this

---

[32] Michael C. Short, quoted in Andrew F. Tully, 'Yugoslavia: France Faulted for Limiting Targets During Kosovo Conflict', 22 October 1999, <www.rferl.org/nca/features/1999/10/F.RU.991022140550.html>, accessed 28 June 2001.

[33] General Klaus Naumann, examined before the House of Commons Defence Committee, Fourteenth Report: Lessons of Kosovo Volume II. Minutes of Evidence and Appendices, 7 June 2000, p. 148.

[34] Kenneth R. Rizer, 'Bombing Dual-Use Targets: Legal, Ethical, and Doctrinal Perspectives', 1 May 2001, <www.airpower.maxwell.af.mil/airchronicles/cc/Rizer.html>, accessed 15 February 2002; Ward Thomas, *The Ethics of Destruction: Norms and Force in International Relations* (Ithaca: Cornell University Press, 2001), p. 165; and Adam Roberts, 'NATO's "Humanitarian War" over Kosovo', *Survival* 41: 3 (1999).

[35] Klaus Naumann, interview given to Channel Four's 'War in Europe' series, Frontline, 29 February 2000, <www.pbs.org/wgbh/pages/frontline/shows/kosovo/etc/script2.html>, accessed 25 June 2002. The NAC debated Clark's request to launch the first strike of the war against the Yugoslav capital on 30 March, but it did not

comment, senior NATO officials were worried that public opinion in the West would cease to support the air campaign if NATO killed – however unintentionally – significant numbers of civilians.

The Alliance's political leaders shared these concerns. Geoffrey Hoon who replaced George (now Lord) Robertson as UK Secretary of State for Defence after the Kosovo crisis, in reply to a question as to why NATO did not go 'downtown' on the first night, justified the restraint in expressly legal terms. He stated, 'there were clear constraints in international law . . . We did not attack, for example, civilian targets, pure and simple. We did not conduct any kind of terror campaign which has been a feature of aerial warfare in the past.'[36] It might be argued that political concerns about Alliance cohesion and not legal constraints explain NATO's restraint. However, a choice does not have to be made as to the relative weight to be accorded these factors in shaping the internal decision-making process within the Alliance to pursue a campaign of graduated escalation. What is crucial to the argument advanced here is that whatever the strategic rationale for decisively striking Yugoslavia at the beginning of the campaign, NATO members could not plausibly defend this strategy to their domestic publics. The 1949 Geneva Convention and Protocol 1 exist to protect civilians against a repeat of the horrors of strategic bombing during the Second World War. And given NATO's humanitarian justifications for its intervention in Kosovo, it could not be seen to be resorting to means that compromised these. This illustrates that not all law relating to the conduct of armed conflict is radically indeterminate: there are clear legal rules prohibiting 'terror bombing', and as Hoon claimed, this placed a clear limit on targeting.

Further evidence for the operation of these legal and moral restraints is supplied by Short's wish-list of targets that he was prevented from striking by NATO political authorities:

> There were still military and political targets in Belgrade I'd like to have gone after. Clearly, I'd like to have dropped the Rock and Roll bridge [the bridge where Serbs gathered to express popular defiance

---

reach a decision, leaving it to Solana to decide. See Dana Priest, 'The Battle Inside Headquarters: Tension Grew With Divide Over Strategy', 21 September 1999, <www.Washingtonpost.com>, accessed 3 July 2001.

[36] Geoffrey Hoon MP, examined before the House of Commons Defence Committee, Fourteenth Report: Lessons of Kosovo Volume II. Minutes of Evidence and Appendices, 7 June 2000, pp. 169, 174.

of NATO's bombing]. There were other bridges across the Danube that we would like to have dropped. There were economic targets, factories, plant capabilities that had dual capacity for producing military goods and civilian goods . . . There was still part of the power grid that we hadn't hit. Even if we went after everything we wanted, it was incremental, slowly ratcheting up . . . Air war . . . is designed to go after that target set, as rapidly and as violently and with as much lethality as possible. Just stun the enemy. And we never stunned them, from my perspective.[37]

President Jacques Chirac boasted after the war that any bridges left standing on the Danube were down to him. There were cases where a government refused to attack a target because its lawyers would not approve this. However, in most of these situations, that nation's planes stayed on the ground whilst others attacked the target.[38] But in the case of the Danube bridges, France opposed any NATO state targeting them. Nevertheless, it is apparent from Short's comments above that targeting restraints were relaxed as NATO struggled to coerce the Milosevic regime into accepting its terms. The tactical air war against Serb forces in Kosovo had not prevented the mass expulsion of the Kosovar Albanians. And in the absence of the political will within the Alliance to deploy ground forces to Kosovo to contest Serb control of the province, NATO's only military option was to escalate against the political and economic base of the regime. SACEUR was given broad authority to strike what targets he wanted, but he had to get permission from political authorities where there were high risks of civilians being harmed. As NATO took on targets in the highest category of 'collateral damage', there was increasing political controversy within the Alliance over the selection of these.

A good example of this disagreement is the attack on 21 April against the Headquarters of Milosevic's ruling Socialist Party (it also housed the offices of Milosevic's daughter's radio and television station). This target fell within the highest category of 'collateral damage' and Clark sought approval from his political masters to attack it. In a revealing statement of which nations were running the targeting policy, the document estimating a direct casualty figure of 50 to 100 employees and a further 250 civilians who were at potential risk was circulated to

---

[37] Lt. General Michael C. Short, Interview given to Channel Four's 'War in Europe' series, Frontline, <www.pbs.org/wgbh/pages/frontline/shows/kosovo/interviews/short.html>, pp. 15–16, accessed 28 June 2001.
[38] Ignatieff, *Virtual War*, p. 199.

London, Paris and Washington.[39] France initially objected to the strike 'noting that the party headquarters also housed Yugoslav television and radio studios'.[40] The US argued that the headquarters was really an alternative base for the regime, and that it was a legitimate military target. The Chairman of the US Joint Chiefs of Staff recalls that winning this argument 'was tough . . . We kept at it. Persistence wore them down, and I think they eventually saw exactly what we were talking about.'[41] Were French political and military officials persuaded by the force of the arguments mobilised by their US counterparts to accept that this action was in conformity with IHL? Or did non-legal factors such as US political pressure lead France to acquiesce in this choice of target?

The question of what constitutes a legitimate military target under Protocol 1 was raised again two days later when US planes attacked the headquarters of Radio Televisija Srbije (RTS) killing sixteen civilian technicians. Article 52(2) defines these as 'objects which by their nature, location, purpose or use make an effective contribution to military action'.[42] Even if this requirement is satisfied, Article 51(5)(b) prohibits attacks 'which may be expected to cause incidental loss of civilian life, injury to civilians, damage to civilian objects, or a combination thereof, which would be excessive in relation to the concrete and direct military advantage anticipated'.[43] NATO's attack against RTS was justified by NATO spokesman Colonel Konrad Freytag at a press conference the next day in the following terms: 'Our forces struck at the regime's leadership's ability to transmit their version of the news and to transmit their instruction to the troops in the field.'[44] Solana confirmed this latter rationale in a letter written to AI on 17 May 1999. The Secretary-General wrote that it was a legitimate target because the television and radio stations were 'being used as radio relay stations and transmitters to support the activities of the FRY military and special police forces, and therefore they represented legitimate military targets'.[45] According to Ignatieff, the UK's military lawyers were not persuaded that attacking

---

[39] Dana Priest, 'Bombing by Committee: France Balked at NATO Targets', 20 September 1999, <www.Washingtonpost.com>, accessed 3 July 2001; and Tim Judah, *Kosovo: War and Revenge* (London: Yale University Press, 2000).

[40] Priest, 'Bombing by Committee'.      [41] Quoted in Judah, *Kosovo*, p. 268.

[42] Quoted in Adam Roberts and Richard Guelff, *Documents on the Laws of War*, 3rd edn (Oxford: Oxford University Press, 2000), p. 450.

[43] Quoted in Roberts and Guelff, *Documents on the Laws of War*, p. 449.

[44] Quoted in Amnesty International, 'NATO/Federal Republic of Yugoslavia', p. 39.

[45] Letter written to Amnesty International by NATO's Secretary-General, 17 May 1999, quoted in Amnesty International, 'NATO/Federal Republic of Yugoslavia', p. 39.

RTS could be justified under Protocol 1 and its planes remained on the ground.[46] However, the significance of this should not be exaggerated since the UK did not try to veto the US from attacking RTS.

NATO's decision to target key aspects of Milosevic's power structure also involved hitting specific industrial targets that were chosen because they were run by his cronies. Speaking off the record, one NATO officer is reported as saying: 'if you blow up some things near and dear to him – or to somebody close to him – then that could have an effect'.[47] For example, the attacks against the oil and gas industry were publicly justified as choking off the supplies of oil and gas to the 3rd army in Kosovo, but the strikes were also aimed at hurting Dragan Tomic, Director of Yugo Petrol, and a close ally of Milosevic. Similarly, a missile attack on 9 April destroyed the Zastava automotive plants in Kragujevac whose Director, Milan Beko, was a close supporter. Four days earlier NATO had struck a tobacco warehouse and factory in Nis. The reason behind this strike was to hurt Milosevic's son who was a key player in the Yugoslav tobacco industry.[48]

Since the outset of the campaign, Short had wanted to turn the lights out in Belgrade. According to William Arkin, senior US Air Force commanders had argued for the electrical grid to be hit from the outset of the campaign. He quotes one official as saying 'Shutting down electricity . . . along with the distribution elements of POL [petroleum, oil, and lubricants] can impose paralysis on the regime rapidly by stressing power supplies for things like communications systems, air defenses, transportation, TV, and radio.'[49] However, a decision to attack the grid was resisted by NATO governments, especially the French, which worried about the civilian consequences and feared that this would stiffen the resistance of the Serbs.[50] The US had attacked Iraqi power sources during the 1991 war and it is estimated that this resulted in the indirect deaths of as many as 100,000 Iraqi civilians through the loss of power, water and sewage facilities.[51] As Milosevic showed no sign of blinking, there was pressure from the US to strike the grid. The

---

[46] Ignatieff, *Virtual War*, p. 207.
[47] Quoted in E. Schmitt and S. L. Myers, 'NATO Said to Focus Raids on Serb Elite's Property', *New York Times*, 19 April 1999.
[48] Schmitt and Myers, 'NATO Said to Focus Raids on Serb Elite's Property'.
[49] Quoted in William Arkin, 'Smart Bombs, Dumb Targeting?', *Bulletin of the Atomic Scientists* 56: 3 (2000), <www.thebulletin.org/issues/2000/mj00/mj00arkin.html>, accessed 15 June 2001.
[50] Daalder and O'Hanlon, *Winning Ugly*, p. 125.
[51] Thomas, *The Ethics of Destruction*, p. 166.

Americans wanted to strike electrical lines that would have disrupted power supplies for days, but the French opposed this. In the end, it was agreed that the US would use a new specialised CBU-munition that would short out electrical lines but not damage the power transmission stations themselves.[52] According to Dana Priest, French reservations were overcome when the Chairman of the Joint Chiefs 'showed his French counterparts how it would work. He even described what kind of backup electricity would be available to hospitals.'[53] However, as Ward Thomas points out, keeping the power down 'required repeated strikes . . . and such a predictable pattern of sorties against fixed targets was seen as posing an increasing threat to the safety of NATO pilots'.[54] Finally, on 24 May, NATO used heavier munitions and knocked out the five major power transmission stations themselves. This disrupted electricity and water supplies across the country for days. Ignatieff argues that it was 'the single most effective military strike of the campaign . . . Hitting it . . . sent a powerful message to the civilian population. After the grid was destroyed, both the political elite and the people knew that NATO had secured control of the regime's central nervous system.'[55] This was the 'Sunday punch' that Short had wanted from the beginning, and the fact that NATO political leaders had finally consented to it was a sign of their growing desperation to bring the war to a satisfactory end.

There is evidence that the legal advisers at NATO, and in national capitals, were uncomfortable with the decision to attack the power grid. Ignatieff captures the dilemma that confronted NATO leaders:

> The extraordinary fact about the air war was that it was more effective against civilian infrastructure than against forces in the field. The irony here was obvious: the most effective strike of the war was also the most problematic. Hitting the grid meant taking out the power to hospitals, babies' incubators, water-pumping stations. The lawyers made this clear to Clark. As one of them recalled, 'We'd have preferred not to have to take on these targets. But this was the Commander's call.'[56]

The implication is that military considerations were allowed to trump legal ones. But to state it in these terms is to overlook the fact that the law is open to interpretation. Consequently, the question to ask is whether

---

[52] Priest, 'Bombing by Committee'; and Daalder and O'Hanlon, *Winning Ugly*, p. 145.
[53] Priest, 'Bombing by Committee'.   [54] Thomas, *The Ethics of Destruction*, p. 166.
[55] Ignatieff, *Virtual War*, p. 108; and Arkin, 'Smart Bombs, Dumb Targeting?'
[56] Ignatieff, *Virtual War*, p. 108.

NATO was able to furnish a reasonable defence for attacking the grid that was justifiable under Protocol 1. Whatever the difficulties in squaring the laws of war with actions that deprived the civilian population of water and electricity, NATO argued that the power grid was a legitimate military target. Without electricity, the integrated air defence system and command and control networks supporting the Yugoslav army in Kosovo were paralysed.[57] As NATO spokesman Shea stated, 'Command and control or a computer in military hands without electricity simply becomes a mass of metal, wire and plastic.'[58] And in response to the charge that NATO was cutting off vital power supplies to hospitals and other civilian services, it was argued that the Serbs had back-up generators powered by diesel fuel. Shea stressed that it was Milosevic's choice as to whether he used 'his remaining energy resources: on his tanks or on his people'.[59]

Even if it is accepted that the power grid was a legitimate military target, there is the further question as to whether NATO violated the prohibition in Protocol 1 against indiscriminate attacks. It will be recalled that these are defined as strikes 'which may be expected to cause incidental loss of civilian life, injury to civilians, damage to civilian objects, or a combination thereof, which would be excessive in relation to the concrete and direct military advantage anticipated'. NATO's disruption of power supplies might have weakened the Yugoslav 3rd army in Kosovo, but was this gain proportional to the harm inflicted on civilians? The answer to this question turns on whether we focus on the direct or the indirect injury caused by attacks against dual-use targets. The US Air Force argues that attacking a state's electricity plants meets the proportionality requirement because it only counts direct harm.[60] This is an implicit admission that defining the loss of life and injury in indirect terms would render such strikes illegal and illegitimate. As Kenneth R. Rizer of the US Air University acknowledges, 'it might be very difficult to find a concrete and direct military advantage that outweighed the tens of thousands of civilian deaths that might be indirectly caused from loss of electricity'.[61] By interpreting the harm inflicted by strikes against dual-use facilities in such narrow terms, the US Air Force can continue

---

[57] See 'Final Report to the Prosecutor by the Committee Established to Review the NATO Bombing Campaign Against the Federal Republic of Yugoslavia', pp. 24–5, <www.un.org/icty/pressreal/nato061300.htm>, accessed 14 July 2001.
[58] Quoted in M. R. Gordon, 'NATO Air Attacks on Power Plants Pass a Threshold', *New York Times*, 4 May 1999.
[59] Quoted in Gordon, 'NATO Air Attacks on Power Plants'.
[60] Rizer, 'Bombing Dual-Use Targets'.    [61] Ibid.

to attack those targets whose destruction it views as central to its core doctrinal goal of 'indirectly targeting civilian morale'.[62] In the words of the Air Force Basic Doctrine Document, 'Strategic attack objectives often include producing effects to demoralize the enemy's leadership, military forces, and population, thus affecting an adversary's capability to continue the conflict.'[63] What is evident from this discussion is the scope for conflicting judgements as to what is permitted under Protocol 1 in terms of dual-use targeting. How, then, should we decide between these divergent legal interpretations?

## Resolving law's indeterminacy over Kosovo?

The fundamental legal issue at stake over NATO's bombing campaign is whether the Alliance acted within the permissible limits of Protocol 1. There was no disagreement among the contending actors as to what the appropriate legal rules were; nor was there any attempt to deny the binding character of these. The controversy existed over what counted as a legitimate target and whether the proportionality rule had been satisfied. In its legal interpretation of the case, HRW concluded that whilst there was no evidence of war crimes, 'NATO [had] violated international humanitarian law.'[64] The Executive Director of the organisation, Kenneth Roth, in a letter to *The Guardian* on 1 December 2000, set out his view on the reasoning behind NATO's targeting strategy:

> NATO bombed the civilian infrastructure not because it was making a significant contribution to the Yugoslav military effort but because its destruction would squeeze Serb civilians to put pressure on Milošević to withdraw from Kosovo. Using military force in this fashion against civilians would violate the 'principle of distinction' – a fundamental principle of international humanitarian law – which requires military force to be used only against military targets, not against civilians or civilian objects.[65]

Roth's judgement that NATO acted illegally rested on the proposition that NATO's targeting of civilian assets, justified on the grounds that they supported military operations, masked its real intent of hitting targets that would break civilian morale. In addition to the selection of

---

[62] Ibid.    [63] Ibid.
[64] Human Rights Watch, 'Civilian Deaths in the NATO Air Campaign', p. 2.
[65] Kenneth Roth, Letters, *The Guardian*, 1 December 2000.

dual-use targets, HRW argued that NATO could have done more to protect Serb civilians: by selecting different weapons (cluster bombs were singled out as being too indiscriminate in their effects and depleted uranium weapons were identified as posing a long-term risk to the health of the population); by providing greater warning of attacks against strategic targets in the FRY; and by pilots flying at lower altitudes to permit more effective target discrimination. The latter two criticisms raise the question as to whether the goal of maximising the safety of NATO aircrews (no pilot was lost during the 78-day campaign) was achieved at the expense of exposing civilians to excessive risks. HRW concluded that NATO was morally responsible for not doing more to minimise the risk to non-combatants. However, it fully acknowledged that NATO political and military leaders had not deliberately killed Serb civilians and therefore there were no grounds in international law for specific war crimes trials against individuals.

Reviewing the same evidence and applying the legal framework of Protocol 1, a harsher judgement was reached by Amnesty International. It charged NATO with 'the unlawful killings of civilians'. It called for the International Criminal Tribunal for the former Yugoslavia (ICTY) to investigate its allegations, with a view to bringing anyone to trial 'against whom there is sufficient admissible evidence'.[66] It was the decision on 23 April to attack the radio and television station that killed sixteen civilians which it singled out as a deliberate attack on a civilian object, and hence a 'war crime'.[67] In his letter to AI on 17 May 1999, Solana, it will be recalled, had emphasised that RTS facilities were being used to support the activities of the military and police forces, and hence the station constituted a legitimate military target. However, AI claims in its report of June 2000 that it was told at a briefing in Brussels by NATO officials in February 2000 that this referred to other aspects of the RTS network and not to the 23 April 1999 attack against the headquarters. The rationale for this strike was to disrupt Milosevic's control of propaganda that NATO argued directly supported Serb military operations. This assessment was confirmed by the US Defense Department in its report on the bombing campaign. It concluded in January 2000 that the bombing was justified because it was 'a facility used for propaganda purposes'.[68] This justification was also employed by British

---

[66] Amnesty International, 'NATO/Federal Republic of Yugoslavia', p. 26.
[67] Amnesty International, 'NATO/Federal Republic of Yugoslavia', p. 23.
[68] Amnesty International, 'NATO/Federal Republic of Yugoslavia', p. 40.

Prime Minister Tony Blair, who claimed that the media 'is the apparatus that keeps him [Milosevic] in power and we are entirely justified as NATO allies in damaging and taking on those targets'.[69] Within hours of the NATO attack, the Serb propaganda machine was back in business raising the question as to whether such an attack constitutes 'an effective contribution to military action' under Article 52(2). According to the interpretation of Protocol 1 supplied by the International Committee of the Red Cross (ICRC), 'an attack which only offers potential or indeterminate advantages' would fail to satisfy this requirement. The ICRC construes the language of 'concrete and direct military advantage' in Article 51(5)(b) to mean that 'the advantage concerned should be substantial and relatively close rather than hardly perceptible and likely to appear only in the long term'.[70] This leads AI to allege that 'NATO deliberately attacked a civilian object, killing 16 civilians, for the purpose of disrupting Serb television broadcasts in the middle of the night for approximately three hours'.[71]

Faced with these and other allegations, the then chief prosecutor of the ICTY, Louise Arbour, created a special committee to review whether there was a case to answer (the membership of this committee has not been made public). Based on this published report, her successor Carla Del Ponte stated before a meeting of the Security Council on 3 June 2000 that 'Although mistakes were made by NATO, I am very satisfied that there was no deliberate targeting of civilians or unlawful military targets.'[72] The review committee set up by Arbour had access to the reports by both HRW and AI, but it reached a very different conclusion to these organisations on the legal conduct of the air campaign. In response to the charge that NATO had violated the laws of war and even committed war crimes, the committee judged that there was insufficient evidence to support an investigation by the Office of the Prosecutor. It admitted that 'errors of judgment' may have occurred and that 'certain objectives for attack may be subject to legal debate', but 'neither an in-depth investigation related to the bombing campaign as a whole nor investigations related to specific incidents are justified. In all cases, either the law is not sufficiently clear or investigations are unlikely to result

[69] Quoted in 'Final Report to the Prosecutor', p. 22. Blair's public endorsement of the attack against the RTS can be contrasted with the doubts expressed privately by some UK military lawyers as to whether this was a legitimate target under Protocol 1.
[70] Quoted in Amnesty International, 'NATO/Federal Republic of Yugoslavia', p. 42.
[71] Amnesty International, 'NATO/Federal Republic of Yugoslavia', p. 42.
[72] Quoted in NATO Press Release 2000(060), 7 June 2000, <www.nato.int/docu/pr/2000/p00-060e.htm>, accessed 25 June 2002.

in the acquisition of sufficient evidence to substantiate charges against high level accused or against lower accused for particularly heinous offences.'[73] A careful reading of the report reveals some ambiguity on the question of whether the strike against RTS was legally justified. The committee considered that if the justification for the attack was purely propaganda purposes, then it 'may not meet the "effective contribution to military action" requirement in Protocol 1'. Set against this, it argued contrary to the report of the US Department of Defense that whatever the propaganda value of the target, the primary goal of the attack was 'disabling the Serbian military command and control system and to destroy the nerve system and apparatus that keeps Milošević in power'.[74] What the committee failed to address was whether taking television and radio off the air for a few hours satisfied the proportionality requirement. The report also accepted without question NATO's rationale that attacks against power sources were legally justified because they fed the command and control structures of the FRY's army and security forces.

The chief prosecutor's decision, based on the report of the special committee, not to pursue further investigations into the legal conduct of Operation Allied Force (OAF) might be taken as an authoritative determination that NATO adhered to the laws of war, the implication being that the report submitted to Del Ponte reflected the 'correct legal view' as against the interpretations offered by HRW and AI. Alternatively, as Paolo Benvenuti argues, the review committee's interpretation of the law might be cited as an example of defective legal reasoning.[75] This chapter has argued strongly against accepting either of these positions. Disagreements over the interpretation of the law are not resolvable through appeals to some neutral and objective process of legal reasoning. This is not to say that all interpretations are equally valid, since what can legitimately be advanced as legal is constrained by past precedents, rules of procedure, and shared normative precepts. This still leaves an important space of indeterminacy within which conflicting but plausible legal claims contend for validation. In domestic society, we rely on judges and jurors to decide between principled legal arguments, but at the international level there is no final court of appeal that is recognised as the authoritative decision-maker when it comes to the application of

---

[73] 'Final Report to the Prosecutor', p. 28.    [74] 'Final Report to the Prosecutor', p. 23.
[75] Paolo Benvenuti, 'The ICTY Prosecutor and the Review of the NATO Bombing Campaign against the Federal Republic of Yugoslavia', *European Journal of International Law* 12: 3 (2001).

international law. The closest approximation at the global level is the International Court of Justice (ICJ). Higgins, who now serves as a judge on this body, wrote in 1994 that its findings are accepted by states as authoritative pronouncements on what the state of international law is.[76] There are three reasons for bestowing this authority on the ICJ. First, it has procedural legitimacy under the UN Charter; second, it is representative with each of the fifteen national judges being elected for a seven-year term by the General Assembly. Third, the court brings together fifteen experienced judges who do not serve as representatives of their government and who are required to justify their decisions publicly.

Yet let us imagine for a moment that the ICJ was to rule on whether NATO breached international humanitarian law and that this verdict supported the findings of the committee established by the prosecutor of the ICTY. Would critics of NATO's conduct, such as AI and HRW, endorse the ICJ's judgement? No, they would challenge this ruling on legal grounds in the same manner they criticised the decision of the prosecutor not to pursue an investigation into NATO's bombing campaign. This illustrates the force of Simpson's contention that 'Determination does not end indeterminacy'. Citing the ICJ's judgement in the *Anglo-Norwegian fisheries case*, he writes:

> The *Anglo-Norwegian Fisheries* case resulted in a finding in favour of the Norwegian method of delineation as an exception to the general rule. This is a 'result' but the deeper issue is surely whether this result was required by the legal materials or whether (a) either the British or Norwegian positions were equally plausible interpretations of the rules or (b) some external or extra-legal factor entered the reasoning and determined the outcome (e.g. the interests of Norwegian coastal fisherman.)[77]

The same questions can be posed in relation to the special committee's investigation into NATO's bombing campaign. Was the position taken by the ICTY 'required by the legal materials' or did some 'extra-legal factor' enter the decision-making process? A cynical assessment of the latter is that any other conclusion would have put the international tribunal on a collision course with its most powerful backers. As Diana Johnstone argued, 'It was hardly conceivable that the ICTY would allow itself to get too interested in crimes committed by the NATO powers

---

[76] Higgins, *Problems and Process*, p. 202.
[77] Simpson, 'The Situation on the International Legal Front', 462.

who provide it with funding, equipment and investigators.'[78] This instrumentalist conception of the law ignores the fact that the ICTY review committee was required for its own credibility to provide arguments that satisfied accepted standards of legal reasoning. There are grounds for criticising its interpretation of the law, but the report cannot be dismissed as a mere rationalisation of NATO policy. A better understanding of this case is that the conflicting legal determinations reached by the ICTY on the one hand, and HRW / AI on the other, represented equally defensible legal readings of Protocol 1.

In making their criticisms of NATO's actions over Kosovo, the human rights NGOs accepted the legitimacy of the existing legal framework of IHL. But this case illustrates how limited this is as an instrument for protecting civilians in armed conflict. The international lawyer Peter Rowe is particularly critical of the law on the question of whether dual-purpose targets can legitimately be attacked. He considers that, 'It is when civilians are most likely to be placed in danger that Protocol 1, designed to protect them, shows its faults.'[79] By codifying ideas of legitimate agency in war, Protocol 1 allocates enormous power to state actors whilst disempowering the moral claims of civilians. This is where CLS has an important contribution to make since it alerts us to the taken-for-granted assumptions that constitute the givens of legal discourse. Writing in a different context, David Kennedy deconstructs the ICJ's Advisory Opinion on nuclear weapons to reveal the judges' deafening silence on the wider political and moral context. He writes:

> The Nuclear Weapons Opinion offers a mirror for international law at century's end ... most of all we find a polemic for the law itself, claiming now both to embrace the perils of nuclear war and hold them at bay ... But in the end, if we wish to speak more about nuclear weapons, we must speak more about the law, speak in a way this case is silent, about the law which emboldens states as warriors and structures deterrence as rational.[80]

---

[78] Diana Johnstone, 'The Berlin Tribunal', 21 June 2000, <www.emperors-clothes.com/articles/Johnstone/berlin.htm>, accessed 20 June 2002.

[79] Peter Rowe, 'Kosovo 1999: The Air Campaign – Have the Provisions of Additional Protocol I Withstood the Test?', *International Review of the Red Cross*, No. 837, 31 March 2000, p. 4, <www.icrc.org/icrceng.nsf/4dc394db5b54f3fa4125673900241f2f/5815a62298ea0cff412568d30033d627?OpenDocument>, accessed 28 June 2001.

[80] David Kennedy, 'The *Nuclear Weapons* Case', in Laurence Boisson de Chazournes and Philippe Sands (eds.), *International Law, the International Court of Justice and Nuclear Weapons* (Cambridge: Cambridge University Press, 1999), p. 472.

The same criticism can be levelled at the chief prosecutor's determination that NATO acted legally in its bombing campaign. It is the shared normative values that legitimate such a judgement that need exposing to public scrutiny. To paraphrase Kennedy, these enable the use of force and structure the inadvertent but foreseeable death of civilians as acceptable.

## Conclusion

It is evident from this study of the Kosovo bombing campaign that legal considerations shaped the possibilities of action. It is too sweeping a statement to claim as realism does that states can always find a convenient legal rationale to justify any course of action. States will on occasion ignore the need to legally justify their positions, but such actions carry costs, and sensitivity to this leads most states most of the time to recognise the importance of providing sound legal rationales. This is why constructivism places such an emphasis on studying the justifications and public reasoning process since this constitutes the possibilities of political action. It follows that the lack of available legitimating reasons will constrain state behaviour unless those states, which have the power to do so, dispense with reasoned argument and rely on brute force. As this examination of NATO's targeting policy shows, even the world's most powerful military alliance recognised the need to justify its actions before the court of domestic and world public opinion. And the fact that Alliance leaders knew that they would be called upon to defend their choice of targets was an inhibiting factor on what could be attacked. This burden of legal justification fell particularly heavily on NATO because it comprises democratic states that had to answer before domestic publics and a global media ever ready to expose a gap between the humanitarian rationale behind the intervention and the means employed.

The contention that legal constraints inhibited NATO's bombing strategy should not be read as supporting the 'law as rules' approach. It is a fantasy to think that there is an objective or proper view of the law that good men and women of sound legal reasoning apply. If this were the case, then it would be necessary to argue that the dispute between NATO and HRW/AI over the legal conduct of OAF is resolvable because one side was applying flawed legal reasoning. In fact, what this case demonstrates is that agreement on the relevant legal rules is no guarantee that actors will agree on their application in particular cases. The fact that AI and HRW drew radically different conclusions from applying the same body of law illustrates the problem of legal indeterminacy. The New Haven school tried to resolve this problem by establishing human dignity as the universal moral precept that should be employed to decide between conflicting legal claims. The problem is that recourse to this principle would not settle disputed legal issues because both its meaning and application to specific cases would be deeply contested. AI and HRW would claim their interpretation of the law to be the valid one, but this cannot be legally determined by reference to the goal of human dignity or any other conception of the good. Both human rights organisations – especially AI – were too dogmatic in arguing that NATO's actions clearly breached IHL. They mobilised a strong and persuasive case against NATO, but the legal materials of the case are not sufficient to warrant a definite legal determination.

AI and HRW challenged NATO on the legal terrain of Protocol 1, but they missed the opportunity to issue a deeper moral challenge against the hidden assumptions that underpin the laws of war. Focusing solely on the legal question of what counts as a legitimate military target excludes crucial ethical questions. Determining that NATO's conduct was lawful does not mean that it was just. As Ignatieff argues, moral questions 'stubbornly resist being reduced to legal ones, and moral exposure is not eliminated when legal exposure is'.[81] The limits of the legal discourse are illustrated by the vexed normative question as to whether NATO governments should have exposed their military personnel to increased risks in order to provide greater protection to civilians. There is an inescapable tension between the risks that states accept to their militaries and the safety they can extend to non-combatants. The reports by AI and HRW criticise NATO for not flying its planes at lower altitudes to permit better target discrimination and for not giving warning when preparing to attack dual-purpose facilities (as required under Article 57(2)(c) of Protocol 1).[82] The rationale behind both these military operating procedures was the safety of NATO aircrews. The moral challenge of balancing the risks faced by combatants and civilians cannot be decided by an application of the law. But if civilians are to be better safeguarded in the future, changing the laws of war could facilitate this.

NATO was able to justify its targeting of the FRY's dual-use civilian infrastructure because Protocol 1 is ambiguous on whether this is

---

[81] Ignatieff, *Virtual War*, p. 199.
[82] Amnesty International, 'NATO/Federal Republic of Yugoslavia', pp. 7, 15.

permitted. Advocates of CLS would argue that this supports their general thesis of radical indeterminacy. They would seek to expose how the laws of war are structured in such a way as to empower state interests at the expense of human values. Protocol 1 is too enabling of state power, but the conclusion should not be to bemoan the value of law. Rather, what is required is to look for ways to change the existing legal framework so as to reduce the indeterminacy that NATO was able to exploit so effectively over Kosovo. Were Protocol 1 to be amended to significantly constrain what can legitimately be targeted in terms of dual-purpose facilities (such as a state's electricity generating facilities), it would reconstitute the boundaries of legitimate agency, and represent an important shift in the balance between sovereign rights and human rights.[83] The Independent International Commission on Kosovo recommended in its report that the ICRC prepare a new legal convention to govern military operations justified on humanitarian grounds.[84] The problem is that it is very difficult to imagine states agreeing to such a restriction on their freedom of action, even if this was restricted to cases of humanitarian intervention. The attraction of the language of Protocol 1 in the eyes of governments and the military is its very ambiguity on the question of what is a legitimate target. It is highly unlikely, for example, that the US Air Force would support any change that challenged its doctrinal commitment to attacking targets that contribute to civilian morale.

There are two further significant obstacles to tightening up the loopholes in Protocol 1. The first is that effectively raising the legal standard of civilian protection in future humanitarian interventions would require states to accept increased risks to their militaries. However as the Independent International Commission on Kosovo pointed out, 'There is a delicate balance here, as countries are being asked to take risks for humanitarian purposes, and may be reluctant to do so.'[85] This concern is borne out by the case of Kosovo. The determination of the major NATO governments that OAF would be casualty-free rested uneasily with their claim to be protecting human rights. The commitment to force protection led to bombing being selected as the means of intervention, and it shaped the conduct of the air campaign. Ignatieff argues that NATO's

---

[83] This argument is developed in Shue, 'Bombing to Rescue?'

[84] Independent International Commission on Kosovo, *The Kosovo Report: Conflict, International Response, Lessons Learned* (Oxford: Oxford University Press, 2000), pp. 183–4.

[85] Independent International Commission on Kosovo, *The Kosovo Report*, p. 184.

'riskless warfare'[86] contradicted the human rights imperative because it assumed that 'our lives matter more than those we are intervening to save'.[87] Revising the laws of war to better safeguard non-combatants depends critically upon changing this mind-set, especially among US political and military leaders. The second roadblock to establishing higher standards for the military conduct of humanitarian intervention is that states might oppose this because of concerns that it could expose their forces to an increased risk of prosecutions for war crimes. This concern drives the Bush Administration's virulent opposition to the International Criminal Court (see David Wippman, chapter 7, in this volume) and this objection could easily frustrate any movement in the direction of changing Protocol 1.

It is apparent that significant barriers stand in the way of changing the laws of war to enhance civilian immunity in war. However, these should not prevent the global human rights community from seeking to persuade governments and the military to accept greater restrictions on what can be legitimately targeted in future cases of humanitarian intervention. The outcome of such a campaign will determine whether the innocent can be better protected the next time a state, or group of states, decide to go to war in defence of human rights.

---

[86] This concept belongs to Paul Kahn upon whose argument Ignatieff builds. See Paul W. Kahn, 'War and Sacrifice in Kosovo', *Report from the Institute for Philosophy & Public Policy* 19:2/3 (1999), <www.puaf.umd.edu/IPPP/spring_summer99/kosovo.htm>, accessed 25 August 2001.
[87] Ignatieff, *Virtual War*, p. 162.

# 9 International financial institutions

*Antony Anghie*[1]

The International Monetary Fund (IMF) and the World Bank ('Bank' or WB), comprise the two major international financial institutions (IFIs). The IFIs exercise enormous power over the workings of the international financial system as reflected in the fact that half the world's population and two-thirds of its governments are bound by the policies they prescribe.[2] This chapter attempts to examine the relationship between law and politics as it manifests itself in the operations of these powerful institutions. Realists view these institutions principally as mechanisms by which powerful states further their own interests. By way of contrast, Beth Simmons, adopting a neoliberal institutionalist approach, studies the IMF in terms of the factors which lead states to co-operate with each other to create a legal regime regulating monetary affairs, the reasons why 'legalization of monetary relations helps governments make credible policy commitments to market actors,'[3] and, further, the conditions under which compliance with the system is likely. And Michael Barnett and Martha Finnemore, working within the constructivist school, examine international organisations (IOs) as powerful independent actors and seek to account for the 'dysfunctional, even pathological, behavior'

---

[1] Many thanks to Chris Reus-Smit and anonymous reviewers for extremely helpful comments.
[2] Ute Pieper and Lance Taylor, 'The Revival of the Liberal Creed: The IMF, the World Bank, and Inequality in a Globalized Economy', in Dean Baker, Gerald Epstein, and Robert Pollin (eds.), *Globalization and Progressive Economic Policy* (Cambridge: Cambridge University Press, 1998), p. 37. See also David Held and Anthony McGrew, 'The Great Globalization Debate: An Introduction', in David Held and Anthony McGrew (eds.), *The Global Transformations Reader: An Introduction to the Globalization Debate* (Cambridge: Polity Press, 2000), pp. 1–44.
[3] Beth A. Simmons, 'The Legalization of International Monetary Affairs', *International Organization* 54: 3 (2000), 574.

of IOs.[4] This approach contends that IOs acquire a life of their own in the course of their operations, and define tasks and functions quite independent of the intentions of the states which created them in the first place.[5]

My discussion takes this proposition seriously. IOs such as the IFIs strive to preserve and further their own interests and their autonomy, even while, inevitably, they must serve the purposes of the states that created them. The tension that arises between the concern of IOs to preserve their autonomy, and the attempts of states, particularly powerful states, to further their own interests through the IOs, constitute and animate, in important ways, the 'politics' of IFIs.[6] The politics of the IFIs are also significantly shaped by the immense controversies generated by the impact of IFI policies on developing states, and IFI attitudes towards human rights and environmental issues.

This chapter adopts a 'legal' perspective in exploring how the IFIs deal with these challenges. That is, I examine the IFIs as creations of international law which are provided by that law with an independent legal personality and operate within a realm governed by international law. Barnett and Finnemore do not give much emphasis to the legal dimension of these organisations.[7] As this chapter suggests, their omission may be entirely justifiable. Nevertheless, the question demands some attention. After all, IOs are, unlike states, emphatically *creations* of international law, and their constituent documents, their articles of agreement, are formulated to ensure that the IOs perform the function for which they were created. Further, given that the IOs are international bureaucracies that rely for the authority they exercise on their 'rational-legal' character, as Barnett and Finnemore, following Max Weber, assert, then it is important to focus on the legal dimensions of these actors.[8]

---

[4] Michael N. Barnett and Martha Finnemore, 'The Politics, Power, and Pathologies of International Organizations', *International Organization* 53: 4 (1999), 699.

[5] This is one of the key arguments made by Barnett and Finnemore, 'The Politics, Power, and Pathologies of International Organizations'.

[6] Institutionalists also emphasise the importance of the IO being independent in order to be effective. See Kenneth W. Abbott and Duncan Snidal, 'Why States Act Through Formal International Organizations', *Journal of Conflict Resolution* 42: 1 (1998).

[7] As Finnemore and Toope point out, further, law does not do very much work in Simmons' analysis either. See Martha Finnemore and Stephen J. Toope, 'Alternatives to "Legalization": Richer Views of Law and Politics', *International Organization* 55: 3 (2001), 751. My own analysis focuses on a different set of questions from those proposed in the same article by Finnemore and Toope regarding the role of law.

[8] Barnett and Finnemore, 'The Politics, Power, and Pathologies of International Organizations', 707–8.

If we take seriously the idea that IOs are important independent actors, then we might ask a series of further questions. What are the interests or identities of the IFIs, and to what extent and in what ways does law play a role in formulating and shaping, expanding and confining those interests? What limitations does law impose upon the actions of these extremely important international actors, the IFIs? Further, given the IO concerns to preserve their independence, to what extent and in what ways does international law constrain powerful states in their actions within these organisations? This chapter attempts to elucidate some of the questions of the relationship between law and politics by focusing on such issues. Of course scholars, while writing within one of these traditions, nevertheless borrow from the others. And it is perhaps by drawing on realist, institutionalist, and constructivist perspectives that an examination of the law/politics relationship in the context of the IFIs might suggest the inadequacies and strengths of each of these approaches.

This chapter commences, then, with an examination of the constitutional structures of the IFIs, and the particular blend of law, politics, and technocracy that is embodied in these structures. The third section examines legal aspects of the ways in which the functions of the IFIs have altered over time, and the criticisms made of the IFIs by human rights and environmental lawyers on the one hand, and by critics of IFI lending and structural adjustment policies on the other. The fourth section examines how the IFIs have responded to this challenge in part through a deployment of legal norms that suggest an affinity between IFI operations and other areas of international law such as human rights law. My conclusion is that while the IFIs, and especially the Bank, may attempt to demonstrate that new developments in international law have significantly shaped their operations, these claims have only a partial and problematic validity.

## The legal framework regulating the IFIs

The World Bank and the IMF were essentially created in 1944 at the Bretton Woods Conference for the broad purpose of co-ordinating and managing international monetary and financial matters. Although united in achieving these general goals, the two institutions were constituted to perform distinctive but complementary functions. The World Bank was to 'assist in the reconstruction and development of territories',[9] to 'promote private foreign investment',[10] and to 'promote the long-range balanced growth of international trade'[11] among other such duties. The IMF was to 'promote international monetary cooperation', to 'facilitate the expansion and balanced growth of international trade', 'to promote exchange stability, to maintain orderly exchange arrangements among members' and to generate confidence among the members by 'making the general resources of the Fund temporarily available to them under adequate safeguards'.[12] While the Bank was intended to provide long-term financing for development projects, the IMF was expected to provide only short-term financial assistance to member states suffering from transitory monetary problems relating, for example, to balance of payments problems.

The IFIs are creations of international law, specifically, international treaty law. Their constituent documents, their respective articles of agreement, provide them with independent legal personality and a system of governance, outline a set of functions and provide them with specific powers to enable them to perform those functions. In broad terms, the law governing the IFIs may be found in two distinct realms: first in the articles of agreement, the constituting documents of the institutions, and second, in the larger universe of international law which creates the environment in which these international institutions operate and which bestows the institutions with certain rights and responsibilities. In addition, of course, this larger universe of international law also contains within it other bodies of international law such as international human rights law and international environmental law, that are connected in complex ways with the law directly applicable to the IFIs.

The basic governance structure of the two IFIs is very similar. The Bank has a president and all the powers of the Bank are vested in a board of governors;[13] the day-to-day running of the Bank is entrusted, however, to the executive directors of the Bank.[14] Similarly, the IMF is headed by a managing director and is administered by its executive directors. Both institutions have adopted a weighted voting system which is based

---

[9] Articles of Agreement of the International Bank for Reconstruction and Development (hereafter Articles of Agreement of the World Bank), *United Nations Treaty Series* 2 (1947), Article I(i).

[10] Articles of Agreement of the World Bank, Article I(ii).

[11] Articles of Agreement of the World Bank, Article I(iii).

[12] Articles of Agreement of the International Monetary Fund, *United Nations Treaty Series* 2 (1947), Article I.

[13] Articles of Agreement of the World Bank, Article V.2.

[14] Articles of Agreement of the World Bank, Article V.4.

on contributions made by the members. Under this system, the United States exercises roughly 17 per cent of the vote; China and India each exercise roughly 3 per cent of the vote.

It is hardly possible to dispute that these institutions are intensely political institutions, notwithstanding their attempts to suggest otherwise. Nevertheless, the IFIs have formulated specific images of 'law' and 'politics' to present themselves as neutral, and apolitical. Whatever the deficiencies of these images, it is by developing and deploying them that these institutions attempt in part to legitimise their actions and establish their particular authority.

The Bank and the IMF, are, like the World Health Organisation (WHO) and International Labour Organisation, specialised agencies – international institutions established for the purpose of co-ordinating and advancing the international community's efforts in a particular field. Clearly, however, the Bank and the IMF are treated as unique organisations, as reflected by the relationship agreements between the IFIs and the UN which suggest that the IFIs are to be effectively immune from control by the United Nations. Thus the agreement between the Fund and the UN states that the Fund, because of its special responsibilities 'is, and is required to function as, an independent international organization'.[15] IFI independence is further stressed by the fact that, unlike states, the IFIs are not legally bound by decisions made by the Security Council. Rather, they are required, in the conduct of their activities, to have 'due regard for decisions of the Security Council'.[16] This protection from 'political interference', seen here as emanating from the UN, is also evident in a number of other provisions which deal with the specific activities of the organisation.[17]

Not only is the Bank protected against political interference by these techniques, but the Bank itself is prohibited from engaging in any political activity: 'The Bank and its officers shall not interfere in the political affairs of any member; nor shall they be influenced in their decisions by the political character of the member or members concerned. Only

---

[15] Agreement between the United Nations and the International Monetary Fund, *United Nations Treaty Series* 16 (1948), 330, Article I.

[16] Agreement between the United Nations and the International Bank for Reconstruction and Development, *United Nations Treaty Series* 16 (1948); and Agreement between the United Nations and the International Monetary Fund, Article VI. The relationship agreements between other specialised agencies such as the WHO and the UN make no reference to the effect of Security Council decisions on the agency.

[17] See Agreement between the United Nations and the International Bank for Reconstruction and Development, Article IV.3.

economic considerations shall be relevant to their decisions.'[18] The IMF Articles of Agreement lack such an explicit prohibition. Nevertheless, the interpretations of various provisions of the articles have led several authorities, including, most notably, the distinguished former General Counsel of the Fund, Sir Joseph Gold, to conclude that the IMF too cannot interfere in the political affairs of a member state and should base its policies solely on economic criteria.[19]

Given that the IFIs are created by sovereign states, the further problem presents itself of how the IFIs can remain unaffected by the attempts of these states to pursue their interests through the institution. This fundamental problem was recognised by the creators of the IFIs. On the one hand, the British and the US agreed on a weighted voting system, in order to control the Bretton Woods Institutions.[20] On the other hand, the British wanted to ensure that the IFIs would operate on the basis of strictly technical and objective considerations, arguing that 'So far as practicable . . . we want to aim at a governing structure doing a technical job and developing a sense of corporate responsibility to all members, and not the need to guard the interests of particular countries.'[21] Thus, the politicisation of the IFIs from *within* is ostensibly prevented by a provision which requires all officers of the IFIs to exercise their voting power according to the Articles of Agreement of the Bank.[22] This provision could appear somewhat unrealistic, given that the officers, the executive directors, are appointed by member states.[23] Nevertheless, the importance of the IFIs being independent, technical institutions was heavily stressed by John Keynes himself, who

---

[18] Articles of Agreement of the World Bank, Article IV.10.

[19] See Herbert V. Morais, 'The Globalization of Human Rights Law and the Role of International Financial Institutions in Promoting Human Rights', *George Washington International Law Review* 33: 1 (2000), 89, n. 107. This position is also expressed in International Monetary Fund, *Good Governance: The IMF's Role* (Washington, DC: IMF, 1997), p. 4.

[20] See the account of the beginnings of the IMF given in the classic work, Kenneth W. Dam, *The Rules of the Game* (Chicago: University of Chicago Press, 1982), p. 110.

[21] This submission by the British is extracted in Dam, *The Rules of the Game*, p. 111.

[22] Articles of Agreement of the World Bank, 5.5(c).

[23] This is especially the case since voting power was exercised by sovereign states. The United States, as noted earlier, exercises 17 per cent of the voting power of the Fund and the Bank. The US executive director who exercises this power is nevertheless characterised as owing her duty 'entirely to the Bank and to no other authority'. Articles of Agreement of the World Bank, 5.5(c). The problem inherent in operating an international institution which is at the same time a creation of member states and yet independent of the specific interests of those states, and especially the most powerful states, is reflected here. The same tension is found in Article 48(2) of the UN Charter which requires UN member states to carry out UN decisions 'directly and through their action in the appropriate international agencies of which they are members'. UN Charter, Article 48(2).

eloquently and presciently warned of the dangers of the politicisation of the IFIs.[24]

The idea that the IFIs are apolitical and could detach themselves from international politics, from the political imperatives of the sovereign states which constituted the entity in the first place, was based on the theory of functionalism which was classically formulated by David Mitrany in his work, *A Working Peace System*.[25] Functionalism has been usefully summarised by Bartram Brown as follows:

> Functionalism is a theory of international organization which holds that a world community can be best achieved, not by attempts at the immediate political union of states, but by the creation of non-political international agencies dealing with specific economic, social, technical or humanitarian functions. Functionalists assume that economic, social and technical problems can be separated from political problems and insulated from political pressures.[26]

Seen within this framework, the function of law is to create an independent agency immune from politics and operated strictly according to the technocratic responsibilities it is supposed to fulfil. In these different ways, the IFIs are supposed to embody the rational-legal authority of classic bureaucracies. This is the legal basis of the autonomy ostensibly enjoyed by IFIs, an autonomy which they have exercised by, for example, presenting themselves as the ultimate arbiters of scientific knowledge about how to achieve development or monetary stability.[27] IFIs exercise their authority by creating the analytic framework, the social reality that plays an important role in shaping state behaviour in that particular field.[28] Indeed, the knowledge produced by these institutions can make special claims of authority precisely because they are seen to be generated by apolitical, expert institutions that are independent in their approach and analysis. The knowledge generated by these institutions takes on the rational (and implicitly, therefore, universal) character of

---

[24] Dam, *The Rules of the Game*, pp. 113–14.

[25] David Mitrany, *A Working Peace System: An Argument for the Functional Development of International Organisation* (London: Royal Institute of International Affairs, 1943).

[26] Bartram S. Brown, *The United States and the Politicization of the World Bank: Issues of International Law and Policy* (New York: K. Paul International, 1992), pp. 14–15.

[27] Thus one *World Development Report* (the important annual publication of the World Bank) is called, precisely, *Knowledge for Development*. See World Bank, *World Development Report 1998/98: Knowledge for Development* (New York: Oxford University Press for the World Bank, 1999).

[28] Barnett and Finnemore, 'The Politics, Power, and Pathologies of International Organizations', 710–15.

the institutions themselves.[29] The appearance of independence is crucial to the rational-legal authority that the IFIs claim to wield, and the governing law of the IFIs attempts, however inadequately, to ensure and protect this independence.

## Politics and the changing role of the IFIs

The functions performed by the IMF and Bank have evolved dramatically in the fifty years since they first came into existence. The IMF, which was created for the purpose of managing monetary stability (principally through the par value mechanism) and which provided only short-term financial assistance to enable member states to overcome temporary balance of payment problems, has become a major lending institution. The Bank, which was to assist in the reconstruction of countries devastated by the Second World War, has evolved into the principal development institution and assumes jurisdiction over a vast number of areas of domestic policy in ways that could hardly have been contemplated at the time of its creation. What are the politics generated by these changes, and what is the role that law plays in formulating and regulating these politics?

It is clear now that both IFIs have in effect become managers of economic policies of the developing countries. In this capacity, the IFIs have required developing countries seeking their assistance to embark upon the radical restructuring of their economies through 'structural adjustment programmes' (SAPs). Structural adjustment, in broad terms, involves reduction in government spending, liberalisation of the economy, privatisation, and devaluation.[30] These programmes are designed to increase efficiency, expand growth potential, and increase resilience

---

[29] Thus, for example, I have argued that the claims of development discourse to be scientific, universal, and objective may be attributed, in important respects, to the fact that it is produced by an international institution that presents itself as possessing these characteristics, rather than by colonial powers intent on pursuing their interests. I have explored this argument in detail in studies of the Mandate System of the League of Nations, the progenitor, in important respects, of the World Bank. See Antony Anghie, 'Colonialism and the Birth of International Institutions: Sovereignty, Economy and the Mandate System of the League of Nations', *New York University Journal of International Law and Politics* 34: 3 (2002), 513; and Antony Anghie, 'Time Present and Time Past: Globalization, International Financial Institutions, and the Third World', *New York University Journal of International Law and Politics* 32: 2 (2000), 243.

[30] See Poul Engberg-Pedersen et al. (eds.), *Limits of Adjustment in Africa: The Effects of Economic Liberalization, 1986–94* (Copenhagen: Centre for Development Research in association with James Currey, 1996), p. ix.

to shocks.[31] Critics of such programmes have argued that they are designed with little regard for the specific needs of the particular country concerned (the cookie cutter approach) and as such are inherently defective. The SAPs often have massively detrimental consequences for the most disadvantaged in recipient countries; health services are affected, food and fuel prices increase, and unemployment intensifies. 'IMF' riots have taken place in African and Latin American countries where these programmes were implemented.[32] In addition to the social and political instability caused by these programmes, they have produced uncertain benefits. More broadly, critics argue, the economic programmes designed by the IFIs work in the interests of the advanced industrialised nations who are the major shareholders of the IFIs.[33] Furthermore, the IFIs, it is argued, have exacerbated the debt crisis confronting many developing countries,[34] and, moreover, have used their power over developing country economic policy to ensure that the interests of foreign creditors take precedence over the needs of the people of these countries.[35]

Surveying the expanding operations of the IFIs over the last few decades, in the context of developments in international law, human rights and environmental lawyers have added to the criticisms made by economists and sociologists by arguing that IFI policies are indifferent, if not hostile, to human rights and environmental concerns. Rights set out in the Covenant on Economic and Social Rights, which includes the right to health and education, for example, have been undermined by IFI SAP policies.[36] In particular, many of the African countries which submitted to IFI structural adjustment policies are now even worse off than they were initially, and are deeper in debt, and the IFIs have given

---

[31] Sigrun I. Skogly, 'Structural Adjustment and Development: Human Rights – An Agenda for Change', *Human Rights Quarterly* 15: 4 (1993), 751, citing a World Bank paper.

[32] See Michel Chossudovsky, *The Globalization of Poverty: Impacts of IMF and World Bank Reforms* (London: Zed Books, 1997); and Skogly, 'Structural Adjustment and Development', 763.

[33] Thus the noted economist Jagdish Bhagwati speaks of the 'Wall Street–Treasury Complex'. See Jagdish Bhagwati, 'The Capital Myth: The Difference Between Trade in Widgets and Dollars', *Foreign Affairs* 77: 3 (1998), 11–12.

[34] Susan Strange, *Mad Money: When Markets Outgrow Governments* (Ann Arbor: University of Michigan Press, 1998).

[35] Thus the IMF has been described (by executive directors of the IMF, no less) as the 'creditor community's enforcer' and as 'being used by the commercial banks in the collection of their debts'. See Devesh Kapur, 'The IMF: A Cure or a Curse?', *Foreign Policy* 111 (1998), 123.

[36] J. Oloka-Onyango, 'Beyond the Rhetoric: Reinvigorating the Struggle for Economic and Social Rights in Africa', *California Western International Law Journal* 26: 1 (1995), 1.

priority to debt repayment as opposed to the provision of the basic welfare services necessary for survival.[37] Furthermore, the Bank sponsored several large infrastructure projects which threatened to cause massive environmental damage and involved the 'resettlement' of thousands of people.

Another strand of criticism voiced by human rights scholars focuses on a related issue – the Bank's policy of lending to countries based only on economic criteria. The most notorious example of this took place in the 1960s, when the Bank made loans to both South Africa and Portugal, this despite the authoritarian and racist policies practised by both governments at the time, and despite General Assembly resolutions calling upon all specialised agencies to deny 'technical and economic assistance' to those two countries.[38] In justifying its position, the Bank relied, predictably, on Article IV.10 which prohibited the Bank from interfering in the internal political affairs of a state.[39] Since this time, human rights advocates and lawyers have argued that the IFIs should incorporate human rights considerations into their decision-making. It is notable, however, that while these two forms of critique are closely interrelated, they are distinct. The first focuses on the impact of SAPs on economic and social rights. The second focuses more on the violation of civil and political rights by recipient countries, on the support given by the IFIs to dictatorial regimes such as South Africa under apartheid.

In more recent times, the manner in which the IMF handled the Asian crisis has given rise to further criticisms. The causes of the Asian crisis are complex.[40] But as a consequence of that crisis, the powerful Asian economies of Korea and Thailand, for example, which had made enormous progress in the previous decade or so, and which were exemplars of the 'Asian miracle' were compelled to resort to the IFIs for financial assistance. The collapse of the Asian economies provided the IFIs with a novel opportunity to apply their economic disciplines to these states.[41] The IFIs offered the desperately required assistance, but only on

---

[37] Thus in Tanzania, 'where 40% of people die before the age of 35, debt payments are six times greater than spending on health care'. David Ransom and Margaret Bald, 'The Dictatorship of Debt', *World Press Review* 46: 10 (1999), 6, 7.

[38] For an account, see Lawyers Committee for Human Rights, *The World Bank: Governance and Human Rights* (New York: Lawyers Committee for Human Rights, 1995), pp. 28–9.

[39] Lawyers Committee for Human Rights, *The World Bank*, p. 29.

[40] For differing accounts see for example, Robert Hormats, 'Reflections on the Asian Crisis', *International Lawyer* 34: 1 (2000), 193.

[41] These disciplines had been applied extensively to African, Asian, and Latin American countries over the previous two or three decades.

condition that the recipient state met specific economic goals and implemented prescribed economic and institutional reforms.[42] The technique of 'conditionality' is intended to ensure that the assistance given will resolve the problem and that, furthermore, the IFIs' resources will be properly protected. This technique has been used to profoundly shape the internal and external policies of the recipient state. Furthermore, as the General Counsel of the IMF notes, 'at the behest of creditor countries, the scope of Fund conditionality has gradually expanded'.[43]

In a work published in August 1997 entitled *Good Governance: The IMF's Role*, the IMF affirmed that 'the IMF's judgments should not be influenced by the nature of a political regime of a country, nor should it interfere in domestic or foreign politics of any member'.[44] Only a few months later, the IMF was demanding from Korea a fundamental reorientation of its economy, involving higher taxes and interest rates, reduced spending, and a contractionary macro-economic policy.[45] Martin Feldstein argues that the IMF seized upon a liquidity crisis in Korea to impose, in effect, a farreaching series of changes which extended well beyond the immediacies of the problem and which should properly have been decided by political processes within the country itself.[46] The reforms required by the Fund during the Asian crisis dealt with a huge variety of subjects involving, in some cases, garlic monopolies, taxes on cattle feed, and new environmental laws.[47] Prominent economists such as Jeffrey Sachs and Martin Feldstein argued that the IMF policies made the situation worse. Notably, the Bank was explicitly critical of the IMF's policies, in a well-publicised dispute between the two institutions. The Bank indeed took the opportunity to provide welfare loans, almost as though to negate the devastating social effects of IMF policies. In addition to all this, it is clear that the IMF's prescribed conditionalities were not 'objectively' and 'impartially' structured

---

[42] This basically involves the use of 'Conditionality': under the Fund's articles, the Fund may provide financial assistance to member states, but subject to conditions which ensure that the problem will be solved and the Fund's resources will be protected. See Articles of Agreement of the International Monetary Fund; and François Gianviti, 'The Reform of the International Monetary Fund (Conditionality and Surveillance)', *International Lawyer* 34: 1 (2000), 107.

[43] Gianviti, 'The Reform of the International Monetary Fund', 114.

[44] International Monetary Fund, *Good Governance*, p. 4.

[45] Martin Feldstein, 'Refocusing the IMF', *Foreign Affairs* 77: 2 (1998), 26. For a detailed and graphic account of the IMF–US Treasury bail-out of Korea and its consequences, see Paul Blustein, *The Chastening: Inside the Crisis that Rocked the Global Financial System and Humbled the IMF* (New York: Public Affairs, 2001), particularly chapters 5 and 7.

[46] Feldstein, 'Refocusing the IMF'.     [47] Kapur, 'The IMF: A Cure or a Curse?', 114.

according to the needs of the recipient country and the concern to protect the interests of the Fund. Rather, various scholars have argued, the conditions were prescribed by major shareholders intent on furthering their own interests: both Feldstein and Devesh Kapur argue that the conditionalities demanded from South Korea, involving the opening up of South Korea's automobile and financial markets, were the result of pressures exercised by the United States and Japan.[48]

These then, are the major allegations against the IFIs: that they are run in the interests of the most powerful states; that they ignore the obligations of international human rights and environmental law;[49] that they expand their functions well beyond legally prescribed limits; and that they interfere dramatically in the internal affairs of recipient states.

The argument that the IFIs are run in the interests of the most powerful states would suggest the validity of realist and institutionalist understandings of the IFIs. Nevertheless, as the work of scholars such as Robert Wade makes clear, these interpretations may not be completely adequate. First, the international legitimacy of the IFIs, inasmuch as it can be asserted at all, depends, as Keynes had foreseen, on their ability to present themselves as neutral, technocratic, and independent. Second, as Wade points out, powerful states such as the United States seek to control the IFIs in order to pursue their national interests through the IFIs. And yet, as Wade argues:

> the US needs to structure and operate within the organizations in a way that maintains the organizations' appearance of acting according to rules decided by the collective member governments rather than according to discretionary US judgments. If not, the organizations lose the legitimacy of multilateralism and are less likely to achieve US objectives.[50]

It is clear, furthermore, that the officials of the IFIs themselves are intent on preserving their institutional autonomy as best they can, and see themselves very much as international civil servants furthering the

---

[48] See also Robert Wade, 'The Coming Fight Over Capital Flows', *Foreign Policy* 113 (1998–99), 47–8. The extent of the US involvement in the IMF bail-out of South Korea is suggested in Blustein, *The Chastening*.

[49] For a detailed comparative study of the relationship between the IFIs and human rights issues, see Daniel D. Bradlow, 'The World Bank, the IMF, and Human Rights', *Transnational Law and Contemporary Problems* 6: 1 (1996), 47.

[50] Robert Hunter Wade, 'US Hegemony and the World Bank: The Fight over People and Ideas', *Review of International Political Economy* 9: 2 Summer (2002), 202.

cause of the international community, rather than simply acting as a cover for the policies of hegemonic powers.[51]

The IFIs confront, then, a series of distinct but related challenges. First, at a very basic level, as Barnett and Finnemore argue, the IFIs seek to play an important role in contemporary international relations. Second, they seek to maintain what independence they can, notwithstanding the demands of their most powerful members. Third, they strive to respond to changes taking place within the international system, changes which are reflected in new and evolving norms of international law. It is within this matrix of issues that the next section examines the strategies used by the IFIs – which differ in important respects – in addressing these criticisms, and their specific use of international legal doctrines for these purposes.

## The IFIs and good governance

Given that the IFIs were created in 1944, before the emergence of the UN and significant bodies of law such as international human rights law and international environmental law, important questions have arisen as to how those new bodies of law affect the operations of the IFIs. Furthermore, both the IFIs have been significantly involved in drafting commercial laws in states that have drawn on their resources. This increasing engagement by the IFIs in law reform in recipient countries has occurred under the rubric of 'technical assistance', and the IFIs have been stressing the importance of the 'rule of law' and 'good governance' for the purposes of achieving development and economic stability. The legal norms generated at these different levels have been used, paradoxically, to both challenge and support the legitimacy of the IFIs.

The Bank and the IMF have responded differently to the evolution of international law relating, for example, to human rights and the environment. Since the massive criticisms generated by the South African episode, the Bank has recognised that its international legitimacy would be seriously undermined by assertions that its operations are governed strictly by its articles of agreement to the extent that the articles prevail against developing international norms. Thus it has sought to incorporate these new norms within its operations by arguing that this was permitted by the articles.

---

[51] Wade, 'US Hegemony and the World Bank', 217–19.

Technically, human rights law still only binds states, an anomaly that many scholars are now examining, given that IOs and multinational corporations are such prominent international entities whose actions certainly have an impact on human rights.[52] The Bank, apparently intent on appearing a good international citizen, has not relied on this relatively formalist argument to assert its independence of human rights law. Rather, the Bank, in a formidable and comprehensive literature produced by Ibrahim Shihata, who was the Bank's General Counsel, has argued that it can properly take human rights issues into account when such issues affect 'development', as the promotion of development is one of the Bank's central purposes.[53] Thus, anything which impinges on 'development' can be properly considered in the Bank's deliberations. This approach enabled the Bank, at least in theory, to retain its position that it was not being influenced by political considerations or interfering with the internal political affairs of a state. Thus Shihata argued that 'the Bank should not allow political factors or events, no matter how appealing they may seem to be, to influence its decisions unless . . . it is established that they have direct and obvious economic effects relevant to the World Bank.'[54] Similarly, Shihata argued that since the emergence of environmental law and the concept of 'sustainable development', environmental protection has become inextricably linked with development concerns and, as such, it is legitimate for the Bank to take environmental factors into account when making decisions.[55] In these ways, the Bank has formulated a technique of appearing to accommodate human rights and environmental considerations in its operations without departing from the fundamental premise that it is bound strictly, only by its articles of agreement.

Notably, furthermore, the concept of 'good governance' has been powerfully deployed by the Bank to legitimise its actions and extend its range of operations. 'Good governance', now a ubiquitous term both in international law and international relations scholarship, is ambiguous enough to support very different types of initiatives and strategies. In

---

[52] For recent work on this subject see Peter T. Muchlinski, 'Human Rights and Multinationals: Is There a Problem?', *International Affairs* 77: 1 (2001); Chris Jochnick, 'Confronting the Impunity of Non-State Actors: New Fields for the Promotion of Human Rights', *Human Rights Quarterly* 21: 1 (1999).

[53] Articles of Agreement of the World Bank, Article I(i).

[54] Ibrahim Shihata, *The World Bank in a Changing World: Selected Essays*, volume II, compiled and edited by Franziska Tschofen and Antonio R. Parra (Dordrecht: Martinus Nijhoff, 1995), p. 560.

[55] Shihata, *The World Bank in a Changing World*, pp. 50–4.

international human rights law, it has been associated with the creation of a system of government that is accountable and transparent and that is supported by a vibrant and effective civil society and by democratic institutions which uphold and promote the rule of law.[56] The Bank first articulated the concept of governance in a 1989 study of Sub-Saharan Africa.[57] The Bank, when seeking to account for the dismal development record of many recipient African countries (and by implication the dismal record of the Bank) concluded that this could be attributed to the lack of good governance in those countries. In making this argument, the Bank in effect sought to refute economists who argued that the Bank had prescribed inappropriate policies that had simply exacerbated rather than alleviated poverty. The violation of economic and social rights inherent in the intensification of poverty, furthermore, was also the fault of the lack of governance and not the fault of the Bank: the causes of failure were to be located at the local level and not the international level.

Having defined the problem in this way, the Bank sought to remedy it by initiating a new and comprehensive campaign to promote 'good governance' and, thereby, human rights.[58] The linkage between governance, as so conceived, and human rights is suggested by the Bank:

> The World Bank helps its client countries build better governance. This assistance in improving the efficiency and integrity of public sector institutions – from banking regulation . . . to the court system – has a singularly important impact on creating the structural environment in which citizens can pursue and continue to strengthen all areas of human rights.[59]

The shift to governance suggested a new target for IFI management. Previously, the IFIs had insisted on focusing on economic factors in devising their policies. Now, by asserting that economic success depended on good governance, on the political system of a country, the IFIs could

---

[56] See generally Linda C. Reif, 'Building Democratic Institutions: The Role of National Human Rights Institutions in Good Governance and Human Rights Protection', *Harvard Human Rights Journal* 13: 1 (2000).

[57] World Bank, *Sub-Saharan Africa: From Crisis to Sustainable Growth: A Long-term Perspective Study* (Washington, DC: World Bank, 1989).

[58] The Bank defines governance in technical terms, referring to it as the exercise of authority over a country's resources, and the ability of a government to formulate and implement policy. See World Bank, *Governance and Development*, Report No. 10650 (Washington, DC: World Bank, 1992).

[59] World Bank, *Development and Human Rights: The Role of the World Bank*, Report No. 23188 (Washington, DC: World Bank, 1998), p. 11.

justify formulating an entirely new set of initiatives that sought explicitly to reform the political institutions of a recipient state. Thus, the Bank's governance campaign has focused on creating a system of government which is accountable, transparent, and democratic; this includes initiatives to reform judiciaries, enhance participation in decision-making, formulating environmental policy, restructuring the public service and governmental auditing functions, and even strengthening the role and effectiveness of the press.[60] In this way, the Bank can be seen as furthering civil and political rights. Thus, instead of being seen as violating human rights, the IFIs, through their engagement with governance issues, present themselves as upholding human rights. At the same time, the Bank maintains a certain distance from human rights by suggesting that it promotes the 'structural environment' in which human rights can be furthered, rather than claiming to directly promote human rights. In addition, in promoting development, the Bank claims to be instrumental in advancing social and economic progress.[61] Of course, this presumes that Bank policies further all the important social and economic goals encompassed by the term 'development'. By equating its own controversial and problematic economic policies with the promotion of human rights, the Bank basically reinterprets the character and content of these rights, rendering them in a way which is consistent with the neoliberal economic policies furthered by the Bank.[62] What this approach obscures is the possibility that the IFIs themselves, precisely through these policies, are arguably responsible for human rights violations. The further and fundamental point is that, under the rubric of technical intervention in governance issues which have an impact on the economy, the Bank is in effect playing a massively interventionary role in the internal political affairs of a state, a practice which is at odds with Article IV.10. By arguing that it can assume jurisdiction over any activity which affects 'development', the Bank can exercise authority over virtually any activity it pleases in the name of promoting good governance, and hence, development. In this way, the Bank has used the concept of good governance, first, to suggest the affinities between its activities and general international law, thus enhancing its legitimacy; and second, to develop new roles and functions that are arguably inconsistent with its own

---

[60] See World Bank, *Development and Human Rights*, p. 17.
[61] See World Bank, *Development and Human Rights*, p. 2.
[62] James Gathii, 'Good Governance as a Counter-Insurgency Agenda to Oppositional and Transformative Projects in International Law', *Buffalo Human Rights Law Review* 5 (1999), 107.

articles of agreement, the same articles which, it claims, prevent it from directly adhering to developments in international law more generally.

The IMF, a more conservative organisation than the Bank, has, albeit in more guarded terms, adopted the concept of governance with respect to its own sphere of action. Thus the IMF claims to confine itself to 'economic aspects of governance' which are directly connected to matters which the IMF focuses on in fulfilling its purposes. While appearing limited, the issues that the IMF can thus address are comprehensive and go to the very centre of economic policy-making. Thus the IMF can address institutional reforms of the treasury, budget preparation and approval procedures, tax administration, accounting and audit mechanisms, exchange, trade and price systems, and aspects of the financial system, taxation, banking sector laws and regulations, and the establishment of free and fair market entry.[63] The IMF modestly defers to the Bank in areas in which the Bank has comparative expertise, such as public enterprise reform, civil service reform, property rights, contract enforcement and procurement practices. The IMF's strength, in many respects, is its concern to focus on fewer issues, although this hardly makes it less powerful than the Bank, since the issues that the IMF controls are central to the economic system of a country. While the actions of the IMF clearly have an impact on human rights issues,[64] the IMF has been far less engaged than the Bank with human rights issues. It maintains that its focus is on monetary matters, and these are quite distinct and far removed from human rights issues, whereas in the Bank's case, the Bank argues that its principal concern – development – promotes human rights.[65] Thus the IMF has produced far less literature on these complex issues; while the Bank has written several reports on questions of governance, the IMF has produced a twelve-page pamphlet.[66] In general, the IMF is less concerned to address the arguments made by its critics.[67]

The invocation and elaboration of the concept of good governance has a cost. Good governance requires, crucially, the rule of law, a proper and effective system of accountability and democratic decision-making.

[63] International Monetary Fund, *Good Governance*, p. 4.
[64] Balakrishnan Rajagopal, 'Crossing the Rubicon: Synthesizing the Soft International Law of the IMF and Human Rights', *Boston University International Law Journal* 11 (1993), 81.
[65] Morais, 'The Globalization of Human Rights Law'; Bradlow, 'The World Bank', 72–3.
[66] For example, the World Bank report, *Governance and Development*, only one of several, is sixty pages long.
[67] For a recent account which emphatically asserts the IMF's independence of general international law, see Robert Hockett, 'From Macro to Micro to "Mission-Creep": Defending the IMF's Emerging Concern with the Infrastructural Prerequisites to Global Financial Stability', *Columbia Journal of Transnational Law* 41: 1 (2002), 153.

These points are stressed by the IFIs themselves, particularly the Bank,[68] and they act as important justifications for the law reform projects that the Bank undertakes in developing countries. The problem is that the IFIs are lacking in all these important respects, and critics and commentators on the IFIs have raised the question of how the IFIs measure up to the standards they prescribe as being essential for good government. The lack of accountability of the IFIs is the subject of increasing scrutiny and criticism. Thus Ngaire Woods and Kapur have pointed to the fact that the countries most affected by IFI policies are generally the least represented on the executive boards of the IFIs;[69] and that the IFI activities have expanded enormously, while their accountability has declined, as even the mechanisms in place are inadequate.[70]

From a legal point of view, the IFIs lack any system of effective accountability. Eminent lawyers who have occupied very senior legal positions in the IFIs have produced a comprehensive, considerable, and distinguished literature outlining the law governing the IFIs and their operations.[71] The fact remains, however, that there is no system of independent judicial review to ensure that the IFIs comply with their own articles of agreement. The only provision in the articles of each which touches on this issue essentially provides that any dispute as to the interpretation of the articles will be resolved by the executive board. Given that it is the same board which ostensibly makes the decisions which raise the issue of the interpretation in the first place, this whole system is built on a fundamental conflict that annuls entirely the notion of a 'rule of law'.

It is now a commonplace perception that the IFIs are run for the benefit of the richer countries. The IFIs are no longer seen as independent organisations operating according to strictly technocratic considerations.[72] Arguably, the voting structure of the IFIs, which gives the G7 control of the IFIs, has explicitly permitted this; however, as already noted, the articles of agreement included provisions designed to protect the

---

[68] The World Bank, *Governance: The World Bank's Experience*, Development in Practice Series, Report No. 13134 (Washington, DC: World Bank, 1994), p. vii.
[69] See Ngaire Woods, 'Making the IMF and the World Bank More Accountable', *International Affairs* 77: 1 (2001); Kapur, 'The IMF: A Cure or a Curse?'
[70] Woods, 'Making the IMF and the World Bank More Accountable'.
[71] See for example, Joseph Gold, *The Rule of Law in the International Monetary Fund* (Washington, DC: International Monetary Fund, 1980). Sir Joseph was General Counsel of the IMF. See also Shihata, *The World Bank in a Changing World*, volumes I and II. Dr Shihata was General Counsel of the World Bank.
[72] See Gianviti, 'The Reform of the International Monetary Fund', 115–16.

IFIs from becoming simply a vehicle by which powerful states could pursue their own interests.[73] Furthermore, the principle that the IFIs are independent organisations is extremely important to the self-image of the officials of the IFIs themselves, as Wade suggests in his account of the struggles between the Bank and the US Treasury Department over the roles of Joseph Stiglitz and Ravi Kanbur in the work of the Bank. It is because of this that any departure from this model of neutrality and independence becomes noteworthy. Thus it is interesting that even the *Economist* was constrained to observe that 'in recent years, the Fund and the Bank have been hijacked by their shareholders for overtly political ends'.[74] As this comment would suggest, the politicisation of the IFIs is perceived as a deviation from their proper function, and the collapse of the idea that the IFIs are independent technocratic organisations exacerbates the credibility gap they confront.

As a consequence of these developments, the IFIs are suffering from a legitimation crisis that is attributable in part to their deviation from the legal norms they espouse. Their politicisation from within appears to depart from the spirit of the articles of agreement which they cite as their governing instrument. And the IFIs themselves do not comply with the standards of 'good governance' that they prescribe for developing countries when extolling the virtues of the rule of law and transparency. The IMF, once again, is less active than the Bank in responding to this problem. The Bank has attempted to make its operations more transparent and to win the support of non-governmental organisations. For example, it has set up a tribunal to ensure that any project it funds meets its environmental guidelines. In all these different ways, the Bank has attempted to establish equivalents of accountability, which nevertheless remain short of the legal accountability which they prescribe for governments.

## Conclusions

In terms of the broad themes of this volume, then, it is clear that legitimacy is important to the IFIs, and that law plays a crucial role in attempts by IFIs to legitimise themselves and consolidate and expand their power. Just as the economists in the Bank have embraced evolving concerns about poverty, the environment, empowerment, and good

[73] This is what Abbott and Snidal term 'dirty laundering' – a process which, they note, may incur long-run costs. Abbott and Snidal, 'Why States Act', 13.
[74] 'Sick Patient, Warring Doctors', *Economist*, 18 September 1999.

governance in their writings, so too have the lawyers at the Bank attempted to demonstrate that the Bank is a progressive international citizen that seeks in its operations to accommodate, if not further, the emerging norms of international human rights law and international environmental law. In this respect, the Bank's approach provides an interesting study of how international law may affect the operations of an important international actor *even in circumstances where that actor continues to maintain that such norms are not strictly binding on its operations.* The IMF is more reluctant to present itself in this way.

This apparent accommodation, however, is not without its own ambiguities, for it is clear that the Bank is opportunistic and characterises its relationship with general international law in such a way as to expand its operations and assert thereby its relevance and importance. Thus the Bank interprets human rights and environmental standards in ways consistent with its own articles of agreement and its principal purpose of bringing about development. In effect, the Bank adopts a self-serving interpretation of international human rights law, that enables it to further its own neoliberal agenda in a number of different ways. By linking human rights with governance and then stressing the importance of 'governance' for 'development', the Bank justifies programmes directed at reforming the political institutions and practices of a country, thereby interfering in the political activities of the developing state in a manner prohibited by its articles of agreement.

The legitimacy of the IFIs is crucially based on their ability to present themselves as independent. On the whole, the staff of the IFIs, while sharing the neoliberal faith of the United States and other G7 countries, pride themselves on their professionalism and independence and strongly resist any suggestion that they are merely lackeys of the United States and other powerful nations.[75] This presents an ongoing challenge to the IFIs, given the governance system provided for in the articles of agreement, and in particular the system of weighted voting. Seen in this perspective, the IFIs confront a danger, for by expanding their jurisdiction, they may simply expand thereby the range of issues and activities, previously regarded as beyond the competence of IFI management, that powerful states will seek to influence through the IFIs. In these circumstances, the IFIs may choose to argue that international law limits their actions, this in order to prevent powerful states from using the institution to pursue their own interests in ways that undermine the credibility

---

[75] See Wade, 'US Hegemony and the World Bank'.

and legitimacy of the IFIs. Legal norms, then, are deployed strategically by IFIs to pursue and legitimise their actions in a number of different ways. These strategies, however, present their own problems. The IFI initiatives regarding 'the rule of law' and 'good governance' raise awkward questions as to how the IFIs themselves comply with the standards and procedures they prescribe; the manner in which the IFIs respond to these challenges will play a crucial role in consolidating the credibility and legitimacy of the IFIs.

IO independence may be compromised in a number of different ways. But it is only by viewing IOs as actors intent on preserving the independence on which their authority depends, that we may acquire a sense of the complex politics of the IFIs and the crucial role that law plays in managing and shaping the politics of these immensely important actors.

# 10 Law, politics, and international governance

*Wayne Sandholtz* and *Alec Stone Sweet*

The politics of international law are inextricably linked to the issue of governance. In this chapter we approach the central themes of the book by considering this vexed issue, developing four key arguments. First, we define and conceptualise *institutions* and *governance* so that any alleged distinction between *law* and *politics* becomes untenable or irrelevant. Our claim here directly addresses two of the three questions put forward by Christian Reus-Smit (in chapters 1 and 2) as animating this book: How should we think of international law and international politics? What is the relationship between the two? Our empirical discussion responds to the third question: How does rethinking these categories enable us better to understand contemporary international relations? We agree with Reus-Smit that international law and politics infuse and shape each other, although we understand this relationship somewhat differently. Second, we are concerned with the sources and uses of power in international society. Elaborating on the distinction drawn by Reus-Smit between realist and constructivist approaches, we distinguish normative-ideational power (influence through argumentation and suasion, dear to constructivists) from material-physical power (influence through the manipulation of threats and coercion, emphasised by realists). Third, we develop a relatively abstract model of how institutions emerge and evolve in two kinds of social settings: the *dyadic* and the *triadic*. Finally, we illustrate our theoretical ideas with reference to the development of triadic forms of governance in the context of the General Agreement on Tariffs and Trade (GATT), and of dyadic forms in the case of forcible humanitarian intervention.

Our discussion proceeds as follows. In part one, we define our terms and concepts. In part two, we specify the conditions under which third-party dispute resolution will organise institutional change over time, using the transformation of the international trade regime as a case in point. In part three, we discuss how institutional change takes place in the absence of a third party, and explore the question of humanitarian intervention. In the conclusion, we consider the implications of our arguments for various theoretical projects in international relations and international law.

## Rules, dispute resolution, and institutional change

We seek to explain some of the dynamics of institutional change, by which we mean the emergence of new, or the transformation of existing, rule systems. The basic components of our model operate on three levels of analysis:

- macro level: the rule system, or institutional environment, that enables and sustains social activity;
- micro level: the domain of action and decision making by individual actors;
- meso level: those structures – concrete and organisational, or abstract and discursive – that people create and use in order to coordinate rule systems and purposive action.

### Institutions

Rule systems, or institutions, enable actors to conceive, pursue, and express their interests and desires, but also to co-ordinate those desires with other individuals. We take a broad view on social structure, heavily informed by what has by now become virtually generic social theory.[1] Our conception of macro structure is congruent with what Douglass North calls 'institutions', variously: 'rules of the game', 'customs and traditions', 'conventions, codes of conduct, norms of behavior, statute law, common law, and contracts'.[2] It encompasses James March and Johan Olsen's notion of 'rules': the 'beliefs, paradigms, codes, cultures, and knowledge' that permit us to 'identif[y] the normatively appropriate

---

[1] See Douglass C. North, *Institutions, Institutional Change, and Economic Performance* (Cambridge: Cambridge University Press, 1990); and Walter W. Powell and Paul J. Dimaggio (eds.), *The New Institutionalism in Organizational Analysis* (Chicago: University of Chicago Press, 1992).
[2] North, *Institutions*, pp. 3–6.

behavior'.[3] It is capable of equating norms, as Michael Taylor does, with 'ideologies' and 'culture',[4] and with Harry Eckstein's view of 'culture' as a system of 'mediating orientations ... general dispositions of actors to act in certain ways in sets of situations'.[5] And it can understand 'institutionalized rules', in Ronald Jepperson's terms, as 'performance scripts'.[6]

We see institutions as rule structures. Rules, of course, vary; they can be more, or less, formal, precise, and authoritative; and they may be more or less tied to organisational supports, including enforcement mechanisms.[7] We could array institutions along a continuum. At the left end of the continuum are institutional settings that are relatively informal, with imprecise rules that are not binding on actors, and where there are no centralised monitoring or enforcement mechanisms. (This is not to say that these settings lack rules; social existence of any kind is impossible without norms, even if the norms in place are relatively informal and imprecise.) At the right end of the continuum are institutional contexts defined by rules that are highly formal, specific, and authoritative; these have the attributes that people associate with highly developed legal orders. Other institutions would fall between these two extremes.

At the international level, all established institutional structures would occupy different points on the spectrum.[8] Some international institutions are highly formal, specific, and authoritative. The European

---

[3] James March and Johan Olsen, *Rediscovering Institutions: The Organizational Basis of Politics* (New York: Free Press, 1989), p. 22.
[4] Michael Taylor, 'Structure, Culture and Action in the Explanation of Social Change', *Politics and Society* 17: 2 (1989), 135.
[5] Harry Eckstein, 'A Culturalist Theory of Political Change', *American Political Science Review* 82: 3 (1988), 790.
[6] Ronald L. Jepperson, 'Institutions, Institutional Effects, and Institutionalism', in Powell and Dimaggio (eds.), *The New Institutionalism in Organizational Analysis*, p. 145.
[7] See Alec Stone Sweet, Wayne Sandholtz, and Neil Fligstein, 'The Institutionalization of European Space', in Alec Stone Sweet, Wayne Sandholtz and Neil Fligstein (eds.), *The Institutionalization of Europe* (Oxford: Oxford University Press, 2001).
[8] Alec Stone, in 'What is a Supranational Constitution?: An Essay in International Relations Theory', *Review of Politics* 56: 3 (1994), elaborated a continuum in which the rule structures constituting various international regime forms could be situated. The continuum captures three dimensions: degree of normative precision, degree of formality, and degree of organisational capacity to monitor compliance and punish non-compliance. In a recent special issue of *International Organization*, a research project on the 'legalisation' of international politics adopts, as an analytical/heuristic device or dependent variable, a continuum that largely reproduces these same elements. See Judith Goldstein, Miles Kahler, Robert Keohane, and Anne-Marie Slaughter (eds.), Special Issue on the Legalization of International Politics, *International Organization* 54: 3 (2000).

Union (EU) now resembles, in important respects, a 'constitutionalised', quasi-federal polity.[9] During the same period, the GATT[10] developed an important degree of formality, precision, and authoritativeness, if less than the EU, which its mutation into the World Trade Organisation (WTO) took much further.[11] Much of organised international relations fall further to the left on the continuum. The distinctive institution of modern international law that Reus-Smit describes in chapters 1 and 2 would thus be most developed near the right end of our spectrum.

As one moves along the continuum from left to right, the nature of political activity changes. The left end of the spectrum resembles what international relations scholars have traditionally referred to as 'anarchy', meaning not absence of order but the lack of formal structures of government and authoritative dispute resolution. At the left end, bargaining, negotiation, and coercion are standard modes of interaction. Toward the right side of the spectrum, politics are more structured by legal rules and judicialised dispute resolution. There are 'islands' of such institutionalised rules and governance structures in international relations, including the European Union, the WTO dispute resolution mechanism, and the world of transnational business.[12] As Reus-Smit argues in chapter 1, politics tends to be a qualitatively different activity within the framework of law than outside of it.

In the opening chapter to this volume, Reus-Smit makes a strong case for taking seriously the constitutive power of institutions, arguing that they can shape actors' identities, roles, and, therefore, their interests. Although we accept the logic of this argument, our chapter focuses on the relationship between institutions – law and norms – and observable behaviour, including the development of norm-based argumentation, legal discourse, and 'judicialised' politics. It is exceptionally difficult to assess relationships among institutions, identities, and interests as

---

[9] Eric Stein, 'Lawyers, Judges, and the Making of a Transnational Constitution', *American Journal of International Law* 75: 1 (1981); and Joseph H. H. Weiler, 'The Transformation of Europe', *Yale Law Journal* 100: 7 (1991).

[10] Robert E. Hudec, *Enforcing International Trade Law: The Evolution of the Modern GATT Legal System* (Salem, NH: Butterworth, 1993).

[11] Ernst-Ulrich Petersmann, 'The Dispute Settlement System of the World Trade Organization and the Evolution of the GATT Dispute Settlement System Since 1948', *Common Market Law Review* 31: 6 (1994).

[12] Alec Stone Sweet, 'Islands of Transnational Governance', in Martin Shapiro and Alec Stone Sweet, *On Law, Politics, and Judicialisation* (Oxford: Oxford University Press, 2002).

they evolve in dynamic systems. Although we are comfortable with the notion that rule systems – and the flow of politics within institutions – may alter the identities and preferences of actors, we content ourselves with providing the kind of evidence that those who would make such claims might use. But we do not directly address what we take to be the basic epistemological question: pursuant to some observable alteration of the institutional environment, is a given, stable shift in the observable behaviour of any actor or set of actors best explained by (1) a change in the actors' preferences or identities, or (2) a change in actors' strategies (with preferences fixed)?

Of course, institutions persist because they are in some sense functional constructions, whether in an old-fashioned anthropological or new-fashioned economistic sense. Among other things, they provide people with behavioural guidance, reduce uncertainty and transaction costs, and thereby facilitate social exchange and co-operation. Conceived more sociologically, any social setting, or organisational field, is nothing but a specific set of normative solutions to a specific set of social problems. Even accepting these points, two problems necessarily arise. First, institutions are abstractions. At best they constitute templates or choice-contexts for action. Put differently, because rule structures do not apply themselves, they are always at least relatively indeterminate. The precise nature, scope, and content of relevant duties and obligations can only be known (if at all) through processes of interpretation and application. Second, institutions, partly because they are abstract, can, in and of themselves, be a source of disputes that erupt between individuals. That is, a dispute may reveal tensions and inconsistencies within rule structures, at least with respect to that dispute. Thus, to the extent that any normative construct is in fact relevant to a particular situation, decision, or action, it can never be innocent of politics and the exercise of power.

In short, rule structures are at the heart of any dispute that might interest social scientists, for two reasons. First, the inevitable gap between general rules and specific actions means that the application of rules is always subject to interpretation and contestation. Second, because no complex rule system provides comprehensive solutions to conflicts among all of its constituent components, tensions and contradictions among norms are also commonplace, and likewise fuel debate. When normative disputes of these kinds arise, actors bring to bear both normative and material powers, and thus the distinction between law and politics vanishes.

242

### Actors and action

Whenever individuals interact with each other, they inevitably build norm-based structures, rules of language and action considered appropriate to a given set of interactions. We assume that in these interactions, people are rational, in the sense of being utility maximisers. Within constraints imposed by institutions, resource limitations, and imperfect information, actors will seek to develop optimal strategies with which to pursue their interests. The game theoretic point that rules systems structure strategic calculation (a change in the rules of the game will always lead to different play, and thus different outcomes), simply privileges institutions as crucial factors generating political outcomes. Further, institutions possess the capacity to help mitigate imbalances of material or physical power between actors. Indeed, normative systems typically announce rules that either (1) do not take into account such asymmetries, or (2) invoke principles (such as equity or fairness) that give advantages to the weaker party. We do not deny that seemingly 'power-neutral' norms often reflect underlying distributions of power. Our point is rather the contrary: norms are always implicated in politics. Last, in situations where information is imperfect in some meaningful way, institutions will be all the more important[13] to how actors make sense of their world and select courses of action.

If we see actors as bearers of interests, that is not all we see. Rationality, in the utility-maximising sense, is not the only logic of action (or micro-foundation) relevant to institutional change. As a diverse set of social scientists have noticed and begun to theorise,[14] norms tend to develop in processes that are both incremental and path dependent. The deep structures of this process are cognitive and pre-social: human beings have native or 'instinctual' capacities for language. Indeed, we would argue that the ability to think about rules in complex ways – reasoning from precedent and weighing contradictory norms – is as innately human as the 'language instinct'.[15] Robert Sugden points out that 'ordinary people with limited rationality' find little difficulty in solving co-ordination problems that the fully rational players in game theory

---

[13] See North, *Institutions*.

[14] For example March and Olsen, *Rediscovering Institutions*, chapter 2; Alec Stone Sweet, 'Judicialization and the Construction of Governance', *Comparative Political Studies* 32: 2 (1999); and Robert Sugden, 'Spontaneous Order', *Journal of Economic Perspectives* 3: 4 (1989).

[15] The phrase borrows the title of a superb book by Steven Pinker, *The Language Instinct* (New York: W. Morrow, 1994).

find intractable, and suggests that the ability to work with conventions and norms is innate, even biological.[16] We observe people reasoning and talking about rules in every kind of social group. That observation lends some *prima facie* credibility to the notion that normative reasoning, based on analogies that link rules to situations, is at least as innate and fundamental to humans as utilitarian calculation.

For cognitive psychologists, analogical reasoning is the process through which people 'reason and learn about a new situation (the *target* analog) by relating it to a more familiar situation (the *source* analog) that can be viewed as structurally parallel'.[17] The ability to construct analogies is widely considered to be an innate part of thinking.[18] Unfamiliar situations, those that individuals cannot understand through their generalised knowledge, stimulate the formation of analogies, which are used to conceptualise *and* to find solutions to problems.[19] The set of potential source analogs is defined jointly by (1) the specific, immediate problem to be resolved (or situation to be conceptualised), and (2) the past experiences of the individuals constructing the analogy. Foreshadowing somewhat, we view normative deliberation, including legal argumentation and judging, as a species of analogical reasoning: actors reason from existing institutions (the equivalents of source analogs), to characterise the interplay of new fact contexts and interests raised by a dispute (the target analog), and to find an appropriate solution to it.[20] As Reus-Smit argues in chapter 2, actors simultaneously engage in purposive and instrumental logics (maximising) and in logics of obligation and justification (or normative reasoning).

---

[16] Sugden, 'Spontaneous Order', 89, 95.

[17] Keith Holyoak and Paul Thagard, 'The Analogical Mind', *American Psychologist* 52: 1 (1997), 35.

[18] Mark Keane, *Analogical Problem Solving* (Chichester, UK: Ellis Horwood Ltd, 1988); Stella Vosniadou and Andrew Ortony (eds.), *Similarity and Analogical Reasoning* (Cambridge: Cambridge University Press, 1989); Keith Holyoak and Paul Thagard, *Mental Leaps: Analogy in Creative Thought* (Cambridge, MA: MIT Press, 1995); and Richard Mayer, *Thinking and Problem Solving: An Introduction to Human Cognition and Learning*, 2nd edn (New York: W. H. Freeman & Co, 1992).

[19] Keane, *Analogical Problem Solving*, p. 103.

[20] See James Murray, 'The Role of Analogy in Legal Reasoning', *UCLA Law Review* 29: 4 (1982); Cass Sunstein, 'On Analogical Reasoning', *Harvard Law Review* 106: 3 (1993); Garry Marchant, John Robinson, Urton Anderson, and Michael Schadewald, 'Analogical Transfer and Expertise in Legal Reasoning', *Organizational Behavior and Human Decision Processes* 48: 2 (1991); and Garry Marchant, John Robinson, Urton Anderson, and Michael Schadewald, 'The Use of Analogy in Legal Argument: Problem Similarity, Precedent, and Expertise', *Organizational Behavior and Human Decision Processes* 55: 1 (1993).

## Dispute resolution and governance

Typical sources of conflicts can be listed but need not detain us much. An actor may succumb to temptations to renege on promises made in order to obtain advantage (the prisoner's dilemma). As circumstances change, actors may come to different views on the legitimacy of the existing rules that govern a relationship, and seek to replace those with new ones. Or, as norms evolve, and social interactions become more complex, actors may disagree about if and how a specific set of rules is to be applied to the situation in which they find themselves. Last, some rule systems offer actors more than one normatively defensible means of resolving a conflict, even when the disputants agree about the nature or type of dispute they are in.

Institutions facilitate dispute resolution. They do so in three ways. First, at the level of the single actor, a norm can prevent disputes from arising in the first place, by providing individuals with behavioural guidance, and by structuring choices concerning compliance. Second, once a dispute has erupted, norms may provide the contracting parties with the materials for settling the dispute on their own, dyadically as it were, to the extent that norms furnish the bases for evaluating both the disputed behaviour and potential solutions to the conflict. Third, existing rule systems help third-party dispute resolvers do their jobs, by providing templates for determining the nature of the dispute and an appropriate solution.

We define governance as the process through which rule systems are adapted to the needs and purposes of those who live under them.[21] Modes of governance are social mechanisms for constructing rules and for applying them to concrete situations. Given changing circumstances, all social systems require such mechanisms if they are to reproduce themselves. We focus here on how two types of governance serve both to resolve disputes and to evolve institutions. Both are meso-level structures that, under certain conditions, will forge linkages between macro abstractions and micro particularities. To the extent that they operate with effectiveness, they will help to bind together, and mediate between, the domain of rules and the domain of action, giving institutions at least a measure of determinacy that they would otherwise lack.

The first structure, the argumentation framework, is cognitive and discursive. Argumentation frameworks (what Anglo-Saxon lawyers

---

[21] Stone Sweet, 'Judicialization and the Construction of Governance'.

often call doctrine) organise how disputants make normative claims and engage one another's respective arguments. Following Giovanni Sartori,[22] these structures can be analysed as a series of inference steps, represented by a statement justified by reasons (or inference rules), that lead to a conclusion. Legal frameworks typically embody inconsistency, to the extent that they offer, for each inference step, both a defensible argument and counter-argument, from which contradictory – but defensible – conclusions can be reached.

Although we have argued that rule systems, including law, are indeterminate, argumentation frameworks provide a measure of (at least short-term) systemic stability, to the extent that they condition how actors pursue their self-interest, social justice, or other values through normative deliberation. To be effective in this discursive politics, actors have to be able to identify the type of dispute in which they are involved, reason through the range of legal norms that are potentially applicable, and assess available remedies and their consequences. Argumentation frameworks, being a formalised analog, help actors do all of these things, and more. They require actors not only to engage in analogic reasoning, but in argumentation. Considered in more sociological terms, they are highly formal, meso-level structures that connect institutions (such as the law) to the domain of individual agency, by sustaining deliberation about the nature, scope, and application of norms. In culturalist terms, they enable specifically placed social actors to adjust abstract 'guides to action' to 'the relentless particularity of experience',[23] on a continuous basis.

The second structure is the triad, where two parties to a dispute delegate their conflict to a third party for resolution. All forms of dispute resolution can be classified as either dyadic or triadic. The distinction is straightforward. In dyadic contexts, the parties to a dispute seek to define a solution between themselves, that is, without recourse to an external mediator, arbitrator, or judge. In that sense, we might think of dyadic settings as formally anarchic (which is not to say without order), because there exists no authoritative dispute resolver outside the dyad. Dyadic dispute resolution can thus take multiple forms: imposition (a stronger party coerces a weaker one), negotiation, persuasion. Such forms of dispute resolution are ubiquitous; we see them between spouses, between labour and management, in many interstate conflicts,

---

[22] Giovanni Sartori, 'A Formal Model of Legal Argumentation', *Ratio Juris* 7: 2 (1994).
[23] Eckstein, 'A Culturalist Theory of Political Change', 795–6.

and so on. Moreover, describing a dispute resolution process as dyadic does not mean that only two actors are involved. Multilateral disputes (that is, involving more than two parties), can be seen as a collection of linked bilateral relationships. The label 'dyadic' simply refers to the absence of an outside adjudicator.

Triadic dispute resolution, naturally, embraces all settings in which, in addition to the parties themselves, there is a 'third party' (which can also be a collectivity of multiple actors, including enforcers), who assists in finding, or authoritatively determining, resolution of the dispute. To move from dyadic to triadic systems of dispute resolution is to move from anarchy to hierarchy. Empirically, forms of triadic dispute resolution vary along a continuum that roughly stretches from mediation to arbitration to adjudication. As we move left to right on this continuum, the authority of the triadic entity, *vis-à-vis* the parties, is enhanced and institutionalised in ever more formal rules and procedures.

We view judging as a species of analogic reasoning which produces marginal adjustments to the law over time. Further, to the extent that judgements are motivated with reasons, and to the extent that some minimally robust conception of precedent operates, dispute resolution will serve not only to construct the law but to delineate argumentation frameworks. Where adjudication is both intensive and effective, prior records of decision-making, curated by legal actors as precedents, will cluster and congeal in argumentation frameworks. These frameworks will organise normative deliberation and analogical reasoning, and help to reinforce the authority of the triadic entity.

Under certain conditions, dispute resolution will provoke normative innovation. Where these conditions are met, the sequence – rule structures > social exchange > disputing > dispute resolution (through normative deliberation or delegation to a third party) > rule-making > institutional change > social exchange – will tend to reproduce itself in a self-reinforcing process. We will try to defend these claims in the next two sections.

## Triadic dispute resolution and governance

The causal relationship between triadic dispute resolution (TDR) and rule innovation is well-known, and has been theorised in quite diverse theoretical languages.[24] If the triadic entity resolves disputes in a

---

[24] For example, H. L. A. Hart, *The Concept of Law*, 2nd edn (Oxford University Press, 1994), chapter 7; Karl Llewellyn, 'The Normative, the Legal, and the Law-Jobs: The

minimally respectable (rather than arbitrary or a fraudulent) manner, and gives reasons for her decisions, then these decisions will contain materials for consolidating existing, or building new, norms. Given two conditions, TDR is likely to generate powerful pedagogical – or positive feedback – effects, to be registered on subsequent social exchange and dispute resolution. First, actors must perceive that they are better off in a world with TDR than without it. If they do, and if they are rational, they will evaluate the rulefulness of any potential action and anticipate the probable outcome issuing from TDR. Second, the dispute resolver must understand that her decisions have some authoritative – that is, precedential – value.

If these conditions are met, then the more people go to a triadic entity, the more that entity will exercise authority over the relevant rule system. A virtuous circle is thereby constructed: to the extent that TDR is effective, it will reduce the costs of social exchange; as social exchange increases in scope, so will the demand for the authoritative interpretation of rules; as TDR is exercised, the body of rules that constitutes normative structure steadily will expand, becoming more elaborate and differentiated; these rules then will feed back onto dyadic relationships, structuring future interactions, conflict, and dispute resolution.

If exercised on an ongoing and effective basis, TDR is likely to constitute a crucial mechanism of social cohesion and change, by propagating and sustaining the development of expansive argumentation frameworks. To put it in constructivist terms, triadic governance will help to co-ordinate the complex relationship between structures and agents,[25] helping to constitute and reconstitute both over time. In rationalist terms, the move from the dyad to the triad replaces games, like the prisoner's dilemma or chicken, with an entirely different strategic context. Although game theorists have begun to notice the challenge,[26] they have had difficulty modelling 'triadic'.[27]

Problem of Juristic Method', *Yale Law Journal* 49: 8 (1940), 1373; Alf Ross, *On Law and Justice* (London: Stevens and Sons, 1958); Martin Shapiro, 'Stability and Change in Judicial Decision-Making: Incrementalism or *Stare Decisis*?', *Law in Transition Quarterly* 2: 3 (1965); and Stone Sweet, 'Judicialization and the Construction of Governance'.

[25] Anthony Giddens, *The Constitution of Society: Outline of the Theory of Structuration* (Berkeley: University of California Press, 1984).

[26] For example, Randall L. Calvert, 'Rational Actors, Equilibrium, and Social Institutions', in Jack Knight and Itai Sened (eds.), *Explaining Social Institutions* (Ann Arbor, MI: University of Michigan Press, 1995).

[27] See the exchange between Alec Stone Sweet, 'Rules, Dispute Resolution, and Strategic Behavior', *Journal of Theoretical Politics* 10: 3 (1998) and Georg Vanberg, 'Reply to Stone Sweet', *Journal of Theoretical Politics* 10: 3 (1998).

We now examine the impact of TDR on the international trade regime, an arena in which judicial power had been initially, and by design, excluded. By judicial power, we mean the capacity of a triadic dispute resolver to authoritatively determine the content of a community's normative structure. In the GATT, an international treaty established rules governing relations between states; yet the regular use of TDR led to the mutation of these relations, and a new regime was thereby constituted. We use the term 'judicialisation' as shorthand for this mutation.

## The judicialisation of the international trade regime

When the GATT (1948) entered into force and was institutionalised as an organisation, 'anti-legalism' reigned.[28] Diplomats excluded lawyers from GATT organs and opposed litigating violations of the treaty. In the 1950s, TDR emerged in the form of the panel system. Panels, composed of three to five members, usually GATT diplomats, acquired authority through the consent of two disputing states. In the 1970s and 1980s, the system underwent a process of judicialisation. States began aggressively litigating disputes; panels began treating the treaty as enforceable law, and their own interpretations of that law as constituting authoritative precedents; jurists and trade specialists replaced diplomats on panels. The process generated the conditions necessary for the emergence of the compulsory system of adjudication now in place in the WTO.

### Normative structure and dispute resolution

The GATT is the most comprehensive commercial treaty in history, today governing more than five-sixths of world trade. In the 1955–74 period, membership jumped from 34 to 100 states; 124 states signed the Final Act of the Uruguay Round (establishing the WTO) in 1993. The treaty's core provision is a generalised equal treatment rule, the most favoured nation (MFN) principle, which rests on reciprocity: each party to the GATT must provide to every other party all the advantages provided to other trading partners. The treaty further prohibits, with some exceptions, import quotas. The organisation also supports an interstate forum for legislating trade law: eight 'rounds' have reduced most tariffs to the point of insignificance and, less successfully, restricted non-tariff barriers to trade.

The treaty exhorts members to settle their disputes dyadically, in accordance with GATT rules. The potential for a trade conflict to move

---

[28] Olivier Long, *Law and its Limitations in the GATT Multilateral Trade System* (Boston: Martinus Nijhoff, 1985), pp. 70–1; and Hudec, *Enforcing International Trade Law*, p. 137.

to a triadic stage was implied: if state A could demonstrate that it had suffered damages due to violations of GATT law committed by state B, state A could be authorised by the GATT membership as a whole to withdraw advantages or concessions that it would normally be required to accord state B. Almost immediately, however, member states invented the panel system to resolve disputes.

As institutionalised in the 1950s, the system blended mediation and consensual adjudication, against a backdrop of ongoing dyadic dispute resolution. Defendants could not be compelled to participate in TDR. By denying consent, a state could block the construction of a panel, reject proposed panelists, and refuse to allow a ruling to be reported. Relative to compulsory forms of adjudication, the system appeared grossly inefficient. The original function of panels, however, was to facilitate dyadic conflict resolution, not to punish violators or to make trade law. Diplomats, trade generalists who saw expedience in flexible rules and detriment in rigid ones, sat on panels. When mediation failed, panels could, with the consent of the disputants, resolve conflicts according to relevant treaty provisions.

Before 1970, states did not exploit the connection between TDR and rule-making. But, being both imprecise and rigid, the regime's normative structure proved insufficient to sustain optimal levels of trade over time. The treaty mixes a few hard obligations (the MFN norm and tariff schedules) with a great many statements of principle and aspiration. Despite its flexibility, important GATT provisions could be revised only by unanimous consent. Although the success of the GATT was partly due to normative imprecision – the more vague a rule, the easier it was for states to sign on to it – textual imprecision was often locked in by the unanimity requirement. The tension is obvious. Achieving optimal levels of exchange partly depends on the continuous adaptation of abstract rules to concrete situations, but the GATT legislator was ill-suited to perform this adaptation for the trade regime.

### Building the triad

Beginning in 1970, the largest trading states turned to the panel system not just to resolve their trade conflicts, but to make trade policy. After falling into desuetude in the 1960s (only seven complaints filed), TDR exploded into prominence afterwards. Of the 207 complaints filed through 1989, 72 per cent were filed after 1969, and 56 per cent after 1979. The four largest trading states – Canada, the EC, Japan, and the

US – dominated panel proceedings: in the 1980s, over 80 per cent of all disputes registered involved two of these four states.

The expansion of global exchange, and the domestic political consequences of that expansion, broadly explain the renaissance of TDR. Bilateral exchange among the big four (Canada, the EC, Japan, and the US) rose from $15 billion in 1959, to $44 billion in 1969, to $234 billion in 1979, to $592 billion in 1989. As trade redistributed resources and employment across productive sectors within national economies, domestic actors mobilised to protect their interests. And as these economies came to produce virtually the same products for export (for example, electronics, automobiles, food products), trade relations were easily interpreted in zero-sum terms.

By 1970, new forms of protectionism had proliferated, the Gold Standard currency regime was rapidly disintegrating, and the American trade deficit had become chronic. The need for clearer rules and better compliance was acute. At the same time, the GATT legislator had failed to liberalise certain crucial sectors (for example, agriculture), to dismantle the mosaic of non-tariff barriers that had emerged in response to tariff reduction (for example, restrictive licensing policies and production standards), and to regulate other practices that distorted trade (for example, subsidies). Led by the US, which was also groping for ways to reduce its trade deficit, governments turned to the panel system.[29]

Three general motivations animated the move to TDR. In the vast majority of instances, states initiated complaints in order to induce other states to modify their domestic trading rules. As we will see, GATT panels proved to be a relatively effective means of doing so. Second, states appealed to panels in order to alter, clarify, or make more effective existing GATT rules. This motivation overlaps the first, since virtually all trade disputes are translatable into a general argument about the meaning and application of specific treaty provisions. Disputants worked to convince panels to adopt their versions of GATT rules, in order to encourage the spread of practices they considered lawful and to discourage practices they considered unlawful. Third, while difficult to verify,

---

[29] Disputants tend to litigate what diplomats failed to legislate. Conflicts over agriculture and subsidies paralysed trade negotiations, and they also dominated TDR processes after 1970. Of 115 complaints filed in the 1980s, 51 (44 per cent) concerned trade in agricultural goods. Of the 44 disputes filed citing one of the GATT codes, 21 (or 48 per cent) relied on rules found in the subsidies code.

governments sometimes participated in TDR to delegitimise – and thus facilitate the revision of – their own trade practices.[30]

To maximise their success, governments had a powerful interest in replacing diplomats and generalists with lawyers and trade specialists. The Americans understood this immediately; the Nixon Administration turned GATT litigation over to trade lawyers in 1970. By that year, the enormous complexity of trade disputes – the resolution of which requires determining (a) the extent to which a specific domestic law or administrative practice conforms with treaty provisions, and (b) the extent to which, in cases of non-conformity, such a law or practice had caused, or might cause, trade distortions – was far beyond the capacity of anyone but the lawyer and the expert. Once introduced by the Americans, lawyerly discourse perpetuated itself. Lawyers filed detailed legal briefs, attacking or defending particular national policies; faced with detailed questions, panels gave detailed answers; lawyers then understood the reasoning supporting such answers as guidelines for future litigation strategies. The EC and Japan initially resisted the move to legalism; but they became active participants after being bombarded with complaints by the US and Canada. By the early 1980s, all of the major trading states had armed their Geneva staffs with permanent legal counsels.

## Triadic governance

In activating TDR, GATT members delegated to the panel system an authority that is inherently governmental. As panels exercised this authority, they generated three sets of political outcomes; these outcomes can only be explained by attending to the dynamics of TDR.

First, panels altered the terms of global exchange by provoking, with their decisions, the modification of national trading rules. If complied with, every decision declaring a national rule or practice inconsistent with GATT rules concretely impacts the lives of importers, exporters, consumers, and producers. Activating TDR worked in favour of plaintiff

---

[30] In 1988, the US instituted proceedings against the EC's payment regime for oilseed processing. A panel ruled that the programme both discriminated against foreign processors and functioned as an indirect subsidy for EC producers. France, invoking the consensus norm, sought to suppress the decision but the EC adopted the ruling over France's objection. The EC then replaced the payment system with a new one. In effect, the EC had used TDR to delegitimise an outmoded, costly programme of which France had blocked revision within internal EC law-making processes. Complaint #179, US v. EC (22 April 1988). Complaints have been assembled and numbered chronologically in Hudec, *Enforcing International Trade Law*, Appendix. We use Hudec's reference system to refer to cases in this and subsequent notes.

states: plaintiffs enjoyed a success rate of 77 per cent in the 1948–89 period, rising to 85 per cent in the 1980s. The rate of compliance with adverse decisions was 74 per cent in the 1980–9 period.

To resolve many of the most complex disputes, panels had no choice but to reach far into national jurisdictions. Thus, a panel ruled that a US law providing a special administrative remedy for patent infringement claims involving imported goods violated the GATT since defendants stood a better chance of winning in district courts.[31] To arrive at this decision, panelists investigated US litigation rates and judicial outcomes, concluding that biases in the administrative procedure constituted a discriminatory bias affecting trade. In separate cases, panels required Canada to force provincial governments to remove taxes on foreign gold coins, and to force provincial liquor boards to change regulatory practices favouring domestic alcoholic beverages.[32]

Panels reinforced their influence over policy outcomes by elaborating guidelines for state compliance. In explaining why a given national practice was or was not inconsistent with GATT obligations, panels suggested GATT-consistent versions of the practices in question. (Such behaviour inheres in triadic rule-making.) In 1986, to take just one instance, the EC attacked the Japanese system of taxation for alcoholic beverages.[33] The system, which classified products into dozens of categories corresponding to different tax rates, resulted in importers paying higher taxes than Japanese producers for similar products. The panel declared the system to be inconsistent with the treaty, and announced a general rule: national tax schemes must treat all 'directly competitive' products equally. It then elaborated a hypothetical system based on equal treatment, demonstrating precisely what a lawful system would look like. The Japanese subsequently adopted a system similar to the panel's.

Second, in response to the exploitation of TDR by states for their own political purposes, panels reinvented themselves as judges, the authoritative interpreters of the regime's normative structure. This process can be tracked and measured. As the number and complexity of complaints grew, panels produced longer decisions and increasingly precise interpretations of treaty provisions.[34] In complicity with GATT litigators,

[31] Complaint #162, EC v. US (29 April 1987).
[32] Complaint #132, South Africa v. Canada (3 July 1984); complaint #139, EC v. Canada (12 February 1985).
[33] Complaint #154, EC v. Japan (6 November 1986).
[34] In the 1948–69 period, the average length of reported rulings was seven pages; in the 1970–9 period, the average length rose to fifteen pages; after 1985, the average reached

citations to past decisions became increasingly common and expected. Once constructed as a precedent-based discourse about the meaning of GATT rules, panel decisions became a fundamental source of those rules. (Such rule-making took place despite the absence of a doctrine of *stare decisis* in international law, and despite the refusal of the member states to formally recognise the precedential value of decisions.) Certain treaty provisions (for example, the MFN norm, rules governing taxation and quotas) emerged as sophisticated, relatively autonomous domains of legal discourse, replete with their own stable of argumentation frameworks.[35] By the 1980s at the latest, the rules in these domains could *only* be understood in light of the argumentation frameworks curated by the panels. Although the substance of this law is far beyond the scope of this chapter, panels ratcheted up national responsibility to justify any claimed exceptions to liberal trading rules which, among other things, served to expand the grounds for future complaints.

Panels also generated rules governing their own jurisdiction.[36] By the end of the 1980s a stable case law asserted that, among other things, panels could:

- not only review the consistency of national acts with the treaty, but could also detail what kinds of similar, if hypothetical, acts might violate GATT rules;
- announce answers to questions not raised by plaintiffs, but which were nevertheless relevant to other trade disputes;
- report a ruling even if the dispute on which it was based had become moot (for example, as a result of prior dyadic settlement), in order to clarify GATT rules and thus facilitate future dyadic and triadic dispute resolution.

---

forty-eight pages. Robert E. Hudec, 'The Judicialization of GATT Dispute Settlement', in M. H. Hart and D. B. Steger (eds.), *In Whose Interest?: Due Process and Transparency in International Trade* (Ottawa: Center for Trade Policy and Law, 1992), p. 11.

[35] Breaking down GATT complaints filed in the 1980s with reference to the article of the Agreement in dispute provides some indication of the relative density of these areas. In 115 filings, disputants invoked specific parts of the Agreement 212 times. Four areas of the law account for 71 per cent of total claims: the MFN norm (arts. 1 and 2, 21 per cent); non-discrimination in taxation and regulation (art. 3, 10 per cent); elimination of quotas (arts. 11, 13, 34 per cent); and nullification or impairment of benefits (art. 23, 6 per cent). Of the 66 instances in which the special codes were invoked, the codes on subsidies were involved 41 times (62 per cent). See Alec Stone Sweet, 'The New GATT: Dispute Resolution and the Judicialization of the Trade Regime', in Mary L. Volcansek (ed.), *Law Above Nations: Supranational Courts and the Legalization of Politics* (Gainesville: University Press of Florida, 1997).

[36] Hudec, *Enforcing International Trade Law*, pp. 258–65.

Third, judicialisation processes reconstructed how states understood the nature of their own regime. States reacted to the development of a rule-oriented mode of governance not by suppressing it, but by adjusting to it. Their lawyers filed more and increasingly legalistic complaints, and their diplomats ratified judicialisation in official agreements. Thus, the 1979 'Understanding' on dispute settlement placed the GATT's system on legal footing for the first time, codified dispute settlement procedures, and gave legal force to panel reports. In 1981, citing the overwhelming complexity of litigation facing panelists, states permitted the establishment of a Legal Office charged with rationalising procedures and providing support for panel members. And in the Uruguay Round (1986–92), states asked an autonomous group of experts to study how TDR could be strengthened. The fruit of their efforts was the legal system of the WTO.

The Final Act of the Uruguay Round transformed the GATT into the WTO, providing for a system of compulsory adjudication of disputes. The new rules: automatically confer jurisdiction to panels upon the reception of a complaint; no longer permit unilateral vetoes of any stage by either party; and provide for a broad range of measures to punish non-compliance. An independent appellate body is charged with handling appeals from panels. The body is composed of seven members who possess 'demonstrated expertise in law'.

Undeniably, the move from consensual to compulsory TDR could not have taken place without a convergence in the preferences of the most powerful trading states. The US had advocated more efficient dispute settlement since the 1970s. The Americans had even taken measures in domestic law to unilaterally punish those who blocked or refused to comply with GATT decisions; and the move provoked the EU to adopt similar measures. Facing a trading world in which GATT rules might be enforced unilaterally by the most powerful states, the rest of the world joined the US and Europe in working to strengthen multilateralism.

But, if converging state interests were crucial to the enhancement of TDR in the GATT, judicialisation generated the context necessary for that convergence. Judicialisation is socialisation. As states gained experience with dispute settlement, as panels performed their dispute resolution functions, as a stable case law enhanced legal certainty, GATT members could afford to view triadic rule-making as a useful, cost-effective guarantor of regime reciprocity. In the 1980s, states did not consider abolishing the panel system, but debated how best to enhance it. By the end of the decade, a collective future without effective TDR was no longer a serious option.

## Dispute resolution and normative change in the dyadic context

Though islands of triadic dispute resolution have emerged in international relations, most international interactions are dyadic. Disagreements between international actors are sometimes subject to resolution by a third party, through arbitration, mediation, or referral to supranational courts or other formal mechanisms. But in many instances, when actors contest the appropriateness of specific acts, or debate the meaning of relevant norms, they do not or cannot refer the dispute to an outside arbiter. Instead, each disputant seeks to persuade her rival, and third parties, that her understandings of the rules and of the disputed acts are correct. International actors deploy both arguments and material power to bring others to their view. At one extreme, those with sufficient power resources can impose their preferred solutions on other actors, though they will simultaneously offer arguments designed to show that their choices are also normatively justified. At the other extreme, when no single actor can impose a solution, normative arguments about what course of action is justified are crucial in establishing consensus.

The regular deployment of material resources, whether as incentive or punishment, underlies the persistent image of international relations as structured fundamentally by relations of power. The realist and neorealist traditions deny that norms and suasion play any independent role in international politics; actors offer arguments and invoke norms, but only as decoration for what they would have done in any case. Material structures are the only ones that count. Thus the powerful do what they will and the weak accept what they must.

We argue that even actors with the greatest material resources do not operate outside of normative structures. In the dyadic portions of international relations, where there is no authoritative dispute resolver, the dynamic of normative evolution is not simply reducible to the exercise of power. Three related arguments support this assertion. First, the range of disputes that can be settled by the unilateral application of material power or coercion is restricted and probably shrinking. Indeed, military force (the ultimate currency in realist and neorealist approaches) is simply not a factor in the vast majority of disputes. Indeed, the frequency of wars among great powers has been in secular decline, and

256

essentially non-existent since the Second World War. Thus the great powers can impose armed *faits accomplis* in a small set of instances, and these (in practice) only *vis-à-vis* weak or collapsed states. Second, in the far more common situations where military force is not an option, the great powers operate within a set of institutions (rules) most of which they did not devise but rather inherited. They must therefore employ persuasion, and for that they must assert their claims in terms of existing argumentation frames. Third, to the extent that powerful actors internalise the rules, their values, goals, and choices are shaped from within by normative structures that have been 'domesticated', a point to which we return in the conclusion.

## Normative change in the dyadic context

In both dyadic and triadic settings, the inevitable gap between rules and actions generates disputes. As actors seek to resolve disputes, they reason by analogy, invoke precedents, and give reasons, whether their audience is a judge or a set of other governments. Two significant differences, however, distinguish dyadic international relations from triadic. First, in the dyadic realm, the dispute resolution process is less formalised. As a consequence, it often resembles interstate bargaining, as governments seek to persuade, and pressure, each other. Because the process in general is less formal, the body of precedents available to disputants is less formalised, which means that precedent establishes a broader, less clearly delineated argumentation frame. Second, because the discursive frame is more open and the process non-formalised, the deployment of power resources is less mediated by institutions than it is in a triadic setting.

Even so, the evolution of international norms in dyadic contexts follows a cyclical pattern similar to the one we saw in the triadic context. The cycle begins with the constellation of existing norms, which provides the normative structure within which actors decide what to do and evaluate the behaviour of others. Because rules cannot cover every contingency, and because conflicts among rules are commonplace, actions regularly trigger disputes. The arguments are about which norm(s) apply, and what the norms require or permit. Actors assert analogies between the act in question and some set of prior cases. When the analogy is persuasive, other actors will agree that the current dispute should fall under the same norms that covered the earlier (analogised) cases. But the argument does not end there, for it remains to be determined what the norms require in the present instance. Again, players argue by analogy with similar cases, in order to establish how the rules should apply to the case in dispute (if there are mitigating factors, if the case qualifies as an exception, and so on).

Even powerful states must make their case in terms of an existing normative context. And even governments of the most dominant states do not always prevail in these normative debates. As an illustration, the case of the United States in its post-Cold War 'unipolar moment' is quite instructive. The United States has not always been able to win important arguments, for example, with respect to Iraq. Even important friendly states (France, Germany, Russia) refused to support Security Council authorisation of the use of force against Iraq. The United States and its allies proceeded with war anyway, and the arguments about the effect of the war on international norms will continue for some time. Though other states were unable to prevent the US-led invasion of Iraq, they will be able to penalise the United States for what many governments view as a violation of international rules.

The outcome of any discourse is to change the norms under dispute. If everybody agrees that the norms apply without qualification, then the norms have been strengthened and the scope of their application clarified. If the relevant actors agree that the disputed act qualifies as a justified exception to the norms, then the scope of their application has also been clarified (the proliferation of exceptions, of course, can weaken a rule, which is also a norm change). If the participants in the discourse fail to reach consensus (as with Iraq), then that also modifies the norms in question, leaving their status weakened or ambiguous. In contrast with the triadic situation, where judges must make a decision, in the dyadic context, nothing compels actors to reach a determination. Thus disagreements over the meaning of the rules, and over the justifiability of specific acts, can continue unresolved over long periods of time.

The crucial point, however, is that the cycle of normative change has completed a turn. In a given normative structure, actions trigger disputes. Argument ensues, grounded in analogies with previous cases. The outcomes of these discourses (which also include the deployment of power) modify the rules, whether by making them stronger or weaker, clearer or more ambiguous. The cycle returns to its starting point, the normative structure, but the normative structure has changed. The altered norms establish the context for subsequent actions, disputes, and discourses.

## The case of forcible humanitarian intervention

Since 1990, a series of humanitarian crises has thrown into relief a tension between two sets of fundamental international norms. On the one hand, sovereignty rules traditionally prohibited intervention in the internal affairs of other states; on the other, the international community has clearly made human rights a matter of collective concern and universal norms. The question that pits these concerns against each other is: under what conditions may armed intervention be justified to halt massive human rights abuses occurring within the territory of a sovereign state? The society of states has confronted that question directly in several cases over the past decade; we assess a series of such cases beginning with the question of safe havens in northern Iraq in 1991 and ending with East Timor in 1999.

The resulting disputes over humanitarian intervention have generated precisely the kind of cycle we theorised above: rules provide the social context for action, specific acts trigger disputes, disputes provoke discourses, and discourses lead to modification of the rules. As a result of this evolution, international society has developed rules that permit, though they do not require, forcible intervention to halt grievous, widespread human rights violations.[37]

The United Nations Security Council has provided the chief institutional forum for the disputes and discourses over the legitimacy of humanitarian intervention.

Precedent works in the dyadic world roughly as it does in the triadic, through the creation of analogies. If humanitarian intervention was permitted in A, and the case of B is similar in important respects, then there is a plausible justification for intervening in B. Put differently, once the Security Council has permitted intervention in one case, it becomes much more difficult to argue that the rules prohibit intervention in a similar instance. Furthermore, when states do object to a proposed intervention, they must offer counter-arguments permitted by the argumentation framework. Each subsequent similar decision strengthens the discursive weight of the emerging norm. Thus participants in Security Council deliberations devise their arguments in light of that body's prior decisions (as parties pleading before a court in the triadic setting fashion their arguments with a view to prior judgements and opinions).

[37] See Wayne Sandholtz, 'Humanitarian Intervention: Global Enforcement of Human Rights?', in Alison Brysk (ed.), *Globalization and Human Rights* (Berkeley: University of California Press, 2002).

The proposition that participants in Security Council debates will develop and use argumentation frameworks by deploying analogies and precedents is not as obvious as it might appear. Indeed, Security Council members face substantial incentives to deny that precedents play any part in their decision-making, for at least two reasons. First, the members of any given Security Council will prefer to maximise their own discretion. They will therefore tend to deny the notion that their decisions should be constrained by what an earlier Council may have determined. This is especially true since the composition of the fifteen-member Security Council regularly changes (aside from the five permanent members). This is not the same as the normal turnover in personalities sitting on a court or in a legislature, because it is not just the individuals but the countries represented that rotate.

Second, with specific reference to humanitarian intervention, Security Council members will consistently attempt to maximise the normative protections of state sovereignty, and to minimise any dilution of them. The reason for this is straightforward: ambassadors in the Security Council represent the governments of states, which have an interest in preserving their own autonomy from outside intervention. From the perspective of any given government, any precedent must be seen as potentially dangerous, in that it could weaken their immunity against future interventions. For both reasons, we expect to find generalised resistance to the idea of precedent in Security Council decision-making.

Given the incentives to avoid both creating and referring to precedent, any evidence of such activity will offer strong support for our argument. Issues relating to sovereignty and the use of force within the territory of another state constitute hard cases for our theory of normative evolution. The evidence shows, however, that Security Council members, denying it all the while, create and consider precedent. The representative of Zimbabwe captured this paradox in his remarks during a discussion of the proposed intervention in Somalia: 'Any unique situation and the unique solution adopted create of necessity a precedent against which future, similar situations will be measured.'[38] We take the use of precedent as evidence of an emerging argumentation framework.

---

[38] United Nations Security Council, Provisional Verbatim Record of the Three Thousand One Hundred and Forty-Fifth Meeting, 3 December 1992, S/PV.3145, p. 7.

## Rule contexts

Sovereignty norms are the fundamental constitutive rules of international society. Two sovereignty-related rules erect a *prima facie* barrier to forcible humanitarian intervention. The first, a constitutive precept of international law, establishes exclusive internal jurisdiction. The second is the ban on the use of violence: no state may resort to force of arms in its interactions with other states. Non-intervention norms find expression in the UN Charter, especially in Article 2(7), which forbids the UN organisation (or, in the prevailing interpretation, its member states) 'to intervene in matters which are essentially within the domestic jurisdiction of any state'. The ban against intervention has been reinforced in 'soft law', through a series of General Assembly resolutions, including the 1950 Peace Through Deeds Resolution, the 1957 Declaration Concerning the Peaceful Coexistence of States, the Declaration on Inadmissibility of Intervention in Domestic Affairs of States and Protection of their Independence and Sovereignty (1965), and the Declaration on Principles of International Law Concerning Friendly Relations and Cooperation Among States in Accordance with the Charter of the United Nations (1970).

United Nations rules against the use of force also create a presumption against the legitimacy of armed humanitarian intervention. Article 2(4) enunciates the famous injunction against the use or threat of force. The Charter provides only two explicit exceptions to this prohibition. The first is 'individual or collective self-defence' (Art. 51), and the second is UN action, when mandated by the Security Council, to halt 'threats to the peace, breaches of the peace, and acts of aggression' (Chapter VII). Thus the Charter does not identify enforcement of human rights as one of the permissible justifications for the use of force. Legal scholars have nevertheless argued that forcible humanitarian intervention is clearly compatible with central objectives of the UN and that the absence of a prohibition makes it permissible.[39]

International human rights norms have undergone steady development since the Second World War; they also find expression in the United Nations Charter and in other UN conventions and declarations. The preamble to the Charter affirms a common 'faith in fundamental human rights, in the dignity and worth of the human person, in the equal

---

[39] Fernando R. Tesón, *Humanitarian Intervention: An Inquiry into Law and Morality*, 2nd edn (Irvington-on-Hudson, NY: Transnational Publishers, 1997).

rights of men and women'. Article 1 of the Charter enumerates the purposes of the UN, which include the achievement of 'international cooperation . . . in promoting and encouraging respect for human rights and for fundamental freedoms for all without distinction as to race, sex, language, or religion' (Article 1(3)). Article 55(c) declares that the United Nations 'shall promote . . . universal respect for, and observance of, human rights and fundamental freedoms', and in the following article 'all Members pledge themselves to take joint and separate action in cooperation with the Organization for the achievement' of those purposes (Chapter IX, Article 56).

The members of the UN followed up with a series of declarations and conventions that spelled out a range of human rights, starting with the Convention on the Prevention and Punishment of the Crime of Genocide (1948), and the Universal Declaration of Human Rights (1948). In Jack Donnelly's account,[40] formal rule-making culminated with the International Covenant on Economic, Social, and Cultural Rights and the International Covenant on Civil and Political Rights (both in 1966). Treaties on special topics followed, including women's rights (1979), torture (1984), and the rights of children (1989). Still, by the mid-1990s, though 'norms and the process of norm creation have been almost completely collectivized', and monitoring has moved somewhat in that direction, 'implementation and enforcement remain almost exclusively national'.[41] In short, though the UN Charter does not explicitly provide for collective enforcement of human rights, there were clearly grounds to argue that using force against massive abuses was consistent with the purposes of the institution.

## Disputes, discourse, precedent

International sovereignty rules are fundamentally in tension with universal human rights norms. Rule conflicts are brought to the surface by actors who dispute the appropriate course of action in a specific circumstance. During the 1990s, a series of cases triggered Security Council debates on humanitarian intervention. Instances of humanitarian intervention did occur before 1990, but we focus on the post-1990 cases, for two reasons. First, in the pre-1990 cases, when the Security Council

---

[40] Jack Donnelly, 'State Sovereignty and International Intervention: The Case of Human Rights', in Gene M. Lyons and Michael Mastanduno (eds.), *Beyond Westphalia? State Sovereignty and International Intervention* (Baltimore: Johns Hopkins University Press, 1995), p. 123.
[41] Donnelly, 'State Sovereignty and International Intervention', p. 146.

was involved, it was asked to condone or condemn interventions that had already been carried out unilaterally (for instance, by India in East Pakistan, France in Central Africa, Vietnam in Cambodia, and Tanzania in Uganda).[42] In contrast, in the 1990s, the Security Council was asked to consider multilateral interventions under UN mandate before the fact. Even in controversial instances of multilateral intervention by groups of states without explicit Security Council authorisation (northern Iraq, Kosovo), the UN had already debated and taken specific actions in response to serious human rights concerns.

Second, the end of the Cold War and the collapse of the Soviet Union reconfigured the international political context. Prior to 1990, the superpowers would veto any proposed intervention out of Cold War politico-strategic concerns, thus excluding humanitarian intervention from multilateral decision-making in the UN. Since 1990, the Security Council has been able to debate and often reach consensus in cases that previously would have been deadlocked by the US–Soviet rivalry. In addition, the nature of interventions changed. Before 1990, interventions were generally unilateral; after that date, most interventions have been multilateral.

The Security Council is the primary forum in which states debate norms of humanitarian intervention. Though the speeches offered by delegates are usually carefully scripted and involve generous doses of posturing and pretence, the statements offered in Security Council meetings do expose the normative arguments that actors deploy in order to shape the rules. Participants understand that their statements become part of a larger discourse and a permanent record, and frame normative claims in an effort to shape that discourse, as well as the inevitable accumulation of precedent, in ways compatible with their perceived interests and values. We have examined the transcripts of Security Council debates on proposals for humanitarian intervention in nine cases: Liberia, Iraq (the safe havens), Bosnia, Somalia, Haiti, Rwanda, Sierra Leone, Kosovo, and East Timor. These cases include all of the post-1990 interventions in which humanitarian objectives were central. In two of them (Bosnia, Somalia), the Security Council authorised intervention by

---

[42] These are the four cases commonly identified as instances of humanitarian intervention pre-1990, though scholars disagree as to which ones should count. Tesón, *Humanitarian Intervention*, includes Uganda, Central Africa, East Pakistan, and the US invasion of Grenada. Nicholas J. Wheeler, *Saving Strangers: Humanitarian Intervention in International Society* (Oxford: Oxford University Press, 2000), includes East Pakistan, Cambodia, and Uganda. Sean D. Murphy, *Humanitarian Intervention: The United Nations in an Evolving World Order* (Philadelphia: University of Pennsylvania Press, 1996), includes East Pakistan, Central Africa, and Uganda.

UN ('blue helmet') forces. In six cases (Bosnia, Somalia, Haiti, Rwanda, Sierra Leone, East Timor), it authorised or expressed approval for (after the fact) armed interventions carried out by coalitions of member states ('multilateral forces'). In two cases (Iraq, Kosovo) member state coalitions conducted forcible humanitarian interventions without specific Security Council mandates but in the context of ongoing Security Council efforts to deal with major human rights disasters.[43]

It bears keeping in mind that there are powerful reasons not to expect the use of precedent in Security Council discussions. Indeed, we find explicit and implicit attempts to avoid the setting of precedent. Explicit efforts typically took the form of statements by national representatives to the effect that in authorising intervention, the Security Council was not establishing precedent for future cases. Implicit attempts to suppress the formation of precedent involved statements that emphasised the 'exceptional', 'singular', or 'unique' situation confronting the Security Council. By declaring that a given intervention is unique, states assert that from the particulars of an exceptional case one cannot derive general norms or principles. Such arguments are intended to foreclose the drawing of analogies from one case where intervention was permitted to a subsequent set of circumstances. No future case could ever match the 'singular' features of, say, Somalia. But of course no two cases ever match in all of their details; the question is whether actors construct analogies between a few salient features of two cases that are, by definition, unique. The answer is that they do, because argument by analogy and precedent is an inherent feature of normative reasoning.

We analysed the verbatim transcripts of twenty-two meetings of the Security Council in which the topic of discussion was intervention to halt or alleviate large-scale human rights abuses in nine countries. Meetings of the Security Council are debates only in a loose sense. That is,

---

[43] This brief summary necessarily omits many of the nuances relevant to individual cases. For instance, we have included the case of Iraq even though the Security Council did not expressly authorise forcible intervention to create the 'no-fly zones'. In Resolution 688, the Council addressed major human rights abuses occurring within Iraq and ordered that country to allow unimpeded access by humanitarian relief organisations. In Liberia and Sierra Leone, the Security Council declined to consider authorising intervention by UN forces during the periods of most intense human rights violations, despite requests that it do so. Instead, the Security Council endorsed the intervention carried out by a multinational force sponsored by and composed of members of the Economic Community of West African States (ECOWAS); the intervention force bore the acronym ECOMOG (ECOWAS Monitoring Group). On Liberia, see David Wippman, 'Enforcing the Peace: ECOWAS and the Liberian Civil War', in Lori F. Damrosch (ed.), *Enforcing Restraint: Collective Intervention in Internal Conflicts* (New York: Council on Foreign Relations Press, 1993).

members of the Council, and delegations that request to offer statements to it, do not engage in direct exchanges of arguments and counterarguments in order to win votes. Some delegates speak before the vote, and some speak after. The speeches are more like set pieces, as the members essentially know in advance what the outcome of the vote will be. Indeed, the serious debating and negotiating take place prior to the meetings, in bilateral conversations or in 'informal consultations' of the Security Council as a whole. Nevertheless, the official statements do reveal the normative stances adopted by the various states, as they seek to imprint their interpretations of the norms on the public record.

We found direct or indirect attempts to negate the precedential value of the decision being taken in six meetings, involving four cases (Iraq, Bosnia, Somalia, and Haiti). Indirect efforts include statements highlighting the uniqueness of the present case, so as to cut off analogies and diminish its potential significance as precedent. An example comes from the statement of the Spanish delegate during discussion of the resolution to authorise a multinational intervention force for Haiti: 'It must be stressed that this decision is an exceptional one, taken in response to the singular circumstances attending the Haitian crisis.'[44] Direct efforts include explicit disavowals that the current decision would create any precedent for future situations, like the following statement by the Indian delegate in the meeting authorising forcible intervention in Somalia: 'The present action should not, however, set a precedent for the future.'[45] A statement by China regarding Somalia incorporates both direct and indirect approaches: 'It is our understanding that this authorization is based on the needs of the unique situation in Somalia and should not constitute a precedent for United Nations peace-keeping operations.'[46]

More striking is the frequency with which speakers in the Security Council made positive references to precedent. Table 1 reports all thirty such references that we found in the twenty-two meetings. Of these, twenty-two drew analogies with earlier cases. Nineteen of these concerned previous Security Council decisions on humanitarian intervention; the other three references were to Nazi Germany (2) or South Africa. The remaining eight statements regarding precedent were

[44] United Nations Security Council, Provisional Verbatim Record of the Three Thousand Four Hundred and Thirteenth Meeting, 31 July 1994, S/PV.3413, p. 19.
[45] United Nations Security Council, S/PV.3145, p. 51.
[46] United Nations Security Council, Provisional Verbatim Record of the Three Thousand One Hundred and Eighty-eighth Meeting, 26 March 1993, S/PV.3188, p. 22.

Table 1 *Uses of precedent in United Nations Security Council deliberations*

| Date | Agenda topic | Precedent | Speaker's country | UN Doc. |
|---|---|---|---|---|
| 5 April 1991 | Iraq | South Africa | United Kingdom | S/PV.2982:64–65 |
| 13 Aug 1992 | Bosnia | Somalia | Zimbabwe | S/PV.3106:18 |
| 13 Aug 1992 | Bosnia | Nazi Germany | Austria | S/PV.3106:26 |
| 19 Nov 1992 | Liberia | Somalia | Sierra Leone | S/PV.3138:56 |
| 3 Dec 1992 | Somalia | Iraq, Bosnia | Austria | S/PV.3145:31 |
| 3 Dec 1992 | Somalia | Future – Bosnia | Austria | S/PV.3145:32 |
| 3 Dec 1992 | Somalia | Future | Hungary | S/PV.3145:48 |
| 3 Dec 1992 | Somalia | Future | Zimbabwe | S/PV.3145:7 |
| 31 Mar 1993 | Bosnia | Future | France | S/PV.3191:4 |
| 4 June 1993 | Bosnia | Kuwait | Venezuela | S/PV.3228:25 |
| 6 June 1993 | Somalia | Bosnia | Pakistan | S/PV.3229:7 |
| 6 June 1993 | Somalia | Future – Cambodia, Yugoslavia | Venezuela | S/PV.3229:17 |
| 6 June 1993 | Somalia | Future – Bosnia, Cambodia | Russia | S/PV.3229:22 |
| 8 June 1994 | Rwanda | Nazi Germany | Czech Republic | S/PV.3388:3 |
| 22 June 1994 | Rwanda | Somalia | New Zealand | S/PV.3392:7 |
| 15 July 1994 | Haiti | General past practice and principles | Sec. General | S/1994/828:5–6 |
| 31 July 1994 | Haiti | Future | New Zealand | S/PV.3413:22 |
| 26 Mar 1999 | Kosovo | Bosnia | Bosnia | S/PV.3989:14–15 |
| 26 Mar 1999 | Kosovo | General recent precedents of action by regional organisations | Slovenia | S/PV.3989:3 |
| 10 June 1999 | Kosovo | Cambodia | Netherlands | S/PV.4011:13 |
| 10 June 1999 | Kosovo | Rwanda | Canada | S/PV.4011:13 |
| 10 June 1999 | Kosovo | Bosnia | Malaysia | S/PV.4011:16 |
| 10 June 1999 | Kosovo | Bosnia | Bahrain | S/PV.4011:19 |
| 10 June 1999 | Kosovo | Croatia | Croatia | S/PV.4011 (resumption):12 |
| 10 June 1999 | Kosovo | Slovenia, Croatia, Bosnia | Albania | S/PV.4011 (resumption):14 |
| 11 Sept 1999 | E. Timor | Somalia, Rwanda, Bosnia, Kosovo | Italy | S/PV.4043 (resumption):13 |
| 11 Sept 1999 | E. Timor | Kosovo | Italy | S/PV.4043 (resumption):14 |
| 11 Sept 1999 | E. Timor | Kosovo | Austria | S/PV.4043 (resumption):27 |
| 11 Sept 1999 | E. Timor | Future precedent | Singapore | S/PV.4043 (resumption):20 |
| 25 Oct 1999 | E. Timor | Rwanda, Somalia, Haiti, Zaire | Canada | S/PV.4057:17 |

prospective in nature, that is, they expressed a hope that the current case would establish precedent for other specific crises or for the future more generally. This is strong evidence that, even in settings where one might not expect it, actors regularly refer to analogies and precedents as they engage in collective normative reasoning.

In substantive terms, the resolutions approved in these meetings have clearly pushed the development of norms permitting forcible intervention to halt human rights violations.[47] In Bosnia and Somalia, the Security Council created precedents for deploying armed force to assist in the delivery of emergency relief supplies. The Somalia case, in addition, broke new ground by authorising intervention in a crisis that did not pose any real threat to international peace and security. With the intervention in Haiti, the Security Council established that the UN could act to restore to power a democratically elected government. Its decisions on Haiti and East Timor, and its refusal to condemn the NATO bombing campaign on behalf of Kosovo, showed that the UN could authorise humanitarian intervention by multinational forces under national command.[48]

## Emergence of an argumentation framework

In short, a rudimentary argumentation framework has evolved in the domain of forcible humanitarian intervention. It is now established that forcible intervention is permissible, though not required, when abuses of human rights are massive, that is, both grievous and numerous. No standard of grievousness exists, but in all of the cases considered here, the abuses included serious bodily violence (rape, torture, mutilation) and deaths. Other kinds of human rights violations (detention without filing charges, arbitrary arrest) do not justify forcible responses. Though there is no precise threshold for 'massive', it is clear that occasional

[47] We are not arguing that the interventions did in fact effectively curtail human rights abuses. Indeed, the Security Council did not explicitly authorise intervention to assist the Kurds or the Kosovar Albanians, though in both cases it did not condemn the actions of multinational intervention forces. The Security Council essentially opted not to act on the horrendous human rights violations occurring in Liberia and Sierra Leone, and offered too little, too late to affect the genocide being carried out in Rwanda.

[48] The Security Council discussed in March 1999 a draft resolution proposed by Russia, Belarus, and India to condemn the NATO bombing campaign against Yugoslavia as a violation of international law and demand an immediate cessation. The resolution was defeated by twelve votes to three, only China, Namibia, and Russia voting in favour. Voting against the resolution were Argentina, Bahrain, Brazil, Canada, France, Gabon, Gambia, Malaysia, Netherlands, Slovenia, the United Kingdom, and the United States. A solid majority was therefore unwilling to condemn the intervention, though the point was vigorously contested by other states.

human rights violations, even continuing over a period of years, will not invite armed intervention (other kinds of international response being available). Conversely, opponents of intervention in a specific case can argue that the abuses are not sufficiently widespread or serious to justify military action against the offending state.

The argumentation framework also makes the case for intervention stronger when a human rights crisis includes a transnational dimension, by fomenting armed conflict in neighbouring states, or even by creating large flows of people fleeing from danger or forcibly expelled from their homes. The counter-argument, of course, is that a particular crisis is entirely internal to a country, in which case non-intervention norms should apply (although the international community can provide assistance to refugees without intervening militarily). Even so, it is clear that many states regard governments engaged in massive human rights violations as having forfeited their sovereignty-based claims to immunity from outside intervention.

A blanket non-intervention argument based simply on sovereignty is clearly no longer valid. The cases decided in the 1990s will make it much less plausible for governments to argue, in response to future large-scale human rights violations in some part of the world, that international norms prohibit intervention. Other potential exclusions have also been weakened. 'Legal' intervention need not depend on a request or even agreement from the target state. UN-led forces (blue helmets) are not the only valid mode of intervention; the UN can also authorise groups of willing states or regional organisations to carry out interventions under national command.

Finally, the record of Security Council deliberations and decisions is not the only indicator that an argumentation framework has emerged. It is by now almost universally accepted among legal scholars that forcible intervention to halt massive human rights abuses can be permissible under international law. Indeed, among the publicists, the debate has already moved on to fleshing out more of the details – conditions, exceptions, qualifications – of the argumentation framework.[49]

---

[49] The legal literature is too voluminous to cite comprehensively; representative works include Menno T. Kamminga, *Inter-State Accountability for Violations of Human Rights* (Philadelphia, PA: University of Pennsylvania Press, 1992); Laura W. Reed and Carl Kaysen, *Emerging Norms of Justified Intervention* (Cambridge, MA: American Academy of Arts and Sciences, 1993); Lori F. Damrosch, *Enforcing Restraint: Collective Intervention in Internal Conflicts* (New York: Council on Foreign Relations Press, 1995); Murphy, *Humanitarian Intervention*; Oliver Ramsbotham and Tom Woodhouse, *Humanitarian*

## Conclusion

Two summary points deserve emphasis. First, we deny any inherent, theoretically significant, distinction between how international and
domestic regimes operate. Put simply, the range of variation is as
great within categories of *domestic* and *international* as between these
categories, and mainstream international relations theory has woe-
fully failed to distinguish, theoretically, one kind of rule system from
another.[50] Colombia, Sierra Leone, and Somalia are hardly states at all,
in the Waltzian[51] sense of being centralised; while in the international
system there exist zones constituted by highly institutionalised modes
of governance. Further, national politicians, interacting in domestic political contexts, can be more jealous of their prerogatives than statesmen
negotiating with one another on the global stage; and supranational
courts can be more effective on a day-to-day basis than many national
jurisdictions.

Second, we would like this chapter to be read as an attempt to for-
malise some important insights of process-based approaches to law,[52]
and to give better micro-foundations to rule-oriented constructivism.[53]
Neorationalist perspectives (game theory and rational choice) on international regimes and legal systems have contributed to our understanding of why and how actors build new institutional arrangements
to help them achieve joint purposes. But neorationalism, to the extent
that it fails to provide a convincing account of why and how normative
discourse and legal institutions develop a 'life of their own', has not been
able to explain certain crucial dynamics of institutional change.[54] Our
differences with neorationalists do not reduce to an argument about
the status of rationality. We assume that all actors are rational (in the
sense of seeking to maximise their subjective utility given both cognitive and institutional limits), but take seriously the view that strategic

*Intervention in Contemporary Conflict: A Reconceptualization* (Cambridge: Polity Press, 1996);
Tesón, *Humanitarian Intervention*; and Wheeler, *Saving Strangers*.
[50] Friedrich V. Kratochwil, *Rules, Norms, and Decisions: On the Conditions of Practical and
Legal Reasoning in International Relations and Domestic Affairs* (Cambridge: Cambridge University Press, 1989); and Stone, 'What is a Supranational Constitution?'
[51] Kenneth N. Waltz, *Theory of International Politics* (New York: Random House, 1979).
[52] For example, H. H. Koh, 'The 1998 Frankel Lecture: Bringing International Law Home',
*Houston Law Review* 35: 3 (1998).
[53] For example, Nicholas Onuf, 'The Constitution of International Society', *European Journal of International Law* 5: 1 (1994).
[54] See the exchange between Vanberg, 'Reply to Stone Sweet', and Stone Sweet, 'Rules,
Dispute Resolution, and Strategic Behavior'.

action is heavily conditioned by existing institutional arrangements and normative uncertainty.

A more generic issue raised here is whether theoretical primacy should be assigned, a priori, to normative-ideational rather than material-physical power. At times, these two types of influence (or types of resources for action) may be in opposition to one another, as when one excludes the use of the other. More often, they are interlinked, with their relative importance varying according to the social context. In triadic settings, formal dispute resolution procedures and bodies of precedent substantially mediate the effects of material power resources. Indeed, some systems of triadic dispute resolution may explicitly seek to dilute, if not eliminate, the effects of material disparities, by forcing parties to engage in normative suasion within structures of precedent and argumentation. In dyadic contexts, material power is presumptively less mediated, but may nonetheless be shaped and constrained by normative structures.

If powerful states dictate international rules and change them as they please, then we need only focus on material power relations and the analysis need go no further. To be sure, powerful countries often exercise the greatest influence on the rules of international society. Indeed, we take it as axiomatic that in any social system, institutions, 'or at least the formal rules, are created to serve the interests of those with the bargaining power to devise new rules'.[55] Powerful actors (rich countries, large transnational companies) can offer payoffs to those who agree to their preferred rules, and they can inflict costs on those who refuse. More subtly, but perhaps more pervasively, powerful actors shape the broader intellectual and cultural environment within which other actors make their way. It is not necessarily the case that leading states actively manipulate ideas and culture for their own benefit; the point is closer to the Gramscian one that simply by virtue of their size and reach, leading states produce much of the scientific, legal, and cultural environment within which other actors live.

Still, the emergence and evolution of international norms can have an impact even on powerful states through various mechanisms. We have focused on mechanisms associated with norm-based conflict and organised dispute resolution in this chapter, but of course there are others. The development of international rule structures (like rights), for example, can offer transnational actors, and a state's own subjects, new

[55] North, *Institutions*, p. 16.

possibilities for pursuing their political interests. Much of the action in modern international law concerns how international norms are noticed, absorbed, and used politically within the legal frameworks of states. Citizens, groups, firms, non-governmental organisations, and governmental officials may then be led to alter their own cognitive schema, values, and decision-making in light of such processes. This dynamic deserves more attention in light of the themes raised by this volume,[56] and in light of the constructivist claim that international norms are basic to how states' values, objectives, and identity are constructed and evolve over time.[57]

---

[56] But see Koh, 'The 1998 Frankel Lecture'; Andrew P. Cortell and James W. Davis, Jr, 'How Do International Institutions Matter? The Domestic Impact of International Rules and Norms', *International Studies Quarterly* 40: 4 (1996); and Andrew P. Cortell and James W. Davis, Jr, 'Understanding the Domestic Impact of International Norms: A Research Agenda', *International Studies Review* 2: 1 (2000).

[57] Nicholas Onuf, *World of Our Making: Rules and Rule in Social Theory and International Relations* (Columbia: University of South Carolina Press, 1989); and Alexander Wendt, *Social Theory of International Politics* (Cambridge: Cambridge University Press, 1999).

# 11 Society, power, and ethics

## Christian Reus-Smit

In his early guise as a student of international law, Hans Morgenthau
stressed the difference between 'political' and 'non-political' international law. The latter, which encompassed rules governing 'respect to
diplomatic privileges, territorial jurisdiction, extradition, wide fields of
maritime law, arbitral procedure, and so forth', fell outside the political realm because it reflected 'the permanent interests of states to put
their normal relations upon a stable basis by providing for predictable
and enforceable conduct with respect to these relations'.[1] Political international law included the remaining panoply of international rules,
from treaties of alliance to grand legalistic schemes for collective peace
and security. These were deemed 'political' because they reflected underlying social forces, most notably the prevailing balance of power
and configuration of states' interests. Such rules, Morgenthau insisted,
were 'always precarious; the interests which they are supposed to serve
appear permanent and definite, whereas they are actually exposed to
continuous change and are more or less uncertain; and consequently,
the rights and duties established by them appear to be clearly determined, whereas they are subject actually to the most contradictory
interpretations'.[2]

The perspective on the politics of international law advanced in previous chapters differs from Morgenthau's in three important respects.
First, we share his concern with the impact of underlying 'social forces'
on the nature and practice of international law, and we understand these
forces in political terms. But our conception of the socio-political realm

[1] Hans J. Morgenthau, 'Positivism, Functionalism, and International Law', *American Journal of International Law* 34: 2 (April 1940), 279.
[2] Morgenthau, 'Positivism, Functionalism, and International Law'.

is more expansive than his. As I sought to capture in chapter 2, we see politics as encompassing more than the material and the instrumental, as having significant idiographic, purposive, and ethical dimensions. Second, while we acknowledge that some fields of international law are more stable than others, due to the enduring needs they serve and the uncontroversial nature of the rules they embody, our perspective denies the bifurcation of international law into 'non-political' and 'political' forms. For instance, only by comprehending the multiple faces of political liberalism can we account for the form, practice, and content of the modern international legal order, and the impact of this politics, and the conflicts and controversies it has engendered, has left its mark on every aspect of that order. Third, for Morgenthau the relationship between politics and law is a one-way street – politics shapes law, not the reverse.[3] Preceding chapters suggest, however, that international law 'feeds back' to constitute politics. This is more than the constraint emphasised by neoliberals; it includes the restraints of sanction and self-interest, but also the distinctive 'logic of argument' through which legal norms and discourse condition actors' identities, interests, and strategies.

In this final chapter, I conclude by considering, in a preliminary fashion, the implications of the book's approach for thinking about society, power, and ethics in international relations. My principal reason for adopting such a focus is that ideas about the nature of, and relationship between, international politics and law necessarily condition, and are conditioned by, these three concepts. The meaning of realist and rationalist views on the politics of international law for each of them has been well canvassed, but we have said little so far about the implications of our broadly 'constructivist' perspective. My second reason is that ideas about society, power, and ethics together form a central matrix around which key debates in the discipline of International Relations revolve. Our judgements about the existence, nature, and salience of social bonds among international actors affect our understanding of the nature, exercise, and centrality of power (and vice versa), and our assumptions about society and power condition our views about international ethics. Reflecting on the implications of our conception of the politics of international law for this ideational matrix thus starts to build a bridge to these central issues animating the field.

[3] Morgenthau, 'Positivism, Functionalism, and International Law', 275–6.

## Society

The perspective advanced in previous chapters is predicated upon, and serves to reinforce, the idea that international relations and world politics take place within a social domain. As soon as one speaks of the politics of international law, and pays more than cursory attention to law as a 'variable' in its own right, one is *per force* assuming more than crude systemic relations among states; one is assuming the existence of an international or world society. In Kenneth Waltz's starkest of systemic depictions of international relations, neither international law nor society rates a mention, and the concept of socialisation is reduced to the harsh lessons states learn when they ignore the principles of self-help and maximising relative power.[4] Opening the door to international law renders such imagery unsustainable, as law is a social not a material fact, and to the extent that its operation has material dimensions or consequences, these are dependent upon the complex of intersubjective meanings that constitute international law as a distinctive social practice. Yet stating that recognition of international law implies a conception of society beyond the state tells us little about how that society is to be understood. Different views about the politics of international law lead to, and draw upon, different conceptions of international society.[5]

To date, most writing on the nature of international or world society has been done by scholars of the 'English School', with constructivists making crucial contributions over the past decade. The perspective on the politics of international law advanced here, however, problematises the contours and substance of English School debate about the nature of international law and society, with particular implications for the ongoing debate between pluralists and solidarists.[6]

Hedley Bull captured the central insight of the English School in the evocative title of his classic work *The Anarchical Society*. Sovereign states can form more than systems; even in the absence of a central authority, they can form societies. 'A *society of states* (or international society) exists', he argued, 'when a group of states, conscious of certain common

---

[4] Kenneth N. Waltz, *Theory of International Politics* (New York: Random House, 1979).

[5] This is nicely addressed in David R. Mapel and Terry Nardin's volume *International Society: Diverse Ethical Perspectives* (Princeton: Princeton University Press, 1998).

[6] Some of the ideas developed in this section were rehearsed in Christian Reus-Smit, 'Imagining Society: Constructivism and the English School', *British Journal of Politics and International Relations* 4: 3 (October 2002).

interests and common values, form a society in the sense that they conceive themselves to be bound by a common set of rules in their relations with one another, and share in the working of common institutions'.[7] While this insight unites English School scholars, pluralists and solidarists differ markedly over precisely how international society is to be further understood, with important implications for how they see international law. Bull set the terms of the pluralist/solidarist debate when he observed that there is a fundamental distinction between those who see international society as bound together in solidarity by common values and purposes and those who hold that states have a plurality of different purposes and that society rests solely on the observance of common rules of coexistence.[8]

The pluralist conception of international society and law is most succinctly articulated by Terry Nardin. International society, he contends, is a practical association, 'a relationship among those engaged in the pursuit of different and possibly incompatible purposes, and who are associated with one another, if at all, only in respecting certain restrictions on how each may pursue his own purposes'.[9] It is thus a society of coexistence, one based, in Robert Jackson's words, 'on the values of equal sovereignty, territorial integrity, and non-intervention of member states'.[10] These rules are upheld by a system of 'authoritative practices' that enable states to 'rub along together'.[11] It is these practices, in fact, that enable us to speak of international society as a 'society'. In Nardin's words, it is 'constituted by the forms and procedures that states are obliged to observe in their transactions with one another'.[12] Principal among these practices is the system of international law, which 'consists of rules distilled from the common practices of the society of states, expressing more precisely and explicitly the terms of association embodied in them'.[13]

---

[7] Hedley Bull, *The Anarchical Society: A Study of Order in World Politics*, 2nd edn (London: Macmillan, 1995), p. 13, emphasis in original.
[8] Hedley Bull, 'The Grotian Conception of International Society', in Herbert Butterfield and Martin Wight (eds.), *Diplomatic Investigations: Essays in the Theory of International Politics* (London: George Allen and Unwin, 1966), p. 52.
[9] Terry Nardin, *Law, Morality, and the Relations of States* (Princeton: Princeton University Press, 1983), p. 9.
[10] Robert Jackson, *The Global Covenant: Human Conduct in a World of States* (Oxford: Oxford University Press, 2000), p. 178.
[11] James Mayall, *World Politics: Progress and Its Limits* (Cambridge: Polity Press, 2000), p. 29.
[12] Nardin, *Law, Morality, and the Relations of States*, p. 15.
[13] Nardin, *Law, Morality, and the Relations of States*, p. 187.

For solidarists, this view of international society is deeply problematic. International society is more than a practical association; it exhibits – or is starting to exhibit – characteristics of a 'purposive association'. Such an association exists, they contend, when 'there is some consensus about the substantive moral purposes which the whole society of states has a duty to uphold'.[14] This would be evident, for instance, if states 'reached an agreement about a range of moral principles such as individual human rights, minority rights, responsibilities for nature and duties to other species which they believe they should promote together'.[15] Unlike its pluralist counterpart, the solidarist conception of international society has a strong aspirational dimension: solidarists move constantly between advocating a set of normative principles and making empirical claims about their emergent status in existing international society.[16] Solidarists also question the idea that international society should rightly be considered a society of states, suggesting instead that normatively and empirically it should be seen as a society of individuals and peoples; a world society, therefore. All of this has important implications for the relationship between international society and international law. Where pluralists see the laws of coexistence as constitutive of, and coextensive with, international society, solidarists hold that there is an ethical universe beyond the state that is, and ought to be, constitutive of international society and its law. Nowhere is this clearer than in their attitude towards humanitarian intervention. For pluralists the principle of non-intervention is a cardinal rule of international law; for solidarists the cosmopolitan principles of human rights must take precedence when states commit crimes against humanity.[17]

The perspective advanced in this book casts doubt on this dichotomous rendering of the debate about international society and law. The first problem is the pluralist notion that international society can be equated with law – 'international society is not merely regulated by international law but *constituted* by it'.[18] This view simultaneously overstates international law's status as a social practice – citing it as the

---

[14] Andrew Linklater, *The Transformation of Political Community: Ethical Foundations of the Post-Westphalian Era* (Cambridge: Polity Press, 1998), pp. 166–7.
[15] Linklater, *The Transformation of Political Community*, pp. 166–7.
[16] Nicholas Wheeler handles these two dimensions of solidarism artfully and systematically in his *Saving Strangers: Humanitarian Intervention in International Society* (Oxford: Oxford University Press, 2000).
[17] Wheeler, *Saving Strangers*, pp. 12–13.
[18] Terry Nardin, 'Legal Positivism as a Theory of International Society', in Mapel and Nardin (eds.), *International Society*, p. 20, emphasis in original.

definitive foundation of international society – and underestimates that status by ignoring the social embeddedness of international law, the fact that it is a practice that evolves within a given socio-historical context. None of this book's contributors would wish to deny the centrality of international law to the fabric and functioning of international society, but as noted in chapter 2 we share Philip Allott's view that law 'presupposes a *society* whose structures and systems make possible the mutual conditioning of the public mind and the private mind, and the actual conditioning of the legal and the non-legal'.[19] Our illustration of this view appears in my own discussion of the role that political liberalism played historically in the constitution of the modern system of international law, and in my fellow contributors' discussions of the ways in which politics, in its varied dimensions, conditioned international legal developments in diverse areas, even if politics itself was framed by the broader legal order. Because pluralists ignore the socially rooted nature of international law, they have no way to account for its emergence.[20]

The second problem concerns the pluralist characterisation of international law as essentially a system of rules for interstate coexistence, a position that has both empirical and normative dimensions. Pluralists treat it as fact that rules of coexistence define international law *per se*, and caution against solidarist principles corroding these rules, a view that echoes Bull's early prioritising of order over justice.[21] Yet even if one holds that international law is best understood as a system of rules, the twentieth-century development of international law has seen the codification of a vast array of purposive norms, from world trade law to international humanitarian law. More than this, though, the perspective advanced here complements views that international law is more than a system of rules, it is a social process. The modern international legal system is distinguished by its distinctive discourse of autonomy, multilateral form of legislation, and language and practice of justification, and preceding chapters have shown the salience of these features in diverse cases. The crucial thing for our purposes, however, is that a dialogue between pluralist and solidarist principles 'lives' in the ongoing discourse of international law as a communicative process.

[19] Philip Allott, 'The Concept of International Law', in Michael Byers (ed.), *The Role of Law in International Politics: Essays in International Relations and International Law* (Oxford: Oxford University Press, 2000), p. 70.
[20] See Christian Reus-Smit, *The Moral Purpose of the State: Culture, Social Identity, and Institutional Rationality in International Relations* (Princeton: Princeton University Press, 1999), pp. 36–9.
[21] Jackson, *The Global Covenant*, p. 181; and Bull, *The Anarchical Society*, pp. 83–94.

We see this in arguments surrounding the creation of the International Criminal Court, over the Kosovo bombing campaign, and in other cases as well. Rather than conceiving international law as a coexistence system, potentially undermined by solidarist politics, our discussions suggest that it is more fruitfully seen as a crucial site within international society for the negotiation of practical and purposive norms. The need for international society to engage in such negotiation was noted by Bull himself when he observed that '[a]ny regime that provides order in world politics will need to appease demands for just change, at least to some degree, if it is to endure; and thus an enlightened pursuit of the goal of order will take account also of the demand for justice'.[22]

The final problem relates to the pluralist isolation of international society and its law as a discrete social realm, with relative autonomy from the actors, structures, and processes of the surrounding world society. This isolation is inherent to the pluralist ontology, which defines international society as a society of states and rules of interstate coexistence as the essence of society, and it is vigorously defended as necessary for the development of a 'political theory of international relations understood as a "society" with its own distinctive standards of conduct'.[23] A growing body of international relations scholarship suggests, however, that these commitments are unsustainable. Arguing that core principles of international society, such as sovereignty, non-intervention, and self-determination, are inherently variable, constructivists have shown empirically how non-state actors and international organisations have worked to shape the domestic and international normative contexts in which states constitute their identities, interests, and strategies.[24] These conclusions are reinforced by the findings of previous chapters. We see in the development of legal norms banning anti-personnel landmines, in the politics of the climate change regime, in the relationship between international norms and Japanese policies towards migrants, and elsewhere as well that international society and its legal order are penetrated and structured by the wider politics of world society.

While the above criticisms have focused on the pluralist strand of the English School's account of international society and law, they should

---

[22] Bull, *The Anarchical Society*, p. 91.    [23] Jackson, *The Global Covenant*, p. 97.
[24] Margaret Keck and Kathryn Sikkink, *Activist Beyond Borders: Advocacy Networks in International Politics* (Ithaca: Cornell University Press, 1998); and Thomas Risse, Stephen Ropp, and Kathryn Sikkink (eds.), *The Power of Human Rights: International Norms and Domestic Change* (Cambridge: Cambridge University Press, 1999).

not be read as a validation of the solidarist position. The perspective advanced here encourages us to think of society beyond the state as more than the law of coexistence, as comprising social forces that are constitutive of that law. It encourages us to break with the very reduction of international law to rules of coexistence, to see international law as a critical site for the negotiation of pluralist and purposive values. And it encourages us to see international society as a highly penetrated domain of world society, the latter being the terrain in which the constitutive social forces that spawned international law as an institution, and which force the negotiation of pluralist and purposive values, are substantially rooted. Much of this will be grist for the solidarist mill, such as the argument about the penetration of international society by world society. But in destabilising the pluralist pole of the English School debate, our perspective challenges the dichotomous reasoning that has oriented solidarist thought as much as pluralist.

## Power

The prevailing 'realist' understanding of the relationship between power and international law has a distinctive logic, consisting of four interlinked ideas: (1) power is defined 'possessively', as a tangible resource that states command individually; (2) it is understood almost exclusively in terms of material resources, most notably guns and money; (3) politics is defined as a struggle for power, so understood; and (4) a dichotomy is drawn between international politics and law, with the latter subordinated to the former. These ideas not only dominate the realist imagination within the discipline of International Relations, they also have a remarkable grip on prominent strands of public discourse about power in the contemporary world. The problem from the perspective advanced here, however, is that this 'possessive-materialist' view of power and law has no way to accommodate the power *of* international law. If power is possessive and material, if politics is simply about the acquisition of such power, and if law is nothing more than an epiphenomenal expression of such politics, what room is left for international law as a socially constitutive practice?

The perspective advanced in previous chapters speaks to a radically different conception of power, a 'social' conception.[25] The starting point

---

[25] The perspective advanced here is elaborated in Christian Reus-Smit, *American Power and World Order* (Cambridge: Polity Press, 2004), chapter 2.

for such a conception is the view that power is ubiquitous, both in the sense that it is a necessary characteristic of all social agency, and in the sense that it is a prerequisite for social goods and evils, for both freedom and oppression. As Anthony Giddens observes, '[a]t the heart of both domination and power lies the *transformative capacity* of human action, the origin of all that is liberating and productive in social life as well as all that is repressive and destructive'.[26] The crucial departure for the social conception is to view power as 'relational' not possessive. Instead of seeing it as something actors 'own' as atomistic individuals, it is to be seen as something they gain only within relationships. Power 'can develop only through *exchange* among the actors involved in a given relation. To the extent that every relation between two parties presupposes exchange and reciprocal adaptation between them, power is indissolubly linked to negotiation: *it is a relation of exchange, therefore of negotiation*, in which at least two persons are involved.'[27] The lone individual, living outside of society but possessing abundant material resources, cannot be said to have power in any politically meaningful sense. It is only when an actor seeks to have a transformative effect in relation to other actors that they can be said to have, or not to have, power; and it is only in this relational context that the resources they conscript, material or otherwise, will have meaning or salience.

Scholars are divided about whether power ought to be contrasted with force or whether it encompasses force. The former position holds that power is the capacity to extract compliance from others, and while the threat of force can help induce such compliance, the exercise of force is evidence of non-compliance. 'Unlike power', Robert Jackman contends, 'force does not induce compliance; the exercise of force is instead an admission that compliance cannot be induced by other noncoercive means.'[28] For most international relations scholars this view is unlikely to compel, as it jars too readily with our deepest intuitions that when states use violence to achieve their ends they exercise, or seek to exercise, power. It is thus more fruitful, I would suggest, to see a continuum between ideal types of authoritative and coercive power, the former resting on legitimacy, the latter on force. The crucial thing, however,

---

[26] Anthony Giddens, *A Contemporary Critique of Historical Materialism: Volume One, Power, Property, and the State* (Berkeley: University of California Press, 1981), p. 51, emphasis in original.
[27] Michel Crozier and Erhard Friedberg, *Actors and Systems: The Politics of Collective Action* (Chicago: University of Chicago Press, 1980), pp. 30–1, emphasis in original.
[28] Robert W. Jackman, *Power Without Force: The Political Capacity of Nation-States* (Ann Arbor: University of Michigan Press, 1993), p. 30.

is that authoritative power is stable and conducive to sustained governance, whereas coercive power is inherently unstable and subject to the vagaries of command, threat, and sanction. As Charles Merriam wrote, power 'is strongest when it employs the instruments of substitution and counter attraction, of allurement, of participation rather than exclusion, of education rather than of annihilation'.[29] In contrast, as Edmund Burke famously observed, 'the use of force alone is but *temporary*. It may subdue for a moment, but it does not remove the necessity of subduing again; and a nation is not governed, which is to be perpetually conquered.'[30]

In all social systems, there is an inevitable 'pull' towards the authoritative end of the power continuum, even if coercion persists. The reason is that power is most effective, durable, and reliable when it has two qualities – when it is deemed legitimate, and when it is structured – and both of these qualities increase towards the authoritative end of the continuum. When power is considered legitimate, 'compliance is no longer motivated by simple fear of retribution, or by calculation of self-interest, but instead by an internal sense of moral obligation: control is legitimate to the extent that it is approved or regarded as "right"'.[31] When power is structured, it becomes routinised and predictable. 'The exercise of power', Jackman writes, 'requires a degree of *continuity* to the relations between participants, in other words, some history to the relationship. The exercise of power also assumes a degree of *regularity* to the relationship between participants.'[32] The principal means by which power is legitimised and structured in social systems is through institutions. This is so because the rules, norms, and decision-making procedures that comprise institutions are 'legitimators', in the sense that they specify categories of agency and action that are socially sanctioned, and they are 'structuring principles', in the sense that rules and norms prescribe categories of agency and action that are to be observed across time and space. On the latter point, Giddens goes so far as to say that the 'most important aspects of structure are rules and resources recursively involved in institutions'.[33]

[29] Charles Merriam, *Political Power* (New York: McGraw-Hill, 1934), p. 180.
[30] Edmund Burke, 'On Conciliation with the Colonies', in *Speeches and Letters on American Affairs* (London: J. M. Dent and Sons, 1908), emphasis in original.
[31] Ian Hurd, 'Legitimacy and Authority in International Politics', *International Organization* 53: 2 (Spring 1999), 387.
[32] Jackman, *Power Without Force*, p. 39, emphasis in original.
[33] Anthony Giddens, *The Constitution of Society: Outline of the Theory of Structuration* (Berkeley: University of California Press, 1984), p. 24.

While much ado is made about the differences between 'society within' and 'society beyond' the state, this obscures the fact that we also see in international society power drawn towards the authoritative end of the continuum. This is partly because dominant states wish to sanctify and regularise their rule, and partly because the vast majority of states prefer legitimate and structured power to the vicissitudes of coercion and conflict. As in 'domestic' societies, authoritative power in international society is generated and structured through institutions, and not surprisingly we see institutional orders of various sorts evolving in all historical societies of states. Underlying historically contingent social forces have determined the types of international institutions that have risen to prominence in particular epochs, and as we saw in chapter 2 the rise of political liberalism internationally was critical in the development of modern international law and the paired institution of multilateralism.

Previous chapters have highlighted several ways in which power in the contemporary world is legitimised and structured by the institution of international law. Here it is useful to distinguish between international law's regime of rules and its processes. With regard to the former, the international legal order conditions power in three ways: it codifies norms of legitimate agency that endow certain polities with sovereign rights and legal personality; it establishes hierarchies of authority among recognised sovereign states, as evident in the existence and powers of the United Nations Security Council and in weighted voting rights in international financial institutions; and it enshrines rules and norms of legitimate action, governing everything from maritime borders to the use of force. With regard to its processes, the international legal order conditions power relations through two mechanisms: its distinctive mode of multilateral legislation, which invokes and enacts the principles of self-legislation and non-discrimination to discipline the expression of power; and its peculiar language and practice of justification, through which states and other actors use rhetorical and analogical reasoning to interpret existing norms and license new ones, thus constructing and reconstructing the bounds of normatively permissible agency and action.

The case-studies presented in previous chapters suggest that these legitimising and structuring effects operate across a broad spectrum of issues. It is most illuminating, however, to consider them in relation to one of the traditional, nineteenth-century prerogatives of sovereign states: the right to wage war. Addressing the issue of *jus ad bellum*, Dino Kritsiotis explains in chapter 3 how through a protracted 'legislative' process in the first half of the twentieth century an ineffectual international norm proscribing war was replaced by a relatively robust norm banning the use of force. More interesting, though, is his discussion of the development of the legal norms that define exceptions to this ban. Here, he concludes, 'International law is here best seen as a discursive exercise, in which states are able to make, address, and assess justifications and it is through this process that international law can develop and store its own "self-knowledge", working practices, and conditions for regulating international recourses to force'.[34] Turning to the question of *jus in bello*, Nicholas Wheeler shows how NATO's use of force in the Kosovo bombing campaign was significantly conditioned by prevailing international legal rules and modes of reasoning. '[E]ven the world's most powerful military alliance', he concludes, 'recognised the need to justify its actions [through legal argument] before the court of domestic and world public opinion. And the fact that Alliance leaders knew that they would be called upon to defend their choice of targets was an inhibiting factor on what could be attacked.'[35]

In a social system that lacks a central authority with the capacity to forcefully discipline the expression of power, it is always possible for states or other actors to resort to coercion and force to achieve their ends, to step outside the institutionally structured universe of authoritative power relations. Adolf Hitler, Osama Bin Laden, and other sociopaths are testimony to such a possibility. Strong incentives exist, however, for states and other actors to shy away from the exercise of naked, coercive power. A comprehensive discussion of these incentives is beyond the scope of this conclusion, but three observations merit noting.

First, in a highly interdependent world, characterised by webs of co-operation across multiple issue-areas, the framework of institutionalised power relations is dense and extensive, and we can expect the vast majority of actors who lack the resources to impose their will, and who would prefer not to be imposed upon, to be strongly committed to this framework. Second, a hegemon, such as the United States, has a greater capacity to impose its will through the exercise of coercion, but even here the incentives to work within the institutional order are significant. For much of the post-1945 period the United States had an ideological commitment to the rule of international law and the maintenance of a multilateral order, playing a significant role in the construction of

---

[34] Dino Kritsiotis, chapter 3, this volume, p. 49.
[35] Nicholas Wheeler, chapter 8, this volume, p. 213.

the present institutional order. Research has also shown that it was in America's long-term interests to sponsor and sustain such an order: 'multilateralism provides a relatively cheap, stable organisational form. In exchange for a loss of some power over decision making and probably some decrease in distributional benefits, the hegemon gains a stable decision making forum.'[36] Finally, a unilateralist, anti-institutionalist turn in American foreign policy, which now appears to be occurring, may well be dysfunctional to American interests. If Washington persistently exits from international legal rules and multilateral processes, America's social identity is likely to become disassociated from the normative structures of international society, thus eroding the 'soft power' it so cherishes. And since in the absence of a major catalytic shock to the system most other states can be expected to have an ongoing functional, if not ideological, commitment to maintaining and augmenting those structures, the United States may find itself on the 'social margins', with a reduced not expanded, costly not efficient, range of political and diplomatic options.

## Ethics

As conceptions of international politics and law vary, so too do conceptions of international ethics. Realist notions of politics as a struggle for power, and law as an epiphenomenal expression of politics, are linked to the idea that the only viable form of international ethics is the prudent pursuit of the national interest.[37] Rationalist conceptions of politics as utility-maximisation, and law as a functional solution to co-operation problems, encourage an ethics of coexistence, based on respect for states' individuality and autonomy.[38] Cosmopolitanism, at least in its Kantian form, views politics as rational over the *longue durée*, and law as a vehicle for emancipation, leading to a universal ethics of solidarity.[39] What implications does the perspective on the politics of international law advanced in preceding chapters have for thinking about international ethics? This final section takes up this issue, focusing on

---

[36] Lisa L. Martin, 'The Rational Choice of Multilateralism', in John Gerard Ruggie (ed.), *Multilateralism Matters: The Theory and Praxis of an Institutional Form* (New York: Columbia University Press, 1993), p. 111.

[37] Morgenthau's fourth principle of political realism represents a classic statement of this position. *Politics Among Nations: The Struggle for Power and Peace*, 6th edn (New York: McGraw-Hill, 1985), p. 12.

[38] Nardin, *Law, Morality, and the Relations of States*, chapter 12.

[39] Immanuel Kant, *Perpetual Peace and Other Essays* (Indianapolis: Hackett Publishing, 1983).

two sub-questions: What does our perspective tell us about the role of ethics in international relations? And does it encourage a particular ethical standpoint?

The first of these warrants less attention than the second, as answers have been well anticipated by previous chapters. Our understanding of politics incorporates ethics within its idiographic, purposive, and moral dimensions, as well as in the interstitial dialogue between its four faces (including the instrumental). We have also seen how procedural ethics are embedded in the normative structure of international society, in the most fundamental norms governing how states ought collectively to formulate rules of coexistence and co-operation. More significant, however, is the nature of modern international law as an instantiation of a distinctive ethics, and as an ethical frame itself. As we saw in chapter 2, the ethics of political liberalism casts a long shadow over the international legal order, perhaps most significantly in its foundational principles of sovereign equality, self-legislation, and non-discrimination. In fact it is precisely this connection between liberalism and modern international law that has drawn realist ire, based as it is on a supposedly false analogising of the domestic and international realms.[40] A recurrent, yet subterranean, theme in many of our case-studies, is the way in which modern international law operates as an ethical frame, as a discursively and normatively structured site for the conduct of delimited ethical argument and the negotiation of legally codified ethical principles. This is not to reduce ethics to law, which leaves no basis on which to critique 'the law', but rather to see international law as an institutional locale in which established norms and privileged modes of reasoning condition social dialogue about existing and desired norms, a dialogue that includes claims about the right and the good.

On the question of whether our perspective encourages a particular ethical standpoint, the remaining discussion concentrates on its implications for one prominent form of contemporary ethical theorising about international relations – communicative ethics. To canvass its implications for all theories of international ethics, or even the most prominent, would be desirable but impractical within available space. This aside, though, it is particularly interesting to concentrate on communicative ethics, as some of its leading exponents have seen a natural affinity

---

[40] See George F. Kennan, 'Diplomacy in the Modern World', in Robert J. Beck, Anthony Clark Arend, and Robert D. Vander Lugt (eds.), *International Rules: Approaches from International Law and International Relations* (Oxford: Oxford University Press, 1999).

between 'constructivist' perspectives on international relations and the ethics of dialogue.[41]

The assumed connection between constructivist empirical theory and communicative ethics lies in their shared concern with the dynamics of social communication, which is reinforced by the intellectual debt they both owe to key communicative action theorists, particularly Jürgen Habermas. Both build upon a core idea of communicative action theory, the notion of 'universal pragmatics'. Stated in the simplest of terms, this holds that when actors communicate with one another to reach an understanding, they necessarily assume 'that the validity claims they reciprocally raise are justified'.[42] For constructivists, this insight enables the development of an *empirical* theory of norm formation, one that emphasises the way in which actors negotiate new norms by 'grafting' them discursively to established intersubjective meanings, a process clearly evident in the analogical aspect of international legal reasoning and discourse. For communicative ethicists, the idea of universal pragmatics provides the basis for an *ethical* theory of norm formation. A rule or norm can only be considered legitimate if it satisfies the principle of 'universalisation'. In Habermas' words, this means that '[a]ll affected can accept the consequences and the side effects its *general* observance can be anticipated to have for the satisfaction of *everyone's* interests (and these consequences are preferred to those of known alternative possibilities for regulation)'.[43] The fact that constructivists embrace a familiar ontology was quickly noted by communicative ethicists within International Relations, but they also criticised constructivists, rightly or wrongly, for not moving beyond empirical theory.[44]

The perspective on the politics of international law advanced in previous chapters destabilises this assumed fit between constructivist empirics and communicative ethics in two important respects. First, although

---

[41] See, in particular, Mervyn Frost, *Ethics in International Relations: A Constitutive Theory* (Cambridge: Cambridge University Press, 1996); Richard Shapcott, *Justice and Community in International Relations* (Cambridge: Cambridge University Press, 2001); and Robyn Eckersley, *The Green State: Rethinking Democracy and Sovereignty* (Cambridge, MA: MIT Press, 2004).

[42] Jürgen Habermas, *Communication and the Evolution of Society* (Boston: Beacon Press, 1979), p. 3.

[43] Jürgen Habermas, *Moral Consciousness and Communicative Action* (Cambridge, MA: MIT Press, 1991), p. 65, emphasis in original.

[44] See Richard Shapcott, 'Solidarism and After: Global Governance, International Society, and the Normative "Turn" in International Relations', *Pacifica Review* 12: 2 (2000); and Christian Reus-Smit, 'In Dialogue on the Ethic of Consensus: A Reply to Shapcott', *Pacifica Review* 12: 3 (2000).

at a deep ontological level the two share a common view about the logic of intersubjective communication, our analyses suggest that the actual communicative processes that accompany the production, interpretation, and reproduction of international law differ, perhaps not surprisingly, from the ideal type posited by communicative action theory. Second, communicative action theorists would describe such processes as 'distorted' forms of communication – corrupted by unrepresentative patterns of participation, penetration of particularistic interests, or strategic bargaining – and conclude that the norms generated will lack legitimacy, affecting their durability and salience, and cannot be considered normatively 'valid'. The problem is that these 'distorted' processes do, in fact, often produce rules and norms that international actors deem legitimate and which our own moral intuitions tell us are right, good, or just.

Previous chapters indicate two principal ways in which actual communicative processes in international relations depart from the ideal. The first involves the question of participation. Habermas insists that communicative processes must include *all* those affected by a proposed norm in a concrete practical discourse. For instance, 'a norm cannot be considered the expression of common interest simply because it seems acceptable to some of them [those concerned] under the condition that it be applied in a nondiscriminatory fashion'. Nor can a valid norm be deduced from a fictitious 'original position', such as that proposed by John Rawls.[45] It is clear, however, that the processes of international law almost never meet this exacting standard, yet over time rules and norms are constructed that not only command widespread assent but, in some cases, attain the status of *opinio juris*. Sometimes actors in the communicative process of negotiating an international legal regime decide that strong rules require the non-participation of certain actors. As David Wippman explains in his chapter, states negotiating the Rome Statute of the International Criminal Court opted for a stronger court, even if this meant the non-involvement of the United States. We have also seen a trend in recent years to open the processes of international norm formation to include non-state actors, a development that has had a crucial impact on the development of rules in fields such as climate change, anti-personnel landmines, and international criminal law. Before we could see this trend as a move toward Habermas' ideal, we would need to be confident that the expanded yet relatively random

---

[45] Habermas, *Moral Consciousness and Communicative Action*, p. 66.

participation that it involves is closer to an ideal speech situation than the more regimented representational processes of traditional multilateral forms of international legislation.

The second departure involves the issue of 'crisis' norm formation. Notwithstanding what was said above, it is easiest to imagine Habermas' ideal being realised in situations of planned institutional design, involving 'prepcoms' and formal conferences. Yet international norm formation also takes place in crisis situations. States and other actors often negotiate new rules and norms in response to the practical ethical dilemmas that accompany instances of social breakdown, from interstate war to pathological practices such as genocide.[46] As we saw in Wheeler's analysis of the Kosovo bombing campaign, such norm formation takes place through informal processes of public legal and ethical argument, processes that transcend the boundaries between international society and world society. Crises also provide focal points for international lawyers in their efforts to determine the nature of emergent international norms, and in doing so their interpretations help to constitute those norms. Also focusing on NATO's Kosovo campaign, Hilary Charlesworth condemns the discipline of International Law for 'regarding "crises" as its bread and butter and the engine of progressive development of international law'.[47]

If the actual processes of international communicative action contradict the theoretical ideal, should we conclude that the rules and norms they generate are normatively invalid? To do so would be to ignore some of our deepest moral intuitions. For most of us, proscribing the use of anti-personnel landmines, enhancing international criminal law, or circumscribing the use of force are defensible social goods, irrespective of whether their negotiation satisfied the principle of universalisation. We can still be asked to provide robust ethical defences of these norms, but one thing is clear: such defences will have to reach beyond the procedural tenets of communicative ethics to some other more substantive body of ethical thought. A similar point has been made by Agnes Heller, though from a different angle. She asks whether the principle of universalisation, even if enacted as Habermas prescribes, can always be said to yield morally acceptable norms. What if '[e]veryone concerned can agree to accept the norm that every man and woman over sixty years

[46] See Heather Rae, *State Identities and the Homogenization of Peoples* (Cambridge: Cambridge University Press, 2002), chapter 6.
[47] Hilary Charlesworth, 'International Law: A Discipline of Crisis', *The Modern Law Review* 65: 3 (May 2002), 391.

of age should be abandoned in the desert to die of starvation'.[48] She argues, correctly in my mind, that this cannot be considered a normatively valid norm, and that the only way to ensure that the principle of universalisation does not yield such norms is to qualify it with other non-procedural values, such as freedom and/or life.

The upshot of all of this is that the perspective on the politics of international law articulated here highlights not only the centrality of ethics to the complex entanglement of politics and law in contemporary world society, but also the problem of seeing a necessary affinity between constructivist empirics and communicative ethics. The problem, as we have seen, is more than the fact that our analyses have shown that legal rules and norms evolve through 'distorted' processes of communicative action. It is that when confronted with the question of whether this makes these norms morally invalid we are more likely to doubt the veracity of international communicative ethics than our own moral intuitions.

## Conclusion

It was once commonplace for International Relations scholars to engage in systematic and extended reflections on the nature of politics. Some thought it necessary to preface their treatises with a chapter on the subject, others felt so motivated as to write whole books on the topic.[49] Curiously, few scholars of the subject now feel so compelled. This is partly because the economistic view of politics as strategic action has been so thoroughly internalised by many scholars as to be beyond question, and partly because political reflection and argument have been marginalised as unscientific pursuits. The cost of this neglect of the political (or its reduction to strategic action) has been the growing reification of our theoretical frameworks, their increasing remoteness from the richness and complexity of lived political experience. It is the poverty of this reification that motivated this book. As explained in the introduction, the reduction of politics to material power or strategic action, and law to a simple epiphenomenon or functional expression, seem to miss much that is fascinating about the contemporary politics of international law. To capture more of this richness and complexity,

---

[48] Agnes Heller, *Beyond Justice* (Oxford: Basil Blackwell, 1987), p. 240.
[49] Good examples of this tendency are E. H. Carr's *The Twenty Years' Crisis, 1919–1939: An Introduction to the Study of International Relations*, 2nd edn (London: Macmillan, 1946); Morgenthau's *Politics Among Nations*; and J. D. B. Miller's *The Nature of Politics* (London: Duckworth, 1962).

our strategy has been to reflect anew on the nature of politics, the institution that we call international law, and their mutual constitution. All scholarship that moves beyond simple description towards theory must strike a balance between parsimony and complexity. The ideas of politics as interstitial, international law as a historically contingent institutional practice and process, and the two as reciprocally implicated, push towards the complexity end of the spectrum. Our claim, however, is that this opens a wider window on the politics of international law than narrower conceptual portals.

The danger, of course, with reconsidering ideas so fundamental as international politics and law is that it brings a host of related ideas into question, much as pulling a loose thread puckers a cloth. This final chapter has considered the implications of our perspective on the politics of international law for thinking about society, power, and ethics. My discussion has by no means been exhaustive, concentrating on specific debates or arguments in each of these areas. It has shown, however, that our findings destabilise the English School's dichotomous debate about the nature of international society, validate and reinforce a social conception of power, and problematise views that see an affinity between constructivist theories and communicative ethics. While largely suggestive, each of these discussions pushes the broad church of constructivist theory on to largely unexplored terrain. It links a perspective on the politics of international law rooted in constructivist social theory to broad discussions of international society within the English School; it ties constructivist insights to a systematic conception of power; and it contributes to the largely neglected project of relating constructivist empirical theory to reflections on international ethics.

# Bibliography

Abbott, Kenneth W., 'Modern International Relations Theory: A Prospectus for International Lawyers', *Yale Journal of International Law* 14: 2 (1989), 335–411.

Abbott, Kenneth W. and Snidal, Duncan, 'Why States Act Through Formal International Organizations', *Journal of Conflict Resolution* 42: 1 (1998), 3–32.

Abbott, Kenneth, Keohane, Robert O., Moravscik, Andrew, Slaughter, Anne-Marie, and Snidal, Duncan, 'The Concept of Legalization', *International Organization* 54: 3 (2000), 408–9.

Acheson, Dean, 'Remarks before the American Society of International Law', *Proceedings of the American Society of International Law* 57 (1963).

Adler, Emanuel, 'Seizing the Middle Ground: Constructivism in World Politics', *European Journal of International Relations* 3: 3 (1997), 319–63.

Agreement between the United Nations and the International Bank for Reconstruction and Development, *United Nations Treaty Series* 16 (1948), 342–56.

Agreement between the United Nations and the International Monetary Fund, *United Nations Treaty Series* 16 (1948), 326–40.

Albin, Cecilia, *Justice and Fairness in International Negotiation*, Cambridge: Cambridge University Press, 2001.

Allott, Philip, 'The Concept of International Law', in Michael Byers (ed.), *The Role of Law in International Politics: Essays in International Relations and International Law*, Oxford: Oxford University Press, 2000, pp. 69–89.

Amnesty International, 'NATO/Federal Republic of Yugoslavia: "Collateral Damage" or Unlawful Killings? Violations of the Laws of War by NATO during Operation Allied Force', June 2000, <www.web.amnesty.org/ai.nsf/index/Eur700182000>.

Anghie, Antony, 'Time Present and Time Past: Globalization, International Financial Institutions, and the Third World', *New York University Journal of International Law and Politics* 32: 2 (2000), 243–90.

— 'Colonialism and the Birth of International Institutions: Sovereignty, Economy and the Mandate System of the League of Nations', *New York University Journal of International Law and Politics* 34: 3 (2002), 513–633.

## Bibliography

Annan, Kofi, 'Two Concepts of Sovereignty', *The Economist* (18–24 September 1999), 81.

Arend, Anthony Clark, 'Do Legal Rules Matter? International Law and International Politics', *Virginia Journal of International Law* 38: 2 (1998), 107–53.

Arkin, William, 'Smart Bombs, Dumb Targeting?', *Bulletin of the Atomic Scientists* 56: 3 (2000), 46–53, <www.thebulletin.org/issues/2000/mj00/mj00arkin.html>.

Articles of Agreement of the International Bank for Reconstruction and Development, *United Nations Treaty Series* 2 (1947), 134–204.

Articles of Agreement of the International Monetary Fund, *United Nations Treaty Series* 2 (1947), 39–132.

Barnett, Michael N. and Finnemore, Martha, 'The Politics, Power, and Pathologies of International Organizations', *International Organization* 53: 4 (1999), 699–732.

Beck, Robert J., 'International Law and International Relations: The Prospects for Interdisciplinary Collaboration', *Journal of International Legal Studies* 1: Summer (1995), 119–49.

Beier, J. Marshall, 'Anti-Personnel Landmines and Customary Law: The Case of India', unpublished manuscript, Toronto: York University, 2000.

Beiner, Ronald, *Political Judgement*, London: Methuen, 1983.

Benesch, Susan, McGrory, Glenn, Rodriguez, Cristina, and Sloane, Robert, 'International Customary Law and Antipersonnel Landmines: Emergence of a New Customary Norm', in International Campaign to Ban Landmines, *Landmine Monitor Report 1999: Toward a Mine-Free World*, New York: Human Rights Watch, 1999, pp. 1020–36.

Benvenuti, Paolo, 'The ICTY Prosecutor and the Review of the NATO Bombing Campaign against the Federal Republic of Yugoslavia', *European Journal of International Law* 12: 3 (2001), 503–30.

Bhagwati, Jagdish, 'The Capital Myth: The Difference Between Trade in Widgets and Dollars', *Foreign Affairs* 77: 3 (1998), 7–12.

Blustein, Paul, *The Chastening: Inside the Crisis that Rocked the Global Financial System and Humbled the IMF*, New York: Public Affairs, 2001.

Bodin, Jean, *Six Books of the Commonwealth*, Oxford: Basil Blackwell, 1967.

Bolton, John, 'Speech Two: Reject and Oppose the International Criminal Court', in Alton Frye (ed.), *Toward an International Criminal Court?: Three Options Presented as Presidential Speeches*, New York: Council on Foreign Relations, 1999, 37–52.

Bowett, Derek, *Self-Defence in International Law*, Manchester: Manchester University Press, 1958.

Boyle, Francis A., 'The Irrelevance of International Law: The Schism Between International Law and International Politics', *California Western International Law Journal* 10: 1 (1980), 193–219.

Bozeman, Adda, *Politics and Culture in International History*, Princeton: Princeton University Press, 1961.

Bradlow, Daniel D., 'The World Bank, the IMF, and Human Rights', *Transnational Law and Contemporary Problems* 6: 1 (1996), 47–90.

Brierly, J. L., 'International Law and Resort to Armed Force', *Cambridge Law Journal* 4: 3 (1932), 308–19.

Brown, Bartram S., *The United States and the Politicization of the World Bank: Issues of International Law and Policy*, New York: K. Paul International, 1992.

Brownlie, Ian, *International Law and the Use of Force by States*, Oxford: Clarendon Press, 1963.

— 'International Law at the Fiftieth Anniversary of the United Nations: General Course on Public International Law', *Hague Recueil* 255 (1995–I).

— *Principles of Public International Law*, 5th edn, Oxford: Clarendon Press, 1998.

Brunnee, Jutta and Toope, Stephen J., 'International Law and Constructivism: Elements of an Interactional Theory of International Law', *Columbia Journal of Transnational Law* 39: 1 (2000), 19–74.

Bukovansky, Mlada, *Legitimacy and Power Politics: The American and French Revolutions in International Political Culture*, Princeton: Princeton University Press, 2002.

Bull, Hedley, 'The Grotian Conception of International Society', in Herbert Butterfield and Martin Wight (eds.), *Diplomatic Investigations: Essays in the Theory of International Politics*, London: George Allen and Unwin, 1966, pp. 51–73.

— *The Anarchical Society: A Study of Order in World Politics*, 2nd edn, London: Macmillan, 1995.

Burke, Edmund, 'On Conciliation with the Colonies', in *Speeches and Letters on American Affairs*, London: J. M. Dent and Sons, 1908, pp. 76–141.

Buzan, Barry, 'From International System to International Society: Structural Realism and Regime Theory Meet the English School', *International Organization* 47: 3 (1993), 327–52.

Byers, Michael, *Custom, Power and the Power of Rules: International Relations and Customary International Law*, Cambridge: Cambridge University Press, 1999.

— 'The Laws of War, US-Style', *London Review of Books* 25: 4 (20 February 2003), <www.lrb.co.uk/v25/n04/print/byer01_html>.

Calvert, Randall L., 'Rational Actors, Equilibrium, and Social Institutions', in Jack Knight and Itai Sened (eds.), *Explaining Social Institutions*, Ann Arbor, MI: University of Michigan Press, 1995, pp. 57–93.

Campbell, Leah, 'Defending Against Terrorism: A Legal Analysis of the Decision to Strike Sudan and Afghanistan', *Tulane Law Review* 74: 3 (2000), 1067–96.

Caron, David D., 'The Legitimacy of the Collective Authority of the Security Council', *American Journal of International Law* 87: 4 (1993), 552–88.

Carr, E. H., *The Twenty Years' Crisis, 1919–1939: An Introduction to the Study of International Relations*, 2nd edn, London: Macmillan, 1946.

Cassese, Antonio, 'Terrorism is Also Disrupting Some Crucial Legal Categories of International Law', *European Journal of International Law* 12: 5 (2001), 993–1001.

*Bibliography*

Charlesworth, Hilary, 'International Law: A Discipline of Crisis', *The Modern Law Review* 65: 3 (May 2002), 377–92.
Charlesworth, Hilary and Chinkin, Christine, *The Boundaries of International Law: A Feminist Analysis*, Manchester: Juris Publishing, 2000.
Charney, Jonathan, 'The Persistent Objector Rule and the Development of Customary International Law', *British Yearbook of International Law* 56 (1985), 1–24.
Chayes, Abram, *The Cuban Missile Crisis*, New York: Oxford University Press, 1974.
Chayes, Abram and Slaughter, Anne-Marie, 'The ICC and the Future of the Global Legal System', in Sarah B. Sewall and Carl Kaysen (eds.), *The United States and the International Criminal Court: National Security and International Law*, Lanham, MD: Rowman & Littlefield, 2000, pp. 237–47.
Checkel, Jeff, 'The Constructivist Turn in International Relations Theory', *World Politics* 50: 2 (1998), 324–48.
Chimni, B. S., *International Law and World Order: A Critique of Contemporary Approaches*, Newbury Park: Sage, 1993.
Chinkin, Christine, *Third Parties in International Law*, Oxford: Clarendon Press, 1993.
Chomsky, Noam, *The New Military Humanism: Lessons from Kosovo*, Monroe, ME: Common Courage Press, 1999.
Chossudovsky, Michel, *The Globalization of Poverty: Impacts of IMF and World Bank Reforms*, London: Zed Books, 1997.
Cohen, William S. and Shelton, Henry H., Joint Statement on 'Kosovo After-Action Review', Hearings of Senate Armed Services Committee, 14 October 1999.
Condorelli, Luigi, 'A propos de l'attaque américaine contre l'Iraq du 26 juin 1993', *European Journal of International Law* 5: 1 (1994), 134–44.
*Consolidated Treaty Series* 205 (1907).
*Corfu Channel Case* (Merits): United Kingdom v. Albania (1949) *ICJ Reports* 4.
*Corfu Channel Case* (Pleadings), Vol. III.
Cortell, Andrew P. and Davis, James W. Jr, 'How Do International Institutions Matter? The Domestic Impact of International Rules and Norms', *International Studies Quarterly* 40: 4 (1996), 451–78.
— 'Understanding the Domestic Impact of International Norms: A Research Agenda', *International Studies Review* 2: 1 (2000), 65–87.
CR 99/15 (translation), Verbatim Record of 10 May 1999, <www.icj-cij.org/icjwww/idocket/iyall/iyall_cr/iyall_icr9915_19990510_translation.htm>.
Crawford, James, 'Foreword', in Michael Byers (ed.), *Custom, Power and the Power of Rules: International Relations and Customary International Law*, Cambridge: Cambridge University Press, 1999.
Cronin, Bruce, 'The Paradox of Hegemony: America's Ambiguous Relationship with the United Nations', *European Journal of International Relations* 7: 1 (2001), 103–30.

Crozier, Michel and Friedberg, Erhard, *Actors and Systems: The Politics of Collective Action*, Chicago: University of Chicago Press, 1980.

D'Amato, Anthony, 'Israel's Air Strike Upon the Iraqi Nuclear Reactor', *American Journal of International Law* 77: 3 (1983), 584–88.

Daalder, Ivo H., and O'Hanlon, Michael E., *Winning Ugly: NATO's War to Save Kosovo*, Washington, DC: Brookings Institution, 2000.

Dam, Kenneth W., *The Rules of the Game*, Chicago: University of Chicago Press, 1982.

Damrosch, Lori F., *Enforcing Restraint: Collective Intervention in Internal Conflicts*, New York: Council on Foreign Relations Press, 1995.

Davies, Norman, *Europe: A History*, Oxford and New York: Oxford University Press, 1996.

Dinstein, Yoram, *War, Aggression and Self-Defence*, 3rd edn, New York: Cambridge University Press, 2001.

Donnelly, Jack, 'State Sovereignty and International Intervention: The Case of Human Rights', in Gene M. Lyons and Michael Mastanduno (eds.), *Beyond Westphalia? State Sovereignty and International Intervention*, Baltimore: Johns Hopkins University Press, 1995, pp. 115–46.

Douzinas, Costas, *The End of Human Rights*, Oxford: Hart, 2000.

Dworkin, Ronald, *Law's Empire*, Cambridge, MA: Belknap Press, 1986.

Eckersley, Robyn, *The Green State: Rethinking Democracy and Sovereignty*, Cambridge, MA: MIT Press, 2004.

Eckstein, Harry, 'A Culturalist Theory of Political Change', *American Political Science Review* 82: 3 (1988), 789–804.

Engberg-Pedersen, Poul et al. (eds.), *Limits of Adjustment in Africa: The Effects of Economic Liberalization, 1986–94*, Copenhagen: Centre for Development Research in association with James Currey, 1996.

'Explanation of Vote by Ambassador Dr. Mahmoud Darem on the Resolution on Anti Personnel Landmines', internal Egyptian government document, The Permanent Mission of Egypt to the United Nations, 1998.

Farer, Tom J. and Gaer, Felice, 'The UN and Human Rights: At the End of the Beginning', in Adam Roberts and Benedict Kingsbury (eds.), *United Nations, Divided World: The UN's Roles in International Relations*, 2nd edn, Oxford: Clarendon Press, 1993, pp. 240–96.

Feldstein, Martin, 'Refocusing the IMF', *Foreign Affairs* 77: 2 (1998), 20–33.

Fernández de Gurmendi, Silvia A., 'The Role of the International Prosecutor', in Roy S. Lee (ed.), *The International Criminal Court: The Making of the Rome Statute*, The Hague and London: Kluwer Law International 1999, pp. 175–88.

*Filartiga v. Pena-Irala*, United States Court of Appeals, Second Circuit, 630 F. 2nd 876 (1980).

'Final Report to the Prosecutor by the Committee Established to Review the NATO Bombing Campaign Against the Federal Republic of Yugoslavia', <www.un.org/icty/pressreal/nato061300.htm>, accessed 14 July 2001.

## Bibliography

Finalized Draft Text of the Elements of Crimes, PCNICC/2000/1/Add. 2, New York: United Nations, 2 November 2000.

Finnemore, Martha, 'Are Legal Norms Distinctive?', *New York University Journal of International Law and Politics* 32: Spring (2000), 699–705.

Finnemore, Martha and Toope, Stephen J., 'Alternatives to "Legalization": Richer Views of Law and Politics', *International Organization* 55: 3 (2001), 743–58.

*Fisheries Case, ICJ Reports 1951.*

Fiss, Owen M., 'Objectivity and Interpretation', *Stanford Law Review* 34: 4 (1982), 739–63.

Franck, Thomas M., 'Who Killed Article 2(4)? Or: Changing Norms Governing the Use of Force by States', *American Journal of International Law* 64: 4 (1970), 809–37.

— *The Power of Legitimacy Among Nations*, New York: Oxford University Press, 1990.

— *Fairness in International Law and Institutions*, Oxford: Clarendon Press, 1995.

— *Recourse to Force: State Action Against Threats and Armed Attacks*, Cambridge: Cambridge University Press, 2002.

Freedman, Lawrence and Gamba-Stonehouse, Virginia, *Signals of War: The Falklands Conflict of 1982*, Princeton: Princeton University Press, 1991.

French, Howard W., '"Japanese Only" Policy Takes Body Blow in Court', *New York Times* (15 November 1999).

Frost, Mervyn, *Ethics in International Relations: A Constitutive Theory*, Cambridge: Cambridge University Press, 1996.

Frowein, Jochen Abr. and Krisch, Nico, 'Article 39', in Bruno Simma (ed.), *The Charter of the United Nations: A Commentary*, 2nd edn, Oxford and New York: Oxford University Press, 2002, pp. 719–26.

Gathii, James, 'Good Governance as a Counter-Insurgency Agenda to Oppositional and Transformative Projects in International Law', *Buffalo Human Rights Law Review* 5 (1999), 107–74.

Gianviti, François, 'The Reform of the International Monetary Fund (Conditionality and Surveillance)', *International Lawyer* 34: 1 (2000), 107–16.

Giddens, Anthony, *A Contemporary Critique of Historical Materialism: Volume One, Power, Property, and the State*, Berkeley: University of California Press, 1981.

— *The Constitution of Society: Outline of the Theory of Structuration*, Berkeley: University of California Press, 1984.

Gold, Joseph, *The Rule of Law in the International Monetary Fund*, Washington, DC: International Monetary Fund, 1980.

Goldstein, Judith, Kahler, Miles, Keohane, Robert, and Slaughter, Anne-Marie (eds.), Special Issue on the Legalization of International Politics, *International Organization* 54: 3 (2000).

Gong, Gerrit W., *The Standard of 'Civilization' in International Society*, Oxford: Clarendon Press, 1984.

Gordon, M. R., 'NATO Air Attacks on Power Plants Pass a Threshold', *New York Times*, 4 May 1999.

Grams, Rod, Senator, 'Is a UN International Criminal Court in the US National Interest?', Statement at the Hearing before the Subcommittee on International Operations of the Committee on Foreign Relations, United States Senate, 105th Congress, 2nd Session (23 July 1998).

Gray, Christine, *International Law and the Use of Force*, Oxford: Oxford University Press, 2000.

Greenwood, Christopher, 'The Concept of War in Modern International Law', *International and Comparative Law Quarterly* 36: 2 (1987), 283–306.

— 'International Law and the United States Air Operation Against Libya', *West Virginia Law Review* 89: 4 (1987), 933–60.

— 'The Administration of Occupied Territory in International Law', in Emma Playfair (ed.), *International Law and the Administration of Occupied Territories: Two Decades of Israeli Occupation of the West Bank and Gaza Strip*, Oxford: Clarendon Press, 1992.

— 'The International Court of Justice and the Use of Force', in Vaughan Lowe and Malgosia Fitzmaurice (eds.), *Fifty Years of the International Court of Justice: Essays in Honour of Sir Robert Jennings*, Cambridge: Cambridge University Press, 1996, pp. 373–85.

Grotius, Hugo, *The Law of War and Peace: De Jure Belli ac Pacis Libri Tres*, New York: Bobbs-Merrill, 1925.

Grubb, Michael and Depledge, Joanna, 'The Seven Myths of Kyoto', *Climate Policy* 1: 2 (2001), 269–72.

Grubb, Michael with Vrolijk, Christiaan, and Brack, Duncan, *The Kyoto Protocol: A Guide and Assessment*, London: Royal Institute of International Affairs and Earthscan, 1999.

Grubb, Michael and Yamin, Farhana, 'Climatic Collapse at The Hague: What Happened, Why, and Where Do We Go From Here?', *International Affairs* 77: 2 (2001), 261–76.

Gurowitz, Amy, 'Mobilizing International Norms: Domestic Actors, Immigrants, and the Japanese State', *World Politics* 51: 3 (1999), 413–45.

— 'Mobilizing International Norms: Domestic Actors, Immigrants, and the State', unpublished manuscript, 2003.

Haacke, Jürgen, 'Theory and Praxis in International Relations: Habermas, Self-Reflection, Rational Argument', *Millennium* 25: 2 (1996), 255–89.

Habermas, Jürgen, *Communication and the Evolution of Society*, Boston: Beacon Press, 1979.

— *Moral Consciousness and Communicative Action*, Cambridge, MA: MIT Press, 1991.

— *Between Facts and Norms: Contributions to a Discourse Theory of Law and Democracy*, trans. W. Rehg, Cambridge: Polity, 1996.

— *The Inclusion of the Other: Studies in Political Theory*, ed. C. Cronin and P. De Greiff, Cambridge, MA: MIT Press, 1998.

Bibliography

Haley, John Owen, *Authority Without Power*, New York: Oxford University Press, 1991.

Halliday, Fred, *Rethinking International Relations*, Basingstoke: Macmillan, 1994.

Hanami, Tadashi, 'Japanese Policies on the Rights and Benefits Granted to Foreign Workers, Residents, Refugees and Illegals', in Myron Weiner and Tadashi Hanami (eds.), *Temporary Workers or Future Citizens? Japanese and US Migration Policies*, New York: New York University Press, 1998, pp. 211–37.

Harris, D. J., *Cases and Materials on International Law*, 5th edn, London: Sweet and Maxwell, 1998.

Hart, H. L. A., *The Concept of Law*, Oxford: Clarendon Press, 1961.

— *The Concept of Law*, 2nd edn, Oxford: Oxford University Press, 1994.

Held, David and McGrew, Anthony, 'The Great Globalization Debate: An Introduction', in David Held and Anthony McGrew (eds.), *The Global Transformations Reader: An Introduction to the Globalization Debate*, Cambridge: Polity Press, 2000, pp. 1–44.

Heller, Agnes, *Beyond Justice*, Oxford: Basil Blackwell, 1987.

Henkin, Louis, 'The Reports of the Death of Article 2(4) are Greatly Exaggerated', *American Journal of International Law* 65: 3 (1971), 544–8.

— *How Nations Behave: Law and Foreign Policy*, 2nd edn, New York: Columbia University Press, 1979.

— *International Law: Politics and Values*, Dordrecht: Martinus Nijhoff, 1995.

Higgins, Rosalyn, *The Development of International Law Through the Political Organs of the United Nations*, London: Oxford University Press, 1963.

— 'Policy Considerations and the International Judicial Process', *International and Comparative Law Quarterly* 17: 1 (1968), 58–84.

— *Problems and Process: International Law and How We Use It*, Oxford: Clarendon Press, 1994.

Hockett, Robert, 'From Macro to Micro to "Mission-Creep": Defending the IMF's Emerging Concern with the Infrastructural Prerequisites to Global Financial Stability', *Columbia Journal of Transnational Law* 41: 1 (2002), 153–94.

Hollis, Martin, 'Say it With Flowers', in James Tully (ed.), *Meaning and Context: Quentin Skinner and his Critics*, Cambridge: Polity Press, 1988, pp. 135–46.

Holyoak, Keith and Thagard, Paul, *Mental Leaps: Analogy in Creative Thought*, Cambridge, MA: MIT Press, 1995.

— 'The Analogical Mind', *American Psychologist* 52: 1 (1997), 35–44.

Hook, Glenn D. and Weiner, Michael A., 'Introduction', in Glenn D. Hook and Michael A. Weiner (eds.), *The Internationalization of Japan*, London: Routledge, 1992, pp. 1–12.

Hook, Glenn D. and Weiner, Michael A. (eds.), *The Internationalization of Japan*, London: Routledge, 1992.

Hoon, Geoffrey, MP, examined before the House of Commons Defence Committee, Fourteenth Report: Lessons of Kosovo Volume II. Minutes of Evidence and Appendices, 7 June 2000.

298

Hopf, Ted, 'The Promise of Constructivism in International Relations Theory', *International Security* 23: 1 (1998), 171–200.

Hormats, Robert, 'Reflections on the Asian Crisis', *International Lawyer* 34: 1 (2000), 193–9.

Hudec, Robert E., 'The Judicialization of GATT Dispute Settlement', in M. H. Hart and D. B. Steger (eds.), *In Whose Interest?: Due Process and Transparency in International Trade*, Ottawa: Center for Trade Policy and Law, 1992, pp. 9–43.

— *Enforcing International Trade Law: The Evolution of the Modern GATT Legal System*, Salem, NH: Butterworth, 1993.

Human Rights Watch, 'Civilian Deaths in the NATO Air Campaign', <www.hrw.org/reports/2000/nato/>, accessed 11 January 2000.

— 'Clinton's Landmine Legacy', *Human Rights Watch Reports* 12: 3 (June 2000), <www.hrw.org/reports/2000/uslm/>.

Human Rights Watch and Physicians for Social Responsibility, *Landmines: A Deadly Legacy*, New York: Human Rights Watch, 1993.

Hurd, Ian, 'Legitimacy and Authority in International Politics', *International Organization* 53: 2 (Spring 1999), 379–408.

Hurrell, Andrew, 'International Law and the Changing Constitution of International Society', in Michael Byers (ed.), *The Role of Law in International Politics: Essays in International Relations and International Law*, Oxford: Oxford University Press, 2000, pp. 327–47.

ICBL (International Campaign to Ban Landmines), *Landmine Monitor Report 1999: Toward a Mine-Free World*, New York: Human Rights Watch, 1999, <www.icbl.org/lm/1999/>.

— *Landmine Monitor Report 2000: Toward a Mine-Free World*, New York: Human Rights Watch, 2000, <www.icbl.org/lm/2000/report/LMWeb-24.php3#P18173_2403557>.

— *Landmine Monitor Report 2001: Toward a Mine-Free World*, New York: Human Rights Watch, 2001, <www.icbl.org/lm/2001/report/>.

— *Landmine Monitor Report 2002: Toward a Mine-Free World*, New York: Human Rights Watch, 2002, <www.icbl.org/lm/2002>.

ICTY (International Criminal Tribunal for Former Yugoslavia), Press Release, Address by the Registrar of the ICTY, Mr Hans Holthuis, to the Plenary of the Preparatory Commission of the International Criminal Court During its Seventh Session (6 March 2001).

Ignatieff, Michael, *Virtual War: Kosovo and Beyond*, London: Chatto and Windus, 2000.

Igorev, Aleksandr, and Dvali, Georgiy, 'Minefields Will Separate Russia from Georgia', Moscow Kommersant in Russian, FBIS Reports (12 April 2000), p. 3.

Independent International Commission on Kosovo, *The Kosovo Report: Conflict, International Response, Lessons Learned*, Oxford: Oxford University Press, 2000.

Bibliography

*Interhandel Case*: Switzerland v. United States (1959) *ICJ Reports* 6 (per President Klaestad and Judge Spender).

International Committee of the Red Cross, 'Banning Anti-Personnel Mines: The Ottawa Treaty Explained', Geneva: ICRC, 1998.

International Monetary Fund, *Good Governance: The IMF's Role*, Washington, DC: IMF, 1997.

Iwasawa, Yuji, 'Legal Treatment of Koreans in Japan: The Impact of International Human Rights Law on Japanese Law', *Human Rights Quarterly* 8: 2 (1986), 131–79.

— 'The Domestic Impact of Acts of International Organizations Relating to Human Rights', Draft Paper, Second Trilateral Symposium, Swiss Hotel Atlanta, 24–26 March 1996.

— 'The Impact of International Law on Japanese Law: Revolution or Accommodation', SJD Dissertation, University of Virginia, 1996.

— *International Law and Human Rights in Japanese Law*, Oxford: Clarendon Press, 1998.

Jackman, Robert W., *Power Without Force: The Political Capacity of Nation-States*, Ann Arbor: University of Michigan Press, 1993.

Jackson, Robert, *Quasi-States: Sovereignty, International Relations, and the Third World*, Cambridge: Cambridge University Press, 1990.

— *The Global Covenant: Human Conduct in a World of States*, Oxford: Oxford University Press, 2000.

Japan Federation of Bar Associations, *Utilizing International Human Rights Covenants in the Courtroom* (Hotei ni ikaso kokusai jinken kinyuko), Tokyo: Japan Federation of Bar Associations, 1996.

Jepperson, Ronald L., 'Institutions, Institutional Effects, and Institutionalism', in Walter W. Powell and Paul J. Dimaggio (eds.), *The New Institutionalism in Organizational Analysis*, Chicago: University of Chicago Press, 1991, pp. 143–63.

Jgrenaya, Vacho, 1999, 'Peaceful Caucasus: Toward a Future Without Landmines', Regional Landmine Conference, Tbilisi, Georgia, 5–7 December 1999, in ICBL, *Landmine Monitor Report 2000*, New York: Human Rights Watch, 2000, <www.icbl.org/lm/2000/report/LMWeb-24.php3#P18173_2403557>.

Jochnick, Chris, 'Confronting the Impunity of Non-State Actors: New Fields for the Promotion of Human Rights', *Human Rights Quarterly* 21: 1 (1999), 56–79.

Johnstone, Diana, 'The Berlin Tribunal', 21 June 2000, <www.emperorsclothes.com/articles/Johnstone/berlin.htm>, accessed 20 June 2002.

Johnstone, Ian, 'Treaty Interpretation: The Authority of Interpretative Communities', *Michigan Journal of International Law* 12: 2 (1991), 371–419.

Judah, Tim, *Kosovo: War and Revenge*, London: Yale University Press, 2000.

Kahn, Paul W., 'War and Sacrifice in Kosovo', *Report from the Institute for Philosophy & Public Policy* 19: 2/3 (1999), <www.puaf.umd.edu/IPPP/spring_summer99/kosovo.htm>.

— 'American Hegemony and International Law. Speaking Law to Power: Popular Sovereignty, Human Rights, and the New International Order', *Chicago Journal of International Law* 1: 1 (2000), 1–18.

Kamminga, Menno T., *Inter-State Accountability for Violations of Human Rights*, Philadelphia, PA: University of Pennsylvania Press, 1992.

Kant, Immanuel, *Perpetual Peace and Other Essays*, Indianapolis: Hackett Publishing, 1983.

Kapur, Devesh, 'The IMF: A Cure or a Curse?', *Foreign Policy* 111 (1998), 114–29.

Katzenstein, Peter J., *Cultural Norms and National Security: Police and Military in Postwar Japan*, Ithaca: Cornell University Press, 1996.

— *The Culture of National Security*, Ithaca: Cornell University Press, 1996.

Katzenstein, Peter J. and Tsujinaka, Yutaka, *Defending the Japanese State: Structures, Norms and the Political Responses to Terrorism and Violent Social Protest in the 1970s and 1980s*, Cornell East Asia Series 53, Ithaca: East Asia Program, Cornell University, 1991.

Kawashima, Yasuko, 'A Comparative Analysis of the Decision-making Processes of Developed Countries toward $CO_2$ Emissions Reduction Targets', *International Environmental Affairs* 9: 2 (1997), 95–126.

Keane, Mark, *Analogical Problem Solving*, Chichester, UK: Ellis Horwood Ltd, 1988.

Keck, Margaret and Sikkink, Kathryn, *Activist Beyond Borders: Advocacy Networks in International Politics*, Ithaca: Cornell University Press, 1998.

Kennan, George F., 'Diplomacy in the Modern World', in Robert J. Beck, Anthony Clark Arend, and Robert D. Vander Lugt (eds.), *International Rules: Approaches from International Law and International Relations*, Oxford: Oxford University Press, 1996, pp. 99–106.

Kennedy, David, 'The Disciplines of International Law and Policy', *Leiden Journal of International Law* 12: 1 (1999), 9–134.

— 'The *Nuclear Weapons* Case', in Laurence Boisson de Chazournes and Philippe Sands (eds.), *International Law, the International Court of Justice and Nuclear Weapons*, Cambridge: Cambridge University Press, 1999, pp. 462–72.

Keohane, Robert O., 'The Demand for International Regimes', in Stephen D. Krasner (ed.), *International Regimes*, Ithaca: Cornell University Press, 1983, pp. 141–72.

— *International Institutions and State Power: Essays in International Relations Theory*, Boulder: Westview, 1989.

— 'International Relations and International Law: Two Optics', *Harvard International Law Journal* 38: 2 (1997), 487–502.

Kirgis, Frederic, Jr, 'Custom on a Sliding Scale', *American Journal of International Law* 81: 1 (1987), 146–51.

Kirsch, Philippe and Holmes, John T., 'The Rome Conference on an International Criminal Court: The Negotiating Process', *American Journal of International Law* 93: 1 (1999), 2–12.

Klotz, Audie, *Norms in International Relations: The Struggle Against Apartheid*, Ithaca: Cornell University Press, 1995.

*Bibliography*

— 'Norms Reconstituting Interests: Global Racial Equality and US Sanctions Against South Africa', *International Organization* 49: 3 (1995), 451–78.

Koh, H. H., 'The 1998 Frankel Lecture: Bringing International Law Home', *Houston Law Review* 35: 3 (1998), 623–81.

Koschmann, J. Victor, 'Asianism's Ambivalent Legacy', in Peter J. Katzenstein and Takashi Shiraishi (eds.), *Network Power: Japan and Asia*, Ithaca: Cornell University Press, 1997, pp. 83–110.

Koskenniemi, Martti, *From Apology to Utopia: The Structure of International Legal Argument*, Helsinki: Finnish Lawyers, 1989.

— 'The Politics of International Law', *European Journal of International Law* 1: 1/2 (1990), 4–32.

— 'Faith, Identity, and the Killing of the Innocent: International Lawyers and Nuclear Weapons', *Leiden Journal of International Law* 10: 1 (1997), 137–62.

— 'Letter to the Editors of the Symposium', *American Journal of International Law* 93: 2 (1999), 351–61.

Krajnc, Anita, 'Anti-Personnel Landmines and Customary Law: The Case of Egypt', unpublished manuscript, University of Toronto, 2000.

Krasner, Stephen D., *Sovereignty: Organized Hypocrisy*, Princeton: Princeton University Press, 1999.

Kratochwil, Friedrich V., *Rules, Norms, and Decisions: On the Conditions of Practical and Legal Reasoning in International Relations and Domestic Affairs*, Cambridge: Cambridge University Press, 1989.

— 'How Do Norms Matter?', in Michael Byers (ed.), *The Role of Law in International Politics: Essays in International Relations and International Law*, Oxford: Oxford University Press, 2000, pp. 35–68.

Kritsiotis, Dino, 'The Legality of the 1993 US Missile Strike on Iraq and the Right of Self-Defence in International Law', *International and Comparative Law Quarterly* 45: 1 (1996), 162–77.

— 'The Power of International Law as Language', *California Western Law Review* 34: 2 (1998), 397–409.

— 'Reappraising Policy Objections to Humanitarian Intervention', *Michigan Journal of International Law* 19: 4 (1998), 1005–50.

— 'The Legal Travails of Kind-Hearted Gunmen', *Modern Law Review* 62: 6 (1999), 937–56.

Kubálková, Vendulka, Onuf, Nicholas, and Kowert, Paul (eds.), *International Relations in a Constructed World*, Armonk, NY: M. E. Sharpe, 1998.

Kuznetsov, Vladimir, 'The Ottawa Process & Russia's Position', *Krasnaya Zvezda* (27 November 1997), p. 3, as in *What The Papers Say* (28 November 1997), p. 37.

Lauterpacht, Hersch, *The Function of Law in the International Community*, Oxford: Clarendon Press, 1933.

— 'Neutrality and Collective Security', *Politica* 2: 6 (1936), 133–55.

— 'Sovereignty Over Submarine Areas', *British Yearbook of International Law* 27 (1950), 376–433.

Lawyers Committee for Human Rights, *The World Bank: Governance and Human Rights*, New York: Lawyers Committee for Human Rights, 1995.

*League of Nations Treaty Series* 89.

*Legality of the Threat or Use of Nuclear Weapons*, Advisory Opinion, *ICJ Report 1996*.

'Legalization and World Politics', *International Organization* 54: 3 (2000), Special Issue.

Legro, Jeffrey and Moravscik, Andrew, 'Is Anybody Still a Realist?', *International Security* 24: 2 (1999), 5–55.

Liaison Committee of the House of Commons, United Kingdom: <www.publications.parliament.uk/pa/cm200203/cmselect/cmliaisn/334-i/3012103.htm>, (21 January 2003).

Lietzau, William, 'International Criminal Law After Rome: Concerns from a US Military Perspective', *Law and Contemporary Problems* 64: 1 (2001), 119–40.

Linklater, Andrew, *The Transformation of Political Community: Ethical Foundations of the Post-Westphalian Era*, Cambridge: Polity Press, 1998.

Lisowski, Michael, 'Playing the Two-Level Game: US President Bush's Decision to Repudiate the Kyoto Protocol', *Environmental Politics* 11: 4 (2002), 101–19.

Llewellyn, Karl, 'The Normative, the Legal, and the Law-Jobs: The Problem of Juristic Method', *Yale Law Journal* 49: 8 (1940), 1355–1400.

Long, Olivier, *Law and its Limitations in the GATT Multilateral Trade System*, Boston: Martinus Nijhoff, 1985.

Loughlin, Martin, *Sword and Scales: An Examination of the Relationship Between Law and Politics*, Oxford and Portland, OR: Hart, 2000.

Lumsdaine, David, *Moral Vision in International Politics*, Princeton: Princeton University Press, 1990.

Lutz, Ellen L. and Sikkink, Kathryn, 'International Human Rights Law and Practice in Latin America', *International Organization* 54: 3 (2000), 633–59.

Mannari, Hiroshi and Befu, Harumi (eds.), *The Challenge of Japan's Internationalization: Organization and Culture*, Hyogo, Japan: Kwansei Gakuin University, 1983.

Mapel, David R. and Nardin, Terry, *International Society: Diverse Ethical Perspectives*, Princeton: Princeton University Press, 1998.

March, James and Olsen, Johan, *Rediscovering Institutions: The Organizational Basis of Politics*, New York: Free Press, 1989.

Marchant, Garry, Robinson, John, Anderson, Urton, and Schadewald, Michael, 'Analogical Transfer and Expertise in Legal Reasoning', *Organizational Behavior and Human Decision Processes* 48: 2 (1991), 272–90.

— 'The Use of Analogy in Legal Argument: Problem Similarity, Precedent, and Expertise', *Organizational Behavior and Human Decision Processes* 55: 1 (1993), 95–119.

Martin, David A., 'Effects of International Law on Migration Policy and Practice: The Uses of Hypocrisy', *International Migration Review* 23: 3 (1989), 547–78.

*Bibliography*

Martin, Lisa L., 'The Rational Choice of Multilateralism', in John Gerard Ruggie (ed.), *Multilateralism Matters: The Theory and Praxis of an Institutional Form*, New York: Columbia University Press, 1993, pp. 91–121.

Mayall, James, *World Politics: Progress and Its Limits*, Cambridge: Polity Press, 2000.

Mayer, Richard, *Thinking and Problem Solving: An Introduction to Human Cognition and Learning*, 2nd edn, New York: W. H. Freeman & Co., 1992.

McDougal, Myres S. and Feliciano, Florentino P., *The International Law of War: Transnational Coercion and World Public Order*, revised edn, New Haven: New Haven Press, 1994.

McKibben, Bill, 'Some Like it Hot', *New York Review of Books* 48: 11 (5 July 2001), 35–8.

Memorandum for SEE Distribution, Subject: Commandant's Training Policy for Non-Self Destructing Anti-Personnel Landmines, 26 April 1999, <www.wood.army.mil/CTSC/TRADOC%20NSD-APL.htm>.

Memorandum from Major General John Sylvester, Deputy Chief of Staff for Training, to Commandant, US Army Engineer School, 'Commandant's Training Policy for Non-Self Destructing Anti-Personnel Landmines' (12 August 1999).

Merriam, Charles, *Political Power*, New York: McGraw-Hill, 1934.

Miller, J. D. B., *The Nature of Politics*, London: Duckworth, 1962.

Mitrany, David, *A Working Peace System: An Argument for the Functional Development of International Organisation*, London: Royal Institute of International Affairs, 1943.

Morais, Herbert V., 'The Globalization of Human Rights Law and the Role of International Financial Institutions in Promoting Human Rights', *George Washington International Law Review* 33: 1 (2000), 71–96.

Morgenthau, Hans J., 'Positivism, Functionalism, and International Law', *American Journal of International Law* 34: 2 (April 1940), 260–84.

— *Politics Among Nations: The Struggle for Power and Peace*, 6th edn, New York: McGraw-Hill, 1985.

Mosteky, Vaclav, *Index of Multilateral Treaties: A Chronological List of Multi-Party International Agreements from the Sixteenth Century through 1963*, Cambridge, MA: Harvard Law School Library, 1965.

Muchlinski, Peter T., 'Human Rights and Multinationals: Is There a Problem?', *International Affairs* 77: 1 (2001), 31–47.

Murphy, Sean D., *Humanitarian Intervention: The United Nations in an Evolving World Order*, Philadelphia: University of Pennsylvania Press, 1996.

— 'Terrorism and the Concept of "Armed Attack" in Article 51 of the UN Charter', *Harvard International Law Journal* 43: 1 (2002), 41–51.

Murray, James, 'The Role of Analogy in Legal Reasoning', *UCLA Law Review* 29: 4 (1982), 833–71.

Myjer, Eric P. J. and White, Nigel D., 'The Twin Towers Attack: An Unlimited Right to Self-Defence?', *Journal of Conflict and Security Law* 7: 1 (2002), 5–17.

Nardin, Terry, *Law, Morality, and the Relations of States*, Princeton: Princeton University Press, 1983.

— 'Legal Positivism as a Theory of International Society', in David R. Mapel and Terry Nardin (eds.), *International Society: Diverse Ethical Perspectives*, Princeton: Princeton University Press, 1998, pp. 17–35.

Nash, William L., 'The ICC and the Deployment of US Armed Forces', in Sarah B. Sewall and Carl Kaysen (eds.), *The United States and the International Criminal Court: National Security and International Law*, Lanham, MD: Rowman & Littlefield, 2000, pp. 153–64.

NATO Press Release 2000(060), 7 June 2000, <www.nato.int/docu/pr/2000/p00-060e.htm>, accessed 25 June 2002.

NATO Press Release M-NAC-1(99)51, 'The Situation in and around Kosovo', 12 April 1999, <www.nato.int/docu/1999/p99-051e.htm>.

NATO Press Release NAC-S(99)64, 'Washington Summit Communiqué', 24 April 1999, <www.nato.int/docu/pr/1999/p99-064e.htm>.

Naumann, Klaus, examined before the House of Commons Defence Committee, Fourteenth Report: Lessons of Kosovo Volume II. Minutes of Evidence and Appendices, 7 June 2000.

Naumann, Klaus, Interview given to Channel Four's 'War in Europe' series, Frontline, 29 February 2000, <www.pbs.org/wgbh/pages/frontline/shows/kosovo/etc/script2.html>, accessed 25 June 2002.

Newell, Peter, 'Who "CoPed" Out in Kyoto: An Assessment of the Third Conference of the Parties to the Framework Convention on Climate Change', *Environmental Politics* 7: 2 (1998), 153–9.

— *Climate for Change: Non-State Actors and the Global Politics of the Greenhouse*, Cambridge: Cambridge University Press, 2000.

*Nicaragua Case*: Nicaragua v. United States (1986) *ICJ Reports* 14.

North Sea Continental Shelf Cases, *ICJ Reports 1969*.

North, Douglass C., *Institutions, Institutional Change, and Economic Performance*, Cambridge: Cambridge University Press, 1990.

*Norwegian Loans Case*: France v. Norway (1957) *ICJ Reports* 9.

O'Brien, William, 'Reprisals, Deterrence and Self-Defense in Counterterror Operations', *Virginia Journal of International Law* 30: 2 (1990), 421–78.

Oberthur, Sebastian and Ott, Hermann E., *The Kyoto Protocol: International Climate Policy for the 21st Century*, Berlin: Springer-Verlag, 1999.

Office of the Undersecretary of Defense for Policy, 'Report to the Secretary of Defense on the Status of DoD's Implementation of the US Policy on Anti-Personnel Landmines', May 1997, <www.defenselink.mil:80/pubs/landmines/>, accessed 7 April 2000.

Oka, Takashi, *Prying Open the Door: Foreign Workers in Japan*, Washington, DC: Carnegie Endowment for International Peace, 1994.

Oloka-Onyango, J., 'Beyond the Rhetoric: Reinvigorating the Struggle for Economic and Social Rights in Africa', *California Western International Law Journal* 26: 1 (1995), 1–73.

Bibliography

Onuf, Nicholas, 'Do Rules Say What They Do? From Ordinary Language to International Law', *Harvard International Law Journal* 26: 2 (1985), 385–410.

— *World of Our Making: Rules and Rule in Social Theory and International Relations*, Columbia: University of South Carolina Press, 1989.

— 'The Constitution of International Society', *European Journal of International Law* 5: 1 (1994), 1–19.

Onuma, Yasuaki, 'Japanese International Law in the Prewar Period – Perspectives on the Teaching and Research of International Law in Prewar Japan', *The Japanese Annual of International Law* 29 (1986), 23–46.

Oppenheim, Lassa, 'The Legal Relations Between an Occupying Power and the Inhabitants', *Law Quarterly Review* 33: 4 (1917), 363–70.

— *Oppenheim's International Law*, volume II, 7th edn, Harlow, Essex: Longman, 1952.

Optional Protocol on the Involvement of Children in Armed Conflict, UN Doc. A/54/L.84, New York: United Nations, May 2000.

Pak, Katherine Tegtmeyer, 'Immigration Politics in Japan: Differences in Issue Articulation across Levels of Government and Society', American Political Science Association Convention, Chicago, 1995.

Passin, Herbert, 'Overview: The Internationalization of Japan – Some Reflections', in Hiroshi Mannari and Harumi Befu (eds.), *The Challenge of Japan's Internationalization: Organization and Culture*, Hyogo, Japan: Kwansei Gakuin University, 1983, pp. 15–30.

Petersmann, Ernst-Ulrich, 'The Dispute Settlement System of the World Trade Organization and the Evolution of the GATT Dispute Settlement System Since 1948', *Common Market Law Review* 31: 6 (1994), 1157–244.

Philpott, Daniel, *Revolutions in Sovereignty: How Ideas Shaped Modern International Relations*, Princeton: Princeton University Press, 2000.

Pieper, Ute and Taylor, Lance, 'The Revival of the Liberal Creed: The IMF, the World Bank, and Inequality in a Globalized Economy', in Dean Baker, Gerald Epstein, and Robert Pollin (eds.), *Globalization and Progressive Economic Policy*, Cambridge: Cambridge University Press, 1998, pp. 37–63.

Pinker, Steven, *The Language Instinct*, New York: W. Morrow, 1994.

Port, Kenneth L., 'The Japanese International Law "Revolution": International Human Rights Law and its Impact in Japan', *Stanford Journal of International Law* 28: 1 (1991), 139–72.

Porter, Gareth, Welsh Brown, Janet, and Chasek, Pamela S., *Global Environmental Politics*, 3rd edn, Boulder, CO: Westview Press, 2000.

Powell, Walter W. and Dimaggio, Paul J. (eds.), *The New Institutionalism in Organizational Analysis*, Chicago: University of Chicago Press, 1992.

'Presidential Decision Directive 48', <www.pub.whitehouse.gov/ uri-...oma. eop.gov.us/1997/5/16/16.text.1>, accessed 9 June 2000.

'Press Release by the Press Office of the Embassy of the Republic of Iraq, London, 12 September 1990', in E. Lauterpacht, C. J. Greenwood, Marc Weller, and Daniel Bethlehem (eds.), *The Kuwait Crisis: Basic Documents*, Cambridge

International Documents Series, Vol. I (Cambridge: Grotius, 1991), pp. 73–7.

Price, Richard, 'Moral Norms in World Politics', *Pacifica Review* 9: 1 (1997), 45–72.

— 'Reversing the Gun Sights: Transnational Civil Society Targets Land Mines', *International Organization* 52: 3 (1998), 613–44.

— *Anti-Personnel Landmines and Customary International Law*, Report, Ottawa: Canadian Department of Foreign Affairs and International Trade, 2000.

Price, Richard and Reus-Smit, Christian, 'Dangerous Liaisons? Critical International Theory and Constructivism', *European Journal of International Relations* 4: 3 (1998), 259–94.

Priest, Dana, 'Bombing by Committee: France Balked at NATO Targets', 20 September 1999, <www.Washingtonpost.com>, accessed 3 July 2001.

— 'The Battle Inside Headquarters: Tension Grew With Divide Over Strategy', 21 September 1999, <www.Washingtonpost.com>, accessed 3 July 2001.

Provisional Verbatim Record of the 2932nd Meeting, held at Headquarters, New York, on Thursday, 2 August 1990, Security Council, S/PV.2932, New York: United Nations, 1990.

Putnam, Robert, 1988. 'Diplomacy and Domestic Politics: The Logic of Two-Level Games', *International Organization* 42: 3 (1988), 427–60, reprinted in Peter B. Evans, Harold K. Jacobson, and Robert D. Putnam (eds.), *International Bargaining and Domestic Politics: Double-Edged Diplomacy*, Berkeley: University of California Press, 1993, pp. 431–68.

Rae, Heather, *State Identities and the Homogenization of Peoples*, Cambridge: Cambridge University Press, 2002.

Rajagopal, Balakrishnan, 'Crossing the Rubicon: Synthesizing the Soft International Law of the IMF and Human Rights', *Boston University International Law Journal* 11 (1993), 81–107.

Ramsbotham, Oliver and Woodhouse, Tom, *Humanitarian Intervention in Contemporary Conflict: A Reconceptualization*, Cambridge: Polity Press, 1996.

Ransom, David and Bald, Margaret, 'The Dictatorship of Debt', *World Press Review* 46: 10 (1999), 6–8.

Reed, Laura W. and Kaysen, Carl, *Emerging Norms of Justified Intervention*, Cambridge, MA: American Academy of Arts and Sciences, 1993.

*Regina v. Bow Street Metropolitan Stipendiary Magistrate, ex parte Pinochet Ugarte (No. 3)* [1999] 2 All ER 97.

Reif, Linda C., 'Building Democratic Institutions: The Role of National Human Rights Institutions in Good Governance and Human Rights Protection', *Harvard Human Rights Journal* 13: 1 (2000), 1–69.

Reisman, W. Michael, 'The Raid on Baghdad: Some Reflections on its Lawfulness and Implications', *European Journal of International Law* 5: 1 (1994), 120–33.

Repeta, Lawrence, 'The International Covenant on Civil and Political Rights and Human Rights Law in Japan', *Law in Japan* 20 (1987), 1–28.

Report of the Ad Hoc Committee on the Establishment of An International Criminal Court, reprinted in Cherif Bassiouni (compiler), *The Statute of the*

*International Criminal Court: A Documentary History*, Ardsley, NY: Transnational Publishers, 1998.

Reus-Smit, Christian, *The Moral Purpose of the State: Culture, Social Identity, and Institutional Rationality in International Relations*, Princeton: Princeton University Press, 1999.

— 'In Dialogue on the Ethic of Consensus: A Reply to Shapcott', *Pacifica Review* 12: 3 (2000), 305–8.

— 'Human Rights and the Social Construction of Sovereignty', *Review of International Studies* 27: 4 (2001), 519–38.

— 'The Strange Death of Liberal International Theory', *European Journal of International Law* 12: 3 (2001), 573–93.

— 'Imagining Society: Constructivism and the English School', *British Journal of Politics and International Relations* 4: 3 (October 2002), 487–509.

— 'Politics and International Legal Obligation', *European Journal of International Relations* 9: 4 (2003).

— *American Power and World Order*, Cambridge: Polity Press, 2004.

Risse, Thomas, 'International Norms and Domestic Change: Arguing and Communicative Behavior in the Human Rights Area', *Politics and Society* 27: 4 (1999), 529–59.

— '"Let's Argue!": Communicative Action in World Politics', *International Organization* 54: 1 (2000), 1–39.

Risse, Thomas, Ropp, Stephen, and Sikkink, Kathryn (eds.), *The Power of Human Rights: International Norms and Domestic Change*, Cambridge: Cambridge University Press, 1999.

Rizer, Kenneth R., 'Bombing Dual-Use Targets: Legal, Ethical, and Doctrinal Perspectives', 1 May 2001, <www.airpower.maxwell.af.mil/airchronicles/cc/Rizer.html> accessed 15 February 2002.

Roberts, Adam, 'NATO's "Humanitarian War" over Kosovo', *Survival* 41: 3 (1999), 102–23.

Roberts, Adam, and Guelff, Richard, *Documents on the Laws of War*, 3rd edn, Oxford: Oxford University Press, 2000.

Ross, Alf, *On Law and Justice*, London: Stevens and Sons, 1958.

Rousseau, Jean-Jacques, 'On Social Contract or Principles of Political Right', in Alan Ritter and Julia Conway Bondanella (eds.), *Rousseau's Political Writings: New Translations, Interpretive Notes, Backgrounds, Commentaries*, New York: Norton, 1988, pp. 84–173.

Rowe, Peter, 'Memorandum', *Foreign Affairs Committee*, Fourth Report, Kosovo, 23 May 2000.

— 'Kosovo 1999: The Air Campaign – Have the Provisions of Additional Protocol I Withstood the Test?', *International Review of the Red Cross*, No. 837, 31 March 2000, <www.icrc.org/icrceng.nsf/4dc394db5b54f3fa4125673900241f2f/5815a62298ea0cff412568d30033d627?OpenDocument>, accessed 28 June 2001.

Ruggie, John Gerard, 'Multilateralism: The Anatomy of an Institution', in John Gerard Ruggie (ed.), *Multilateralism Matters: The Theory and Praxis of an Institutional Form*, New York: Columbia University Press, 1993, pp. 3–50.

— 'Territoriality and Beyond: Problematizing Modernity in International Relations', *International Organization* 47: 1 (1993), 139–74.

— (ed.), *Multilateralism Matters: The Theory and Praxis of an Institutional Form*, New York: Columbia University Press, 1993.

Ruggie, John and Kratochwil, Friedrich, 'International Organization: A State of the Art on the Art of the State', *International Organization* 40: 4 (1986), 753–75.

Sadako, Ogata, 'Interdependence and Internationalization', in Glenn D. Hook and Michael A. Weiner (eds.), *The Internationalization of Japan*, London: Routledge, 1992, pp. 63–71.

Sandholtz, Wayne, 'Humanitarian Intervention: Global Enforcement of Human Rights?', in Alison Brysk (ed.), *Globalization and Human Rights*, Berkeley: University of California Press, 2002, pp. 201–25.

Sarooshi, Danesh, 'The Powers of the United Nations International Criminal Tribunals', *Max Planck Yearbook of United Nations Law* 2 (1998).

Sartor, Giovanni, 'A Formal Model of Legal Argumentation', *Ratio Juris* 7: 2 (1994), 177–211.

Schachter, Oscar, 'The Legality of Pro-Democratic Invasion', *American Journal of International Law* 78: 3 (1984), 645–50.

— 'Self-Defense and the Rule of Law', *American Journal of International Law* 83: 2 (1989), 259–77.

— *International Law in Theory and Practice*, Dordrecht and Boston: Nijhoff Publishers, 1991.

Scharf, Michael P., 'The ICC's Jurisdiction over the Nationals of Non-Party States: A Critique of the US Position', *Law and Contemporary Problems* 64: 1 (2001), 66–118.

Scheffer, David, 'International Criminal Court: The Challenge of Jurisdiction', Address to the Annual Meeting of the American Society of International Law, 26 March 1999, <www.state.gov/www/policy_remarks/1999/990326_scheffer_icc.html>.

Schmitt, E. and Myers, S. L., 'NATO Said to Focus Raids on Serb Elite's Property', *New York Times*, 19 April 1999.

Schrijver, Nico J., 'Responding to International Terrorism: Moving the Frontiers of International Law for "Enduring Freedom"?', *Netherlands International Law Review* 48: 3 (2001), 271–91.

Schwartz, Eric, 'The United States and the International Criminal Court: The Case for Dextrous Multilateralism', *University of Chicago Journal of International Law* 4: 233 (2003).

Sekine, Masami, 'Guest Worker Policies in Japan', *Migration* September (1991), 49–69.

Sellek, Yoko and Weiner, Michael A., 'Migrant Workers: The Japanese Case in International Perspective', in Glenn D. Hook and Michael A. Weiner (eds.), *The Internationalization of Japan*, London: Routledge, 1992, pp. 205–28.

Bibliography

Shapcott, Richard, 'Solidarism and After: Global Governance, International Society, and the Normative "Turn" in International Relations', *Pacifica Review* 12: 2 (2000), 147–65.
— *Justice and Community in International Relations*, Cambridge: Cambridge University Press, 2001.
Shapiro, Martin, 'Stability and Change in Judicial Decision-Making: Incrementalism or *Stare Decisis?*', *Law in Transition Quarterly* 2: 3 (1965), 134–57.
Shihata, Ibrahim, *The World Bank in a Changing World: Selected Essays*, volumes I and II, compiled and edited by Franziska Tschofen and Antonio R. Parra, Dordrecht: Martinus Nijhoff, 1991–5.
Shimada, Haruo, *Japan's 'Guest Workers'*, Tokyo: University of Tokyo Press, 1994.
Shoichi, Koseki, 'Japanizing the Constitution', *Japan Quarterly* 35: 3 (1988), 234–40.
Short, Lt. General Michael C., Interview given to Channel Four's 'War in Europe' series, Frontline, <www.pbs.org/wgbh/pages/frontline/shows/kosovo/interviews/short.html>, accessed 28 June 2001.
Shue, Henry, 'Bombing to Rescue? NATO's 1999 Bombing of Serbia', in Deen K. Chatterjee and Don E. Scheid (eds.), *Ethics and Foreign Intervention*, Cambridge: Cambridge University Press, 2003.
Simmons, Beth A., 'The Legalization of International Monetary Affairs', *International Organization* 54: 3 (2000), 573–602.
Simpson, Gerry, 'The Situation on the International Legal Front: The Power of Rules and the Rule of Power', *European Journal of International Law*, 11: 2 (2000), 439–65.
Skinner, Quentin, 'Some Problems in the Analysis of Political Thought and Action', in James Tully (ed.), *Meaning and Context: Quentin Skinner and his Critics*, Cambridge: Polity Press, 1988, pp. 97–118.
Skogly, Sigrun I., 'Structural Adjustment and Development: Human Rights – An Agenda for Change', *Human Rights Quarterly* 15: 4 (1993), 751–78.
Slaughter Burley, Anne-Marie, 'International Law and International Relations Theory: A Dual Agenda', *American Journal of International Law* 87: 2 (1993), 205–39.
Slaughter, Anne-Marie and Burke-White, William, 'An International Constitutional Moment', *Harvard International Law Journal* 43: 1 (2002), 1–21.
Slaughter, Anne-Marie, Tulumello, Andrew S., and Wood, Stepan, 'International Law and International Relations Theory: A New Generation of Interdisciplinary Scholarship', *American Journal of International Law* 92: 3 (1998), 367–97.
Sofaer, Abraham D., 'International Law and Kosovo', *Stanford Journal of International Law* 36: 1 (2000), 1–21.
Sprinz, Detlef and Vaahtoranta, Tapani, 'The Interest-based Explanation of International Environmental Policy', *International Organization* 48: 1 (1994), 77–105.

Sprinz, Detlef F. and Weiss, Martin, 'Domestic Politics and Global Climate Policy', in Urs Luterbacher and Detlef F. Sprinz (eds.), *International Relations and Global Climate Change*, Cambridge, MA: MIT Press, 2001, pp. 67–94.

Statement of NATO Secretary-General Lord Geoffrey Robertson, 2 October 2001, <www.nato.int/docu/speech/2001/s011002a.htm>.

Stein, Eric, 'Lawyers, Judges, and the Making of a Transnational Constitution', *American Journal of International Law* 75: 1 (1981), 1–27.

Stone, Alec, 'What is a Supranational Constitution?: An Essay in International Relations Theory', *Review of Politics* 56: 3 (1994), 441–74.

Stone Sweet, Alec, 'The New GATT: Dispute Resolution and the Judicialization of the Trade Regime', in Mary L. Volcansek (ed.), *Law Above Nations: Supranational Courts and the Legalization of Politics*, Gainesville: University Press of Florida, 1997, pp. 118–41.

— 'Rules, Dispute Resolution, and Strategic Behavior', *Journal of Theoretical Politics* 10: 3 (1998), 327–38.

— 'Judicialization and the Construction of Governance', *Comparative Political Studies* 32: 2 (1999), 147–84.

Stone Sweet, Alec, 'Islands of Transnational Governance', in Martin Shapiro and Alec Stone Sweet (eds.), *On Law, Politics, and Judicialisation*, Oxford: Oxford University Press, 2002.

Stone Sweet, Alec, Sandholtz, Wayne, and Fligstein, Neil, 'The Institutionalization of European Space', in Alec Stone Sweet, Wayne Sandholtz, and Neil Fligstein (eds.), *The Institutionalization of Europe*, Oxford: Oxford University Press, 2001, pp. 1–28.

Strange, Susan, *Mad Money: When Markets Outgrow Governments*, Ann Arbor: University of Michigan Press, 1998.

Suganami, Hidemi, 'Japan's Entry into International Society', in Hedley Bull and Adam Watson (eds.), *The Expansion of International Society*, Oxford: Clarendon Press, 1984, pp. 185–99.

Sugden, Robert, 'Spontaneous Order', *Journal of Economic Perspectives* 3: 4 (1989), 85–97.

Sunstein, Cass, 'On Analogical Reasoning', *Harvard Law Review* 106: 3 (1993), 741–91.

Supplementary Memorandum Submitted by Professor Ian Brownlie CBE, QC in House of Commons Foreign Affairs Committee, *Fourth Report: Kosovo*, volume 2: *Minutes of Evidence and Appendices* (2000).

Taylor, Michael, 'Structure, Culture and Action in the Explanation of Social Change', *Politics and Society* 17: 2 (1989), 115–88.

Terrorist Threat to the Americas, Res. 1, Twenty-Fourth Meeting of Consultation of Ministers of Foreign Affairs Acting as Organ of Consultation in Application of the Inter-American Treaty of Reciprocal Assistance, OEA/Ser.F/II.24, RC.24/RES.1/01 (21 September 2001).

Tesón, Fernando R., *Humanitarian Intervention: An Inquiry into Law and Morality*, 2nd edn, Irvington-on-Hudson, NY: Transnational Publishers, 1997.

*Bibliography*

*The Lotus Case, PCIJ Reports 1927*, Series A, Nos 9 and 10.

Thomas, George M., Meyer, John W., Ramirez, Francesco, and Boli, John (eds.), *Institutional Structure: Constituting State, Society, and the Individual*, London: Sage, 1989.

Thomas, Ward, *The Ethics of Destruction: Norms and Force in International Relations*, Ithaca: Cornell University Press, 2001.

Thomson, David, *Europe Since Napoleon*, Harmondsworth: Penguin, 1966.

Toope, Stephen J., 'Emerging Patterns of Governance and International Law', in Michael Byers (ed.), *The Role of Law in International Politics: Essays in International Relations and International Law*, Oxford: Oxford University Press, 2000, pp. 91–108.

Tully, Andrew F., 'Yugoslavia: France Faulted for Limiting Targets During Kosovo Conflict', 22 October 1999, <www.rferl.org/nca/features/1999/10/F.RU.991022140550.html>, accessed 28 June 2001.

Turkey, Ministry of Foreign Affairs, Information Department, 'Joint Statement of the Minister of Foreign Affairs of the Republic of Turkey HE Mr. Ismail Cem and the Minister of Foreign Affairs of the Republic of Bulgaria HE Ms. Nadezhda Mihailova', 22 March 1999, <www.mfa.gov.tr/grupb/bc/bcc99/march/02.htm>, accessed 13 August 2000.

'Turkey's Explanation of Vote on the Draft Resolution Entitled: Convention on the Prohibition of the Use, Stockpiling, Production and Transfer of Anti-Personnel Mines and on Their Destruction', A/C.1/53/L.33, 4 November 1998.

Ueki, Yasuhiro, 'Japan's UN Diplomacy: Sources of Passivism and Activism', in Gerald L. Curtis (ed.), *Japan's Foreign Policy After the Cold War: Coping With Change*, New York: M. E. Sharpe, 1993, pp. 347–70.

UN Document S/PV.2932 (1990).

UN Document S/PV.2955 (16 December 1998).

UN Document S/1998/1181 (16 December 1998) (United States).

UN Document S/2003/350 (21 March 2003) (United Kingdom).

UN Document S/2003/351 (21 March 2003) (United States).

UN Document, Press Release GA/DIS/3096 (11 November 1997).

Unal, Elif, 'Turkey, Greece Agree to Clear Landmines', *Reuters Newswire* (6 April 2001).

United Nations General Assembly Resolution 2625 (XXV), A/RES/2625(XXV), 24 October 1970.

United Nations Security Council, 2346th Mtg., 2 April 1982.

United Nations Security Council, Provisional Verbatim Record of the Three Thousand One Hundred and Forty-fifth Meeting, 3 December 1992, S/PV.3145.

United Nations Security Council, Provisional Verbatim Record of the Three Thousand One Hundred and Eighty-eighth Meeting, 26 March 1993, S/PV.3188.

United Nations Security Council, Provisional Verbatim Record of the Three Thousand Four Hundred and Thirteenth Meeting, 31 July 1994, S/PV.3413.

United States Department of the Army Information Paper, 'PDD-64: Anti-Personnel Landmines: Expanding Upon and Strengthening the US APL Policy', 8 July 1998, cited in Griesdorf, Michael, 'An Alternative Methodology for Constructivism: Measuring the American Adherence to an AP Landmine Ban', unpublished report, Toronto, July 2000.

United States Office of Humanitarian Demining Programs, *Hidden Killers, 1998: The Global Landmine Crisis*, Washington, DC: US Department of State, 1998.

Vanberg, Georg, 'Reply to Stone Sweet', *Journal of Theoretical Politics* 10: 3 (1998), 339–46.

Vogel, Ezra F., 'Pax Nipponica?', *Foreign Affairs* 64: 4 (1986), 752–67.

von Elbe, Joachim, 'The Evolution of the Concept of the Just War in International Law', *American Journal of International Law* 33: 4 (1939), 665–88.

von Martens, G. F., *Summary of the Law of Nations Founded on the Treaties and Customs of Modern Nations*, Philadelphia: Thomas Bradford, 1795.

Vosniadou, Stella and Ortony, Andrew (eds.), *Similarity and Analogical Reasoning*, Cambridge: Cambridge University Press, 1989.

Vrolijk, Christiaan, 'Introduction and Overview', *International Affairs* 77: 2 (2001), 251–60.

Wade, Robert, 'The Coming Fight Over Capital Flows', *Foreign Policy* 113 (1998–9), 41–53.

Wade, Robert Hunter, 'US Hegemony and the World Bank: The Fight over People and Ideas', *Review of Political Economy* 9: 2 Summer (2002), 201–29.

Waltz, Kenneth N., *Theory of International Politics*, New York: Random House, 1979.

Walzer, Michael, *Just and Unjust Wars: A Moral Argument with Historical Illustrations*, 3rd edn, New York: Basic Books, 2000.

Ward, Hugh, 'Game Theory and the Politics of Global Warming: The State of Play and Beyond', *Political Studies* 44: 5 (1996), 850–71.

Ward, Robert, *An Enquiry into the Foundations and History of the Law of Nations from the Time of the Greeks to the Age of Grotius, Volume 1*, London: Butterworth, 1795.

Watts, Arthur, 'The Importance of International Law', in Michael Byers (ed.), *The Role of Law in International Politics: Essays in International Relations and International Law*, Oxford: Oxford University Press, 2000, pp. 5–16.

Wedgwood, Ruth, 'Fiddling in Rome: America and the International Criminal Court', *Foreign Affairs* 77: 6 (1998), 20–4.

— 'Responding to Terrorism: The Strikes Against bin Laden', *Yale Journal of International Law* 24: 2 (1999), 559–76.

— 'Speech Three: Improve the International Criminal Court', in Alton Frye (ed.), *Toward an International Criminal Court?: Three Options Presented as Presidential Speeches*, New York: Council on Foreign Relations, 1999, pp. 53–71.

— 'Courting Disaster: The US Takes a Stand', *Foreign Service Journal* 77: 3 (2000), 34–41.

Weiler, Joseph H. H., 'The Transformation of Europe', *Yale Law Journal* 100: 7 (1991), 2403–83.

*Bibliography*

Weiner, Myron, 'Opposing Visions: Migration and Citizenship Policies in Japan and the United States', in Myron Weiner and Tadashi Hanami (eds.), *Temporary Workers or Future Citizens?: Japanese and US Migration Policies*, New York: New York University Press, 1998, pp. 3–27.

Wendt, Alexander, 'The Agent Structure Problem in International Relations Theory', *International Organization* 41: 2 (1987), 335–70.

— 'Anarchy is What States Make of It: The Social Construction of Power Politics', *International Organization* 46: 2 (1992), 391–426.

— 'Constructing International Politics', *International Security* 20: 1 (1995), 71–81.

— 'Identity and Structural Change in International Politics', in Yosef Lapid and Friedrich V. Kratochwil (eds.), *The Return of Culture and Identity in IR Theory*, Boulder: Lynne Rienner, 1996, pp. 47–64.

— *Social Theory of International Politics*, Cambridge: Cambridge University Press, 1999.

Wendt, Alexander and Duvall, Raymond, 'Institutions and International Order', in Ernst-Otto Czempiel and James N. Rosenau (eds.), *Global Changes and Theoretical Challenges: Approaches to World Politics for the 1990s*, Lexington: Lexington Books, 1989, pp. 51–73.

Weschler, Lawrence, 'Exceptional Cases in Rome: The United States and the Struggle for an ICC', in Sarah B. Sewall and Carl Kaysen (eds.), *The United States and the International Criminal Court: National Security and International Law*, Lanham, MD: Rowman & Littlefield, 2000, pp. 85–111.

Wheeler, Nicholas J., *Saving Strangers: Humanitarian Intervention in International Society*, Oxford: Oxford University Press, 2000.

White, Nigel D., *Keeping the Peace: The United Nations and the Maintenance of International Peace and Security*, 2nd edn, Manchester: Manchester University Press, 1997.

Willoughby, Westel Woodbury, *The Sino-Japanese Controversy and the League of Nations*, Baltimore: Johns Hopkins University Press, 1935.

Wippman, David, 'Enforcing the Peace: ECOWAS and the Liberian Civil War', in Lori F. Damrosch (ed.), *Enforcing Restraint: Collective Intervention in Internal Conflicts*, New York: Council on Foreign Relations Press, 1993, pp. 157–203.

Woods, Ngaire, 'Making the IMF and the World Bank More Accountable', *International Affairs* 77: 1 (2001), 83–100.

World Bank, *Sub-Saharan Africa: From Crisis to Sustainable Growth: A Long-term Perspective Study*, Washington, DC: World Bank, 1989.

— *Governance and Development*, Report No. 10650, Washington, DC: World Bank, 1992.

— *Governance: The World Bank's Experience*, Development in Practice Series, Report No. 13134, Washington, DC: World Bank, 1994.

— *Development and Human Rights: The Role of the World Bank*, Report No. 23188, Washington, DC: World Bank, 1998.

— *World Development Report 1998/98: Knowledge for Development*, New York: Oxford University Press for the World Bank, 1999.

Wright, Quincy, 'The Meaning of the Pact of Paris', *American Journal of International Law* 27: 1 (1933), 39–61.

Yamanaka, Keiko, 'Contesting Immigrant Rights in Japan', *World On the Move* 6: 2 (2000), 8–10.

Yasuhiko, Saito, 'Japan and Human Rights Covenants', *Human Rights Law Journal* 2: 1–2 (1981), 79–107.

Yasutomo, Dennis T., 'The Politicization of Japan's "Post-Cold War" Multilateral Diplomacy', in Gerald L. Curtis (ed.), *Japan's Foreign Policy After the Cold War: Coping With Change*, New York: M. E. Sharpe, 1993, pp. 323–46.

York, Geoffrey, 'Russia Flouts Land-Mine Vow', *Globe and Mail* (4 June 2001).

Zimmern, Alfred, *The League of Nations and the Rule of Law: 1918–1935*, London: Macmillan, 1936.

Zukang, Sha, 'Chinese Comments on the Issue of APL: Excerpts of a Speech Given by Sha Zukang, Ambassador of the PRC for Disarmament Affairs, June 1997', *Beijing Review* (5–11 January 1998), 19–20.

# Index

Acheson, Dean 190
action 5, 25–30
    communicative 25, 38, 92, 286–289
    strategic 18, 28, 30–31, 270, 289
Afghanistan 66, 121, 127
Africa 225, 231
Age of Absolutism 37, 43
Age of Revolutions (1776–1848) 35
aggression 8, 33–36, 50, 115, 171, 174, 188,
        192–193 *see also* force
Albania 58
Albin, Cecilia 31
Albright, Madeleine 186
Algeria 126
Allott, Philip 43, 277
Amnesty International (AI) 191, 203, 208,
        209, 210, 212, 213–214
anarchy 18, 32, 81, 128, 241 *see also*
        'cultures of anarchy'
*Anglo-Norwegian Fisheries* case 115, 211
Angola 117, 118, 121, 125, 126
Annan, Kofi 76
apartheid 122, 226
Arab states 162, 165
Arbour, Louise 209
Argentina 59, 88
argumentation 46, 241, 270
    and the ICC 55, 154–155, 156–160
        framework of 245–248, 254, 259–260,
            267–268
    in Japan 144–145
    logics of 9, 23, 273
Arkin, William 204
Asia 132, 135, 138, 162
Asian financial crisis 226–228
Australia 84, 85, 88, 101, 110
autonomy 45, 197, 218, 223, 260, 284
    institutional 5, 11, 36–38, 40, 228, 277

Balkans 26
Barnett, Michael 217–218, 229
Belgium 58
Blair, Prime Minister Tony 77, 167, 209
Bolton, John 176–179
Bortz, Ana 143
Bosnia 263, 264, 265, 267
Bosnia-Herzegovina 121
Britain *see* United Kingdom
Bulgaria 123
Bull, Hedley 274–275, 277, 278
Burma 125
Burundi 126
Bush Administration 185, 216
Bush, President George H. W. 65, 83, 87
Bush, President George W. 86, 89, 100–101,
        103, 104, 127
Byers, Michael 42–43, 108–109, 123, 124,
        127
Byrd-Hagel resolution 88, 104

Cambodia 121, 181
Canada 84, 85, 127, 160, 250, 252, 253
carbon sinks 84, 86, 88
Carr, E. H. 3, 16, 25
Chayes, Abram 182, 190–191
cheating 18, 29
Chechnya 118–119, 125
China 53, 55, 132, 221
    and landmines 116, 119, 129
    and the ICC 152, 162, 168, 181
Chirac, President Jacques 202
Clark, General Wesley 199, 202, 205
Clean Development Mechanism 84
climate change negotiations 81, 82–90, 95,
        98–104
    Berlin 87, 100
    Bonn 84–85, 86, 87, 88, 99

Kyoto 83, 87, 88, 89, 100, 102
Marrakesh 84
The Hague 84, 87, 88, 99, 102, 103
Clinton Administration 88, 126, 151, 186
Clinton, President Bill 88, 116, 151
coexistence 275, 276, 277, 278, 279, 284, 285
Cohen, William S. 197
Cold War 19, 68, 73, 75–76, 263
collateral damage 197, 202
collective security 72–78
Colombia 126, 269
communication 23, 92–93 *see also* justice
communicative ethics 13, 285–289, 290
complementarity 8, 174–176
compliance 7, 51–52, 56, 122–129, 189, 280, 281
Congo, Democratic Republic of 125
'Connally Reservation' 55, 62
conquest 59, 63
consent 90, 106, 107–109, 120, 122–124, 128, 130, 250
    and jurisdiction 8, 170–174
    and obligation 20, 35, 42, 43
constitutive norms 109–113
constructivism 12, 107–109, 269, 290
    and climate change 87, 98, 104, 105
    and constraint 190
    and ethics 286–289
    and IFIs 217, 219
    and international law 3, 4, 11, 21–24, 40, 122
    and international politics 3–4, 15, 21–24, 213
    and international society 274, 278
    and power 238
    and treaty making 80–82, 90–98
    and triadic governance 248
Convention on Conventional Weapons (CCW) 112
Convention on the Elimination of all Forms of Discrimination Against Women (CEDAW) 140, 142, 145
Convention on the Elimination of Racial Discrimination (CERD) 140, 143
Convention on the Prevention and Punishment of the Crime of Genocide (1948) 168, 262
Convention on the Rights of the Child on Involvement of Children in Armed Conflict 186
Convention Relating to the Status of Refugees 140, 141–143
Corfu Channel Case (1949) 58, 75
cosmopolitanism 7, 21, 24, 284

crimes against humanity 8, 153, 162, 171, 179, 194, 276 *see also* human rights
crises 288
Critical Legal Studies (CLS) 196, 212, 215
Croatia 121
Cronin, Bruce 97, 100
Cuba 47, 190–191
'cultures of anarchy' 95–97
'cultures of relating' 81, 95
customary international law 17, 38, 69, 128, 130
    and consent 20, 107–109
    and constitutive norms 109–113
    and landmines 7, 106–107, 115–124
    and treaty law 143, 187
    determination of 10, 11, 113–115
customary norms 40, 113, 128

decision-making 93, 239
    and humanitarian intervention 68, 71, 263
    and IFIs 20, 226, 232, 233
    and law 190, 193, 247, 271, 284
    and NATO 201, 211
    and the ICC 155, 160–162, 175, 182, 185–187
    and the UN 73, 260
Declaration on Principles of International Law Concerning Friendly Relations and Co-operation Among Nations (1970) 59
Del Ponte, Carla 209, 210
deliberation 5, 24–30, 244, 246, 247
determinacy 56–57, 154 *see also* rules
deterrence 128, 184
developing countries 136, 137, 172
    and climate change 83–85, 87–88, 99, 100, 102, 104
    and IFIs 218, 224–225, 234, 235, 236
discourse 23
    legal 40, 54, 212, 241
dispute resolution 10, 241, 245–246, 247
    and the Panel System 249–256
    dyadic 246–247, 249, 256–258
    triadic 246–256, 270
divine law 37, 43
dyadic dispute resolution *see* dispute resolution

East Timor 61, 263, 264, 267
ECOWAS (Economic Community of West African States) 68
Egypt 117, 118, 121, 122, 162
'English School' of International Relations 13, 274, 290

environment 6, 12, 225, 228, 229–232, 236
Eritrea 121, 125
ethical debate 28, 30
ethics 12, 31, 273, 284–289, 290 *see also*
    morality
Ethiopia 125, 126
ethnic cleansing 189, 199
Europe 26, 33, 43, 161
European Community (EC) 250, 252,
    253
European Union (EU) 240–241, 255
    and climate change 81, 83–84, 88–89, 95,
        102–104
exceptionalism 162, 172, 183, 184, 188

Falkland Islands 59
Feldstein, Martin 227–228
*Filartiga* case 113, 115
fingerprinting 146–147
Finnemore, Martha 11, 217–218, 229
Fitzmaurice, Judge 192
force 28–29, 64–67, 174, 280–281 *see also*
    aggression
    and the US 182, 183
    in international law and practice 5–6,
        46–47, 50–51, 57–61, 68–79, 190, 213,
        261
        exceptions 6, 49–63, 78, 283
        Kosovo campaign 194, 196, 197, 213
foreign workers 136–138, 144
France 103, 161, 168, 181, 202, 203,
    204–205, 252
Franck, Thomas 31, 42, 52, 56, 195
Freytag, Colonel Konrad 203
friendship 96
functionalism 223

game theory 18, 243, 248, 269
General Agreement on Tariffs and Trade
    (GATT) 11, 238, 241, 249–256
Geneva Conventions 171, 198, 201,
    203–212, 214–216
genocide 8, 122, 153, 162, 171, 179
Georgia 118, 125, 128
Germany 89, 103, 161, 170–171, 189
Giddens, Anthony 280, 281
Gold, Sir Joseph 222
governance 10–11, 34, 238, 245
    and IFIs 229–235, 236–237
    triadic 248, 252–256
Greece 120, 189
greenhouse gas emissions 82–88, 89, 100,
    102
Guinea-Bissau 126
Gulf Crisis of 1990–1 74

Habermas, Jürgen 80, 91–95, 98, 286, 287,
    288
Hague Convention 60
Haiti 76, 263, 264, 265, 267
Hart, H. L. A. 42, 177–178
hegemony 97–98, 100
Heller, Agnes 288–289
Henkin, Louis 41, 195
Higashizawa, Yasushi 147
Higgins, Rosalyn 9, 191, 192, 193–194, 195,
    196, 211
Hobbesian culture 81, 95–97
Hoon, Geoffrey 201
human dignity 162, 193, 214
human rights 7–8, 12, 25, 164, 197 *see also*
    crimes against humanity
    and humanitarian intervention 259–260,
        261–268, 276
    and IFIs 225–226, 228, 229–233, 236
    and the Kosovo campaign 189, 215
    in Japan 139–140, 141, 145–147, 148–149
Human Rights Watch (HRW) 189, 191,
    207–208, 209, 210, 212, 213–214
humanitarian intervention 9, 10, 63, 68–72,
    76–77, 197, 215–216, 276
    forcible 238, 259–260, 262–268
    rules of 261–262, 267–268
humanitarian law 9, 111, 112, 160, 164
    *see also* war, laws of
    and NATO 207, 211
    and the Kosovo campaign 189, 203, 212,
        214
humanitarian norms 23

Iceland 84
identity 80, 82, 90, 95–98, 109, 110, 148
    construction of 28, 30–31
    state 27–28, 31, 32, 33, 160–164, 271
Ignatieff, Michael 198, 203, 205, 214, 215
illegitimacy 145
immigrants 136–138, 142, 144 *see also*
    migrants
immigration 131, 132, 136, 137, 138
independence 159, 166, 173
    and IFIs 219, 221, 224, 229, 235, 236, 237
Independent International Commission
    on Kosovo 215
indeterminacy 191, 195, 196, 214, 215
    *see also* Kosovo campaign
India 152, 162, 166, 221
    and landmines 112, 116, 117, 122, 125,
        128
Indonesia 61, 126, 181
information 18, 29
institutional change 238, 239, 243, 247, 269

institutions 12, 238, 239–245, 282
and power 281, 283
autonomy of 5, 11, 36–38, 40, 228, 277
demand for 11, 29–31
integration 132
interest formation 22, 28, 30
interests *see* states
International Committee of the Red Cross
(ICRC) 209, 215
International Court of Justice (ICJ) 58, 76
*Anglo-Norwegian Fisheries* case 115
and international law 211
*Corfu Channel* case (1949) 58, 75
*Lotus* case (1927) 107
*Nicaragua* case 55–56, 62, 63–64, 69–70,
75, 115
*North Sea Continental Shelf* cases 121
*Nuclear Weapons* case (1996) 111–112,
119, 120–121, 128, 212
International Covenant on Civil and
Political Rights (ICCPR) 139, 140,
141, 142, 143, 145, 146, 147, 262
International Covenant on Economic,
Social, and Cultural Rights
(ICESCR) 140, 142, 144, 147, 225,
262
International Criminal Court (ICC) 8–9,
34, 216, 278, 287
establishment of 151–156, 164–166,
187–188
and complementarity 174–176
and the law 176–186
and UN Security Council 166–168
jurisdiction and consent 170–174
legal argumentation 156–160
prosecutor issue 168–170
states involved 160–164
International Criminal Tribunal for
Rwanda 75, 151, 152, 163–164, 169,
178
International Criminal Tribunal for the
Former Yugoslavia 74, 151, 152,
163–164, 169, 178–180, 182, 208,
211–212
international financial institutions (IFIs)
217–219, 235–237 *see also*
International Monetary Fund,
World Bank
and good governance 229–235
legal framework of 219–224
politics of 224–229
international law 11, 39, 44, 45, 271 *see also*
compliance, consent,
constructivism, force, law,
obligation, rationalism, realism

and IFIs 218–219, 220, 225, 236–237
and international politics 4–5, 130, 238
and Japan 131, 132, 134, 139, 140–141,
144–150
and legal institutions 176–181
and national interest 181–186
and non-party states 109, 116–117, 129,
154–155, 159, 171, 172–174, 185,
187
and politics 1–3, 11–12, 14, 15, 272–273
as a process 40–41, 191–197, 277–278,
282
change in 47–48, 52, 66, 68–69, 76, 78–79,
105
and IFIs 229–233
cosmopolitanisation of, 7–8
institution of 32, 35–36, 241
politics of 14, 24, 272–273, 289–290
sources of 107–109
International Law Commission (ILC)
151–152, 164, 168, 170
International Monetary Fund (IMF) 9–10,
34, 217, 219–220, 236
and good governance 229, 233, 235
functions of 224–225, 226–228
structure of 220–222
international organisations (IOs) 217–219,
230, 237
international political economy 9, 12
international politics 4, 14, 256 *see also*
international law, politics
and law 1–3, 15, 110, 130, 273, 279
International Relations 1–3, 12, 14, 273,
286, 289 *see also* 'English School',
theory of 108–109, 269
international society 5, 12, 94, 108,
273–279, 290
and power 238, 282, 290
nature and structure of 13, 32–36, 91,
285
internationalisation 133–138, 141, 144,
148
Iran 132
Iraq 65, 152, 181, 258, 263, 264, 265
and Gulf Conflict 59–60, 76, 77
and landmine 121
Israel 125, 152
Italy 189

Jackman, Robert 280, 281
Japan 7–8, 53, 55, 110, 228
and the GATT 250, 252, 253
migration to 131–133, 148–150, 278
and international law 138–147
and internationalisation 133–138

Japan Federation of Bar Associations
(JFBA) 141, 147
Jennings, Sir Robert Y. 63, 75
judicialisation 249, 255
jurisdiction 261
   and Nicaragua Case 55–56, 62
   and the ICC 153–156, 159, 161, 165, 167,
      168, 170–174, 175, 177, 188
justice 42, 80, 92, 169, 179, 246, 277–278
   communicative 90, 91, 93, 100, 105
   procedural 32, 37–39, 43, 90, 91, 105
justification 119, 128, 213, 234, 244, 283
   for use of force 49, 63, 68, 70, 194, 195,
      261
      NATO 196, 201, 208, 210, 213
   language and practice of 5–11, 36, 40–41,
      154, 164, 195, 277, 282
   realist position on 190, 193

Kahn, Paul 157, 162
Kanbur, Ravi 235
Kantian culture 95–97, 103
Kapur, Devesh 228, 234
Kellogg–Briand Pact (1928) 52–53, 55, 57,
   58, 67
Kennan, George 16
Kennedy, David 212–213
Keohane, Robert 29
Keynes, John 222, 228
Khazakstan 84
Kirgis, Frederic 116, 122
Korea, Republic of 126, 132, 226, 227, 228
Koreans 131, 132, 141–142, 143, 145
Koskenniemi, Martti 196, 197
Kosovo 26–28, 76, 125, 182, 263, 264
Kosovo campaign 74, 174, 197–207,
   213–216, 267, 278, 283, 288 *see also*
   Operation Allied Force
   law's indeterminacy over 191,
      207–213
Kratochwil, Friedrich 23, 40, 41, 91, 194
Kuwait 59, 60
Kyoto Protocol of the Framework
   Convention on Climate Change
   (1997) 6, 83–90, 99, 102, 104, 187
Kyrgyzstan 125

labour 132, 137
landmines 6–7, 125–129
   norm banning use of 106, 109–113,
      123–124, 130, 278
   and *opinio juris* 115–122
Landmines Convention (1997) 962 109,
   110, 116–119
Latin America 132, 149, 162

law 1–3, 92–95, 191, 269, 289 *see also* divine
   law, international law, legal norms
   and politics 157–158, 159, 191, 238
   and the ICC 164–166, 179–181
   national 156–157, 163, 176–178
   natural 37
'law as rules' 9, 191–197, 213
lawyers 159, 288
   and IFIs 225, 226, 234, 236
   and the GATT 249, 252
   and the Kosovo campaign 197–198, 202,
      203, 205
   in Japan 141, 144–145, 147
leadership 97, 135, 183, 184, 185–186, 187
League of Nations 50, 51, 52
legal norms 3, 38
   and climate change 6, 87, 105
   and constructivism 24, 40, 98, 106, 107
   and IFIs 10, 229, 237
   and landmines 6, 106, 278
   and migration to Japan 131, 132, 136,
      138–141, 144, 148–150
   and use of force 9, 283
   evolution of 10, 92, 128
   legitimacy of 81, 92, 287
legalisation 11
'Legalization and World Politics' 11, 19,
   20, 40
legislation 5, 11, 36, 38–39, 277, 282, 288
   *see also* self-legislation
legitimacy 5, 34–35, 37, 48, 90
   and international law 20, 38, 42–43, 120,
      132–133, 145, 157
   and Japan 139, 148
   and power 280–281
   and treaty making 6, 81, 91–95, 98, 105
   of humanitarian intervention 259, 261
   of IFIs 10, 228, 229, 232, 235–237
   of legal norms 6, 81, 92, 287
   of the ICC 172
   of UN Security Council 73
liberalism, political 32, 273, 277, 282, 285
Liberia 68, 76, 263
Libya 65, 73, 152
Lietzau, William 173, 174
Lockean culture 81, 95–97
Lotus Case (1927) 107

Macedonia 125
Manchurian crisis (1931) 53–55, 56–57
McDougal, Myres 192–193
Meiji government 133
migrant rights 7–8, 131, 132, 136, 137, 149
migrants 132, 144, 148, 278 *see also*
   immigrants, Japan

Milosevic regime 199, 202
Milosevic, Slobodan 180, 189, 200,
    202–210
moral argument 90, 93–94, 98–100
moral norms 99, 288
moral purpose 34–35, 192, 276
moral reasoning 96, 105
morality 26, 214, 281
    and constructivism 80, 82, 90
    and power 3, 25
Morgenthau, Hans 1, 3, 16, 17, 45, 272–273,
    284
Mozambique 121
multilateralism 31, 38–39, 100, 120, 255,
    282–284
Myanmar 125

Nakasone, Prime Minister Yasuhiro 135
Nardin, Terry 275
nationality 141–144
naturalisation 145–146
Naumann, General Klaus 200
neoliberal institutionalism 15, 18–21, 80,
    82, 97, 98, 108
    and climate change 86, 89
    and IFIs 217, 219, 228
    and the ICC 152–153
neoliberalism 18–19, 82–90, 94, 95, 97, 102,
    132
neorationalism 269
neorealism 80, 81–90, 98, 102, 256
    and treaty making 91, 92, 94, 95, 97
Nepal 125
Netherlands 103
'New Haven' school of policy science
    192–193, 194, 214
New Zealand 84
*Nicaragua Case* 55–56, 62, 63–64, 69–70, 75,
    115
Nixon Administration 252
non-discrimination 36, 37, 39, 43, 282, 285
non-governmental organisations (NGOs)
    105, 138, 139, 149, 189, 212
    and climate change 83, 84, 101–103
    and the ICC 151, 153, 160, 164, 166, 169
non-intervention 33, 196, 261, 268, 275,
    276, 278
normative reasoning 244, 264, 267
norms
    constitutive 109–113
    customary 40, 113, 128
    humanitarian 23
    legal 3, 38
        and climate change 6, 87, 105
        and constructivism 24, 40, 98, 106, 107

and IFIs 10, 229, 237
and landmines 6, 106, 278
and migration to Japan 11, 131, 132,
    136, 138–141, 144, 148–150
and use of force 9, 283
evolution of 10, 92, 128
legitimacy of 81, 92, 287
moral 99, 288
social 3, 10, 26
    and constructivism 24, 40, 109
    and migration to Japan 131, 132,
    133–136, 148–150
violations of 114, 123
North Atlantic Council (NAC) 199
North Atlantic Treaty Organisation
    (NATO) 26, 67, 120
    and Yugoslavia 9, 26–28, 68, 189–191
        *see also* Operation Allied Force
    and law as rules or process 194–197
    and laws of war 207–213, 283
*North Sea Continental Shelf Cases* 121
Norway 84
*Nuclear Weapons* Case (1996) 111–112, 119,
    120–121, 128, 212
Nuremberg war crimes tribunal 152

obligation 40, 52, 56, 71, 128, 244
    and customary law 107, 114, 115,
    122–124, 130
    and landmine norm 106, 109–113, 120,
    127, 128, 129
    and reciprocity 195
    and states 20, 36
    and the ICC 155, 156, 172
    structure of 5, 11, 36, 41–43
occupation 60–61, 63
Operation Allied Force (1999) 48, 58, 76,
    126, 197–207, 210, 213–215
Operation Desert Fox (1998) 77
Operation Enduring Freedom (2001) 66
Operation Infinite Reach (1998) 66
Operation Iraqi Freedom (2003) 48, 76, 77
Operation Provide Comfort (1991) 48, 68
*opinio juris* 7, 17, 107–108, 122–124, 128,
    129, 130, 287
    politics of 113–122
order 16, 31, 36, 277–278
Organisation for Economic Cooperation
    and Development (OECD) 84, 85,
    88
Organisation of American States (OAS) 67

Pact of Paris (1928) 50, 51
Pak, Katherine 138
Pakistan 125, 128, 162

Passin, Herbert 134
peace 16, 167, 179
Peace of Westphalia (1648) 35
peacekeeping 160, 161, 172, 183–184, 265
Perry, Commodore Matthew 133
persistent objector rule 115, 123–124, 129, 130
Philippines 126, 132
*Pinochet* case 113
politicisation 77, 169–181, 222–223, 235
politics 16–18, 36–37, 120, 241, 242, 243, 273 *see also* international law, international politics
  and international ethics 284–289
  and law 11–12, 14, 157–158, 160, 191, 238, 277
  and the ICC 164–166, 179–181
  and the ICC 153, 154–156
  concept and nature of 1–3, 5, 11, 12–13, 24–29, 80, 289–290
  of IFIs 218, 221–229
Portugal 226
power 15–16, 25, 37–38, 94, 190–191, 238, 242, 270
  in international relations 12–13, 256–257, 273, 279–284, 290
pragmatism 38
precedent 66, 257, 259–260, 262–267, 270
principle of discrimination 198, 207
purposive association 276

Qatar 152

Radio Televisija Srbije (RTS) 203–204, 208–210
rational choice 18, 269
rationalisation 191, 193
rationalism 29, 31, 41, 153, 248
  and international law 11, 18–21, 40, 132, 133
  and international politics 15, 18–21, 284
rationality 28, 30, 32, 81, 92, 94, 243–244, 269
Rawls, John 287
realism 52, 78, 130, 152
  and IFIs 217, 219, 228
  and international law 15–18, 40, 132, 190, 191, 193–194, 213
  and international politics 15–18, 256, 284
  and power 28–29, 238, 279
'reasons for action' 22–23, 114, 123, 153
reciprocity 6, 123, 195, 249, 255

recognition 6, 90
Ribbentrop–Molotov Pact of Non-Aggression (1939) 50
rights 7–8, 49, 62, 71–72
Rio Treaty 67
Rome Treaty *see* International Court of Justice
Roth, Kenneth 207
Rousseau, Jean-Jacques 35
Rowe, Peter 212
Ruggie, John 14–35, 39
rules 48–49, 52, 54, 78, 191–197, 270, 277
  *see also* humanitarian intervention, institutions
  and exceptions 61–78
  and power 270
  coherence of 57, 60
  determinacy of 55–57, 59, 60, 79
Russia 65, 84, 85, 89
  and landmines 116, 117, 118, 119, 125, 126, 128, 129
  and the ICC 152, 168, 181
Rwanda 74, 76, 263, 264

sanctions 51
Scheffer, David 171, 173
security 12, 72–78
self-defence 62, 63–67, 70, 75, 261
self-determination 33, 278
self-interest 38, 91, 94, 95, 96, 179, 246
self-legislation 36, 37, 38, 39, 43, 282, 285
Senegal 125, 126, 161
Serbs 28
Shea, Jamie 198, 206
Shelton, General Henry H. 197
Shihata, Ibrahim 230
Shimada, Haruo 137–138
Short, Lt. General Michael C. 199–200, 201–202, 204, 205
Sierra Leone 76, 263, 264, 269
Simpson, Gerry 196–197, 211
Singapore 168
social norms 3, 10, 26
  and constructivism 24, 40, 109
  and migration to Japan 131, 132, 133–136, 148–150
socialisation 22, 23, 255, 274
Sofaer, Abraham D. 192, 194
Solana, General Javier 199, 200, 203, 208
Somalia 76, 121, 125, 260, 263, 264, 265–267, 269
Sonoda, Sunao 139

South Africa 162, 226
sovereign equality 54, 167, 187, 285
sovereignty 21, 32, 33, 34–35, 37, 45, 47,
   60–61
  and human rights 197, 259–261,
    262
  and international society 275, 278
  and the US 163
Soviet Union 190, 263
Spender, Judge 192
Sri Lanka 117, 125
'standard of civilisation' 33
states 29, 31, 46–50, 81, 95–97, 120 *see also*
   identity, international law
  interests of 31, 81, 108, 109, 215, 272
    and IFIs 222–223, 228–229, 235, 236
    and international law 181–186
    and the ICC 8, 160–164
  system of 32–33, 107, 178, 269
Stiglitz, Joseph 235
strategic bargaining 90, 93–94, 105, 287
structural adjustment programs (SAPs)
   224–226
structuralism, 3
Sudan 66, 121
supervenience 27

Taiwan 132
Tajikistan 126
territorial integrity 57, 58, 275
terrorism 67, 73
Thailand 132, 226
Toope, Stephen 11
torture 113, 115, 116, 121, 122, 262
trade regime *see* General Agreement on
   Tariffs and Trade (GATT)
transaction costs 18, 29, 153, 242
treaty law 81, 107, 110, 130, 141–144,
   220
treaty making 6, 81, 100
  constructivist interpretation 80–82,
    90–98, 105
triadic dispute resolution *see* dispute
   resolution
Turkey 116, 117–118, 119, 120, 123–124,
   125, 128

Uganda 125
Ukraine 84
umbrella group 84, 86, 89
United Kingdom 58, 66, 74, 77, 89
  and IFIs 222
  and the ICC 161, 167–168
  and the Kosovo campaign 203

United Nations 28, 60, 221
United Nations Charter 67, 261–262
  Article 2(4) 57–59, 63, 194, 261
  Article 2(7) 261
  Article 51 62, 65, 67, 194, 261
  Chapter VII 68, 72–74, 261
United Nations Framework Convention
   on Climate Change (UNFCCC)
   (1992) 83–90, 99–100
United Nations General Assembly 261
  Resolution 2131 (XX) (1965) 69
  Resolution 2625 (XXV) (1970) 70
United Nations Human Rights Committee
   142, 145, 147
United Nations Security Council 60,
   72–78, 155
  and humanitarian intervention 68,
    259–260, 262–267, 268
  and the ICC 166–168, 169, 170,
    187
  Resolution 1368 (2001) 66
  Resolution 373 (2001) 66
  Resolution 502 (1982) 60
  Resolution 687 (1991) 77
  Resolution 721 (1992) 73
  Resolution 748 (1992) 73
United States 39, 53, 91, 228, 258
  and climate change 81, 82, 84–90, 92, 95,
    100–101, 102–104
  and IFIs 221, 222, 228, 236
  and international law 65–67, 74, 77,
    283–284
  and landmines 116, 119, 120, 126–127,
    128, 129, 185
  and the GATT 251–252, 253, 255
  and the ICC 55–56, 62, 151–152,
    162–164, 168, 176–181, 186–188,
    287
    and complementarity 174–176
    and national interest 181–186
    jurisdiction of 155, 171–174, 175
    prosecutor issue 169–170
    UN involvement 166–167
  and the Kosovo campaign 26, 198, 203,
    205
Universal Declaration of Human Rights
   (1948) 143, 145, 146, 262
universalisation 286, 288–289
Uruguay Round (1986–92) 249,
   255
Uzbekistan 125

Vietnam War 197
violations of norms 114, 123

von Martens, G. F. 36

Wade, Robert 228, 235
Waltz, Kenneth 269, 274
war 51, 52–57, 109, 111–112, 256, 282
   laws of 9, 189, 191, 198, 206, 209, 214,
      215, 216 *see also* humanitarian law
war crimes
   and NATO 18, 207–208, 209
   and the ICC 153, 162–171, 174, 179, 182,
      185, 216
warfare 110, 111, 112, 128
Washington Summit Communiqué 26
Watts, Sir Arthur 193
Wendt, Alexander 3, 27, 80, 95–97, 98,
   103

World Bank 9–10, 34, 217, 219–220,
   235–236
   and good governance 229–235
   and the IMF 227
   structure and functions of 220–222,
      224–226
World Trade Organization (WTO) 11, 241,
   249, 255

Yemen 152
Yugoslavia, Federal Republic of (FRY) 9,
   125, 128
   Kosovo campaign 26–27, 189–191,
     194–197

Zaire 76

CAMBRIDGE STUDIES IN INTERNATIONAL RELATIONS

84 *Heather Rae*
   **State identities and the homogenisation of peoples**

83 *Maja Zehfuss*
   **Constructivism in International Relations**
   The politics of reality

82 *Paul K. Huth and Todd Allee*
   **The democratic peace and territorial conflict in the Twentieth Century**

81 *Neta C. Crawford*
   **Argument and change in world politics**
   Ethics, decolonization and humanitarian intervention

80 *Douglas Lemke*
   **Regions of war and peace**

79 *Richard Shapcott*
   **Justice, community and dialogue in International Relations**

78 *Phil Steinberg*
   **The social construction of the ocean**

77 *Christine Sylvester*
   **Feminist International Relations**
   An unfinished journey

76 *Kenneth A. Schultz*
   **Democracy and coercive diplomacy**

75 *David Houghton*
   **US foreign policy and the Iran Hostage Crisis**

74 *Cecilia Albin*
   **Justice and fairness in international negotiation**

73 *Martin Shaw*
   **Theory of the global state**
   Globality as an unfinished revolution

72 *Frank C. Zagare and D. Marc Kilgour*
   **Perfect deterrence**

71 *Robert O'Brien, Anne Marie Goetz, Jan Aart Scholte and Marc Williams*
**Contesting global governance**
Multilateral economic institutions and global social movements

70 *Roland Bleiker*
**Popular dissent, human agency and global politics**

69 *Bill McSweeney*
**Security, identity and interests**
A sociology of international relations

68 *Molly Cochran*
**Normative theory in International Relations**
A pragmatic approach

67 *Alexander Wendt*
**Social theory of international politics**

66 *Thomas Risse, Stephen C. Ropp and Kathryn Sikkink (eds.)*
**The power of human rights**
International norms and domestic change

65 *Daniel W. Drezner*
**The sanctions paradox**
Economic statecraft and international relations

64 *Viva Ona Bartkus*
**The dynamic of secession**

63 *John A. Vasquez*
**The power of power politics**
From classical realism to neotraditionalism

62 *Emanuel Adler and Michael Barnett (eds.)*
**Security communities**

61 *Charles Jones*
**E. H. Carr and International Relations**
A duty to lie

60 *Jeffrey W. Knopf*
**Domestic society and international cooperation**
The impact of protest on US arms control policy

59 *Nicholas Greenwood Onuf*
**The Republican legacy in international thought**

58 *Daniel S. Geller and J. David Singer*
**Nations at war**
A scientific study of international conflict

57 *Randall D. Germain*
**The International organization of credit**
States and global finance in the world economy

56 *N. Piers Ludlow*
**Dealing with Britain**
The Six and the first UK application to the EEC

55 *Andreas Hasenclever, Peter Mayer and Volker Rittberger*
**Theories of international regimes**

54 *Miranda A. Schreurs and Elizabeth C. Economy (eds.)*
**The internationalization of environmental protection**

53 *James N. Rosenau*
**Along the domestic–foreign frontier**
Exploring governance in a turbulent world

52 *John M. Hobson*
**The wealth of states**
A comparative sociology of international economic and
political change

51 *Kalevi J. Holsti*
**The state, war, and the state of war**

50 *Christopher Clapham*
**Africa and the international system**
The politics of state survival

49 *Susan Strange*
**The retreat of the state**
The diffusion of power in the world economy

48 *William I. Robinson*
**Promoting polyarchy**
Globalization, US intervention, and hegemony

47 *Roger Spegele*
**Political realism in international theory**

46 *Thomas J. Biersteker and Cynthia Weber (eds.)*
**State sovereignty as social construct**

45 *Mervyn Frost*
**Ethics in International Relations**
A constitutive theory

44 *Mark W. Zacher with Brent A. Sutton*
**Governing global networks**
International regimes for transportation and communications

43  *Mark Neufeld*
    **The restructuring of international relations theory**

42  *Thomas Risse-Kappen (ed.)*
    **Bringing transnational relations back in**
    Non-state actors, domestic structures and international institutions

41  *Hayward R. Alker*
    **Rediscoveries and reformulations**
    Humanistic methodologies for international studies

40  *Robert W. Cox with Timothy J. Sinclair*
    **Approaches to world order**

39  *Jens Bartelson*
    **A genealogy of sovereignty**

38  *Mark Rupert*
    **Producing hegemony**
    The politics of mass production and American global power

37  *Cynthia Weber*
    **Simulating sovereignty**
    Intervention, the state and symbolic exchange

36  *Gary Goertz*
    **Contexts of international politics**

35  *James L. Richardson*
    **Crisis diplomacy**
    The Great Powers since the mid-nineteenth century

34  *Bradley S. Klein*
    **Strategic studies and world order**
    The global politics of deterrence

33  *T. V. Paul*
    **Asymmetric conflicts**
    War initiation by weaker powers

32  *Christine Sylvester*
    **Feminist theory and International Relations in a postmodern era**

31  *Peter J. Schraeder*
    **US foreign policy toward Africa**
    Incrementalism, crisis and change

30  *Graham Spinardi*
    **From Polaris to Trident**
    The development of US Fleet Ballistic Missile Technology

29  *David A. Welch*
**Justice and the genesis of war**

28  *Russell J. Leng*
**Interstate crisis behavior, 1816–1980**
Realism versus reciprocity

27  *John A. Vasquez*
**The War Puzzle**

26  *Stephen Gill (ed.)*
**Gramsci, historical materialism and International Relations**

25  *Mike Bowker and Robin Brown (eds.)*
**From Cold War to collapse**
Theory and World Politics in the 1980s

24  *R. B. J. Walker*
**Inside/Outside: International Relations as political theory**

23  *Edward Reiss*
**The Strategic Defense Initiative**

22  *Keith Krause*
**Arms and the state**
Patterns of military production and trade

21  *Roger Buckley*
**US–Japan Alliance Diplomacy 1945–1990**

20  *James N. Rosenau and Ernst-Otto Czempiel (eds.)*
**Governance without government**
Order and change in world politics

19  *Michael Nicholson*
**Rationality and the analysis of international conflict**

18  *John Stopford and Susan Strange*
**Rival states, rival firms**
Competition for world market shares

17  *Terry Nardin and David R. Mapel (eds.)*
**Traditions of international ethics**

16  *Charles F. Doran*
**Systems in crisis**
New imperatives of high politics at century's end

15  *Deon Geldenhuys*
**Isolated States**
A comparative analysis

14  *Kalevi J. Holsti*
**Peace and war**
Armed conflicts and international order 1648–1989

13  *Saki Dockrill*
**Britain's policy for West German rearmament 1950–1955**

12  *Robert H. Jackson*
**Quasi-states**
Sovereignty, International Relations and the Third World

11  *James Barber and John Barratt*
**South Africa's foreign policy**
The search for status and security 1945–1988

10  *James Mayall*
**Nationalism and international society**

 9  *William Bloom*
**Personal identity, national identity and International Relations**

 8  *Zeev Maoz*
**National choices and international processes**

 7  *Ian Clark*
**The hierarchy of states**
Reform and resistance in the international order

 6  *Hidemi Suganami*
**The domestic analogy and world order proposals**

 5  *Stephen Gill*
**American hegemony and the Trilateral Commission**

 4  *Michael C. Pugh*
**The ANZUS crisis, nuclear visiting and deterrence**

 3  *Michael Nicholson*
**Formal theories in International Relations**

 2  *Friedrich V. Kratochwil*
**Rules, norms, and decisions**
On the conditions of practical and legal reasoning in international relations and domestic affairs

 1  *Myles L. C. Robertson*
**Soviet policy towards Japan**
An analysis of trends in the 1970s and 1980s

Lightning Source UK Ltd.
Milton Keynes UK
UKOW02f0310190516

274560UK00001B/209/P